Delinking, Relinking, and Linking Writing and Rhetorics

Praise for this book

This is much anticipated book that investigates a less explored area of rhetoric and writing in a non-Western and indigenous context. Well-crafted arguments from Dr. Marohang Limbu's comprehensive research help build a strong and compelling case to study indigenous identities from a thought-provoking perspective.

**– Yowei Kang, PhD, Assistant Professor
National Taiwan Ocean University, Taiwan**

This is an important and ambitious work that crosses linguistic, cultural, and geographic boundaries. In doing this transdisciplinary scholarship, Limbu is making key contributions to indigenous and scholarly communities. In bridging these areas, his scholarship informs work in writing and language studies, cultural rhetorics, and globalization.

**– Steven Fraiberg, PhD, Associate Professor
Michigan State University, USA**

The book, based on the fieldwork in four countries (Nepal, India, UK, and USA) across four continents, on the development of Sirijanga script and Limbu culture and history promises to bring deep insights, relying on oral history, archival and archeological research, and interviews, on how culture and traditions of an indigenous people survived inhospitable political regimes in Nepal and India, and how the community and network of activists across contingents are working to preserve and expand it after the advent of open political regimes in South Asia.

**– Mahendra Lawoti, PhD, Professor
Western Michigan University, USA**

Limbu's groundbreaking book informs indigenous rhetorics and provides a new methodology for ethnohistorical research. Scholars looking to understand how to ground their research in indigenous contexts can employ his "delinking, relinking and linking" methodology to connect with various populations.

Limbu's historical uncovering of Himalayan Yakthung writing traditions, oral history, and culture makes the case that global digital communities can help span local, regional, and transnational contexts and inform indigenous rhetorics in surprising new ways.

– **Gustav Verhulsdonck, PhD, Assistant Professor**
Central Michigan University, USA

Marohang Limbu has done a superb job at canvassing his own delinking, relinking, and linking theory in Yakthung's writing, rhetoric, and customary traditions, and this book adds a milestone and becomes invaluable asset in the history of Yakthung writing and rhetorics.

– **Ambar J. Limbu, Associate Professor**
Tribhuvan University, Nepal

This book is an extremely rich, immensely persuasive, and utterly compelling piece of substantive Yakthung writing and rhetoric documentation, including analyses and interpretations. It demonstrates the immense power of Marohang's delinking, relinking, and linking theory in the context of the 21st century both in academic and popular cultures.

– **Govinda B. Tumbahang, PhD, Former Governor**
Region No. 1, Nepal

Marohang Limbu has explored Yakthung Indigenous historical cultural artifacts, oral texts, and documents and analyzed and interpreted the way they have never been done until the 21st century. This book will contribute a lot and will add a milestone in the history of Himalayan Yakthung Indigenous studies.

– **Arjun Limbu, Associate Professor**
Limbuwan Study Center, Nepal

Marohang Limbu's book is judicious, informed, and incisive, inviting the enthusiast into a serious of critical engagement with even the most difficult selections while avoiding the simplistic categories that mar too many anthologies. In this book, Limbu makes compelling arguments on the exploration, interpretation, and documentation of Himalayan Indigenous writing and rhetorics ever anybody has done to the ground reality.

– **Balkrishna Mabuhang, Associate Professor**
Tribhuvan University, Nepal

This book offers an analytical framework for making an interventionist inquiry into the epistemological territory of the Yakthung indigeneity which has been unfairly shadowed and distorted for centuries. As this book opens up a new phase of methodological approaches to the indigenous practices of reading and writing, it makes a theoretical contribution to the existing literature in the field of Himalayan indigenous writing and rhetoric.

**– Dilli Bikram Edingo, Research Scholar
York University, Canada**

The book delves into invention, interventions, and reinvention of the Sirijanga script and writing system through Dr. Limbu's delinking, relinking, and linking theoretical lens. Limbu's book delinks paracolonization, relinks ancestral customary institutional traditions, and links them with other local and global Indigenous and non-Indigenous epistemologies in the context of the 21st century networked world. This book is and always will be an excellent source of information for academicians, scholars, and common readers.

– Buddhi L. Khamdak, PhD, Sikkim University, India

Delinking, Relinking, and Linking Writing and Rhetorics

Inventions and Interventions of the Sirijanga Syllabary

Marohang Limbu (Yakthung)

STAR SCHOLARS NETWORK

YAKTHUNG SAPSAK ACADEMY

KHAMDHAK PUBLICATIONS

STAR SCHOLARS
N E T W O R K

First Published 2021
by
STAR Scholars
In collaboration with
Open Journals in Education
Yakthung Sapsak Academy and
Khamdhak Publications

Category
Cultural Studies/Himalayan and
Indigenous Studies/Global Rhetorics

Typeset in Garamond

Project Director
Krishna Bista

Series Editor
Uttam Gaulee

Copyeditor
Renee Prvulov

Proofreader
Halley Deyo

Typeset by:
codeMantra
(Project Manager - Karthik)

Cover Design
Srdjan Marjanovic

Author
Marohang Limbu

ISBN: 978-1-7364699-1-0

© STAR Scholars

Library of Congress Control Number: 2021900775

Delinking, Relinking, and Linking Writing and Rhetorics: Inventions and Interventions of the Sirijanga Syllabary

Library of Congress US Programs, Law, and Literature Division

Cataloging in Publication Program
101 Independence Avenue, S.E.
Washington, DC 20540-4283

Printed in the United States of America

DEDICATION

My Parents

Subedar Major Ganga Lal Limbu (Yakthung)
Chandramati Yakyuk (Yakthung)

The 19ᵗʰ Century's Yakthung Historians and Lexicographers

Jobhansing Limbu
Chyangresing Phedangba
Ranadhoj Limbu
Jit Mohan

Contents

About the author

Marohang Limbu (Yakthung), PhD is Associate Professor in the Department of Writing, Rhetoric, and American Cultures at Michigan State University, USA. Dr. Limbu is the editor-in-chief and founding editor of *Journal of Global Literacies, Technologies, and Emerging Pedagogies*. He has co-edited *Emerging Pedagogies in the Networked Knowledge Society: Practices Integrating Social Media and Globalization* (2013), *Digital Rhetoric and Global Literacies: Communication Modes and Digital Practices in the Networked World* (2014), and *Integration of Cloud Technologies in Digitally Networked Classrooms and Learning Communities* (2016). Dr. Limbu published several journal articles that focus on cloud technologies, crowd pedagogies, digital rhetorics and emerging pedagogies, global indigenous rhetorics, and Himalayan Yakthung Indigenous rhetorics.

Marohang Limbu's current research interests include digital rhetorics, multimodal rhetorics, cloud and crowd pedagogies, global Indigenous rhetorics, minority rhetorics, and Himalayan Indigenous customary institutional rhetorics.

Reviewers

The following Yakthung Suhang activists supported the publication and distribution of this book in Asia, Australia, and Europe

We applaud Dr. Marohang Khawahang Limbu (Yakthung) for this historical exploration and documentation of Yakthung Indigenous writing and rhetorics (language, literacy, and Sirijanga writing system). Dr. Limbu, as an insider Yakthung researcher, has opened our minds and will serve the purpose of Yakthung Indigenous studies. This book, we believe, preserves, promotes, and institutionalize our Yakthung Indigenous rhetorical traditions. We sincerely express our heartfelt gratitude to him.

Lokendra Tabebung Yakthungba, Damak 6/UK
Narendra Mabohang Yakthungba, Dharan 15/UK
Dilsing Menyangbo Mennimang Yakthungba, Jhapa/UK
Jaya Mademba Yakthungba, Itahari/UK
Kamal Dhoj Anchhangbo Yakthungba, Dharan 16/UK
Dhan K. Samyangkham Yakthungba, Jhapa/KSA
Kul Prasad Limbu Menyangbo, Kathmandu, Nepal

Acknowledgments

This research and writing would not have been possible without the support of Writing, Rhetoric, and American Cultures, Dr. Delia Koo Endowment (Research) Award, Asian Studies Center, College of Arts and Letters, International Studies Programs, Michigan State University, USA and Limbuwan Study Center, Nepal/UK. I express my heartfelt gratitude to Drs. Jeff Grabill, Malea Powell, Bill Hart Davidson, Jackie Rhodes, and Kate Birdsall for supporting my research and travel funds in multiple ways.

Among many others, I sincerely thank Yakthung scholars, writers, and community leaders, such as Arjun Limbu, Dr. Chaitanya Subba, Dr. Mohan Tumbahang, Chancellor Til Bikram Nembang, Balkrishna Mabuhang, Ambar Jang Limbu, Yehang Laoti, Manjul Yakthumba, Prem Khajum, Dr. Kamal Tigela, Harkajang Kurumbang, Arjun Mabuhang, and Bharat Tunghang, for providing me with invaluable Yakthung books, monographs, archival materials, and Yakthung documents. My gratitude goes to Ganga Kimdang Athpahariya, Lasemahang Limbu, and Namlinghang Limbu for their unconditional support and encouragement to accomplish this arduous book project.

Among many others, I would like to thank B. B. Muringla, Dr. Buddhi L. Khamdak, Karan Lingden, G.M. Subba, Ganesh Limbu (MLA), Riwaz Ninglekhu, Lakhi Khapung, Suraj Subba, Khagendra Chabegu, Nar Prasad Lumphungwa, Bhima Khapung, Rashna Kimdang, Dilu Kimdang, Bishnu Singak, and Ram Tumbahamphe for their unconditional support to gather data, facts, figures, archival materials, and information. Finally, I would like to thank my students: Fiona Maguire, Gabrielle White, Halley Deyo, Lasemahang Limbu, Naomi Johnson, Olivia Caswell, Renee Prvulov, and Stephie Minjung Kang for reading, copyediting, and proofreading the manuscript.

Introduction

Western and non-Western (local) mainstream cultures colonized Indigenous cultures across the world. Both Western colonizers and local para-colonizers became successful in the construction of Indigenous knowledge, cultures, and peoples. For centuries, both Westerners and local para-colonizers, by force or coercion, labelled, distorted, and destroyed Indigenous cultural, linguistic, and religious identities for colonial purposes. By distorting and displacing Indigenous epistemologies, dominant local para-colonizers (para-colonization is a situation where both colonizers and colonized coexist) and Western cultures constructed social traditions, economic conditions, and academic institutions to serve only the colonial purposes. This is one of the reasons why our global and local social, economic, and academic institutions have been misinterpreting Indigenous identities, such as Indigenous epistemologies, ontologies, axiologies, histories, and customary institutional traditions for centuries. As a result, both para-colonizers and Indigenous communities are falling apart in local and global social and academic spaces. Hence, there is an urgency to critically inquire, debate, discuss, document, and institutionalize the endangered Indigenous customary institutions, folk traditions, performative rhetorics, and traditional customary epistemologies, etc. (see also Cushman, 2013; Hufford, 1991; Noyes, 2004; Powell, 2012).

In relation to inquiring, exploring, discovering, and sharing Indigenous knowledges, delinking, relinking, and linking Indigenous customary traditions, languages, epistemologies, ontologies, axiologies, and rhetorics have become Indigenous-centered methodology, for the way we address Indigenous perspectives, challenges, and issues are local, discursive, and contingent. For instance, when we study Southeast Asian Yakthung Indigenous cultures, we encounter multiple layers of para-colonial ideologies that smear Yet Hang (eight kings) and Thibong Yakthung Suhang (10 Yakthung chieftains) Indigenous identities, subjectivities, and epistemologies. Due to Khas Aryan internal suppression, Indian oppression, and Western cultural colonization, Yakthungs have lost their cultural, linguistic, Mundhumic, and *khambong-lungbong* (land-based) identities. In terms of the use of Khas Aryan in this book, Hari Budhathoki, a Khas scholar and activist, condemns the use of the "Khas Aryan" collective identity. Budhothoki claims that the Khas are historically, culturally, geo-culturally, and religiously different from "Indo-Aryans";

they (Khas) claim to be "Tibeto-Khas." The Khas people follow "Masta" religion, not Hindu. He further contends that Aryans have been abusing and capitalizing the Khas identity (Aryan have used the "Khas Aryan" in the Nepali Constitution) for the Aryan's benefits in Nepal for centuries (H. Budhathoki, personal communication, December 7, 2020). I, however, will use the term Khas Aryan in this book, for the new Nepali constitution (2072 BS) uses the term Khas Aryan. Again, to the point, Yakthung Indigenous peoples, in this context, have become the prey of preys due to the local, regional, and Western colonization. For instance, Indian culture became prey of Western culture; Nepali Khas Aryan culture became prey of Indian and Western cultures; and Yakthung Indigenous culture became prey of Khas Aryan, Indian, and Western cultures. This local and global cultural colonization endangers Yakthung Suhang customary institutions, for Yakthungs currently are not in the position to unambiguously distinguish their Yet Hang and Thibong Yakthung customary cultural traditions.

At present, Yakthungs reside in Nepal, India (Sikkim, Darjeeling, Kalimpong (Kalebung), Manipur, Nagaland, Arunachal Pradesh, and Assam, etc.), Bhutan, Bangladesh, Thailand, Burma, the UK (United Kingdom), the USA (United States of America), and Hong Kong to mention a few. Even though Yakthungs currently reside across the world, they are one of the major Indigenous peoples of the South Asian Himalayan region. The ancient South Asian Hindu culture, including Western cultures, knew and still know them as "Kiratas" or "Kirats" (see Chattopodyaya, 2015, p. 8; Kainla, 2059 BS; Limbu, 2017; Lunminthang, 2016; Raj, 2011; Rosati, 2017; Roy, 2015; Tumbahang, 2007, 2013). After the unification of greater Nepal, the Nepali government recognized the eastern regions of Kathmandu as Kirat (Kõich/ Kõits, Khambu, and Yakthung) regions, such as Wallo Kirat or Kõich region (Near East Kirat from Kathmandu), Majha Kirat or Khambu region (Middle East Kirat from Kathmandu), and Pallo Kirat or Yakthung region (Far East Kirat from Kathmandu). Though South Asian Hindu culture (Aryans) call/ed Yakthungs, the Kirats, the term Kirat or Kirata or Kirant, including Limbu, Subba, Tsong, and Raya/Rai, does not exist in *Yakthung pa:n* (Yakthung language) and in Yakthung Mundhums. When Yakthungs converse in *Yakthung pa:n*, they do not use Kirat, Kirata, or Kirant. For instance, in Hodgson's collection (1845–1857), "Limbu" is frequently used in the Nepali texts (in the Devanagari script); whereas, "Yakthung" is used in Yakthung texts (in the Sirijanga script). According to Yakthung Mundhum, Yakthungs, including their non-Yakthung *phu-ne-nusa* (brothers and sisters), are also known as Sawa Yet Hangs (eight sons of Lahadangna and Suhampheba; later, they stayed with their mother, according to Yakthung Mundhum), for Mundhum states that Sawa Yet Hangs spread across the world. However, South Asian Khas Aryans or Indian (Hindus) called Yakthungs, Khambus, Kõiches (Kõits), Yakkhas, and other Himalayan Indigenous peoples Kirats. Later, Westerners, including Khas Aryans called Yakthungs, Khambus, Kõiches, Yakkhas, and other Himalayan Indigenous peoples as Kirats or Kiratas or Kirants. Hence,

Yakthungs, Khambus, Kõiches, Yakkhas, Athpahariyas, and Southeast Asian Himalayan Indigenous peoples had/have been known as Kirats for centuries (Chattopodyaya, 2015, p. 8; Lunminthang, 2016; Raj, 2011; Rosati, 2017; Roy, 2015; Schlemmer, 2003/04; Sprigg, 1959, 1989, 1999; van Driem, 1987).

Concerning the Kirat history, they (the Kirats) had ruled over South Asian and Southeast Asian regions for centuries. According to Hodgson's collection, it is believed that 28 Kirati Kings or many other sources claim that 32 Kirati Kings (32 generations) had ruled with Yalambar being the first Kirat King and Gasti being the last one. The Kingdom of Kirat spread from Nepal to Southeast Asia; it is believed that the Kingdom of Kirat spread up to Northeast India and beyond, and this might be one of the reasons why the Bodos of Assam (India) claim that Yalambar had been their king. Though the Kingdom of Kirat spread up to Southeast Asia (Northeast India), it is believed that the capital was located in the central part of Nepal, i.e. the Kathmandu Valley. The Kirat reign collapsed in about 300–400 when the Lichchhavis invaded them from Baisali of the ancient Northern India. The Lichchhavis, however, are considered to have been a sub-group of Kirats (A. Limbu, personal communication, June 3, 2017; Limbu, 2017; Sprigg, 1989; Tumbahang, 2068 BS). After Lichchhavi had displaced the Kirat reign, the majority of Kirats migrated to the eastern part of Kathmandu, which had already been the homeland of Yakthungs, Yakkhas, Khambus, and Kõiches (Limbu, 2017; Mabuhang, 2014; Subba, 2015). However, Yakthungs, as I mentioned before, do not identify themselves as Kirats, but as Yakthungs. According to Yakthung Mundhum (folklore), Yakthungs are the descendants of Sawa Yet Hangs and Susuwa Lilim Yakthungs (Mundhumic terms) or the descendants of Yet Hangs and Thibong Yakthungs. Even though Mundhum introduces Yakthungs as Sawa Yet Hangs and Susuwa Lilim Yakthungs, they introduce themselves as Yakthungs or Yakthung Suhangs, their language as *Yakthung pa:n*, and their homeland as Yakthung laje. Yakthungs have been shifting their identities in this order: Sawa Yet Hang (Mundhumic term), Susuwa Lilim Yakthung (Mundhumic term), Yet Hang, Thibong Yakthung, Yakthung Suhang or Yakthung. However, non-Yakthungs, such as Khas Aryans, Bhutias, Indians, and Westerners, gradually labelled, displaced, and destroyed their original identities.

Historically, by the 17th century, the Khas Aryans (local para-colonizers) started establishing their own small nation in Nepal, and they gradually became the dominant culture and nation in the western part of Nepal, known as the Gorkha (Gurkha) Kingdom. The Gorkhas (Khas Aryans) gradually started invading the Malla Kingdoms in the Kathmandu Valley and the Kirat regions (Giuseppe, 1790). The Khas Aryan became one of the most powerful and dominant groups in Nepal by the end of the 18th century. The Khas Aryans conquered the Mallas, Kõiches, and Khambus, and they came under the control of the Gorkha Kingdom. However, Yakthungs (Limbus) became the only allies (co-state) of the Gorkha Kingdom as Gorkhas lost all the 17 Gorkha-Yakthung battles to the Yakthungs. In other words, according to the Nun-Paani Sandhi (Treaty of Salt-Water, literal translation) in 1774, Yakthungs became the only allies of the Gorkha Kingdom, not the conquered citizens of the Gorkha Kingdom. However, after the death of Prithvi Narayan Shah, his sons, grandsons, and descendants disregarded the treaty—the Nun-Paani Sandhi. They could disregard the treaty as they were able to divide Yakthungs in two groups: *samariti* (Gorkha/Khas Aryan statutory law supporters) and *niti* (traditional Yakthung customary institutional tradition supporters) Yakthungs. Gradually, the Khas Aryans, with the help of *samariti* Yakthungs, not only displaced and/or banished Yakthungs from Yakthung laje, but they also destroyed Yakthung cultural, linguistic, religious, and *khambong-lungbong* identities.

During the Sen dynasty (before the Khas Aryan invasion), Yakthungs, including Khambus, Athpahariyas, and Yakkhas, were known as Raya or Rai. Therefore, the Khambus, Athpahariyas, and Yakkhas still identify themselves as Rais; whereas, Yakthungs eventually stopped identifying themselves as Raya or Rai. However, in relation to Raya or Rai identity, Yakthungs still have the Syahamohors (documents given by Sens) that address Yakthungs as Raya or Rai, such as Srijang Raya, Sri Phung (Kum) Raya, Jamun (Sun) Raya, Aitahang Raya, Sri Deb Raya, Shubhawatta Raya, Rainsing Raya, Sunuhang Raya, Ashdeb Raya, and Jasmukhi (Jaikarna) Raya (they were the 10 chieftains in Yakthung laje before/during the Nun-Paani Sandhi). Whereas the Bhutias of Sukhim (Sikkim) also called Yakthungs "Tsong." The political and ideological settings demonstrate that Yakthungs have/had multiple identities, such as Sawa Yet Hang, Susuwa Lilim Yakthung, Yet Hang, Thibong Yakthung Suhang, Raya or Rai, Tsong (Sikkim), Yakthung Suhang or Yakthung, Limbu or Limboo (Sikkim), and Subba.

Although Yakthungs are known as Limbu or Limboo, Subba, Tsong, and Raya, including Kirat, as a part of my delinking, relinking, and linking methodology, I use Yakthung/s or Yakthung Suhang/s in this book. I use Limboo to refer to Sikkimi (Sukhime) Yakthungs, Kirat Yakthung to refer to the Yakthung social institution/s, and Kirat to refer to Kirat-specific historical narratives/documents. In this book, since I am a Yakthung rhetorician, activist, and *tutu-tumyahang*, I use "Yakthungs" and/or "we" interchangeably especially when I feel that my communal presence is instrumental, and I use "Yakthungs" and/or "they" to disengage myself in some circumstances. Similarly, I use para-colonialism, para-colonization, and para-colonizer to refer to Khas Aryan (including Indian) cultural, linguistic, and religious colonization in Nepali and Indian contexts. The critical discussion of local para-colonialism should not be misunderstood like the traditional European and/or Western colonization. In traditional contexts, the colonizers had to leave the colonies, for instance, Britain left the colonies, such as India, Hong Kong, Taiwan, and Nigeria. Likewise, other European colonizers left their colonies. Currently, local colonialism is perceived and practiced or interpreted in "para-colonial" context (Limbu, 2017; Powell, 2002; Vizenor, 1990) in which colonizers and colonized coexist, have to coexist, and will coexist in several countries in the context of the 21st century. Meaning, the para-colonizers are not supposed to leave the places where they have been ideologically and politically oppressing the Indigenous peoples in their ancestral homelands, for instance, Nepal, India, Canada, the USA, Australia to mention a few.

As this book is geared toward Yakthung language, writing, and rhetorics, I want to discuss the Nun-Paani Sandhi, and how it affected Yakthungs, the development of Yakthung language and literacy, and Yakthung customary institutional traditions. As mentioned above, the Nun-Paani Sandhi was/ is a treaty between Yakthung Suhangs (chiefs) and Khas Aryans (Gorkhas) that took place in 1774 (Limbu, 2017, p. 561; see also Lumphungwa Limbu, pp. 55–60). Immediately after the treaty, Khas Aryans started displacing Yakthungs and destroying Yakthung customary traditions, language, writing system, and Mundhum rhetorics. To further destroy and displace Yakthungs, the Khas Aryans and British divided them in three different countries: Nepal, India, and Sikkim in the Treaty of Sugauli in 1816. In this book, I will discuss how the Khas Aryan and British ideologically and politically divided Yakthungs, and displaced their customary traditions, language, literacy, and Mundhum rhetorics. After the Nun-Paani Sandhi, the Khas Aryans divided Kõiches, Khambus, and Yakthungs in three regions: Wallo Kirat (Near East Kirat region from Kathmandu that refers to Kõich region), Majha Kirat (Middle East Kirat region from Kathmandu that refers to Khambu region), and Pallo Kirat (Far East Kirat region from Kathmandu that refers to Limbuwan or the Yakthung laje) for the para-colonial purposes (Kandangwa, 1999, p. 47; Kainla, 2070; Limbu, 2017; Mabuhang, 2014, p. 172; Schlemmer, 2003/2004, pp. 119–143; Subba-Lawati, 2017, pp. 58–66). The Pallo Kirat region had been well known as Yakthung laje for Yakthungs were/are the natives of Yakthung laje; now this region is well known as Limbuwan. Historically, Yakthung laje was comprised of Sikkim, Darjeeling, Kalimpong, Siliguri, Jalpaiguri, Dooars, and the western part of Assam, including some parts of Bangladesh and Bhutan. Currently, Yakthungs live in Yakthung laje (Nepal), Sikkim, Darjeeling, Kalimpong, Bhutan, Assam, West Bengal, Burma, Thailand, Bangladesh, Hong Kong, the UK, the USA, and Canada. During the British colonial era in Southeast Asia, the British dispersed Yakthungs up to Burma, Thailand, and beyond.

Yakthungs have their own script, the Sirijanga script, that was re/designed by King Maarang in the 7th century (see Bhumika by Subba, 1928; Sprigg, 1959, p. 591; Subba, 2015, pp. 99–101; Vansittart, 1991, p. 105) and by King Sirijanga in the late 9th or early 10th century. According to Dor B. Bista (1991) the Khas Aryans (mainly Brahmins), by persuading the Lichchhavi Kings, had destroyed all non-Hindu books and documents after the rise of the Lichchhavi reign. Furthermore, the Khas Aryan practice of destroying non-Hindu books, official documents, genealogy books, Mundhum rhetorics, and archival materials continued until 1990 in Nepal. Hence, the Khas Aryan logic of cultural, linguistic, and religious colonization destroyed all written and oral documents of Indigenous peoples in this region (Bista, 1991; see also Campbell 1842; Kirkpatrick, 1811). In relation to Yakthung language and literacy, due to the lack of adequate research, (lack of the) linguistic competence, and (lack of the) literacy competence in the Sirijanga writing system, Campbell, Mainwaring, Hodgson, Sprigg, and van Driem also misunderstood the Sirijanga script and writing system (Indigenous knowledge and reality); as a result, they constructed knowledge only for the colonial purpose and/or produced incorrect information (Limbu, 2017, 2018; see also Smith, 2012; Sprigg, 1959, 1989, 1999; Tuck & Guishard, 2013; Tuck & Yang, 2018).

As I implied earlier, based on the Old Sirijanga syllabary, the writing system seems to have developed upon the foundation of the ancient Himalayan Indigenous writing system or the Himalayan Indigenous writing system (see Gaur, 1987, p. 113). In the early 18th century, Tye Angsi Singthebe (Yakthungs, in the early 20th century, entitled him Sirijanga II) revived, redocumented, and popularized this script and writing system in Yakthung laje, Sikkim, and India. However, after the Nun-Paani Sandhi, the Khas Aryans (para-colonizers) banned the teaching of *Yakthung pa:n*, the Yakthung writing system, Yakthung customary tradition, and Mundhum rhetorics until 1990 in Nepal. Similarly, the Bhutia Kings also banned the teaching of the Sirijanga script or Yakthung writing system in Sikkim (Sukhim, an independent country then) from the 1740s (the execution of Tye Angsi Singthebe implied) to 1968.

Immediately after the Nun-Paani Sandhi, the Khas Aryans started culturally, linguistically, and politically colonizing and suppressing Yakthungs in Yakthung laje by ignoring the treaty, and the Khas Aryans' political and ideological suppression adversely affected Yakthungs, Yakthung language, and literacy from 1774 to 1990 (until the restoration of so-called democracy) in Nepal. Because of the Khas Aryan's over 240 year-long oppression, the Yakthung culture has become predominantly oral even though the Yakthung writing system had been well-developed before the 18th century (Tye Angsian era's language and literacy implied). Because of the Khas Aryan ideological and political oppression in Yakthung laje, Yakthungs used and still use oral and performance-based Mundhum rhetorics to preserve their culture, language, histories, and Mundhum rhetorics. The Khas Aryans, after the Nun-Paani Sandhi, regularly collected all Himalayan Indigenous (Kirat) people's books, including Yakthung books, pamphlets, Mundhum books, histories, genealogy books, Yakthung Khahun saksak, Syamohors, and Lal Mohars (official documents), and they destroyed all of them (Nembang, 1987; Schlemmer 2003/2004; Subba-Lawati, 2017, pp. 58–66). In relation to Khas Aryan suppression over Yakthung Suhangs in Yakthung laje, the Khas Aryan-centric government captured, tortured, or executed Yakthungs who advocated for their rights to *kipat* (land) or their rights to their ancestral land, language, writing, customary institutional traditions, and Mundhum rhetorics (Limbu et al., 1845 or Hodgson collection, vol. 85; Mabuhang & Tunghang, 2070 BS; Nembang, 1987). Similarly, the Thachhang Lamas with the help of Bhutia King, captured, tortured, and executed Tye Angsi Singthebe, including other

Yakthungs, for his teaching of the Sirijanga writing system, *Yakthung pa:n*, Yakthung Mundhums, and Yakthung religion in the mid of the 18th century (late 30th and early 40th of the 18th century) in Sikkim.

Delinking and relinking Yakthung writing and rhetorics: problem

Only after the establishment of Shree Yakthung Hang Chumlung on July 26, 1925 in Dungrabasti, Kalimpong, *Yakthung phu-ne-nusa* (brothers and sisters) collectively struggled to preserve, document, and institutionalize Yakthung culture, writing, and Mundhum literacies. The collective *Yakthung phu-ne-nusa's* struggle kindled Yakthung Suhang epistemic activities in Yakthung communities. After the foundation of Shree Yakthung Hang Chumlung, Yakthungs networked, collaborated, and wrote several books on Yakthung Mundhums, folklores, Yakthung histories, and grammar books. They established Zambuk Junior Basic School in Dungrabasti, Kalimpong in 1938 in order to teach the Sirijanga script, *Yakthung pa:n*, Yakthung customary cultural traditions, and Mundhum rhetorics (K. B. Sambahamphe, personal communication, May 23, 2018). The teaching of the Yakthung language and writing at Zambuk Junior Basic School for the first time delinked Khas Aryan, Indian, and Western colonial ideology of knowledge construction in the context of the 20th century in Yakthung history. More importantly, after the foundation of Shree Yakthung Hang Chumlung and Zambuk Junior Basic School, Yakthungs, including Yakthung children, started valuing and validating *Yakthung pa:n*, writing system, and Yakthung customary traditions (K. B. Sambahamphe, personal communication, May 23, 2018). Finally, the Sikkimi government (then, an independent country) officially approved the teaching of the Yakthung (Limboo) language in 1968, and the teaching of the Yakthung language started in 1969 in Sikkim (Khamdhak, 2019, pp. 901–902). However, the Khas Aryan-centric discriminatory Nepali government did not recognize the teaching of the Yakthung language and writing in Yakthung laje (Limbuwan), Nepal.

The Khas Aryans banned Yakthungs from the teaching of their language both in formal and informal settings in Yakthung laje, Nepal until the restoration of so-called democracy in 1990. Thereafter, the Khas Aryan-centric Nepali government allowed Yakthungs to teach *Anipa:n* (Limbu language) up to an elementary school level as an optional subject. However, the Khas Aryan-centric government has not yet provided any support to Yakthung language education. Meaning, the Nepali government does not spend a single penny on *Anipa:n* at schools; whereas, the Khas Aryan-centric discriminatory Nepali government spends millions of dollars every year to promote Sanskrit, a dead language (B. Kainla, personal communication, January 3, 2015; Y. Laoti, personal communication, June 3, 2018). During a workshop at Limbuwan Study Center, Bijaypur chapter, Dharan, some of my research informants reported that the Khas Aryan-centric government has approved the teaching and learning of *Yakthung pa:n* at Sanskrit college in Dharan, but Yakthungs, including non-Yakthungs, who are interested in learning *Yakthung pa:n* and Yakthung studies are compulsorily required to take three-to-four Sanskrit courses and also must get passing grades before they take the target language, *Yakthung pa:n* courses. In relation to Indigenous peoples rights to education, United Nations Declaration on the Rights of Indigenous Peoples (UNDRIP) clearly states, "Indigenous peoples have the right to establish and control their educational systems and institutions providing education in their own languages, in a manner appropriate to their cultural methods of teaching and learning"; furthermore, "Indigenous individuals, particularly children, have the right to all levels and forms of education of the State without discrimination" (Article 14.1 & 2, p. 7). Despite being a member of the United Nations, this is how the Khas Aryan-centric Nepali government discriminates against Yakthungs', including other Indigenous peoples', rights to mother-tongue education in Nepal.

Until the early 20th century, none of the governments (Sikkimi, Indian, Nepali, Bhutani, Burmese, and Thai) paid attention to the introduction, preservation, and institutionalization of the Yakthung language in a formal setting. As I stated above, having seen the dire condition of Yakthung culture, language, and literacy, Yakthung community leaders and activists from Kalimpong, India founded Shree Yakthung Hang Chumlung in 1925. The Kalimponge Yakthungs established Shree Yakthung Hang Chumlung not only to teach and learn the Yakthung language, writing, and Mundhum rhetorics, but also to network with other Yakthungs from India, Nepal, Bhutan, Bangladesh, Burma, and Thailand. The main purpose of establishing Shree Yakthung Hang Chumlung was to collectively document, preserve, and disseminate the Yakthung language, literacy, writing system, and Mundhum rhetorics (K. B. Sambahamphe, personal communication, May 23, 2018). After 1925, Yakthungs collectively campaigned to delink the Khas Aryan, Indian, and Western cultural and linguistic colonization; they relinked Sawa Yet Hang and/or Yet Hang customary traditions; they relinked Thibong Yakthung Suhang history and Mundhum epistemologies in local and regional contexts. The relinking of the Sirijanga script, writing, and rhetorics facilitated the development of the Yakthung language, literacy, and Mudhum rhetorics. This setting suggests that Yakthungs from South Asia networked and collaborated to explore Yakthung history, language, literacy, and Mundhum rhetorics and updated them from the early 20th century perspective. In a nutshell, documentation of the Sirijanga script, writing system, Yakthung Suhang histories, and Mundhums not only helped Yakthungs delink Khas Aryan, Indian, and Western cultural and linguistic colonization, but it also facilitated them to relink traditional Sawa Yet Hang knowledge, Susuwa Lilim epistemic practices, Yet Hang insights, and Thibong Yakthung customary cultural traditions. Though the teaching and learning of the Yakthung language had never been formal in any part of the world until the mid-20th century (Yakthung language teaching in Sikkim implied), after the foundation of Shree Yakthung Hang Chumlung, Yakthungs, for the first time, felt the power and prestige of being literate in their own language and writing system.

Despite the fact that Yakthung scholars struggled to restore the Sirijanga script and writing system, the early 20th century Yakthung writing and literacy practices demonstrate how they moved away from the Old Sirijanga script and writing system (will discuss in detail in this book). The reason why Yakthungs stopped using the Old Sirijanga script and writing system was the discontinuation of Yet Hang and Thibong Yakthung Suhang customary traditions, loss of histories, Mundhum narratives, and writing literacies due to the Khas Aryan oppression since 1774 in Nepal and the Bhutia oppression in Sikkim (execution of Tye Angsi Singthebe in 1741 implied). As implied earlier, for more than 240 years, the Khas Aryans, by force or coercion, collected Yakthung books and destroyed all of them and also banned the teaching and learning of the Yakthung language, writing, history, and Mundhum rhetorics. Similarly, when Singthebe was teaching or preaching Yakthung language, writing system, religion, and Mundhum rhetorics in West Sikkim, Thachhang Lamas accused him of plotting against the Sikkimi Bhutia government, such as their language, culture, politics, and religion, and they captured, tortured, and executed him in 1741 (Chemjong, 2003; Limbu, 2016, 2017; Tumbahang, 2007). After the execution of Tye Angsi Singthebe, Yakthungs were hesitant (to encourage their children) to read and write in the Yakthung language and script in Sukhim, for Yakthungs feared the Bhutia ruler/s and Thachhang Lamas' oppression, persecution, and execution. In other words, the execution of Singthebe in 1741 dissuaded Yakthungs from the teaching and learning of the Yakthung language and writing in Sikkim (an independent country then). Therefore, teaching and learning of the Yakthung language in Sukhim (Sikkim) was not also easy as the Bhutia rulers banned the teaching of the *Yakthung pa:n*, writing system, and Mundhum rhetorics until 1968.

As I implied above, during my research, I found some evidence that the Yakthung writing system developed upon the foundation of Himalayan Indigenous cultures (Gaur, 1984, 1987, p. 113) or Kirat culture (Campbell, 1842, 1855; Sprigg, 1959, 1989, 1999; Subba, 1925; van Driem, 1987). Later, due to the constant Khas Aryan oppression, the perception of writing, rhetoric, and culture shifted dramatically. As I stated earlier, Yakthungs started observing their own culture, language, and literacy via the Khas Aryan, Indian, and Western corpuses. Although Yakthung language and literacy has its deepest roots in the ancient Himalayan Indigenous civilization, i. e. the Yet Hang and Thibong Yakthung Suhang civilization, contemporary Yakthung proponents barely invoke their them (Yet Hangs and Thibong Yakthungs); for example, Kirat Yakthung Chumlung's (KYC) decision to exclude "Yakthung" identity in language, race, and history in the upcoming census in 2021 (in Nepal) displaces and destroys Yakthung identity. Hence, Yakthungs (mostly, KYC folks) tend to lean toward Kirat and Limbu, which is ideological and religious, and their ideology or ego and religious faith is displacing and destroying our Yakthung identity. The key conception we have to understand is that Kirat is an exonym (not native) identity; the Hindus (Khas Aryans) called the Himalayan Indigenous peoples the Kirats, which refers to not only Rai, Yakthung, Kõich, Athpahariya, Yakkha, and Dhimal, but all Himalayan Indigenous peoples other than Khas Aryans, and majority of the Himalayan Indigenous peoples do not approve the Kirat identity.

As implied above, Yakthungs could not reintroduce their writing system, language, literacy, and Mundhum rhetorics until 1990 in Nepal. So, they had to depend upon the oral Yakthung Mundhums (Yakthung folklores) to preserve the Yet Hang and Thibong Yakthung customary traditions. In other words, under the Khas Aryan suppression, Yakthung storytelling culture, including performative Yakthung rhetorics and oral-performance-based rhetorics became the medium of transmitting Yakthung history, Mundhum, language, and literacy. As storytelling culture was practiced for centuries, Yakthungs consider their Mundhums as the scriptures of the Sawa Yet Hang, Susuwa Lilim Yakthung, Yet Hang, and Thibong Yakthung cultures. Sadly, Yakthungs have not done any significant research on Yakthung customary rhetorical tradition to critically explore Yet Hang and Thibong Yakthung customary epistemic foundations. They have not yet researched (search again) to critically and analytically study Mundhums and interpret them to explore their historical, spatial, cultural, and political identities for their purposes. As a result, many Yakthungs tend to misconstrue Yakthung Mundhums and historical customary institutional traditions; whereas another group of Yakthungs believe that they are the descendants of Kirats and want to relink their identities to Kirats. The misunderstandings, in the Yakthung communities, exist as they do not have written documents that would reveal their history, culture, writing, and Mundhum rhetorics. So, the Khas Aryans in Nepal, including Bhutias in Sikkim, are solely accountable for the intrusive situations of Yakthungs. The contemporary Yakthung intrusive conditions in Yakthung communities exhibit that knowledge is slippery and culturally constructed through aristocratic (Khas Aryan and Western) dialectical and linguistic interaction within our Yakthung and South Asian Indigenous epistemologies that systemically put the Yakthung language, writing, and rhetorics in exile.

Objectives of the book and research methods

This book is a handbook on the historical development of the Sirijanga script, Yakthung writing and rhetorics, and Yakthung Suhang literacy. The general purpose of this book is to critically examine the inventions, interventions, and reinventions of the Sirijanga script and writing system. In other words, it aims to explore the development of the Sirijanga script, writing system, Mundhum rhetorics and rise-fall-rise of the Sirijanga script and literacy in the South Asian Himalayan Indigenous cultures. Meaning, this book focuses on the politics of writing and rhetoric in Yakthung laje, such as Nepal and

India, including Burma, Thailand, and Bhutan. By using Limbu's (2017) "delinking, relinking, and linking methodology" and ethnohistorical research methodology, this book investigates the history of Yakthung language, writing, and rhetorics. Hence, this book precisely aims to focus on Yakthung studies, including South Asian Himalayan Indigenous studies, such as 1) how to research and digitally document the historical development of endangered language, writing, performative rhetorics and/or oral-performance-based rhetorics, 2) how to critically and analytically study and interpret oral texts, historical artifacts, customary traditions and provide a solid theoretical and historical framework of Indigenous language, writing, and script, 3) how to make Yakthung Indigenous language, writing, and rhetorics more structured and methodological, 4) how to institutionalize Indigenous oral texts, writing, and rhetorics, and 5) how to disseminate them in the local and global contexts in the context of the 21st century's digitally networked global village.

Methodologically, my five-year-long empirical and ethnohistorical research methodologies allowed me to critically map the Yakthung historical, cultural, linguistic, writing, and political conditions as a Yakthung scholar (see also Axtell, 1979; Cushman, 2012, 2013; Harkin, 2010). The ethnohistorical methodology facilitated my research to investigate the historical development of the Sirijanga script and writing traditions. It allowed me to explore Yakthung traditional cultural foundations, current Yakthung cultural conditions, and practices. Via ethnohistorical methodology, I, as an insider (emic approach implied) observed the challenges of the Yakthung language and digital/ multimodal writing practices, such as Yakthung current and archived materials, Yakthung music, paintings, photos, Mundhums, folklores, oral traditions, site explorations, archaeological materials, museum collections, enduring customs, languages, places (names of places—naming and claiming theory and practice implied), and remnants of Yakthung Suhang palaces/ places (see also Cushman, 2013; Kovach, 2009; Lavallee, 2009; McGuire-Adams, 2020; Smith, 2012). During the five-year long research, I went to Assam (Guwahati, Gangapur, Tezpur, Biswanath, Tinsukia, Golaghat), Kalimpong, Sikkim, Darjeeling, Nepal, and the UK to visit/study historical places, libraries, museums, and universities. I met with many historians, linguists, Yakthung activists, community/political leaders, Yakthung Indigenous elders and knowledge keepers, and oral-text experts.

As mentioned above, in this book, I use "Delinking, Relinking, and Linking Methodologies" (Limbu, 2017) to critically study and analyze various facts, figures, data, oral texts, interviews, images, and video files, etc. to unravel how Yakthungs have been delinking Khas Aryan, Indian, and Western colonial ideology; how Yakthungs have been relinking the Yet Hang and Thibong Yakthung Suhang customary institutional epistemologies, narratives, and Mundhum rhetorics, and how they have been linking their Susuwa Lilim Yakthung epistemologies, Yet Hang wisdoms and Thibong Yakthung customary traditions, including current Yakthung cultural, linguistic, and political identities from the local to global levels (Limbu, 2017, pp. 573–575).

Via delinking, relinking, and linking theoretical lens/es, I observe how Yakthungs have been delinking the Khas Aryan-driven Yakthung epistemic activities, how Yakthung Suhangs have been relinking Susuwa Lilim Yakthung and Thibong Yakthung Suhang customary institutional traditions, and how they have been linking Yakthung Suhang rhetorical traditions with other local and global Indigenous and non-Indigenous epistemologies in the context of the 21st century networked world. Via the relinking process, I observe how Yakthung have been relinking Susuwa Lilim Yakthung and Yet Hang epistemologies or Thibong Yakthung Suhang customary institutional foundations. Hence, this book demonstrates how Yakthung Suhang Indigenous peoples are delinking Khas Aryan, Indian, and Western linguistic and cultural colonization, and how they are relinking and reconstructing the Sawa Yet Hang, Susuwa Lilim, Yet Hang, Thibong Yakthung or Yakthung Suhang epistemologies. This book will illuminate what research methodologies, methods, and approaches I have used to demonstrate what Indigenous rhetorical strategies Yakthungs have been utilizing to delink Khas Aryan, Indian, Western colonization, or how they use (have to use) them as tools to explore their traditional customary cultural epistemological (knowledge), ontological (existence), and axiological (value) foundations. In this book, I discuss linking methodology to demonstrate how Yakthungs have been networking, collaborating, institutionalizing, updating, and disseminating their history, language, and literacy (such as Yakthung Suhang customary institutional traditions) from the local, regional to global levels (see also Limbu, 2017, pp. 573–575).

As I implied above, this book critically outlines the historical development of the Sirijanga script, such as its inventions, interventions, and reinventions. It explores the historical foundation of Yakthung writing and rhetorics, such as when the Sirijanga script or writing system was introduced, and what interventions occurred that displaced and destroyed the Old Sirijanga script, writing system, Yakthung language, and literacy. Furthermore, while I went through the delinking, relinking, and linking process especially in the making of this book, I realized that Indigenous research methodologies and composing processes are different from mainstream (Khas Aryan and Western) academic culture/s (also see Smith, 1999; Rigney, 1999; Coombes & Ryder, 2020). Hence, this book exposes my own Yakthung Suhang Indigenous scholarly endeavor, epistemological undertakings, ontological humilities, and axiological perceptions that have informed and shaped my research, writing, and construction of this book. This book, however, does not provide a blueprint on how or what Yakthung Suhang traditional customary epistemologies and ontologies must be (studied, analyzed, interpreted, and documented), but attempts to issue a call for my current and future Yakthung Suhang audience, including Yakthung Indigenous studies audience, how our research theory and practice should look like. Henceforth, this book is a critical contemplation of Yet Hang and Thibong Yakthung Suhang histories in relation to language, writing, and rhetorics, and I have updated them from the 21st century Yakthung Suhang Indigenous scholar's perspective.

Methodologically, I hope this book establishes a leading-edge theoretical and practical conceptions for global Yakthung communities, for it seeks to unfold Yakthung's delinking, relinking, and linking historical foundations, traditional customary traditions, and Yakthung writing and rhetorics. Via delinking, relinking, and linking approaches, this book succinctly reveals how Yakthung Suhangs have preserved, documented, and institutionalized their language, writing, and rhetorics that had been differently (always as inferior) labelled, displaced, and destroyed; later, how Yakthung Suhangs struggled to relink their script, writing system, and Sawa Yet Hang, Yet Hang, and Thibong Yakthung Suhang literacies in the 20th and 21st centuries. Again, this book not only exhibits how Yakthungs have formally institutionalized or are in the process of institutionalizing their language and literacy, but also demonstrates how Yakthungs, including non-Yakthungs, have to orient their children and themselves to promote, institutionalize, and disseminate their language, writing, rhetorics, and Mundhum rhetorics in the context of the 21st century.

Targeted audiences of the book

The intended audience of this book include Yakthungs, Indigenous activists, community leaders, and minority scholars. My targeted audience also include the individual beings who research, write, document, and/or teach global Indigenous studies, and writing and rhetorics. This book will be instrumental for my targeted audience who envision the practice of integrating delinking, relinking, and linking methodologies and pedagogies in research, writing (composition), and pedagogical (classroom) practices. My audience find this book instrumental, for it discusses how Indigenous communities, including linguistic and cultural minorities, can delink cultural, pedagogical, linguistic, and political para-colonization, how they can relink their cultural and linguistic identities and spaces, and how they can link their narratives, stories, histories, and literacies in local and global contexts. This book will be a handbook for Yakthungs, including Indigenous and minority audience, who aim to document, disseminate, maintain, archive, and institutionalize endangered languages, writing, and oral rhetorics. In Yakthung communities, most of the research and documentation done as of now are folktales, narratives, histories, translations, facts, and figures, and there is a lack of critical Yakthung language and literacy research and writing. Furthermore, as critical Yakthung studies or documentation is lacking in Yakthung communities, there is an urgency of critical Yakthung Indigenous research and writing because Yakthung oral texts, performance rhetorics, and/or oral-performance-based Mundhum rhetorics are also on the verge of extinction.

Structure of the book

Chapter 1 offers theoretical and methodological framework of the Sirijanga writing system, writing, rhetorics, and methodologies. It discusses what writing is, and what historical foundations Yakthung writing and rhetoric had gone through in the making of Yakthung Indigenous writing and rhetorics. This chapter seeks to unfold what inventions and interventions (issues and opportunities) took place/s in the making of the Sirijanga writing system. This chapter introduces what delinking, relinking, and linking methodology is and justifies how and why delinking, relinking, and linking methodology is a better research approach to inquire, explore, and institutionalize Yakthung Indigenous writing systems, rhetorical situations, and historical conditions.

Chapter 2 discusses the historical foundation of Yakthung writing and rhetorics. It introduces King Sirijanga (10th century), his re/invention or re/design of the Sirijanga script upon the foundation the King Maarangian writing system (7th century); it also briefly discusses the Mundhum of King Sirijanga and Goddess Nisammang. It further examines King Sirijanga's political, philosophical theories on writing and rhetoric, including Yakthung customary institutional theories and representational Yakthung practices in Yakthung laje. It critically studies the Yakthung Mundhum rhetorics on the development of language and literacy (reading and writing).

Chapter 3 revisits the landscape of the 18th century Yakthung writing and rhetorics. This chapter unveils Tye Angsi Singthebe's contributions to the development of Yakthung writing and rhetoric, such as his relinking of the Sirijanga script, the writing system, Mundhum rhetorics, and traditional customary laws and practices. It also uncovers Singthebe's philosophical and pedagogical theories, his teachings in Yakthung laje and Sukhim (Sikkim) during the early 18th century, and the erosion of Yakthung language and literacies in Yakthung laje. This chapter succinctly exhibits Singthebe's delinking and relinking campaign, his cultural and linguistic theories, philosophies, and how he translated them into practices. Similarly, this chapter unmasks Singthebe's multicultural, transborder, and cross-cultural concepts, theories, and practices, and why and how Tye Angsi Singthebe was one of the greatest linguists, scholars, trans-cultural leaders, transnational/border scholars, and Yakthung Mundhumists in the context of the 18th century.

Chapter 4 discusses the Khas Aryan encroachment into Yakthung laje through the Nun-Paani Sandhi in 1774; then, how they (Khas Aryans) ignored the treaty and how they suppressed Yakthungs in Yakthung laje. The chapter discloses how the Khas Aryans (para-colonizers) gradually divided Yakthungs into *samariti* and *niti*, how they captured, tortured, executed, or banished the Niti Yakthungs, and how Khas Aryan ideology and politics gradually weakened Yakthung collective power. In so doing, this chapter reveals how the Khas Aryans banned Yakthungs from the teaching and learning of their language (*Yakthung pa:n*), Mundhum rhetorics, and writing; and finally, how the Khas Aryans became able to displace and destroy Yakthung cultural and linguistic identities of Yakthungs for 240 years. In this chapter, I, as a Yakthung rhetorician, researcher, and *tutu-tumyahang*, share/d my own lived Yakthung Suhang epistemological experiences in Nepali para-colonial context to inform how I perceive, process, interpret, and project Khas Aryan para-colonial situations. Then, I explain how Khas Aryans use para-colonial ideology to humiliate and hurt Yakthungs, including Indigenous peoples in Nepal.

Chapter 5 examines the Khas Aryan para-colonial politics on how Europeans supported the Khas Aryan hegemony and politics not only to divide and rule Yakthungs, but also to displace, and destroy their (Yakthungs) cultural, linguistic, and historical identities. In other words, this chapter reveals how the British and Khas Aryans divided Yakthungs into three different countries—India, Sikkim, and Nepal in the Treaty of the Sugauli in 1818; then, how they displaced Yakthungs in Southeast Asian countries and destroyed Yakthung Suhang traditional cultural and linguistic identities. The chapter not only evidently exhibits how the Khas Aryans destroyed all Yakthung books, official documents, cultural artifacts and Yakthung archival materials, but also reveals how Europeans gathered Yakthung books and manuscripts and transported them to Europe for colonial purposes.

Chapter 6 discusses the first Yakthung rhetoric and writing wave after the establishment of Shree Yakthung Hang Chumlung (a Yakthung social institution) in Kalimpong in 1925. The chapter scrutinizes why Yakthungs established their social institution, and how they networked, researched, collaborated, and documented Yakthung writing, literacy, and Mundhum rhetorics. This chapter concisely exposes how Yakthung endeavored to delink the Khas Aryan, Indian, and British cultural and linguistic colonization and to relink their Thibong Yakthung and Yakthung Suhang epistemologies via Shree Yakthung Hang Chumlung. It further discusses how Shree Yakthung Chumlung became a crucial *chumlungden* (contact zone) for Yakthungs to network with other Yakthungs from Nepal, Sikkim, India, Bhutan, Bangladesh, Burma, and Thailand, and how Yakthungs contributed to delink Khas Aryan, Indian, and Western cultural and linguistic colonization, to relink Yakthung writing system, histories, and Mundhums, and to link them within Yakthung communities and beyond. Additionally, this chapter briefly discusses the contribution of Lalshor Sendang to the development of Yakthung writing and rhetorics.

Chapter 7 exhibits the remapping of the Sirijanga script, the Sirijanga writing system, and documentation of Yakthung histories and Mundhum rhetorics. It portrays how European soldiers influenced Yakthung soldiers during World War I. This chapter depicts that Yakthungs, for the first time, realized that writing was/is a powerful tool to subvert (para)colonial cultural conditions and political power. This chapter shares the contribution of Bajbir Thalang (Subba) and Phalgunanda Lingden in Yakthung communities. In doing so, this chapter exposes the Indigenous power of resistance, delinking, and relinking approaches for their existence and/or for their Indigenous way of being, becoming, and belonging as Yakthungs in Yakthung laje (both in Nepal and beyond).

Chapter 8 exhibits the influence of other languages, such as Nepali, Hindi, and English on the Sirijanga script and the Sirijanga writing system; it demonstrates how the Old Sirijanga script or the old Yakthung writing system shifted to the new Sirijanga writing system. It stresses how the banning of Yakthung language, writing, and rhetoric and Khas Aryan's destruction of Yakthung books, writing, and Mundhum rhetorics adversely impacted Yakthung writing and rhetorics. This chapter also discusses how R. K. Sprigg's bringing of the old Yakthung documents to Yakthung laje facilitated both the restoration and promotion of Yakthung history, language, and literacy. More importantly, this chapter establishes my critical imagination, interpretation, and analysis of Yakthung archival materials, historical foundations, Mundhums, and existing Yakthung cultural artifacts in relation to transcultural, transborder, and political terrains on how colonized bodies adopt and/or reject, displace and replace own identities, writing and rhetorics.

Chapter 9 examines the second Yakthung rhetoric and writing wave with the emergence of second-generation Yakthung scholars, researchers, and writers. The chapter widely discusses the contributions of the second-generation Yakthung scholars via the Patra-mitrata (networking through traditional post office letters) campaign and popular Yakthung "journals" and "pamphlets." This chapter focuses on how the second-generation Yakthung activists and community leaders contributed to the development of the Yakthung language, writing system, and literacy despite the Khas Aryan suppression in Nepal. The chapter highlights the pressing issues and challenges in developing, re/designing, collaborating, and disseminating Yakthung writing and rhetorics during the Khas Aryan's banning of Yakthung language and literacy. The chapter broadly examines the political tribulations as well as possibilities of delinking, relinking, and linking Yakthung writing and rhetorics in the light of *Yakthung phu-ne-nusa's* communal local and regional networks.

Chapter 10 unravels the history of Yakthung writing and rhetoric in Sikkim (independent country until 1975, now in India), and how Yakthung writing and rhetoric foster and did not foster in Sikkim for a long time. Why Yakthungs, in the late 1960s and early 1970s did not force the urgency of Yakthung language, literacy, and Mundhum rhetorics. This chapter also discusses how the teaching of Yakthung language got the official recognition at school in 1968, and currently, Sikkimi Yakthung are introducing Yakthung studies up to graduate (MA) level (soon to be PhD) in Sikkim. The chapter further discusses how Yakthungs, from other states of India, have been informally promoting and/or informally teaching the Sirijanga writing system, Yakthung culture, and Mundhum rhetorics, in collaboration with Yakthung linguists, scholars, and Mundhumists from Sikkim and Yakthung laje, Nepal. This chapter reveals how the Indian government is disregarding the introduction of the Yakthung language and literacy in Darjeeling, Kalimpong, Assam, and Nagaland; yet, how Yakthungs (from Darjeeling, Kalimpong, Assam, and Nagaland) are struggling to relink and link the Yakthung language and literacy. Finally, this chapter also uncovers how Yakthungs have been promoting their culture, language, and literacy in Bhutan, Burma, and Thailand.

Chapter 11 discusses the establishment of Kirat Yakthung Chumlung in Nepal in 1989, and how Yakthungs have been networking, researching, and advocating for their social, cultural, linguistic, and academic identities. The chapter focuses on how Yakthungs struggled to make their institutional (academic) identities visible from local to global contexts through Limbuwan Study Center, Limbu Bhasha Sahitya Pratisthan, Limbu Saskritik Parisad, Yakthung Sahayog Kosh, and Kirat Yakthung Chumlung-Punarjeevan Kendra. The chapter succinctly scrutinizes how the teaching of Yakthung language in Nepal (and beyond in informal setting) and global Yakthung network (Asia, Europe, North America, Africa, etc.) are delinking Khas Aryan, Indian, and Western cultural colonization. This chapter further discloses contemporary Yakthung cultural and pedagogical issues that Yakthungs have been encountering and also demonstrates ways of addressing them for current and future Yakthung studies, writing, and rhetorics.

Chapter 12 discusses the foundation of Limbuwan Study Center (LSC) and the contemporary sites of Yakthung writing and rhetorics in Nepal, India, and beyond. This chapter exposes how LSC is establishing leading-edge Yakthung academic and popular cultures; how LSC is facilitating the research on diverse Yakthung studies, such as Yakthung language, arts, literature, culture, music, history, politics, and Mundhum rhetorics; how LSC is aiming to pave strategic ways to succeed in academic and popular cultural avenues; and overall, how LSC is critically delinking para(colonization), relinking Yakthung, including Indigenous traditional customary traditions, and linking Yakthung language and literacies from local to global contexts.

Similarly, chapter 13 revisits delinking, relinking, and linking approaches in order to remap, revisit, explore, and institutionalize Yakthung writing and rhetoric in the context of the 21st century. It reveals how Yakthungs shifted from chirography to digitocracy in three decades (from 70s to 90s or after King Palden Thongdup Namgyal officially approved the teaching of the Yakthung language in Sikkim in 1968). It discusses how Yakthung's regional and global network and collaboration facilitated to delink the para-colonialism, mainstream political hegemony, and discriminatory state policies in order to link their cultural and linguistic identities in the center.

Finally, chapter 14 concludes by reiterating delinking, relinking, and linking methodology, compelling theories, leading-edge practices, and exhibiting future directions to the development of the Yakthung language, writing, and rhetoric. This chapter offers how delinking, relinking, and linking methodology and practice assist Yakthungs to strive and thrive in the development the Yakthung language, writing, and rhetorics, such as documentation, dissemination, and maintenance. This chapter provides a solid direction of inclusion, innovation, and global visibility in the local and global contexts.

Part I

Theoretical and methodological framework

1 Historical background of the Sirijanga script, writing, and rhetorics

A history of writing in a glimpse

Writing is one of the oldest forms of communication in the history of human civilization; it is a medium of human communication that embodies language, emotion, history, and identity of any person, community, and nation. Writing is not a language itself, but it is a tool full of signs and symbols that makes language able to be read, studied, and analyzed. Writing as a tool allows communities to construct knowledge and transmit or share it with other audiences. From this perspective, though writing is a very complex entity, writing culture can be the object of study, analysis, and inquiry. Writing reflects any cultural traditions by demonstrating how culture is inscribed, how history, body, and identity are mediated, and how knowledge is established in any particular time and space. This clearly indicates that writing is not only the intersection of self, body, and society, but it is also the intersection of self and audience. Based on the background information, this chapter offers a theoretical and methodological framework of the Sirijanga writing system, Yakthung language, and literacies. To be more specific, this chapter discusses the historical foundations of Yakthung writing and rhetorics, such as what inventions and interventions took place in the development of the Sirijanga script and writing system. Methodologically, this chapter introduces what delinking, relinking, and linking methodology is, and how and why delinking, relinking, and linking methodology is a better research approach for Yakthung and other Indigenous rhetorical studies.

After the invention of writing, people used it to document human activities through different types of signs and symbols. However, writing in the earliest form was not as we write now. People used to mostly carve on rocks, barks, trees, and even printed on leaves. The carvings often represented the earliest peoples' language, emotion, and activities. Hence, through carvings and paintings, early people documented their histories and stories. As the writing system developed slower than the spoken system, people were mostly engaged in painting, carving, and drawing across the world. The early writing systems, let's say in the Bronze Age, were not a sudden invention, but they were a development upon the foundation of earlier paintings, carvings, and drawings. They used ideographic symbols to transmit information; perhaps, it was one of the best forms of communication (Gaur, 1984, 1987; Houston, 2004). Writing or documentation in any form, allowed the ancient societies to document their histories, narratives, and cultural practices.

The more people were civilized, or the more the cultures were developed, the more their demands and expectations also changed. They designed and redesigned letters, characters, and scripts so that they could communicate more effectively both in oral and written forms. When they had to communicate with people (from far and near), they had to engrave signs and symbols. This is how humans gradually developed the writing system, and that kind of writing system satisfactorily represented language, culture, literature, and civilization. In a nutshell, writing was used as a tool to represent language, culture, and philosophy though it changed over time for various reasons. Gaur (1987) states, "[a]ll writing is information storage. It is not the only form of information" (p. 15), and "[i]f all writing is information storage, then all writing is of equal value. Each society stores the information essential to its survival, the information which enables it to function effectively" (p. 15).

In the Bronze Age, writing became more popular in many cultures around the world, including China, India, Near East, and Europe. They steadily influenced each other, including other cultures such as Japan, Korea, and Nigeria (Meroitic Writing System, 2004). During the Bronze Age, writing also emerged in Cuneiform script, Egyptian hieroglyphs, Elamite script, Indus script, Semitic alphabets, Anatolian hieroglyphs, Chinese writing, Cretan and Greek scripts, and Mesoamerica. In this regard, Gaur (1987) states:

> There is in fact no essential difference between prehistoric rock paintings, memoir aids (mnemonic devices), wintercounts, tallies, knotted cords, pictographic, syllabic and consonantal scripts as such …, but only societies at a particular level of economic and social development using certain forms of information storage. (p. 14)

During the Bronze Age, people developed writing to make day-to-day communication easier and more effective. Writing developed through the Bronze Age, Iron Age, Greco-Roman civilizations, Middle Ages, Renaissance, and beyond. Gradually, writing became a medium of human communication that embodied language, emotion, history, and identities of any culture, people, and nation. So, "…writing-in-use and writing-in-context-what might be called the 'pragmatics' of writing … are complex matters and necessitate a comparable depth of interpretation" (Houston, 1984, p. 9). From this perspective, though writing is a very complex entity, writing system or writing culture can be the object of study, analysis, and inquiry (see also Brown & Yule, 1983, pp. 27, 35). Hence, writing is the intersection of self and society; it is the intersection of self and audience. Writing is not only used to embody the intersection of social and cultural hierarchies, such as ruler and ruled, us and other, and superior and inferior, but it is also used to subvert hierarchies.

A historical analysis of the Sirijanga script, writing, and rhetorics

As I implied in the introduction, Yakthungs, also known as Limbus, Kirats (Kiratas), Rayas, Subbas, or Yakthung Suhangs, are one of the Himalayan Indigenous peoples of South Asia and South East Asia. According to Yakthung Mundhum, Yakthungs, including other Indigenous and non-Indigenous peoples, are also considered as Sawa Yet Hangs (Mundhumic term that refers to eight sons of Lahadangna and Suhampheba) or Yet Hangs (eight leaders). Yakthungs primarily reside in Nepal, India (Sikkim, Kalimpong, Darjeeling, Assam, Arunachal Pradesh, Nagaland, and Manipur, etc.), Bhutan, Bangladesh, Burma, and Thailand. Currently, Yakthungs also live in the United Kingdom (UK), Hong Kong, the United States of America (USA), and Canada, etc. Yakthungs have their own distinct Yakthung culture, language—*Yakthung pa:n* (Yakthung language), and writing system—the Sirijanga writing system. In terms of the Sirijanga script and writing system, we do not find any written documents that state who invented the Sirijanga script, and when the Sirijanga script was first designed. Due to an unknown history of the Sirijanga script, I raise a series of questions, such as who invented or designed the Sirijanga script? Who were the audiences, and for what purpose was it designed and used? How did the Sirijanga script serve the general purpose? Did only Yakthungs use this script, or all other Tibeto-Burman language speaking communities used as well in the South(east) Asian regions? Or why was/is this script called the Kirat script or the Kirat Yakthung script? How was the first Sirijanga script written, or how and why did the Sirijanga writing system change over time? Was there any intervention/s in the making of

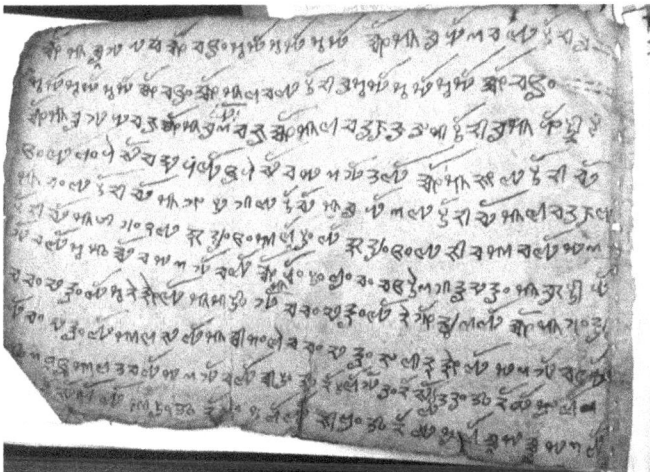

Figure 1 The Old Sirijanga script (Source: The British Library, London).

the Sirijanga script or writing system? If the Old Sirijanga writing system changed, what was the reason behind it?

The Sirijanga writing system was developed during the Sawa Yet Hang (Mundhum-based knowledge) reign or Yet Hang or Indigenous (Kirat) reign in the Himalayan range in Southeast Asia; however, the writing system was not called the "Sirijanga" script then. This script was given various names, such as Kirat script, Kirat Yakthung script, Kirat Yakthung Akchhar, and Limbu script. This script was called the "Sirijanga script" only after 1925 (Shree Yakthung Hang Chumlung implied); however, after 1925, many Yakthungs, including non-Yakthung scholars, still call/ed it the "Kirat script" and "Kirat Yakthung akchhar" (Subba, 1928 implied), and most of the Western scholars still call/ed it the "Kirat script" and "Sirijunga script." I will discuss in detail later in this book.

The Himalayan Indigenous peoples might have developed their writing system to systematize their communication strategies within the Himalayan Indigenous (Kirat) Kingdom and beyond (Laoti, 2005; Limbu, 2016, 2017; Yakthumba, 2062 BS). Based on the research findings, it is believed that the Sirijanga script was invented during the Himalayan Indigenous (Kirat) reign. However, the development of the writing system became very sporadic, uneven, and slow. So, when we study the Sirijanga script and writing system, we theoretically and practically explore that a writing system changes slower than a spoken system. Due to many inventions and interventions in relation to the Sirijanga script and writing system, we still do not exactly know who invented it, or when it was invented. However, it is obvious that the first original Sirijanga script was undeniably different from the Devanagari script and the Brahmi writing system. Based on the phonology, character, and syllabary, it appears that the Old Sirijanga script developed independent of other writing systems, such as the Devanagari (Hindi and Nepali), Ranjana (Newari writing system), and Sambhota (Tibetan) scripts. Meaning, we do not find any influence of the Devanagari script, Ranjana script, and Tibetan scripts on the Old Sirijanga script.

Concerning the phonological features of the Old Sirijanga script, the writing system used to be an /a/-based one, unlike the Devanagari script. Yakthung spoken system is still an /a/-based one. Unlike the Brahmi script, the Old Sirijanga script was written in this order: /ka, ba, a, ma, ta, ya, dha, na, sha, nga, sa, wa, ha, la, ja, pha, kha, ra, cha, yan/ (see figure 5 in chapter 3). The Old Sirijanga writing system and phonological system justify that the Brahmi and Devanagari scripts did not influence the Old Sirijanga script. Moreover, the invention of the Sirijanga script was not a one-time event that one king or person had designed and introduced; the development of the Sirijanga script was a very slow process. The Old Sirijanga script had existed in the South(east) Asian Himalayan cultures before many writing systems were born in this region. In the process of its making, Yakthungs, including other Indigenous peoples, forgot the Old Sirijanga writing system due to the oppressive Khas Aryan regime in Nepal and Bhutia regime in Sikkim. Later,

Yakthungs, in the early and mid-20th century, redesigned and added many characters to the Sirijanga script as they did not know the Old Sirijanga script.

Among many other nations, Yakthungs, including Khambus (Rais), have had very close cultural, linguistic, and political ties with Indian, Tibetan, Lepcha (Lapcha or Rong), and Southeast Asian Indigenous communities. Therefore, they shared, and still share, similar types of cultural, linguistic, and writing systems in the region (Subba, 2015). As I implied earlier, based on the structure of the writing system and phonological features, the Sirijanga script of the 18th century (the Tye Angsian era implied) was still developed independent of other scripts, such as the Devanagari or Brahmi script/s. So, it appears that Tye Angsi Singthebe might have developed the script based on the Old Sirijanga writing system. Perhaps, Yakthungs, Khambus, Kõiches (Kõits), and Yakkhas had written books in this script until the Khas Aryans invaded the Kirat (Kõich, Khambu, and Yakthung) regions. Later, the Khas Aryans destroyed all books in the Kõich and Khambu (Rai) regions. During my research, some of my informants mentioned that when the Gorkhas invaded the Khambus, they handed over many books, such as Khambu genealogies, Khambu history books, Mundhum books, and other important documents to their Yakthung counterparts. Based on the premises, the Himalayan Indigenous (Kirat) civilization might have influenced the Tibetan and South/East Asian writing system/s (see also Gaur, 1987; Brown & Yule, 1983; Scharfe, 2002). My research findings also demonstrate that the Sirijanga, Rong (Lepcha), and Sambhota (Tibetan) scripts seemed to influence each other in their writing system and phonological features. According to Jash Raj Subba (2015), the Himalayan Indigenous cultures from Nepal to Burma had been the Kirat Kingdom (Sawa Yet Hang region—according to Mundhum or Yet Hang region) before the rise of the Lichchhavi reign (they were also a sub-group of Kirats), and that might have been the reason why Tibetans, Bhutias, Lepchas, Khambus, and Yakthungs tend to share similar types of cultural practices, writing systems, and phonological features.

According to the Kirat history, the Indigenous peoples had ruled over the Himalayan regions (over the Himalayan range from Nepal to South or Southeast Asian regions) for centuries, and the Kirat Kingdom had been one of the greatest nations in the history of human civilization (Bista, 1991; Mabohang & Sharma-Dhungel, 2047 BS, p. 29; Mabuhang, 2063 BS, pp. 1–17; Subba, 2015). The Kirat kings ruled over the Himalayan regions for 32 generations (28 generations according to Hodgson collection) starting with "Yalambar" (the first Kirat king) and ending with "Gasti" (the last Kirat king). The Kirat's (also known as Mongoloid people) population spread out mostly in the South Asian and Southeast Asian regions, such as Nepal, India, Bhutan, Burma, and Thailand (Bista, 1991; Subba, 2015). This could be one of the reasons why the Bodos of Assam, India claim that Yalambar had been their king (see also Chattopodyaya, 2015, p. 8; Lunminthang, 2016; Raj, 2011; Rosati, 2017; Roy, 2015). As I already implied above, during the Kirat reign, they had developed their own script and writing system to document their histories, cultural lores, and royal accomplishments. So, when we study the writing systems in this part of the world, such as the Sambhota (Tibetan), Rong (Lepcha), Dzongkha (Bhutani), and Sirijanga scripts, we find similar types of writing systems, especially in (Tibeto-Burman) phonological patterns. Hence, these cultures seem to culturally and linguistically influence each other (the Tibeto-Burman culture and language family implied).

In terms of the modern Sirijanga writing system, although the New Sirijanga script is written like the Devanagari script (Nepali and Hindi) after the foundation of Shree Yakthung Hang Chumlung in 1925 (Bajbir Subba's *Tum Yakthung Ningwaphu Sapla,* 1928 implied), the Old Sirijanga and Tibetan scripts, as discussed above, seem to be similar (from a phonological point of view). While we compare the Old Sirijanga script and the Tibetan script, the Old Sirijanga script or the Old Sirijanga writing system seems to have developed independent from other scripts in the South(east) Asian region; whereas, the Tibetan script might have been influenced by both the Sirijanga and Brahmi scripts (see figure 6). Therefore, the S irijanga s cript m ight have influenced other writing systems in the H imalayan regions, i.e., in the South(east) Asian regions (see Scharfe, 2002). Based on the given premises, King Sirijanga might have redesigned the script or writing system during the late 9th and early 10th centuries based on the script and writing system that Himalayan Indigenous (Kirats) peoples had introduced during their reign. Gaur (1984) states that "[Non-Chinese people's] language, belonging mostly to the Tibeto-Burman group, differ greatly from Chinese, but the majority of their scripts, though in part are the result of independent inventions" (p. 87). More importantly, the Brahmi script might have been influenced by local Himalayan Indigenous writing system, and Kirats had been the Indigenous peoples of Himalayan region in South(east) Asia (see also Chattopodyaya, 2015, p. 8; Raj, 2011; Roy, 2015;). So, there is a strong evidence that supports that the Old Sirijangian writing style might have influenced the S ambhota (Tibetan) writing system, and the Rong writing system.

The Lichchhavis, from Baisali ancient India, invaded the Kirats after they (Lichchhavis) had been invaded and banished by Muslims (Bista, 1991). However, the Lichchhavis are also believed to have been a sub-group of Kirats (Himalayan Indigenous peoples). After the Lichchhavi invasion in the Himalayan Indigenous (Kirat) region (the capital is believed to have been in Kathmandu), the major ruling class (Kirats) were displaced from Kathmandu, and many of them migrated to the eastern part of Kathmandu (Bista, 1991). However, some Kirats continued to live in their original homeland, the Kathmandu valley. Currently, the Kirat (Indigenous) people who live in the Kathmandu valley are now known as Newars (but not all Newars). Some Kirats migrated only up to the eastern part of Kathmandu valley, and other Kirats, such as Gurung, Magar, and some Newars, etc. continued to live in the central part of Nepal (Banepaali, 2075 BS, pp. 107–116; Chemjong, 2003; Kirat league ko bibaran patra, 2008 BS). The Kirats who migrated to the eastern part of Kathmandu were later named as "Wallo Kirats," "Majha

Kirats," and "Pallo Kirats" (see also Mabuhang, 2014). So, the Kirats, who migrated to the eastern part of Kathmandu, settled in different places, which were called "Wallo Kirat" (Near East Kirat from Kathmandu), "Majha Kirat" (Middle East Kirat from Kathmandu), and "Pallo Kirat" (Far East Kirat from Kathmandu). The Wallo Kirat (Kōich) region, geo-politically, ranges from Banepa to the Likhu River; in Wallo Kirat, Kirat people, such as Kōich (Sunuwar), Haayu, Jirel, and Surel reside. Similarly, Majha Kirat (Khambu) region ranges from the Likhu River to the Arun River. In this region, there were more than three dozen different Kirats and were also called Naulakh (nine-hundred thousand) Kirats who were historically known as Khambus or Majha Kirats, and in Majha Kirat, Khambus (Rais) resided and still reside. Whereas, Pallo Kirat (Yakthung) region ranges from the Arun River to the Tista River where 10 Yakthung Chieftains (Thibong Yakthung Suhangs) used to rule; these 10 Yakthung Chieftains were also known as Thibong Yakthung Suhangs. In the Pallo Kirat regions, Yakthungs, Yakkhas, Athpahariyas, Dhimals, Santhals, Rajbansis, Tajpuriyas, Gangais, and Meches, including Sherpas, Bhotes, and Lepchas reside/d. After the Kirats had been displaced from the Kathmandu valley (central Nepal), they founded their own independent nations, such as Magarat, Tamuwan, Khambuwan, and Yakthung laje, etc. (see also Bista, 1991; Mabuhang, 2014).

In relation to writing and literacy in Yakthung laje, Yakthungs continued to practice the Sirijanga script to document their history, culture, and Mundhum rhetorics. They developed diplomatic relationships with their neighbors, such as Khambus, Bhutias, Lepchas, Mallas (Newars), and Lichchhavis. During the new Himalayan Indigenous (Kirat/Yet Hang) reign, they practiced a similar type of writing system that was developed during the great Himalayan Indigenous (Kirat) reign. After the Lichchhavi invasion, the Sirijanga script and/or writing system might have been introduced in Tibet, for it is widely believed that King Songtsen Gampo (or Tong-Tsen-Gam-Po) sent Thonmi Sambhota (a minister) to the south. Thonmi Sambhota might have come to the new Indigenous (Kirat) Kingdom during the 7th century to study of the art of writing; then, the Tibetans introduced the writing system in Tibet. Based on the commonalities between the Sirijanga and Tibetan scripts, specifically in relation to phonological features and writing systems (see figures 5 & 6), I argue that Sambhota might have visited the newer Indigenous (Kirat) Kingdoms and India to learn writing systems in the 7th century. During the Sambhota's visit, King Maarang might have ruled in Yakthung laje; this period had been before the reign of King Sirijanga (10th century). It is also noteworthy to remember that King Maarang redesigned the script during the sixth or seventh century in Yakthung laje (Bhumika by Subba, 1928; Sprigg, 1959, p. 591). Diverse documents suggest that Sambhota might have visited Yakthung laje, the newer Indigenous (Kirat) regions (also known as Sawa Yet Hang or Yet Hang regions, Yakthung Mundhum implied) and India. After his visit to Yakthung laje and India, he introduced the writing system in Tibet. The reason I make this claim is that the Tibetan writing system resembles both the Sirijanga and Bramhi writing systems. Gaur (1987) further states:

> Tibetan civilization as we know it today, and the origin of the Tibetan script, are closely associated with Song-Tsen-Gam-Po, who ruled the country between 620 and 649 AD. Song-Tsen-Gam-Po succeeded in unifying the various tribes, and by doing so, he created a kingdom which spread its influence to China and India. Apart from his political achievements, he introduced paper and ink from China, writing from India [from south], and is generally credited with laying the cornerstones of Tibetan orthography. This later was in itself no mean task. Tibetan belongs to a group of languages entirely unlike the Indian ones and possesses some quite different sounds. (p. 113)

Based on the Tibetan phonological features and writing systems, we can claim that the Yakthung, including Khambu culture and writing system, influenced many neighboring nations in this part of the world. When Tong-Tsen-Gam-Po ruled, the Yet Hangs (Kirats) already had a great empire and had developed their own writing system. Furthermore, Yakthungs, including Kirats, had and still have an /a/-based phonology and an /a/-based writing system as well. If we look at the modern Tibetan writing system, it is also an /a/-based writing system. For my readers' information, Yakthungs had an /a/-based writing system until the 19th century (see the manuscripts written by Limbu et al., 1845–1857 in this book). Similarly, both Tibetan and Yakthung (including, Rai, Tamang, and Sherpa, etc.) languages are tonal and/or glottal-based languages and are /a/-based ones. In relation to the naming and claiming of the Sirijanga script, Kõiches (Sunuwars), Khambus (Rais), and Yakkhas did not use it as much as Yakthungs did because the Lichchhavis and Khas Aryans heavily influenced Kõiches and Khambus.

King Sirijanga (880–915) redesigned the script and popularized it upon the foundation of the writing system that King Maarang reintroduced during his reign (Subba, 2015, pp. 103–110). Based on the time and development of script during the King Maarangian period (i. e. how other scripts were developed during that era), it looks like the Sirijanga writing system was designed and developed during the Indigenous or Yet Hang (Kirat) reign because it (the Old Sirijanga script) does not resemble any other scripts and writing systems (of King Maarangian and King Sirijangian eras). As I stated earlier, the invention of writing did not happen in a single day, but developed over time. For instance, according to Gaur (1984):

> [Non-Chinese people's] language, belonging mostly to the Tibeto-Burman group, differ greatly from Chinese, but the majority of their scripts, though in part the result of independent inventions, betray allegiance to, or at least a knowledge of, Chinese (in some cases also Indian) models. Some scripts are still used, or at least known, as for example the scripts of

Miao or Yao; others have despite the considerable temporary and local importance, long vanished and are partly still undeciphered. (p. 87)

Based upon Gaur's study, we can contend that the Sirijanga script had developed independent of the Chinese, Brahmi, and Devanagari scripts. As I stated earlier, there is a close writing relationship between the Sirijanga and Tibetan scripts, and there might be some similarities with the Miao or Yao writing systems as the ancient Yet Hang or Sawa Yet Hang (Yakthung Mundhum implied) or the Kirat Kingdom extended up to Burma and beyond. As I have been researching the Miao or Yao's (including Southeast Asian) social systems and cultural practices, Yakthung, Miao, Yao, Lao, and Burmese tend to share some cultural norms, values, and practices.

Concerning the Sirijanga writing system or writing practices, the Lichchhavi (they were also a sub-group of Kirats) invasion in the Himalayan Indigenous (Kirat) Kingdom (mainly Kathmandu implied) brought an intervention in the Indigenous (Kirat) nation. The Indigenous (Kirat) people who lived or remained in the same place, for instance, Magar, Gurung, Thakali, and Newar to mention a few, and the Kirats who migrated to the eastern part of Kathmandu could not network on the regular basis with their Indigenous (Kirat) counterparts. Gradually, their cultural practices, writing system, and customary cultural epistemic activities dwindled in the central and western part of Nepal. Most of the Indigenous (Kirat) people who remained in the central and western part of Nepal eventually forgot about their ancient cultural traditions and writing system due to the influence of the Hindu culture and the Devanagari writing system. Since the cultural colonization and/or teaching of Hinduism continued in the western region, they were gradually converted to Hinduism (Bista, 1991). They started valuing, validating, embracing, and practicing Hindu socio-cultural norms and values, and they could not seek their own cultural identities during the discriminatory Khas Aryan reign from the 18th century to the late 20th century.

After Indigenous (Kirat) *phu-ne-nusa* (brothers and sisters), let's say Magars, migrated to the Yakthung laje after 1774, they believed that they were a superior (higher) caste than Yakthungs. So, they did not know that there is not any hierarchy in Yakthung Suhang culture (Indigenous cultures) based on class, caste, gender, or sexuality as they had been disconnected from their Kirat (Sawa Yet Hang or Yet Hang) cultural traditions. The Kirats who lived in the central and western parts of Nepal were suppressed by the Khas Aryans and were banned to learn and teach about their history, culture, language, writing system, and religion. Their cultural, linguistic, and religious identities got distorted, displayed, and destroyed beyond recognition. In a similar fashion, Kôiches and Khambus were also more or less Hinduized by force or coercion (Bista, 1991).

In terms of the development of the script, Tye Angsi Singthebe (1704–1941) who is popularly known as Tye Angsi Sirijanga II, contributed to the promotion of the Sirijanga script and writing system. Though the script and writing system that King Maarang and King Sirijanga redesigned disappeared for almost a thousand years, Singthebe revived and popularized the script and writing system in the 18th century. The scripts and writing systems were different from the Devanagari script (Nepali and Indian scripts). The Old Sirijanga script does not resemble the Devanagari script or Devanagari writing system or Ranjana writing system at all, and it also does not resemble the Brahmi writing system either. However, the Old Sirijanga script and writing system and the Tibetan script and writing system, to some extent, do have some commonalities in the phonological system; for instance, both of them have /a/-based phonological features (see figures 5 & 6). The Old Sirijanga script does not have any signs and/or influence of the Brahmi and Devanagari scripts; whereas, the Tibetan Sambhota script does (Limbu, 2016, 2017; Limbu, et al., 1845; Sprigg, 1958, 1998). The Tibetan script's resemblance to the Old Sirijanga script in relation to phonological features and the Brahmi script in relation to writing systems suggest that Thonmi Sambhota might have borrowed writing systems from both the Sirijanga (Kirat) and Brahmi writing systems (in the 7th century). For instance, he borrowed phonological features from the Sirijanga writing system and writing pattern from the Brahmi script (see figures 5 & 6). Nonetheless, the new Sirijanga script that was redesigned in the early 20th century, though to some extent resembles the Old Sirijanga script, has the influence of the Devanagari script and is different from its predecessor.

The Sirijanga script, inventions, and interventions: theoretical and philosophical perspectives

King Maarang and King Sirijanga redesigned the script upon the foundation of the Himalayan Indigenous (Kirat) script and writing system. By quoting Madan Mani Dikxit, Ambar Jang Limbu (2016) argues that there were six popular scripts during the heyday of Sanskrit (in the South Asian regions), and the Sirijanga script might have been one of them. However, the script we know as the Sirijanga script was not known as the Sirijanga script then, and we do not know what they had called it. It is said that when Yakthungs congregated in the Shree Yakthung Hang Chumlung meeting in 1925 in Dungrabasti, they learned that King Sirijanga invented the script, and Tye Angsi Singthebe (Sirijanga II) redesigned it and was executed for his promoting the script in Sikkim (in the 18th century), and due to the historical reason, they unanimously decided to call the script—Sirijanga script. Henceforth, Yakthung Suhangs started calling the script, the "Sirijanga script." Remarkably, though the meeting at Shree Yakthung Hang Chumlung, Dungrabasti, Kalimpong unanimously decided to call the script, the "Sirijanga script" in 1925, Bajbir Subba, in his *Tum Yakthung Ningwaphu Sapla* (1928), called the script, the "Kirat Yakthung akchhar." Similarly, many Yakthung writers and scholars, still call the script, the "Kirat script," such as A. Campbell, B. Hodgson, R. K. Sprigg, and G. van Driem called it, the "Kirat script" or the "Sirijunga script."

After the first design of the script, the shift in the Sirijanga writing system was not only due to cultural, linguistic, and geo-political reasons within the Himalayan Indigenous (Kirat) nations, but the shift in the Sirijanga writing system was also due to the external influences as well. For instance, King Maarang redesigned the script during the 7th century (Bhumika by Subba, 1928; Sprigg, 1959, p. 591; Subba, 2015, pp. 99–101; Vansittart, 1991, p. 105), and King Sirijanga revised and popularized the script and/or writing system during the 9th century (see Subba, 2015, pp. 103–110). Though writing and literacy, to some extent, flourished from the King Maarangian, King Sirijangian, and Tye Angsian eras, we do not find any strong evidence that supports how the teaching and practice of the Sirijanga script or "Kirat Yakthung script" (Subba, 1928 implied) writing, and literacy shifted over the time (I have discussed the reasons in this book).

In Yakthung laje, Tye Angsi Singthebe (1704–1741) reintroduced, reformed, and popularized the script and writing system. Yakthungs had their books written in *Yakthung pa:n,* including Mundhum books, Yakthung genealogies, histories, narratives, *saksak saplas* (grammar books), and other archival materials. Unfortunately, after the Nun-Paani Sandhi (the Treaty of Salt-Water) in 1774, the Khas Aryans banned Yakthungs from the teaching and learning of the Sirijanga script, writing system, and Mundhum rhetorics. The Khas Aryans collected Yakthung books, including other Khambu and Indigenous books, and destroyed them on a regular basis for centuries until 1990. Those who wanted to resist the oppressions and continued to teach and learn the Sirijanga script, writing, and Mundhum rhetorics were captured, tortured, and executed or banished from Yakthung laje (from their ancestral homeland). The banished Yakthungs were scarcely able to take some books with them to the new places where they settled. During my research, I learned that the European colonial agents, such as Sulzi, Mainwaring, Campbell, and Hodgson, collected old Yakthung books and manuscripts and transported them to European libraries (mainly the British East India Company libraries) for the colonial purposes (see also Campbell, 1842, 1855).

Yakthungs knew the significance of writing and rhetoric; they knew multiple ways of knowledge construction, dissemination, and maintenance. They founded Yakthung social institutions, such as Shree Yakthung Hang Chumlung in 1925 in Dungrabasti, Kalimpong through which they could collectively address Yakthung language and literacy issues they had encountered for centuries. Yakthungs after the foundation of Shree Yakthung Hang Chumlung (July 26, 1925) in Kalimpong struggled to restore the Yakthung language, script (writing system), and literacy (Kandangwa, 1999; Laoti, 2005; Limbu, 2016, 2017). Whereas, Yakthungs also consistently attempted to advocate for the restoration of their writing and rhetorics despite the Khas Aryan subjugation in Nepal and Bhutia oppression in Sukhim (Sikkim). Yakthungs, despite the unfavorable situations in Yakthung laje, networked with Yakthungs from Southeast Asian regions, such as Nepal, India, Bangladesh, Burma, Bhutan, and Thailand to restore their Sawa

Yet Hang insights, Susuwa Lilim Yakthung epistemologies, Yet Hang, and Thibong Yakthung Suhang wisdoms. Yakthungs' collective campaigns after the foundation of Shree Yakthung Hang Chumlung was one of the most important sites of delinking, relinking, and linking Yakthung Suhang epistemologies after the Nun-Paani Sandhi and after the execution of Tye Angsi Singthebe. After the foundation of Shree Yakthung Hang Chumlung, Yakthungs constantly networked and collaborated to delink the Khas Aryan, Indian, and Western cultural colonization in multiple ways in multiple fields (in Yakthung communities). Yakthungs locally and regionally networked to relink Sawa Yet Hang Mundhum rhetorics, and Yet Hang and Thibong Yakthung traditional customary rhetorical traditions. The Yakthung network and collaboration through Shree Yakthung Hang Chumlung empowered them to delink Khas Aryan, Indian, and Western cultural and linguistic colonization. It energized them to relink their Sawa Yet Hang Mundhum epistemologies and Yet Hang and Thibong Yakthung ontological and axiological customary traditions. Overall, the delinking and relinking approaches helped Yakthungs heal from the scars inflicted by Khas Aryans, Indians, Westerners, and Bhutias. It helped them relink the Sirijanga script, writing system, *Yakthung pa:n*, and Sawa Yet Hang, including Thibong Yakthung Mundhum literacies. Furthermore, the delinking, relinking, and linking approach helped them preach, practice, and codify their everyday life, Sawa Yet Hang epistemologies, and Yakthung cultural practices for their (Yakthung) purpose. In other words, it helped Yakthungs delink cultural and linguistic colonization, relink Yet Hang and Thibong Yakthung language and literacy, and link (update) them from the 21st century Yakthung Suhang perspective.

Even though Yakthungs struggled to relink the Sirijanga script and writing system, their rhetorical practices demonstrate how they departed and/or moved away from the Old Sirijanga script and writing practices for not knowing the Old Sirijanga script. In other words, Yakthungs of the early 20th century did not know about the Old Sirijanga script because the teaching of Yakthung language and writing system was banned for centuries in Nepal and Sikkim. In a similar way, the East India Company colonial agents (Europeans), such as Sulzi, Mainwaring, Campbell, and Hodgson collected books from Yakthungs in India and Sikkim for European colonial purposes. Despite the fact that Yakthungs wanted to study their history, writing system, and Mundhum literacies, they did not have any book/s from the King Maarangian, King Sirijangian, and Tye Angsian eras as models to follow. They did not have any Yakthung books as models to follow in relation to the Sirijanga script and writing system. Yakthungs became the prey of the Khas Aryans; they became the prey of mainstream Indian socio-political institutions; they also became prey of Western cultures. So, Yakthungs and Yakthung culture became the prey of the preys. Meaning, Nepali culture and language were colonized by Indian culture and Western culture; Indian culture and language were colonized by Western culture; and Yakthungs and Yakthung culture were/ have been colonized by the Khas Aryans, Indians, and Europeans. The destruction of Yakthungs and Yakthung culture became the proliferation of the Khas Aryan, Indian, and Western para-colonizers. This colonial practice still continues to exist in Yakthung communities whether it is in Nepal, India, Bhutan, Burma, Bangladesh, and beyond.

In the early 20th century, the Yakthung writers, activists, and historians like Bajbir Subba (Thalang), Imansing Chemjong, Kaalusing Papo, Buddhiraj Phago, and Jasman Sangwa wrote Yakthung syllabaries (alphabets), grammar books, and Mundhums. However, the way of the "Kirat Yakthung akchhar" (Subba, 1928) writing system totally digressed from that of the Old Sirijanga script and writing system. Despite the digression in the Sirijanga writing system, the Yakthungs, from the early 20th century, were able to restore the Sirijanga script and writing system. The restoration of the Sirijanga script led the Yakthung communities toward a written culture from an oral-centric Yakthung culture (storytelling culture or oral-performance-based culture). After they had written the books and booklets, they widely distributed them in Yakthung communities, for instance, Nepal, India, Bhutan, Bangladesh, and as far as Burma. It was the first site of the Yakthung campaign to delink the local Khas Aryan, Indian, and European colonization. The campaign rapidly united Yakthungs, for they collectively struggled for the Yakthung Suhang intellectual, cultural, historical, and linguistic progress and prosperity. This campaign facilitated them to delink the local and Western cultural colonization; it helped them unlearn Khas Aryan, Indian, and Western linguistic colonization, and it helped Yakthungs denaturalize their mind, body, and soul. The collective Yakthung struggle helped them relink Thibong Yakthung Suhang language and literacy; it helped them relink Yakthung Suhang customary cultural traditions, including Sawa Yet Hang Mundhumic rhetorical traditions. The Yakthung Suhangs' collective struggle facilitated them to network and link other Yakthungs from different geo-political locations.

As I stated earlier, Yakthungs had well developed culture, rhetoric, and writing in the history of human civilization. Later, local para-colonizers (Khas Aryans and Bhutias) displaced and destroyed the Sirijanga script, writing, culture, space, and identity. The Khas Aryans, Indians and Westerners became quite successful in the epistemic business and in the knowledge making business. In the knowledge making business, they were able to program Yakthungs, including other Indigenous peoples, to ignore their own body, culture, and ethnicity; they disregard/ed their language and rhetoric. The Khas Aryans, Indians, and Europeans programmed Yakthungs in such a way that Yakthungs favor/ed the Khas Aryan, Indian, and European cultures, languages, writing, and rhetorics over their own Yakthung culture, language, and writing. For instance, even today, Yakthungs do not value their own Yakthung culture and tradition; Yakthungs do not validate their own language and literacy. They feel ashamed to speak their own language and practice their Yakthung social norms and values. Gradually, Yakthungs became the shadow of the Khas Aryan, Indian, and European cultural traditions. The problem, we still face is that Yakthungs continue to mimic the Khas Aryan, Indian, and Western cultures, languages, religions, and other institutional practices.

Currently, Yakthungs are collectively networking, collaborating, and documenting their histories, narratives, and Mundhum rhetorics. However, during my five-year-long research, the major issue I noticed was that Khas Aryans, Indians, and Westerners programmed Yakthungs (us) for centuries to see our Sawa Yet Hang, Yet Hang, Thibong Yakthung, and Yakthung cultural traditions through the Khas Aryan and Western lenses. The Khas Aryan, Indian, and Western cultures impaired our ability to distinguish who we are, what our culture is, what the importance of our Mundhum rhetorics is, what the significance of our *Yakthung pa:n* is, and what our cultural-rhetorical tradition is. From this perspective, the Yakthung body has been colonized; the Yakthung mind has been imprisoned, and the Yakthung soul has been caged in the Khas Aryan, Indian, and Western colonial cultural conventions and academic institutions. As a result, Yakthungs have become colonially constructed Yakthung Suhangs (falsely labelled, distorted, and displaced Yakthungs); hence, Indigenous Yakthungs, including other Indigenous peoples have suffered from the definitions and labels imposed upon them (by para-colonizers for centuries). This is because we (Yakthungs) embrace/d Khas Aryan, Indian, and Western cultural values and ideals by ignoring our own Yakthung Suhang customary epistemologies, ontologies, and axiologies. As a result, Yakthung Suhang epistemologies have been trapped in the new settlers' social institutions; Yakthung Suhang axiologies have been imprisoned in the Khas Aryan and European/Western cultures and ideals. Yakthungs have been oriented to value Khas Aryan, Indian, and European cultures and hate their own culture. Yakthungs have been programmed to believe that their language, writing system, culture, and Mundhum rhetorics are inferior to Nepali, Hindi, and English.

Gradually, we (Yakthungs), became hypocrites and became puppets of the colonizers. We preach one thing in public spaces, social media, and practice different one. Meaning, we speak against our para-colonizers and support them in practice. Because of our hypocrisy, our (para)colonizers succeeded in the knowledge making business. For instance, in front of other Yakthungs, we advocate for our language, writing, and culture, and in reality, we discount our own culture, language, and writing system. We do not speak our own language at our homes; we do not encourage our children to speak *Yakthung pa:n*. Based on my own experience, we do not communicate in *Yakthung pa:n* in Yakthung social spaces, workshops, and conferences. Furthermore, we advocate for linguistic and cultural identities, but we are proud of sending our children to English boarding schools, and we spend thousands of dollars on English, Hindi, and Nepali education. We force our children to speak in English, Nepali, and Hindi. Despite the fact that Yakthung language and/or Yakthung studies is taught up to an MA level in Sikkim, I have not yet met any Yakthungs from Nepal, Kalimpong, Darjeeling, Bhutan, and

Assam who have sent their child/ren to Sikkim to study Yakthung studies. There are Yakthung schools and colleges in Sikkim, just adjacent to Yakthung laje (Limbuwan) border; however, Yakthungs still do not consider sending their children to Sikkim to study Yakthung language and literacy.

The Yakthungs of the 21st century have been oriented to distrust themselves (culture, language, and writing) and trust their colonizers' languages and cultures. The modern Yakthung Suhangs psychologically and spiritually became paralyzed; they believe that they need Khas Aryans, Indians, and Europeans to speak for them. In other words, Yakthungs distrust themselves, or they do not trust their own knowledge, history, and Mundhum rhetorics. During my research, I found that Yakthungs usually invite Khas Aryans to give special talks on Yakthung culture and Mundhum rhetorics in Yakthung programs despite the fact that the Khas Aryans do not have even a basic knowledge on Mundhum, Yakthung culture, rhetoric, and writing. Yakthungs have developed a culture where Khas Aryan scholars and Western scholars speak for them, and this practice has become a culture in Yakthung communities. When Yakthungs have to quote for evidence, they quote Khas Aryan, Indian, and Western scholars because they distrust their own Yakthung scholars or Yakthung scholarship. The reason why Yakthungs trust Khas Aryan and Western scholars and distrust themselves is that their mind has been caged in para-colonizers' social institutions; their souls, minds, and intellects have been calibrated to believe that they need (para)colonizers to speak for their history, identity, and Mundhum rhetorics. Yakthungs and Yakthung communities have been taught that their culture, language, and writing were inferior, and they did not want to read, write, and communicate in the inferior language.

Historically, Yakthungs demanded their rights to mother-tongue education and right to ancestral land in 1956 in Limbuwan, Nepal as Yakthungs became well informed citizens through their communal networks, such as Shree Yakthung Hang Chumlung and other social institutions. They (Yakthungs) through Shree Yakthung Hang Chumlung and Zambuk Junior Basic School theoretically and practically learned that writing saves their Sawa Yet Hang, Yet Hang, and Thibong Yakthung customary traditions. They knew that writing opens up the Yet Hang and Thibong Yakthung's imprisoned knowledge, enlightens the disconnected niches, mentors them and their descendants how to survive, and teaches them how to soar in the Yakthung world of conscience and wisdom. On the other hand, the Khas Aryan political institution led by Surya Bahadur Thapa, Badriprasad Thapaliya, Tilbikram Maske, Ganga Prasad Sitaula, and Ganga Dahal revolted against the Yakthung demands. In 1961, King Mahendra Shah and his cronies (Khas Aryans), rather than addressing the demands of Yakthungs, confiscated Yakthungs' right to their ancestral land, known as *kipat* (see Caplan, 1970; Ingnam & Ingnam, 2070 BS; Khajum-Limbu, 2017, pp. 1–21, 2069 BS; Limbu, 2019; Lumphungwa Limbu, 2075 BS, pp. 67–97; Regmi, 1965). Caplan (1970) states that the decline of Limbu (Yakthung) power and prestige in Yakthung laje was the

Khas Aryans well-organized plan to confiscate Yakthung lands. The Khas Aryans' confiscation of the Yakthung land was not a one-time Khas Aryan strategy. The Khas Aryans started the campaign immediately after the Nun-Paani Sandhi in 1774. However, Yakthungs retained their sense of *khambong-lungbong* (land-based) identity until Mahendra Shah and his cronies introduced *Bhumi Sudhar* (land reformation act) (see Caplan, 1970; Lumphungwa Limbu, 2075 BS). The Khas Aryans disregarded the Gorkha Kingdom and Yakthung laje treaty—the Nun-Paani Sandhi; King Mahendra Shah imposed the tyrannical rule—one nation, one language; one nation, one religion; one nation, one costume, etc., and such Khas Aryan ideological campaigns displaced Yakthungs' *khambong-lungbong* identities. In relation to our family's right to ancestral land, while growing up (as a young boy), I used to help my dad, Ganga Lal Limbu to collect land taxes from our subjects in our village. Later, we stopped doing it, but I never asked my dad for the reason.

Currently, I understand that Khas Aryans, including King Mahendra Shah, confiscated Yakthungs' ancestral land, and they continued to ban the Yakthung mother-tongue education (see also Caplan, 1970; Bista, 1991; Regmi, 1965). Mahendra Shah strictly prohibited Yakthungs from the teaching and learning of their language and writing. After I finished my high school degree (10th grade), I found a Yakthung *saksak* (a Yakthung grammar book). My father, Ganga Lal Limbu and uncle, Taul Man Limbu, warned me not to read or even touch the book. They mentioned that if the Khas Aryans found us (Yakthungs) learning to read and write in *Yakthung pa:n* in the Sirijanga script, we would be captured, tortured, executed or banished from Yakthung laje, Limbuwan. This is how the Khas Aryan-centric Nepali government ignored the demands of Yakthungs. Those who revolted against the Khas Aryan government were captured, jailed, humiliated, executed or banished from Yakthung laje, Limbuwan (Limbu, 2016, 2017; Nembang, 1987). The Khas Aryans started the lethal campaign—one country, one culture, one language against Yakthungs, including other Indigenous peoples and linguistic minorities. The Khas Aryans beguiled the campaign—*eutai bhasha, eutai bhesh; eutai raja, eutai desh, eutai dharma* (one language, one costume, one king, one country, one religion); it was absolutely against the rights of Yakthung Indigenous peoples (see ILO Conventions 169). Our Khas Aryan teachers always made us chant the slogans at school, such as:

> *Eutai bhasha, eutai bhesh;*
> *Eutai raja, eutai desh,*
> *Eutai dharma* (one language, one costume, one king, one country, one religion).

I loved to utter the slogans over and over again; our teachers preached us to follow them; we practiced them in our Yakthung communities, and that is how our Khas Aryan-centric government and our Khas Aryan teachers programmed our minds, body, and soul. This is how they made us the shadow of the Khas Aryans; this is how they coerced us to discount our own language, writing, and Mundhum rhetorics. Our Nepali government and teachers, instead of taking care of us (Yakthungs and other Indigenous peoples), they robbed us.

The *Pallo Kirat Limbuwanka Magaharu* (2002) suggests that the Yakthungs have appealed many times for Yakthung rights to Yakthung's *kipat*, Yakthung's inclusion in Nepali governmental positions in the local to central level, political positions, and Yakthung language education to the Parliament, Upper House, and late King Birendra Shah. Yet, Yakthung demands were always misinterpreted and ignored. Instead of negotiating with Yakthungs in a democratic process, Yakthungs received hostile responses only, such as imprisonment, harassment, or even expulsion (from Nepal) from the Khas Aryan-centric Nepali government (see also Nembang, 1987; Lumphungwa Limbu, 2075 BS; Subba, 1995). Even though Yakthungs, along with other ethnic and Indigenous people, are the majority in Nepal, they have already been manacled by the Khas Aryan-constructed academic, social, and political institutions. As Yakthungs learned why their demands were important for them and their future descendants, Yakthungs revolted against the repression of King Mahendra Shah. As the revolt was against the Khas Aryan politics and ideology, the Khas Aryan-centric government sent the Royal Nepali Armed Forces to Yakthung villages in Yakthung laje, Limbuwan. The armed forces captured, tortured, and executed hundreds of Yakthungs indiscriminately in the Limbuwan region (Lumphungwa Limbu, 2075 BS, p. 96; Nembang, 1987, pp. 16–17). Bir Nembang (1987) further portrays that the armed forces captured innocent Yakthungs who were herding cattle and were working in the farms. The armed forces also got many Yakthungs to dig ditches; they shot, killed them (Yakthungs), and buried them in the ditches. Nembang further graphically asserts that the armed forces shot Yakthungs and buried them alive (p. 19). As the Khas Aryans had and still have the political, economic, and military power, they could or still can do anything to Yakthungs and other Indigenous peoples to suppress their voices in Nepal.

Similarly, Yakthungs were never included in local and central administrative, bureaucratic, and political positions. The Khas Aryans selected a few Yakthungs as representative leaders of Yakthungs from Yakthung laje (Limbuwan) who would highly esteem the Khas Aryan political and ideological norms and values. The few selected Yakthung leaders helped the Khas Aryan government to suppress the Yakthung movements. Therefore, neither could Yakthungs challenge the well-established Khas Aryan hegemonic ideology, nor could they move upward from the educational, cultural, economic, and political spaces. As the Khas Aryans have a control over the political power, they appoint the Khas Aryans for the administrative or bureaucratic positions from the local to central levels. The Khas Aryan-centric Nepali government ignores the inclusion and equity of the Indigenous peoples in the political spaces, bureaucratic places, and other decision-making positions (see Subba, 1995). Even after the advent of democracy in 1990 in Nepal, the Khas Aryans constructed and controlled democratic political theories, philosophies, and practices for their purposes. The democracy (post 1990) neither granted Yakthungs, including Indigenous peoples and minorities, the right to preserve their cultural heritages, language, and right to their ancestral lands, nor it included pro-active Yakthungs in the central level political positions, decision-making positions, and/or bureaucratic positions.

The Khas Aryan-centric Nepali government, like in the past, systematically attempts to exterminate Yakthungs and their cultural, linguistic, and Thibong Yakthung rhetorical traditions in Nepal. The Khas Aryan-centric state still does not support the teaching of their language, culture, and Mundhum rhetorics. All Nepalis fought for democracy, inclusion, and equity, and King Birendra Shah bestowed democracy for the peace, progress, and prosperity of Nepal and Nepali people, but the so-called democracy benefitted only the Khas Aryan communities in Nepal. For instance, in relation to the development of language and literacy, *Anipa:n* (Yakthung language subject) has been taught at an elementary level for more than two decades; it has not yet been upgraded to middle school level until now. Ironically, the Khas Aryan government does not provide any logistic support to Yakthung language teachers or multilingual education system. Meaning, the Khas Aryan-centric Nepali government does not provide any benefits, salaries, professional trainings, and pedagogical workshops to *Anipa:n* teachers. The Khas Aryan politics consistently ignores Yakthungs, including other Indigenous communities, their identities, and voices in academic spaces in Nepal. In relation to teaching of *Anipa:n* (Limbu language teaching), Yakthungs have been raising funds from the local Yakthung communities to pay the salary and benefits of Yakthung language teacher/s (Lumphungwa Limbu, 2075; A. Limbu, personal communication, June 3, 2017; Singak, 2069 BS). On the other hand, the discriminatory Khas Aryan government spends billions of dollars every year on the teaching and preservation of the Sanskrit language—a dead language. Hence, the Khas Aryan discrimination against Yakthungs and their culture (including Indigenous peoples) in Nepal is systemic, ideological, and political, and such practices consistently insinuate the ego, "We" (Khas Aryan) as superior and "them" (Yakthungs) as inferior. Similarly, "We" (Khas Aryan) as power who can do whatever "We" want, and "We" do not spend a penny for the development and/or for the preservation of "their" (Yakthung and Indigenous peoples) cultural development. The Khas Aryan-centric Nepali government allows Yakthungs to study the Yakthung language, but they are required to take several Sanskrit courses before they take Yakthung courses. This is how the Khas Aryans have been abusing political, administrative powers in Nepal, and it has been the prevalent practices in Nepal for centuries as a norm in in/visible forms.

The Khas Aryan state's rules, regulations, and policies have been discriminatory from Prithvi Narayan Shah's administration to current date. Meaning, Yakthungs and other Indigenous peoples have been systematically marginalized; they have been prevented from enjoying basic rights; they are prevented from enjoying the state's resources like their mainstream counterparts (Khas Aryans). The Khas Aryan-centric Nepali constitution dominates Yakthungs; it humiliates Yakthungs; it made Yakthungs homeless in their own homes; it made them landless though they live in their own ancestral land. By living in the Yakthung's land and home, the Khas Aryan-centric government humiliates/humiliated the Yakthungs in their own home and land. As Khas Aryans have political power and armed forces, they illegally confiscated Yakthung land, and now they insult Yakthungs in their own ancestral land (see also Caplan, 1970; Ingnam & Ingnam, 2070 BS; Khajum-Limbu, 2017; Limbu, 2019; Regmi, 1965). The Khas Aryan-centric Nepali government rejects Yakthungs' basic needs, demands, and expectations; it (Khas Aryan) demeans Yakthung language, writing, and Mundhum rhetorics. It not only degrades the Sawa Yet Hang and Susuwa Lilim Yakthung cultural norms and values, but it also disgraces the Yakthungs in Yakthung communities in multiple ways in Nepal. The Khas Aryan ideology of a melting-pot concept, such as *eutai desh, eutai bhasha, eutai bhesh, eutai dharma* (one country, one language, one costume, one religion), distorts Yakthung identities, *khambong-lungbong* (land-based) identity, and agency; it destroys Yakthung cultural, linguistic, and Mundhum identities.

The Khas Aryan epistemic game, such as political, academic, ideological game in the Yakthung laje (Limbuwan) region has perpetually been nepotism and favoritism. Since Yakthungs do not possess power from where they can address basic Yakthungs' (Indigenous peoples') needs, demands, and expectations, they cannot channel the Khas Aryan epistemic games. They cannot navigate the Khas Aryan's politics of knowledge construction, for they (Yakthungs) have their own well-developed Yakthung Mundhum-based epistemologies; therefore, the Khas Aryan ideological games are alien to the Yakthungs. The Khas Aryans nepotic games constantly and consistently discard Yakthungs, Yakthung culture, and *khambong-lungbong* identities. The Khas Aryans want to make their political games as murky as possible so that they can tactfully deceive Yakthungs, including other Indigenous peoples, in Nepal.

Historically, the Khas Aryans divided Yakthungs into two major groups: *niti* (traditional Yakthung customary institutional law and practice supporters) and *samariti* (Gorkha/Khas Aryan statutory law supporters) after the Nun-Paani Sandhi in 1774, for they (Khas Aryans) knew that disunity of Yakthung unity would be the proliferation of the Khas Aryans in Yakthung laje. Based on the logic of divide and rule, they (Khas Aryans) classified, labelled, displaced, and destroyed Yakthungs from the late 18th century. Immediately after the Nun-Paani Sandhi, the Gorkhas (Khas Aryans) with the help of the *samariti* Yakthungs captured, tortured, executed, or banished more than 32,000 *niti* Yakthungs from Yakthung laje (see Hodgson collection, vol. 85; Limbu, 2017). After Khas Aryans had banished the *niti* Yakthungs, they gradually destroyed other *samariti* Yakthungs, Yakthung Suhang culture, Yakthung writing system, and Mundhum rhetorics. They, on a regular basis, collected Yakthung books, Mundhum books, history books, genealogy books, and important archival materials and destroyed them (will discuss in detail in this book). They programmed the *samariti* Yakthungs in the Khas Aryan social institutions and coerced them to see from Khas Aryan lenses. They oriented Yakthungs to distaste their own culture and Mundhum rhetorics; if Yakthungs attempted to resist, they were captured, tortured, executed, or banished because the divided Yakthungs were easy to conquer and conquered people/communities were easy to oppress, displace, and destroy (implying *niti* and *samariti* Yakthungs). As the cultural, linguistic, and religious orientation by coercion continued for centuries, Yakthungs (we) disregarded and still continue to discount our culture and language. As I implied earlier, when we (Yakthungs) meet at meetings, conferences, workshops, and workplaces, we do not speak in *Yakthung pa:n* because we have been programmed to believe that it is the inferior language. At the same time, the Khas Aryan and Western cultures forced us to believe that our Yakthung culture is inferior, and our language is inferior (see also Limbu, 2018; B. B. Muringla, personal communication, 2017, 2018).

In my own case, I almost ceased to speak Yakthung language in my early 20s. I even gave up reading and writing in Nepali after I received my bachelor's degrees in 1990. After 1990, I focused only on English (both written and spoken) and wrote several books on digital rhetorics (technology and pedagogy) and global literacies. The Khas Aryan and Western ideologies programmed me to believe that I was one of the best educators, scholars, researchers, and writers, and I ignored my own language, culture, and Mundhum traditional rhetorics. Later, when I searched my own Yakthung Suhang identity in the Khas Aryan and Western institutions, I did not find anything at all. Then, when I looked back to my Yakthung community in research of my Yakthung histories, cultures, and Mundhum traditions in my late 40s, I found out that I was cocooned in Khas Aryan and Western social and academic institutions. Then, this was the moment I theorized the "Delinking, Relinking, and Linking Methodology" to explore my Sawa Yet Hang, Yet Hang, Thibong Yakthung, and Yakthung Suhang epistemologies. Henceforward, I started researching, networking, collaborating, writing, and disseminating Sawa Yet Hang rhetorics, Yet Hang and Thibong Yakthung cultural traditions, and Yakthung Suhang, including Mundhum rhetorical traditions both in traditional writing and multimodal writing.

Delinking, relinking, and linking methodologies: implications on Yakthung language and literacies

Khas Aryans, including Indians and Westerners colonized Yakthungs in the Khas Aryan social institutions for centuries by force or coercion. Khas Aryans banned Yakthungs from the teaching of the Sirijanga script, writing, and Mundhum rhetorics after the Nun-Paani Sandhi (1774). Then, the Khas Aryans persistently oriented Yakthungs to disregard their own language and culture through Khas Aryan social institutions. Henceforward, Khas Aryans culturally and linguistically colonized Sawa Yet Hang, Susuwa Lilim Yakthung, Yet Hang, and Thibong Yakthung epistemologies for centuries. As Khas Aryan (have) colonized Yakthungs for centuries, Sawa Yet Hang Mundhum rhetorical tradition has been petrified; Yet Hang and Thibong Yakthung epistemologies have been paralyzed; and Yakthung Suhang rhetorical tradition has been impaired for centuries. As a result, Yakthungs started viewing themselves from the Khas Aryan, Indian, and Western lenses; they started viewing their language and culture from the Khas Aryan terministic screens. In the context of the 21st century networked global village, Yakthung Suhang knowledge needs to be delinked; Yakthung Suhang knowledge needs to be de-naturalized in multiple fields and in multiple ways (Limbu, 2017). As Walter Mignolo (2007), an Indigenous scholar, contends, "…one strategy of de-linking is to de-naturalize concepts and conceptual fields that totalizes A reality" (p. 459). In Mignolo's own language the process of delinking needs a different epistemic grounding, such as the geo- and body-politics of knowledge and understanding (p. 462). In the process of epistemic delinking in the history of Yakthung Suhang rhetoric and writing, Yakthungs, the descendants of Sawa Yet Hang and Susuwa Lilim Yakthungs, have to culturally, linguistically, ideologically, and pedagogically delink the Khas Aryan body and caste-based politics of knowledge construction (Limbu, 2016, 2017).

Similarly, the relinking process is a form of the Susuwa Lilim epistemic project that occurs simultaneously with delinking process. In this process, Yakthung Suhangs delink the Khas Aryan, Indian, and Western cultural, linguistic, economic, and political colonization and relink Sawa Yet Hang Mundhum epistemologies, Yet Hang and Thibong Yakthung customary cultural traditions. They (Yakthungs) relink Sawa Yet Hang Indigenous knowledge; they relink Yet Hang and Thibong Yakthung civilizations; the relinking approach facilitates to relink Yet Hang and Thibong Yakthung epistemologies by reframing and reformulating Mundhum-based Yakthung epistemologies. The descendants of Sawa Yet Hang, via delinking and relinking research methodologies, critically study the Yet Hang and Thibong Yakthung, including Sawa Yet Hang architecture of Yakthung customary institutions and civilizations. For instance, relinking approach facilitates them to critically study how Yet Hang and Thibong Yakthung created, circulated, and maintained Yakthung customary institutional laws and practices. The relinking process explores the historical and philosophical dimension of Indigenous knowledge, i.e. Sawa Yet Hang and Susuwa Lilim epistemologies, writing, and Mundhum rhetorics. Hence, the delinking and relinking process seeks to reframe Sawa Yet Hang, Yet Hang, and Thibong Yakthung Indigenous knowledge; it seeks the processes and practices of de-naturalizing Khas Aryan, Indian, and Western cultural colonization. Then, it seeks to practice and perpetuate the process of naturalizing, adapting, and solacing Sawa Yet Hang and Susuwa Lilim epistemologies. Similarly, my linking methodology refers to exploring, discovering, and constructing Sawa Yet Hang and Susuwa Lilim knowledge and aligning them to local and global levels in the context of the 21st century digitally networked global village. For the linking approach, we (Yakthungs) should question and contest on our multiple identities and negotiate them from the local to global contexts. In other words, in the linking process, we (Yakthung Indigenous peoples) bring the traditional Yakthung Suhang Indigenous wisdom, histories, and Mundhum rhetorics and update them from the 21st century's perspective. The critical questions, contests, and negotiations on *khambong-lungbong* identities will offer us the Yakthung Suhang historical foundations of our being Yakthung, becoming Yakthung, and physically and/or spiritually belonging to Yakthung laje as *khambong-lungbongsa* Yakthungs. In the linking process, Yakthung Indigenous people will network with other global Indigenous activists, Indigenous scholars, and/ or oral performance-based rhetors, such as *phedangma, yema/ba, and samma/ ba*, etc.—all Yakthung oral ritual performers, including scholars, activists, and writers. Then, they will demonstrate how Indigenous rhetorics should be an alternative pedagogy both in academic, social, and political institutions in Nepal, India, and Southeast Asia, including across the world. It critically studies Yakthung ancestral customary institutional law and practices or may disapprove the hegemonic Western research methodologies, for they (Western research methodologies) are engineered for Western institutions. We (Indigenous Yakthungs) cannot get to our *cho:tlung* (destination) if we use the Western, Khas Aryan, and Indian lenses to explore, question, discover, and/or construct our Yakthung Suhang realities (Limbu, 2017). Hence, delinking, relinking, and linking methodology is a Yakthung Indigenous way of exploring, questioning, and discovering Yakthung ancestral customary laws, norms, values, and ideals.

One of the vital parts of the Yakthung Indigenous research methodology is that our Mundhums, such as among many others, *tangsing takma, cho:tlung, mangena,* and other Mundhums are our research tools; our *phedangma* (Yakthung ritual performer), *yeba* (Yakthung ritual performer), *samma/ba* (Yakthung ritual performer), *tutu-tumyahang* (Indigenous elders or tradition keepers), our ancestral land (space), and history are our research mentors, subjects, and resources. By chanting and rechanting Yakthung Mundhums, our *phedangma, yema/ba, samma/ba,* and *tutu-tumyahang* as mentors can direct us to get to Yakthungs' ultimate *cho:tlung*; they can unravel our distorted Yakthung Indigenous histories, cultural traditions, and *khambong-lungbong* identities. Our land, water, river, and Mundhums as our research resources and subjects make us hear the voices of our ancestors. They make us feel our (Sawa) Yet Hang ancestors, and they make us feel Yet Hang and Thibong Yakthung Suhang culture and civilization. Our Mundhumic Yakthung histories inform us of our *khambong-lungbong* identities, such as who we had been, who we are, and who we should be. Our research methodologies, our subjects, our research tools (as mentioned above), and our intellect orient us that traditions do not exist by themselves, but they have to be communicated, contested, challenged, processed, and constructed for our purpose (Limbu, 2017, p. 574). Our Yakthung Indigenous research tools and methodologies instruct us not to tell the stories to our Yakthung children the way Khas Aryans, including Indians and Westerners, coerced us to tell, but Yakthung Indigenous research methods and methodologies instruct us to tell our Mundhum stories the way they will have been heard in the next hundreds and thousands of years (Limbu, 2017). Importantly, telling our Yakthung Mundhums or Mundhum stories culture formulates and reformulates our and our future Yakthung customary institutional epistemologies in the ways that keeps Yet Hang, Thibong Yakthung, and Yakthung cultural integrities intact (see also Bessarab & Ng'andu, 2010; Clandinin, 2006; Geia, Hayes, & Usher, 2013; Kovach, 2009).

Our collective struggle flourishes our way to *cho:tlung* which is our one of the goals of being Yakthung Suhang, becoming Yakthung Suhang, and belonging to Yakthung laje. We (Yakthungs) understand that the way we present or understand ourselves is not who we actually are, for our body, knowledge, and way of life are constructed in the Khas Aryan, Indian, and Western social institutions (for colonial purposes). Therefore, Yakthungs theoretically, conceptually, and methodologically must understand that we need to delink and unlearn the Khas Aryan, Indian, and Western colonization. We also need to reframe Sawa Yet Hang knowledge and Indigenous peoples' spatial and temporal epistemology from the 21st century global village perspective. The delinking and relinking process is like sowing the seed of Sawa Yet Hang civilization, Susuwa Lilim Yakthung wisdom, and Yakthung Suhang Indigenous epistemologies. This approach will relink our Yakthung Indigenous historical and epistemic foundation, such as Sawa Yet Hang epistemologies, Susuwa Lilim Yakthung civilization, Yet Hang historical tradition, and Thibong Yakthung Suhang wisdom. In so doing, Yakthungs will learn writing and Mundhum rhetorics upon the foundation of Sawa Yet Hang and Susuwa Lilim Yakthung histories and Yakthung Suhang narratives and philosophies (Limbu, 2016, 2017).

One of the pertinent objectives of the delinking, relinking, and linking methodology is to collectively research, discuss the research findings, digitally document them, and institutionalize Yakthung Indigenous rhetorical traditions from the 21st century context. To address our objectives, we need mentors, such as Mundhum, including *tutu-tumyahang, phedangma, samba, yeba/ma,* and historians. For Yakthungs, Mundhum is our mentor, and *tutu-tumyahang, phedangma, samba, yeba/ma* are the purveyors of our Yakthung Mundhum. The reason why I am kin on Yakthung Mundhum and mentors is that they help us channel our Sawa Yet Hang epistemologies, navigate our *khambong-lungbong* identities, and facilitate Yet Hang and Thibong Yakthung Suhang epistemologies upon which our future Yakthung Indigenous descendants, activists, and scholars will be able to reconstruct Yakthung *khambong-lungbong* pedagogies, including inclusive and representational pedagogy (Limbu, 2016, 2017). From this perspective, the delinking, relinking, and linking methodology is not only a way of repairing physical and psychological wounds inflicted by the (para)colonizers, but it is also an intellectual way of delinking, relinking, and linking institutions such as colonial institutions, Yakthung Indigenous customary institutions, and local and global institutions respectively. The delinking, relinking, and linking approach is a process of deconstructing (para)colonial epistemologies and reconstructing Yakthung Indigenous voices, identities, and agencies in the center; it helps us shift our spatial position from the margin to the center. The delinking, relinking, and linking approach is also a method of remembering Yet Hang, Thibong Yakthung Suhang, and Susuwa Lilim Yakthung histories, for if we do not remember (retell) our history (the relinking approach implied), the Khas Aryan brutality may repeat again. Thus, revisiting and re-storytelling is a powerful way of making Khas Aryans stop from suppressing, oppressing, and demeaning the Yakthungs and other Indigenous communities in the context of Nepal. The delinking, relinking, and linking approach is not only a knowledge making process; it is not only a history making process, but it is also our healing process (Limbu, 2017, p. 587). Furthermore, the delinking, relinking, and linking approaches expose Yakthungs, including Indigenous peoples, not only as compartmentalized Yakthungs within Yakthung communities, but also facilitates them to network, collaborate, create, and succeed as contributing global citizens in the context of the 21st century global village.

Part II

Historical development of the Sirijanga script, writing, and rhetorics

2   Classical period

The Sirijanga script, writing, and rhetorics

Revisiting classical Yakthung history, civilization, and rhetorics

The Kirat is an umbrella term that refers to many ethnic groups that reside in the South and Southeast Asian Himalayan regions, such as Nepal, India, Bhutan, Bangladesh, and Burma. They are also known as Himalayan Indigenous peoples or Sawa Yet Hang or Yet Hang (Mundhum implied). They had/have been known as Kiratas or Kirats for thousands of years by the Hindus or South Indian communities; for instance, we find the term Kirat or Kirata in the Mahabharata (see Chattopodyaya, 2015, p. 8; Raj, 2011; Roy, 2015; Subba, 2019). Meaning, the Himalayan Indigenous peoples, such as Kõich (Kõits), Khambu, Yakkha, Yakthung, Haayu, Jirel, Surel, Newar, Dhimal, Magar, Gurung, Tamang, Chaudhari, Koche, Meche, Thami, Thakali, Tharu, Bhote, Lepcha (Lapche), Sherpa, Kulung, and Thulung to mention a few, had been dominant Indigenous peoples who lived in the Himalayan regions ranging from Nepal, Sikkim, Assam, Arunachal, Nagaland, Manipur, Meghalaya, Manipur to Burma. Even though their neighbors from the South, mainly, Khas Aryans from the Southern Indian continent, called them Kirat or Kirata, they did not call themselves Kirat. The term Kirat is not used in Mundhum (implying all Kirat Mundhums, such as Yakthung, Yakkha, Khambu, and Kõit Mundhums). Meaning, they are Indigenous peoples of South Asian Himalayan regions, and they call themselves Kõiches (Sunuwars), Khambus (Rais), Yakkhas, and Yakthungs, including Haayu, Jirel, Surel, Newar, Dhimal, Magar, Gurung, Chaudhari, Koche, Meche, Thami, Thakali, Tharu, Bhote, Lepcha, Sherpa, Kulung, and Thulung (see Baral & Tigela, 2008, p. 3; Banepaali, 2075 BS, pp. 107–116; Chemjong, 2003; Subba, 2015). They also prefer to call themselves as *khambong-lungbongsa* (Indigenous peoples), Sawa Yet Hangs (Mundhum implied), Mongolians, and Tibeto-Burmans. Later, during the Sen reign, the Sen rulers called Yakthungs, including Yakkhas and Khambus Raya or Rai; whereas, Bhutias called Yakthungs Tsong in Sikkim, and the Khas Aryans called Yakthungs Limbu or Subba. Therefore, the terms, Subba, Raya (Rai), Limbu or Limboo, and Tsong are also not Yakthung native terminologies, and we also do not find the terms in Yakthung Mundhum.

As these Himalayan Indigenous peoples have been programmed in the Khas Aryan institutions, they prefer to call themselves in multiple ways, such as *khambong-lungbongsa* (Indigenous peoples), Sawa Yet Hang, Tibeto-Burman, Yakthung, Mongolian, Tsongs, Limboos, and Kirats, etc. Additionally, though the term Kirat referred to only Rai, Limbu, Yakkha, and Sunuwar, recently, some other ethnic groups, such as Thami, Jirel, and some Newar claim to be/to have been Kirats. In terms of Kirats, Dor Bahadur Bista (1991) states:

> Although today, the Kirats are associated particularly with the hilly regions east of Kathmandu Valley, in the ancient period the Kirat regions extended into the western hills as well. They are Mongoloids and spoke a Tibeto-Burmese language, though their descendants have now mixed with other racial groups. The Kirats are thought to have moved from the lower hills through warm, humid, and forested areas, where they practiced a shifting cultivation. (15)

As I mentioned earlier, though Rai, Limbu, Yakkha, and Sunuwar have been considered as Kirats, according to Bista (1991), all Mongoloids and Tibeto-Burmese language speaking Himalayan Indigenous peoples are Kirats (but recently the term "Kirat" has become a contradictory term). It is also believed that the Kirat descendants include all Mongoloid Indigenous groups who speak the Tibeto-Burmese language as their mother-tongues (many Himalayan Indigenous people are reluctant to accept the Kirat identity as well). In this regard, Bista (1991) further argues that any Indigenous peoples who speak Tibeto-Burmese language in South(east) Asia are Kirats; they include "Rai, Limbu, Yakkha, Sunuwar, Jirel, Hayu, Gurung, Magar, Thakali, Thami, and Chepang in the hills, and the Tharu, Danuwar, Bote, Majhi, Dhimal, Meche, Koche in the plains" (p. 17).

In this book, as a part of my delinking, relinking, and linking methodology, I use Yakthungs or Yakthung Suhangs to refer to Limbu or Limboo, Tsong, Subba, Raya/Rai, and Kirat. As I already implied, this chapter briefly introduces the Kirats and Kirat civilization (although this is not the main focus of this book, and many Indigenous communities do not accept this identity); then, it discusses the historical foundation of Yakthung writing and rhetorics. It highlights King Sirijanga (9th and 10th centuries), his re/invention or re/design of the Sirijanga script upon the foundation of the Kirat (Indigenous peoples') writing system (before CE) and the King Maarangian writing system (6th century or 7th century). This chapter further examines King Sirijanga's philosophy on writing and rhetoric, including Yakthung Mundhum theories, philosophies, and practices.

The Himalayan Indigenous peoples or Sawa Yet Hangs (Mundhum implied) or Kirats had/have their own Tibeto-Burman-centric languages and cultures. The Kirats had ruled over Nepal and/or ruled over the Himalayan region (range) from Nepal to Bhutan or up to Burma for centuries, and the Kirat Kingdom was one of the greatest nations in the history of human civilization (there was not any concept of political borders as we do have now). The Kirat kings had ruled up to 33 (or 28 generations, Hodgson collection implied) generations beginning with Yalambar (the first Kirat king) and ending with Gasti (the last Kirat king) (Chattopodyaya, 2015, p. 8; Roy, 2015). They also had developed great Kirat theories, philosophies, Mundhum rhetorics, and their own writing system. The ancient Kirats were one of the Mongoloid races evolved somewhere in the North-Eastern Eurasia during the Ice Age (45,000–40,000 years ago). The Mongoloid races evolved, spread throughout the world from their place of evolution, and presently, they are known as the East Asian Mongoloids of Asia, Indigenous/Autonomous Mongoloids or Native Himalayans of the Hindu-Kush Himalayan region, Mongoloids of Southeast Asia, and Amerindian Mongoloids. The Mongoloid races are Chinese, Japanese, Korean, Burmese, Kirat (the Southeast Asian Himalayan and Hilly Indigenous peoples), American Mongoloids or Native Americans, Alaskan Natives, Aleut, Yu'ik or Inuit people, and Eskimos together comprising one-third of the world's population (Subba, 2015, p. 19; see also Chemjong, 2003; Mishra & Singh, 2002, pp. 285–294). J. R. Subba's (2015) research findings also demonstrate that Kirats are the Mongoloid race and have settled in different parts of Southeast Asia; whereas, other Mongoloids spread across the world (see also Chattopodyaya, 2015, p. 8; Nagarajan, 1993; Raj, 2011; Roy, 2015). Similarly, Anatoly Yakoblave Sherenko came to Nepal in 1978 for archeological research purpose; his research demonstrates that the Kirat people's stone tools (30,000 BC) from Yambu, Budhanilkanth, Kathmandu resemble the stone tools found in Govey of Mongolia, left by Native American Mongoloids. Sherenko named the stone tools as Kirata Stone Tools (as Sherenko quoted in Subba, 2015, p. 19; see also Mabuhang, 2063 BS, pp. 4–5).

In the contemporary Southeast Asian region, the term Kirat refers to Himalayan Indigenous peoples other than Khas Aryans, such as Kôiches, Khambus, Yakkhas, and Yakthungs, including Haayu, Jirel, Surel, Newar, Dhimal, Magar, Gurung, Chaudhari, Koche, Meche, Thami, Thakali, Tharu, Bhote, Lepcha, Sherpa, Kulung, and Thulung in Nepali context (Bista, 1991, pp, 15–17; Chemjong, 2003; Subba, 2015). These diverse Indigenous peoples (Kirats), such as Magar, Gurung, Thakali, and Tharu started settling in the central and western part of Nepal; whereas, Yakthungs, Kôiches, Khambus, Yakkhas, Lepchas, and Athpahariyas settled in the eastern part of Nepal, Sikkim, Bengal, and Northeast India (see also Baral & Tigela, 2008, pp. 11–12). In terms of Dhimal, Santhals, Rajbansis, Tajpuriyas, Gangais, and Meches, as they live/d in the Terai region of Yakthung laje (Limbuwan), they did not come into contact with other Kirat (Indigenous peoples, such as with people from Wallo Kirat, Majha Kirat, and Pallo Kirat. Due to the lack of appropriate research, they thought that they were different from Yakthungs, Khambus, Yakkhas, Athpahariyas, and Kôiches from Wallo Kirat, Majha Kirat, and Pallo Kirat. Similarly, due to the coerced cultural, linguistic, and religious colonization, some Himalayan Indigenous peoples, such as Magar,

Gurung, and Chaudhari also believed that they were different from their Kirat brothers and sisters (Khambu, Yakkha, Yakthung, and Kõich brothers and sisters) for centuries (Bista, 1991, pp. 15–17; Chemjong, 2003; Subba, 2015).

Among many other Indigenous peoples (Mongolians), Khas Aryans labelled, classified, displaced, and destroyed identities of Indigenous peoples, such as Magars, Gurungs, Tamangs, Newars, Kõiches, Khambus, Yakkhas, Yakthungs, Dhimal, Santhals, Rajbansis, Tajpuriyas, Gangais, and Meches. They (Khas Aryans) not only distorted and displaced Indigenous identities, but they also destroyed their philosophies, theories, and Mundhum rhetorics. Currently, they (Indigenous peoples) are stuck in the Khas Aryan colonial cage; they are trapped in the Khas Aryan castic cage; they are programmed in the Khas Aryan colonial politics of knowledge construction. In relation to Yakthung cultural identities, including other Himalayan Indigenous identities, Europeans (English colonizers) supported the Khas Aryans in their para-colonial displacement and destruction of the Indigenous peoples of Nepal. For instance, they (Europeans) supported Khas Aryans to displace and destroy the Malla reign or Malla civilization from the Kathmandu valley (Giuseppe, 1790). Similarly, the British colonizers and mainstream Indians supported the Khas Aryans to displace and destroy Yakthungs, Khambus, Yakkhas, and Kõiches (will discuss later in this book). For instance, Khas Aryans and Europeans, including Indians, systematically divided Yakthung laje and Yakthungs into three countries: India, Sikkim, and Nepal. They dispersed Yakthung collective power in three different countries (will discuss in detail later). They ideologically divided Yakthungs so that it became easier for the Khas Aryans, Indians, and English (British) to rule over them. Gradually, they displaced their *khambong-lungbong* (land-based) identities and destroyed their cultural, linguistic, and religious identities, and finally, we (Yakthungs) became homeless and powerless in their own homeland/s.

In relation to Kirat identity (though it is not their true identity), although the term Kirat refers to many Indigenous groups in Southeast Asia, due to the disconnected histories (as Khas Aryans destroyed all Himalayan Indigenous cultural artifacts and histories), many Mongolians did/do not know if they were Kirats or Sawa Yet Hangs as well (also see Bista, 1991; Chemjong, 2003; Laksamba, 2016; Mabuhang, 2063; Subba, 2015). Many Limboos from Sikkim and some new Yuma Samyo campaigners hesitate to identify themselves as Kirats, but they identify themselves as Subba (Subba), Limbu, or Limboo or Tsong. However, Subba, Limboo, and Tsong were also politically and ideologically created identities for Yakthungs by their local para-colonizers. As the Khas Aryans had called the Himalayan Indigenous peoples Kirats for thousands of years, a few Indigenous groups accepted and still accept the Kirat identity (see the Hodgson collection). After the Nun-Paani Sandhi in 1774, the Khas Aryans also called the Indigenous peoples of Eastern Nepal as the Kirats. At the same time, as I implied earlier, the Khas Aryans also ideologically and politically constructed the Limbu and Subba terms to refer to Yakthungs; whereas, the Bhutias called Yakthungs

Tsongs. Later, to weaken the Indigenous collective power in Sikkim, India, the local and central government required the Indigenous peoples, such as Rai, Limboo, Lepcha, etc., to prove that they have their own unique cultural, linguistic, and religious identities, including writing, to retain the schedule tribe (ST) status or Indigenous status in India. The previously known Kirats or Himalayan Indigenous peoples who had been from the same Indigenous groups for thousands of years have been forced to create diverse cultural, linguistic, and religious identities. This local and central Indian government's divide and rule ideology further divided Indigenous peoples in order to subside their collective cultural, economic, and political power. Hence, because of the Indian political ideology, the Indigenous collective power crumbled into pieces in India, and it is gravely affecting Indigenous unity in Nepal. Unpleasantly, the Indian, Khas Aryan, and British divide and rule ideology has been affecting especially uncritical Indigenous masses in Nepal and India.

Due to the above-mentioned problems, the study of Kirat people, Kirat culture, and Kirat civilization has become one of the compelling and enigmatic research areas. There is an urgent need of delinking, relinking, and linking research methodology and emic research approach on Kirat and Sawa Yet Hang or Yet Hang civilization, and the researchers have to be from the Himalayan Indigenous communities in order to explore the lost civilization, histories, *khambong-lungbong* customary laws and practices, and Sawa Yet Hang Mundhum epistemologies (in the context of the 21st century networked world). The researchers have to create their own Sawa Yet Hang and/or Himalayan Indigenous-centric delinking, relinking, and linking research methodology, non-Western or decolonial methodology (Limbu, 2016, 2017; see also Mignolo, 2007, 2009; Wilson, 2008; Smith, 1999). The Sawa Yet Hang or Himalayan Indigenous-centric delinking, relinking, and linking methodology will facilitate Indigenous research to explore who they had been or who they are, and where they have been residing. The concept of Sawa Yet Hang, Sawa Yet Hang or civilization, Sawa Yet Hang theories and philosophies, and Mundhum rhetorics have become enigmatic to Yakthungs, including local and global citizens. There are enigmatic grounds that have complicated the Sawa Yet Hang studies or Tibeto-Burman studies by making it a more captivating, compelling, and emerging research area in the context of the 21st century. Since the major theme of this book is the historical development of the Sirijanga syllabary and literacy (inventions and interventions), I have chosen not to focus on the Kirat studies or (Sawa) Yet Hang studies in in this book.

King Sirijangian Yakthung era: a glimpse of writing and rhetorics

King Sirijanga (880–915) ruled in the Yakthung laje long after the Lichchhavi invasion in the Kathmandu valley from Baisali of ancient India. After the Lichchhavi invasion, some Kirats had migrated to the eastern part of

Kathmandu valley, which was/is known as the Kirat Pradesh (Kirat region), such as Wallo Kirat, Majha Kirat, and Pallo Kirat, King Sirijanga became one of the dominant Yakthung kings in Yakthung laje. King Sirijanga was a great ruler, scholar, and democratic king. Therefore, Yakthung chieftains from Yakthung laje elected him as their overlord in Yakthung laje. As the overlord of the Yakthung laje, he both continued what King Maarang had introduced and reformed Yakthung social norms and values. Concerning the Yakthung laje, though some Kirats migrated to the new place (Yakthung laje) after the Lichchhavi invasion, the Yakthung laje, including Wallo Kirat and Majha Kirat, however, had been the abode of Sawa Yet Hangs or Kirats for centuries (Bista, 1991; Limbu, 2017; *Pallo Kirat Limbuwan* 2066 BS; Subba, 2015; Tumbahang, 2007, p. 24). As I mentioned above, some Kirats migrated to the eastern part of Kathmandu, some continued to live in Kathmandu (Newars implied), but due to the lack of regular networks among Kirats from the eastern part of Nepal and central or western part of Nepal, they did not realize that they had been *phu-ne-nusa* (brothers and sisters). Those Kirats or Yet Hangs or Sawa Yet Hangs (Mundhum implied) who continued to live in the western part of Nepal, such as Gurung, Magar, and so on gradually forgot about their cultural heritages, including their *phu-ne-nusa*, histories, narratives, and rhetorics because the Khas Aryans ideologically and politically coerced them to accept the Khas Aryan culture, language, and religion (Bista, 1991). Many of them wanted to preserve their language and culture, but Khas Aryans prohibited them from teaching and learning of their language, writing, and Mundhum rhetorics for centuries. As a result, they became the shadows of the Khas Aryans or Hindu culture.

During the 9th century, King Sirijanga had also united many small nations into one great Yakthung laje; the Yakthung laje spread from the Arun River to Darjeeling, Kalimpong, Sikkim, Siliguri, Jalpaiguri, Dooars, and west Assam, ranging from Himalaya region to the Terai region. This is one of the reasons why Yakthungs live in Siliguri, Jalpaiguri, Dooars, Bangladesh, Bhutan, and the Northeast regions of India (Assam, Nagaland, Manipur, Arunachal Pradesh and so on), and they speak *Yakthung pa:n* (Yakthung language). This is one of the reasons why Yakthungs are considered to have been the Indigenous peoples Sikkim, Darjeeling, Kalimpong, Siliguri, Jalpaiguri, Bhutan, Assam, including Arunachal Pradesh, Nagaland, Manipur, and Bangladesh. King Sirijanga, including his predecessors, such as King Maarang, was the well admired king among his subjects. This is one of the reasons why King Sirijanga is always known as a great ruler, diplomat, philosopher, linguist, and rhetor. Based on my five-year-long research and ongoing research inquiries on Yakthung language, writing, and Mundhum rhetorics, I found that King Sirijanga's cultural, political, and pedagogical philosophy profoundly influenced the Southeast Asian regions, such as Nepal, Northeast India, Bhutan, Bangladesh, Burma, and beyond.

As King Sirijanga was a great rhetor and philosopher, he was fond of any form of communication both oral and written, and to systematize the oral

Figure 2 King Sirijanga, re/designer of the Sirijanga script (Sketch: Balkrishna Mabuhang).

and written communication in his kingdom, King Sirijanga redesigned the script upon the foundation of the Himalayan Indigenous (Kirat) writing system or script that had been practiced during King Maarang and Kirat reign (Kandangwa, 1999, pp. 44–55; Laoti, 2005, p. 143; Subba, 1995, p. 294; Subba, 2015, pp. 103–110; Yakthumba, 2062 BS, pp. 26–30). King Maarang had used the script to communicate within Yakthung laje and with other neighboring nations. During the King Sirijangian reign, Yakthungs used to erect stone pillars on the state borders and used to inscribe important information on the stone pillars in this script (Laoti, 2005, p. 143; Subba, 2005), and we still see the remnants of the pillars. This practice (i.e., erecting stone pillars and inscribing on them) was a prevalent system until recently in Yakthung laje; we can still see the tall stone pillars erected in the Yakthung laje (regions).

As mentioned above, King Sirijanga reintroduced the script and writing system and popularized both oral rhetorical communication and written communication during his reign. This script had been popular in the Khambu and Yakthung regions, including Northeast India. Although the script (/a/-based phonology or writing system) had been used by Kirat peoples for a long time, many Kirat (Khambu) communities gradually stopped using it due to the Khas Aryan cultural, linguistic, and religious colonization.

For instance, the Kirat people who continued to live in the western part of Nepal had been culturally, religiously colonized for centuries (Bista, 1991). Consequently, they forgot about their script and writing system as they were forced to pursue the Khas Aryan culture. As a result, Magars, until recently, believed that they were superior caste than Yakthungs; meaning, Magars were Hinduized and followed the Hindu hierarchical caste system. Even the Kirats from Wallo Kirat (Kõich, Danuwar, and Jirel, etc.) and Majha Kirat (Khambus) barely used the script and almost stopped using it because first, the Lichchhavi and Malla cultures heavily influenced them. Later, the Khas Aryan-centric government banned Kõiches (Sunuwars) and Khambus (Rais) from the teaching of the script, writing, and Mundum rhetorics (Khambus call "Mundum"; Yakthungs call "Mundhum"; some Yakthungs in the 18th and 19th century called "Munthum"—Hodgson collection implied). On the other hand, Yakthungs in the Pallo Kirat region, including Sikkim, Kalimpong, and Darjeeling continued to practice the script and writing (despite Khas Aryan and Bhutia's oppression). Yakthungs not only continued to practice the script, but they also documented their major histories, stories, Mundhum rhetorics, and Yakthung cultural rhetorics in this script (Limbu et al., 1845 or Hodgson collection is a good example).

A Mundhum on King Sirijanga and Goddess Nisammang

There is an interesting Mundhum in relation to King Sirijanga and the script he redesigned. According to Yakthung Mundhum, once Nisammang, the Goddess of knowledge, wisdom, and intelligence, asked King Sirijanga to accompany her to the base of the Mt. Phaktanglung (Phaktanglung mountain is situated in Yakthung laje). The Goddess Nisammang took King Sirijanga to a cave in the mountains and offered him a slate with several carvings (letters) on it. The Goddess, Nisammang taught King Sirijanga how to read and write the script and writing system. The King stayed with Nisammang to learn the script and writing system for more than three months. According to the Mundhum, after King Sirijanga had learned how to read and write, the Goddess, Nisammang asked him to take the knowledge and wisdom to his kingdom and teach his subjects the script, writing system, and values of reading and writing (Chemjong, 1982, pp. 40–42; Subba, 2015, pp. 103–110; Tumbahang, 2007). As soon as King Sirijanga got to the palace, he called forth a congregation of his ministers and noble wo/men and recounted his journey to the Mt. Phaktanglung with the Goddess Nisammang and the knowledge he received from Nissamang. King Sirijanga ordered his subjects to devote themselves to the powerful Goddess Nisammang, her message of learning to read and write. According to Yakthung Mundhum, upon the interest of the Goddess, Nisammang, King Sirijanga, his ministers, and noble people spread the teaching of the Sirijanga script and writing system in Yakthung laje. Henceforth, Yakthungs of the Yakthung laje, including Kirat regions, learned to read and write the script and writing system (therefore, this script is called the Sirijanga script).

In terms of the Mundhum on King Sirijanga and Nissamang, many Mundhumists, historians, and scholars state that Yakthungs (especially Yakthung activists and scholars) created this Mundhum so that Yakthungs and non-Yakthungs would be loyal to the Goddess and would devote to read and write the script and writing system. Although the Khas Aryans banned Yakthungs from the teaching and learning of their script, writing, and *Yakthung pa:n*, some Yakthungs continued to read and write as the blessing of the Goddess, Nisammang. Again, the reality was that King Sirijanga, who was a great philosopher, linguist, and scholar, redesigned the Sirijanga script upon the foundation of the King Maarangian writing system. During his reign, King Sirijanga promoted the teaching of Yakthung language, writing, literature, and Mundhum rhetorics. The Yakthung Mundhum demonstrates that King Sirijanga designed the scripts on the slates, stones, and woods. During the reign of King Sirijanga, the script was not only used as a medium to officially communicate within the royal palace and beyond (Yakthung/ non-Yakthung communities), but also document history, narratives, and Mundhum rhetorics. It is commonly believed that King Sirijanga wrote *Kirat Khahun Sapla* and *Kirat Samlo Sapla* in this script (Chemjong, 2003, pp. 22–23; Tumbahang, 2007).

King Sirijanga and Yakthung laje

King Sirijanga is famous for his philosophical and political beliefs in Yakthung land acts. As a visionary Yakthung king, Sirijanga reformed land acts by giving a full administrative authority to local chiefs, which is known as the traditional Yakthung customary institutional laws and practices in Yakthung laje. He empowered the local chiefs so that they could have the control over the lands in Yakthung laje within the parameters of King Sirijangian land acts. In return, he wanted the local Yakthung chiefs to give him military supports to defend Yakthung laje in critical circumstances. According to the Sirijangian Yakthung land act neither the chiefs nor the other common people were allowed to sell their ancestral lands to non-clan members (non-Yakthungs), but rent the land for a certain period of time (Ingnam & Ingnam, 2070 BS; Subba, 2015, p. 110).

King Sirijangian culture was democratic, inclusive, and representational, and during the Sirijangian era, Yakthungs, Dhimal, Santhals, Rajbansis, Tajpuriyas, Gangais, Meches, Lepchas, Sherpas, Lamas, and Bhotes lived in Yakthung laje. The Sirijangian culture did not favor one group of people over another one, such as rich over the poor, son over daughter (*saimundri* is a good example), and able over disable. Yakthung culture was and still is one of the cultures that highly revere/d the position, space, or self-determination of women (Tembe, 2019; Thebe, 2069 BS; also Yakthung Mundhum implied). Our Yakthung cultures highly revere women, for Yakthung culture, according to Yakthung Mundhum, has been nurtured, oriented, and fostered by female leading figures, such as Yuma, Nisammang, Tagera Ningwaphuma, Mujingna-Kheyangna (Mujingna-Muyangna), and Lahadangna to mention a few. Hence, both in Yakthung Mundhum theories and in real cultural practices, female mentors have shaped the Yakthung cultural and rhetorical traditions.

During the research, I went to Nepal, Sikkim, Kalimpong, Darjeeling, Guwahati, Sonitpur, Biswanath, Golaghat, Tinsukia, the UK, and the USA where I got the opportunity to interact with diverse Yakthungs of varied age, gender, sexual orientation, class, creed, and so on. Yakthung Mundhumists or traditional Yakthung Indigenous knowledge keepers, such as *phedangmas, yebas, sammas/bas,* and *tutu-tumyahangs* shared fascinating folklores (Mundhum narratives) during the workshops, informal gatherings, and meetings. According to Yakthung Mundhum/s, female figures, such as Yuma, Tagera-Ningwaphuma, Mujingna-Kheyangna (Mujingna-Muyangna), Lahadangna, Yuma, and many other Mundhumic female figures shaped Yakthung social, cultural, academic, and economic practices; they cherished Yakthungs and Yakthung cultural traditions. They oriented Yakthung cultural ideals, norms, and values; they shaped Yakthung cultural traditions and Mundhum rhetorics in Yakthung communities. They systematized Yakthung pedagogical, political, and business theories and practices, such as they shaped Sawa Yet Hang cultural practices (Mujingna-Kheyangna, Lahadangna, and Ethukna, etc.); they constructed and fostered Susuwa Lilim Yakthung communities (Yuma). They created representational Yakthung communities, cultural patterns, democratic practices, social norms, and values (the Mundhum of Lahadangna and Suhampheba). During the research, I interviewed Vishnu Sing Rai (2019) a professor of linguistics from a Rai community, mentioned that Rais also share similar cultural lores and cultural practices like that of Yakthung Mundhum theories and cultural practices that female figures constructed Rai cultural epistemologies, Munthum theories and cultural practices (V. Rai, personal communication, June 19, 2018).

Yakthung Mundhum experts and traditional Yakthung knowledge keepers argue that we do not find many male characters in Mundhums, and though there are a few male figures, such as Susuwen-Lalawen and Sodhugen Lepmuhang, they do not have dominant roles in the construction of Sawa Yet Hang culture. This is one of the reasons why Yakthungs highly revere women even in the context of the 21st century global village. It is believed that the female individuals, such as Tagera-Ningwaphuma, Mujingna-Kheyangna, Lahadangna, and Yuma, created an egalitarian Susuwa Lilim Yakthung culture where male and female, including non-human beings were and still are treated equally. For instance, males, females, old people, and young children, including animals have their respective spaces in Yakthung Mundhum theories and practices. The Yakthung kings, such as Kings Maarang and Sirijanga also applied Yakthung Mundhum theories and philosophies in practices, and later Thibong Yakthungs and Yakthung Suhangs continued to practice them (Mundhums) as fundamental Yakthung cultural norms and values, and we still follow them in our communities (despite the Hindu and Western cultural dominations).

King Sirijanga was guided by Sawa Yet Hang culture, Yakthung Mundhums, Yakthung socio-political theories, Mundhum philosophies, and Yakthung cultural practices. Therefore, he believed that "the universal truth" was not possible, and the truth was not determined by only a person's sense perceptions and observations, but through discussions, deliberations, interpretations, and negotiations. Because of such democratic philosophical and political beliefs, King Sirijanga as the Overlord of many Yakthung *thums* (nations), always included common people in royal and general discussions (see *Sap Mundhums* or *Kirat Khahun Sapla* and *Kirat Samlo Sapla*) (Tumbahang, 2013, p. 3–4). King Sirijanga not only invited common people during the Royal meetings for the local and state level discussions, but he also welcomed their constructive criticisms, comments, and opinions. Yakthungs (both males and females) invariably supported the practices of democracy by introducing *tutu-tumyahang's* comments and criticism in Yakthung communities. As Yakthung Mundhum philosophies shaped the King Sirijangian socio-cultural theories, political ideologies, and practices, King Sirijanga did not believe in gender and class hierarchies.

King Sirijanga's political theories and cultural practices in Yakthung laje

During the reign of King Sirijanga, there were various classifications of works based on the professionality and expertise of people. Different people were assigned different trades based on their skills, and Yakthung laje citizens executed these duties and responsibilities as assigned. However, unlike South Asian Hindu culture, Yakthung culture did not create caste, class, and gender-centric dichotomies based on the nature of these duties and responsibilities (Tumbahang, 2013). King Sirijanga never introduced class-centered, body-graphic, and gender-centric dichotomies; he, including other Yakthung Hangs also did not introduce cultural dichotomies based on the type of work that people did in Yakthung laje. There was not and still is not any sign of discrimination in Yakthung communities based on gender, sexual orientation, class, and/or profession in Yakthung laje (Subba, 1995; Limbu et al., 1845; Mabuhang & Tunghang, 2070 BS).

According to Sirijangian philosophy, knowledge is epistemic, and people are measures of all things. Meaning, people do not communicate the truth, but we communicate our logic, not the reality. Sirijanga believed that realities themselves are not communicable, but logic; or logos (logic) is negligibly transferable. Hence, King Sirijanga wanted to educate his country people so that people could communicate and network well, or they would understand the importance of education, network, and Mundhum rhetorics. King Sirijanga knew that writing was rhetorical, communication was rhetorical, and knowledge was epistemic; hence, he established the philosophy that writing is rhetorical, epistemic, and social in the sense that writing could not only be used to preserve Mundhum, language, and culture, but also to differently construct, disseminate, and maintain knowledge. Writing and any form of communication, he believed, could be used to network and effectively persuade subjects/audience for various purposes. From that theoretical, philosophical, and practical perspective, King Sirijanga fostered the importance of writing and communication, such as writing as a tool—a tool to create their cultural and communal power and to interconnect within Yakthung laje and beyond. For him, writing was a medium to network with other neighboring kingdoms in local and regional contexts. After the death of King Sirijanga, only sporadic epistemic activities to spread the writing system, were carried out until the emergence of Tye Angsi Singthebe (1704–1741) due to the political, cultural, and religious instabilities in the region/s.

Sirijangian Mundhums and Mundhum rhetorics

Despite the fact that King Sirijanga re/introduced the Sirijanga script, Mundhum rhetorics, and Yakthung philosophies both in oral and written forms during his reign, I did not find any written document/s during my research. What I found during my research were mostly oral texts (Mundhums, folklores, cultural lores). I also did not find any written documents from the 10th century to 17th century in the Sirijanga script. I also did not find any strong political histories, stories, and Mundhum narratives written in other languages other than oral Mundhums. Hence, there is a mystery: why Yakthungs do not have any written documents from the the 10th century (Sirijangian era) to the 18th century (Tye-Angsian era). The mystery is that the Khas Aryans not only had destroyed Yakthung documents beginning from the 18th century to late 20th century, but the non-Hindu books and documents burning campaign began right after the collapse of the Kirat reign (Bista, 1991). Additionally, when the Khas Aryans invaded the Malla, Sen, Khambu, and Yakthung territories, they systemically destroyed Malla, Sen, Khambu, and Yakthung documents, heritages, and resources (see Hodgson collection or Limbu, et al., vol. 85). Hence, with the purpose to destroy Yakthung history, the Khas Aryans burned all Lal Mohars, Syahamohors, books, genealogies, and Mundhum books in Yakthung laje.

Due to the Khas Aryan campaign on Yakthung Indigenous peoples' epistemic erasure, Yakthungs did not know anything about the manuscripts written by Tye Angsi Singthebe in the 18th century because Yakthungs were banned to read and write in their language both in Nepal and Sukkim. Yakthungs did not know anything about the books collected by Hamilton, Manwaring, Campbell, and Hodgson until 1955. When R. K. Sprigg brought some copies of the manuscripts to Nepal in 1955 written by Jobhansing Limbu, Chyangresing Phedangba, Ranadhoj Limbu, and Jit Mohan, including Singthebe, Yakthungs came to know about their books, script, history, and

Mundhum rhetorics. Then, Yakthungs of Kalimpong, Darjeeling, and Sikkim started discussing the manuscripts that European colonizers had collected and transported them (Yakthung books) to Europe for the colonial purposes.

Until 1955, Yakthungs did not even see any books that had been written in the Old Sirijangian script. The manuscripts R. K. Sprigg brought to Yakthung laje were written during the 18th and 19th centuries. To make this idea clear, when we say books written in the Old Sirijanga script, they were not the books written in the 9th and 10th centuries. As I stated earlier, we have King Sirijangian Mundhums and his preaching only in the oral Mundhum forms. Again, the reason why Yakthungs did not have any books in Nepal was that the Khas Aryans collected all Yakthung documents, books, and Mundhum books, and they destroyed them for centuries on regular basis. If Yakthungs did not give the documents, books, or pamphlets to Khas Aryans, they would torture, execute, or banish Yakthungs from Yakthung laje. Similarly, the British colonizers collected most of the Yakthung books from Sikkim, Kalimpong, Darjeeling, including Siliguri, Assam, and Manipur during the East India Company colonial era. For instance, A. Campbell collected dozen of Yakthung books from Ilam Sing Limbu and his family members from Sikkim. In this regard, Spriggs (1959) states:

> In 1842, Dr. Campbell, Superintendent of the Darjeeling Sanitarium, published a reference to a script formerly in use among the Limbus but by that time presumed extinct; in a subsequent article in 1855 he recorded that a Limbu book had a last come into his hands "after many years endeavoring to procure one for the society." (the Asian Society of Bengal, p. 590)

Some Yakthung scholars found old damaged Yakthung books and wrote Yakthung histories, narratives, stories, cultural practices, and Mundhums based on the damaged book/s (they found in Sukhim). However, the original books they found and the books they wrote had been transported to the UK, including other colonial-centric places (libraries) for colonial purposes. Sadly, the teaching and learning of Yakthung writing was not popular among Yakthung communities as well, such as in Sikkim, including Kalimpong and Darjeeling. Yakthungs did not encourage their children to study Yakthung language and script, for the parents knew that Singthebe was executed for his teaching of Yakthung writing and Mundhum rhetorics.

During my research, I learned that Campbell collected more than a dozen books from Ilamsing Limbu and his family members (even after Limbu's death) from Sikkim in the early 1840s. Hodgson also gathered Yakthung books, manuscripts, and original old Yakthung books and requested Yakthung scholars, historians, and Mundhumists to document Yakthung culture, language, Yakthung syllabary, and Mundhum rhetorics (Hodgson collection implied). Finally, he transported them to the UK for colonial purpose. In research of these books, I reached the British Library in London where I found more than a dozen of books collected by Brian Hodgson (will talk about the books later in this book). Despite my arduous effort to look for other old Yakthung books, such as that were collected by Campbell, I failed to find even a single book and did not meet any person who would know the whereabouts of the books. However, I found out that Campbell wrote a few articles on Yakthung script and writing system (Campbell, 1856; Sprigg, 1959; 1998). It is obvious that Europeans collected and took Yakthung documents, books, and manuscripts; and Khas Aryans collected Yakthung documents, books, and manuscripts and destroyed all of them. So, if we find the books collected by European colonizers, such as Campbell and other Europeans, they might uncover the development of Yakthung history, language, and literacy from the 10th century to the 18th century and even before and beyond King Sirijangian and King Maarangian eras. Due to the para-colonial oppression and para-colonial hegemony, Yakthungs have disconnected cultural, linguistic, religious, and Mundhumic identities. I am hopeful that one day, Yakthung scholars and Yakthung studies scholars, researchers, and writers will discover these books, and they will uncover our Kirat and Yakthung Suhangs' disconnected histories, civilizations, and Yet Hang and Thibong Yakthung epistemologies.

3   Tye Angsian era
Reformation of the Sirijanga script, writing, and rhetorics

Tye Angsi Singthebe: the Sirijanga script, language, and literacies in the 18th century in Yakthung laje

Tye Angsi Singthebe (1704–1741) was born and brought up in Sinam, Yangwarak, Yakthung laje. Singthebe was a great Yakthung linguist, educator, historian, and philosopher. Singthebe was popularly known as a religious, spiritual, and Mundhumic forerunner in the history of Yakthung civilization. Singthebe, including his cronies, practiced and popularized the Sirijanga script and writing system that King Maarang and King Sirijanga re/designed (see also Bhumika, Subba, 1928; Subba, 2015, pp. 99–101; Vansittart, 1991, p. 105). Singthebe revived, redesigned, popularized, and disseminated the script in Yakthung laje (Limbuwan), Sikkim, Darjeeling, Kalimpong, and beyond (Yakthumba, 2061 BS, pp. 20–30). Singthebe and his colleagues went from village to village in Yakthung laje to promote the Old Sirijanga script, writing, and Mundhum rhetorics. Their main purpose was to educate Yakthungs, Sherpas, Lepchas (Lapches), and Bhutias on the importance of writing, rhetoric, and Mundhum philosophy. Many documents, both oral and written, suggest that Singthebe was a trans-cultural scholar and was literate in Yakthung, Nepali, Lepcha, Bhutia, Newari, and Hindi. Based on the discussion, this chapter revisits the 18th century Yakthung writing and rhetorics. It discusses Singthebe's philosophical and pedagogical theories and his teachings in Yakthung laje and Sukhim (Sikkim) during the early 18th century. Similarly, this chapter also portrays Singthebe's multicultural, transborder, and cross-cultural theories and practices in the context of the 18th century.

Tye Angsi Singthebe knew the importance of written communication, oral communication, and oral performance-based communication. So, he knew what writing and rhetoric meant to Yakthungs during the critical period of historical, cultural, religious, and linguistic struggles. As Singthebe was a great rhetor, he knew the importance of invention, arrangement, memory, and delivery in order to address and persuade diverse audiences in different contexts. Therefore, he established a robust relationship with Yakthung Suhangs (Yakthung chiefs), and they also supported his campaign to restore and popularize Yakthung language and literacy within Yakthung laje and

Figure 3 Tye Angsi Singthebe (Sirijanga II).

beyond. Throughout his life, Singthebe taught Yakthungs and non-Yakthungs the Yakthung language, Sirijanga script, writing system, religion, and Mundhum rhetorics.

Tye Angsi Singthebe: a translingual, transnational linguist, activist, and philosopher

We do not actually know what kind of education Tye Angsi Singthebe received. However, it is obvious that he had spent most of his life as an educator; he taught writing, rhetoric, and Mundhum rhetorics. As I stated earlier, there is a huge gap in terms of Yakthung writing and literacy—a gap of almost a thousand years between King Sirijanga and Tye Angsi Singthebe. In this regard, Dor Bahadur Bista (1991) states that during the Lichchhavi period, Brahmin priests came into power, and they had a high cultural, religious ritual status at the political level. By misusing the political power, they brought social, linguistic, and religious changes in the Kathmandu Valley and Kõich, Khambu, and Yakthung regions. The social changes that took place during the Lichchhavi period were aggressively implemented in the South Asian Himalayan Indigenous communities. As a result, "Non-Brahmanic literature was destroyed in public book burnings and much of the cultural heritage of the Lichchhavi period was lost in this process.... Many older social institutions were possibly eliminated at this time" (Bista, 1919, pp. 21–22). Perhaps, even after the Lichchhavi reign, non-Brahmanic books might have been burned, and this could be one of the reasons why we do not have old Yakthung books, including other Indigenous books. Despite the fact that there was a thousand-year's gap in the development of Yakthung language and literacy, Singthebe was able to relink the old Yakthung language and literacies. He was one of the Yakthung scholars who strategically bridged the gap between the King Sirijangian Yakthung rhetorical tradition and the 18th century Yakthung Suhang writing and rhetorical tradition (see figure 4).

During my research, I found that the Tye Angsi Sirijangian writing system and that best resembles Yakthung phonology, including other Indigenous peoples' phonologies (/a/-based phonology implied) in South Asian, such as Lepcha, Khambu, Tamang, Sherpa, Magar, and Gurung, etc. The Old Sirijanga script he re/designed, popularized, and disseminated was an /a/-based syllabary (see figures 4 & 5) (see also Campbell, 1955; Hukpa Chongbang, 2071 BS; Kainla, 2071 BS: Laoti, 2005, p. 144; Sprigg, 1989). The Sirijanga script he redesigned resembles the Tibetan phonology, for Tibetan's also have an /a/-based syllabary. During my research, I did not find any scholars who could show me the Tye Angsian Sirijanga documents in Nepal, India, or the United Kingdom (UK). For instance, I met with Yakthung scholars, linguists, historians, and the Sirijanga script re/designers (in the 20th century), and they mentioned that they had heard of the Old Sirijanga script, but none of them could show me how the Old Sirijanga script looked, or how it was/is written (will talk later in this book). The reason the Yakthungs of the 20th century did/do not know about the Old Sirijanga script is because the Khas Aryans systematically destroyed almost all Yakthung books and documents from 1774–1990 in Yakthung laje, and many Yakthung and other Indigenous peoples' books were burned after the collapse of the Kirat Kingdom (Bista, 1991). Similarly, many European colonizers and researchers, such as Hamilton, Manwaring, Campbell, and Hodgson to mention a few, collected Yakthung books and transported them to the UK and Europe. During my research period, I found dozens of Yakthung (including other Indigenous peoples') books and manuscripts, written in their native languages, Nepali, and English in the British Library in London. I, however, failed to find books

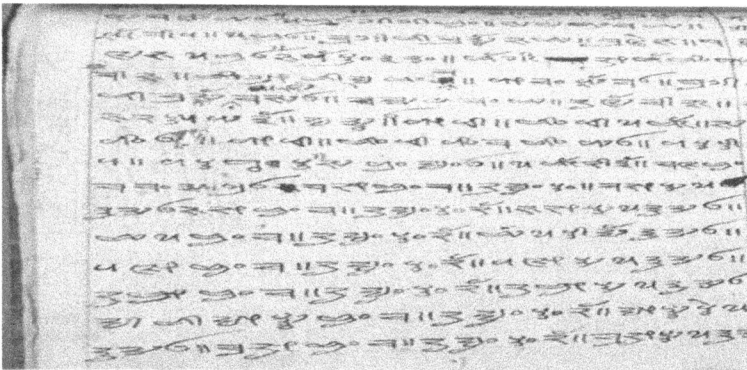

Figure 4 The Tye Angsian Sirijanga script redesigned in the 18th century (Source: The British Library, London).

that Campbell had collected from Ilamsing Limbu and his family members from Sikkim in the early 1840s (but I found some articles that Campbell wrote on Yakthung culture, language, and writing in the early 1840s and mid-1850s). These are some of the reasons why Yakthungs did not know anything about the Old Sirijanga script and writing system until R. K. Sprigg brought some copies of the Hodgson collection to Nepal in 1955.

R. K. Sprigg, who was an expert in the Tibeto-Burman language family, studied Tye Angsian Sirijanga syllabary in the mid-20th century. Sprigg studied both contemporary Yakthung language (phonology), writing system, and the Tye Angsian Sirijanga script. He found that the Tye Angsian Sirijanga script or the Old Sirijanga script was more scientific and systematic than the New Sirijanga script that Yakthungs developed after the foundation of Shree Yakthung Hang Chumlung in 1925 (will talk about it in detail later). Based on his Tibeto-Burman linguistic expertise in relation to the Sirijanga script and *Yakthung pa:n* (Yakthung language), R. K. Sprigg (1959, 1998) claimed that Singthebe was one of the greatest linguists of the 18th century.

When King Sirijanga reintroduced the script in the 9th century, the Yakthung writing and literacy perhaps did not have a much influence on the Yakthung community, for the Bahuns (Brahmans) started burning the non-Hindu books after the foundation of the Lichchhavi reign, or they persuaded the Indigenous peoples that their writing was inferior to the Brahmi script (see also Bista, 1991). In relation to the development of the Sirijanga writing and rhetorics, the period between the King Sirijangian era and the early 18th century remains enigmatic to Yakthung studies scholars until now. In the early 18th century, Singthebe realized that writing and literacy were the backbone for the fundamental development of people, communities, and nations. So, Singthebe went from *thum* to *thum* (region to region), village to village, and door to door to preach the importance of the Sirijanga script, writing system,

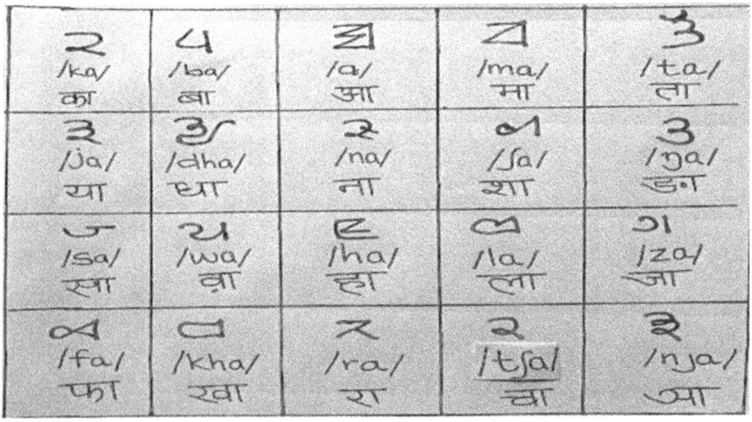

Figure 5 The Tye Angsian Sirijanga Script; /a/-based syllabary redesigned by Tye Angsi Singthebe in the early 18th century.

and Mundhum rhetorics. While he and his cronies were campaigning to encourage Yakthungs and non-Yakthungs on the importance of the Sirijanga script, writing, and religious rhetorics, they reached Sukhim thum (Sikkim). In Sukhim thum, the Bhutias and Thachhang Lamas were attempting to replace Yakthung language, literacies, and religion with that of the Bhutia language, writing system, and religion.

Tye Angsi Singthebe travelled not only all across Yakthung laje (Limbuwan region), Darjeeling, Kalimpong, and Sikkim, but also travelled up to Kathmandu valley. Singthebe is believed to have visited Jagajjaya Malla, Jaya Prakash Malla, Vishnu Malla, and Ranjit Malla, for he had a broader perspective on political magnitudes, diplomatic knacks, and cross-cultural practices. His mantra of the purpose-driven learning was studying anything from inside to outside or outside to inside, for him it was the culture of love, respect, network, progress, and prosperity. Singthebe learned the importance of inclusion, equity, love, and respect from Yakthung Mundhums, Yet Hang, and Thibong Yakthung cultural traditions, for these cultural traditions had always been relative. In Yakthung laje, including in Kirat culture, there were many other ethnic groups who spoke their own languages and practiced their own religions. Kirat kings and later Yakthung kings never imposed their subjects to follow Yumaism and speak or learn *Yakthung pa:n* (Chemjong, 2003; Subba, 2015; Subba, 1995). Singthebe believed that to grow as a civilized human being in local and global (regional) contexts, one had to maintain cordial and congenial relationships with all local and regional fellow beings and communities. Hence, among many others, Singthebe learned Khas Aryan, Newari, Lepcha, Bhutia, and Tibetan languages, oral folklores, and transcultural philosophies. During his time, India was already under the European colonization, and Bhutias, by force or coercion, were suppressing Yakthungs and Lepchas to follow the Buddhism in Sukhim (Khamdak, 2019). The diverse political, cultural, and colonial settings suggest that he got the opportunity to practically observe the colonial logic of knowledge construction, such as what the colonial politics of knowledge construction was, how colonial logic worked in Indigenous communities, and how cultural colonization was a threat to Indigenous communities. Based on these lines of inquiries, Singthebe was determined to educate his followers on the importance of their culture, language, Mundhum rhetorics, and religion. He taught them why it was important for them to preserve their language, history, narratives, and Mundhum rhetorics, and why it was equally important to value and validate other peoples and their cultural traditions.

Tye-Angsian theory of writing and rhetorics

As I stated above, King Maarang and King Sirijanga re/designed the script (writing system) and popularized it. Nonetheless, we do not have any written documents that affirm how many characters, such as consonants, vowels, symbols, and/or syllabaries Kings Maarang and Sirijanga re/introduced.

However, we have plenty of written documents concerning the Old Sirijanga script from the 18th century (Tye Angsian era implied) and the 19th century (Limbu et al., 1845). For instance, the Tye Angsian Sirijanga script (Old Sirijanga script) included 20 syllabaries (see figure 5). The Old Sirijanga script and Tibetan script are both "a" (/a/)-based syllabaries (see figures 5 Sirijanga script & 6 Tibetan script). After Singthebe had redesigned and popularized the Sirijanga script, the teaching of language and writing became popular in Yakthung laje (present Nepal), Darjeeling (then Yakthung laje, now India), Kalimpong (then Yakthung laje, now India), Siliguri, Jalpaiguri and Dooars (then Yakthung laje, now India), and Sikkim (then Yakthung laje and independent country, and now in India).

Tye Angsi Singthebe's teaching of Yakthung writing and Mundhum rhetorics facilitated Yakthungs to document their cultural traditions. The Tye Angsian script (Old Sirijanga script and writing system) was still popular during the 19th century in Yakthung laje, India, Bhutan, and beyond (Campbell in his 1842 mentioned that Limboos did not have script, but in 1855, he mentioned that Limboos had scripts and discussed with evidence, see in Chapter 5). For instance, Jobhansing Limbu, Chyangresing Phedangba, Ranadhoj Limbu, and Jit Mohan (1845–57) used the Old Sirijanga script and Old Sirijangian writing system to document Yakthung history, Mundhum rhetorics, Yakthung cultural practices, Yakthung grammar books (Limbu Alphabets), and Mundhum rhetorics. When I went to the British Library in London in 2016 and 2019, I also found another Yakthung manuscript written in 1867 as well. The Hodgson collection attests that Brian Hodgson gathered many Yakthung books, written in this script, and transported them to the UK for colonial purposes. Most of the books that Hodgson transported to Britain are still available both in hardcopies and micro-films in the British Library in London.

ཀ	/ka/	ཁ	/kʰa/	ག	/ga/	ང	/ŋa/
ཅ	/ʃa/	ཆ	/ʧʰa/	ཇ	/dʒa/	ཉ	/ɲa/
ཏ	/ta/	ཐ	/tʰa/	ད	/da/	ན	/na/
པ	/pa/	ཕ	/pʰa/	བ	/ba/	མ	/ma/
ཙ	/tsa/	ཚ	/tsʰa/	ཛ	/dza/	ཝ	/wa/
ཞ	/ʒa/	ཟ	/za/	འ	/ʕa/	ཡ	/ja/
ར	/ra/	ལ	/la/	ཤ	/ʃa/	ས	/sa/
ཧ	/ha/	ཨ	/a/				

Figure 6 The Tibetan Sambhota script, /a/-based phonology.

By observing the compelling aspects of Yakthung Mundhum rhetorics and philosophy, Singthebe not only introduced the Sirijanga script and writing system (see figures 4, 5, & 7), but also taught the core values of Yakthung culture, religion, and Mundhum rhetorics to Yakthungs and non-Yakthungs. Tye Angsi Singthebe encouraged Yakthungs and non-Yakthungs (especially Lepchas) to learn *Yakthung pa:n*, including their languages, learn to read and write, and teach the Sirijanga script and Mundhum rhetorics because for him writing was one of the most powerful tools to construct knowledge. Singthebe taught Yakthungs and non-Yakthung Mundhum rhetorics in order to create better communities, virtuous *hangs* (rulers), and righteous *tutu-tumyahangs* (citizens). Hence, Singthebe's purpose was not only to spread the teaching of *Yakthung pa:n*, writing, and rhetoric, but also to mentor Yakthung Suhangs to make them effective, efficient, and ethical Yakthung hangs, suhangs, and tutu-tumyahangs. Singthebe's theoretical, philosophical, and practical endeavors demonstrate that he taught about how to create democratic societies, virtuous leaders, citizens, and educators so that they learn to value and validate cultures, languages, and religion.

Tye Angsi Singthebe alleged that we, by respecting other cultures, philosophies, and religions, could get to the *cho:tlung* (destination) of the local and regional peace and prosperity, for Yakthungs always coexisted with other cultures and ethnic groups, such as Khambus, Dhimals, Meches, Tibetans, Bhutias, Lepchas, etc. Singthebe highly valued and respected all cultures and religions. For instance, he not only revered Tibetan, Bhutia, Lepcha, Newar, and Sen cultures, but also profoundly studied their cultural and religious traditions; therefore, he could communicate with Bhutias and Lepchas when he preached in Sikkim. His pedagogical theory and philosophy of valuing other cultures and people made him a multi-faceted transnational scholar, linguist, rhetor, and educator. From this perspective, Singthebe was a multicultural and multilingual scholar and always advocated for the coexistence of all diverse peoples, cultures, languages, and religions. His democratic and inclusive

Figure 7 The Tye Angsian Sirijanga script, re-documented by Jobhansing Limbu, Chyangresing Phedangba, Ranadhoj Limbu, and Jit Mohan (Source: The British Library, London).

advocacy on multiculturalism and multilingualism developed from Yakthung Mundhum rhetorical traditions. Because of his democratic, inclusive, and Mundhum-centric philosophical practices, Singthebe became one of the greatest scholars of the 18th century.

Tye Angsi Singthebe's execution and Erosion of Yakthung language and literacies

By the 18th century, the Bhutias and Thachhang Lamas created such knowledge in Sikkim that Yakthungs were Buddhists, and the Lamas and Bhutias forced Yakthungs to pursue the Buddhist culture, religion, and learn their script and writing system. Singthebe, his colleagues, and Yakthung chieftains from Yakthung laje detested the way the Bhutias and Thachhang Lamas were distorting, displacing, and destroying Yakthung cultural, linguistic, and religious identities, including the Yakthung writing system. The Bhutias and Lamas' oppression prompted Singthebe, including his followers, to go to Sikkim, and he started preaching the importance of their cultural, linguistic, and religious identities. In other words, he taught Yakthungs, including non-Yakthungs (Lepchas), what their culture, writing, and religion, was, and why it was important for them to preserve their cultural, linguistic, and religious identities. While he was preaching in Sikkim, both Yakthungs and non-Yakthungs showed an immense interest to learn Yakthung language, Yakthung rhetorical traditions, and Mundhum rhetorics (Limbu, 2016, 2017).

Since Singthebe was an influential communicator, many Yakthungs and non-Yakthungs pursued what he preached. Although he was a peaceful, courteous preacher, the Thachhang Lamas of Pemayangtse Monastery and Bhutias feared his teaching of the Sirijanga script, writing system, Mundhum rhetorics, and religion. According to Tanka Subba (1989), "[t]he ruling Bhutias in particular always felt threatened by the non-Bhutia communities of Sikkim. The hasty conversion of many Limbus and Lepchas into Buddhism could not give them much assurance about their loyalty to the palace" (p. 43). The Thachhang Lamas and Bhutias revolted against his teaching, for they feared that their culture, religion, and writing would be replaced by the Sirijanga script, writing, religion, and Mundhum rhetorics. Due to the fear of the use of Singthebe's influential preaching, they accused Singthebe of plotting against the Bhutia reign. Thachhang Lamas, with the help of Sikkimi King Tamding Gyalpo, captured, tortured, and executed Singthebe in 1741 (Tumbahang, 2007, pp. 24–25). In this regard, Chemjong (2003) also states:

> In 1741 AD, a learned Limbu man of the Yangwarok district of Northern Limbuwan known as Srijunga Dewangsi [Tye Angsi Singthebe] revived the Kirat Literature and taught the Mundhum religion to all the Kirati people of Limbuwan as well as to those in West Sikkim. The Tibetan Lamas or Tachhang Lamas of the Pemayangtse monastery stood against

this activity of the Limbu learned man. They put him under arrest, bounded him on a tree and shot him to death. (p. 167)

During his short lifespan, Tye Angsi Singthebe travelled near and far and met many great leaders, diplomats, linguists, and writers, for he wanted to learn the foundations of successful political ethics, political strategies, and economic policies. Singthebe networked with scholars, writers, and leaders from different countries in order to share what commonalities and differences they had, for one of his objectives was to spread the Sawa Yet Hang-based Yakthung culture, Mundhum epistemologies, and writing system in local and regional contexts. The purposes of his trips to different kingdoms were to also learn from different scholars, rulers, and commoners from different geo-political locations to reframe Yakthung cultural traditions, customary institutional theories and practices, cross-cultural political rhetorics, Yakthung education system, and Mundhum traditions. Singthebe believed that we could be humane if we would share, respect, and maintain our local, regional, and global friendships.

Interventions in the teaching and learning of Yakthung language, writing, and rhetorics

The Thachhang Lamas' execution of Tye Angsi Singthebe intervened Yakthungs from the teaching of the Sirijanga script, writing system, and Mundhum rhetorics in Sikkim. Though the consequences of Singthebe's execution did not completely wipe out the Yakthung language, writing system, and Mundhum rhetorics, it discouraged the majority of Yakthungs from the teaching and learning of *Yakthung pa:n*, writing, and Mundhum rhetorics in Sikkim. In relation to Yakthung laje (Nepal), the Khas Aryans gradually waged a campaign to destroy Yakthung books and other important documents immediately after the Nun-Paani Sandhi (1774).

The Khas Aryans reprimanded Yakthungs if they learned or promoted the Sirijanga script, writing system, and Mundhum rhetorics. This setting suggests that although Yakthungs, both in Yakthung laje (Nepal) and Sukhim, wanted to promote the Sirijanga script, writing system, and Mundhum rhetorics, the time was not favorable for Yakthungs due to Khas Aryan and Bhutia oppressions in Nepal and in Sikkim respectively. However, Darjeeling and Kalimpong were safe places for Yakthungs to teach, learn, or promote the Sirijanga writing system, Yakthung language, and Mundhum literacies. For instance, Brian Hodgson lived in Kathmandu, but he went to Darjeeling to document Yakthung histories, Mundhum rhetorics, and cultural traditions. Meaning, Hodgson was aware of the Khas Aryan suppression on the non-Nepali (Khas) languages in Nepal. Therefore, Hodgson invited Jobhansing Limbu, Chyangresing Phedangba, Ranadhoj Limbu, and Jit Mohan to document Yakthung histories, narratives, cultural practices, Yakthung grammar books, and Mundhum rhetorics in Darjeeling from 1845 to 1857.

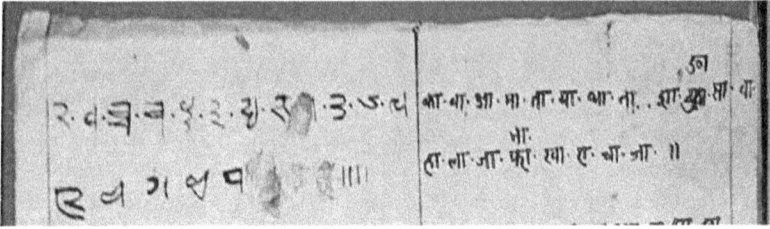

Figure 8 Tye Angsian Sirijanga /a/-based syllabary (Source: The British Library, London).

For readers' information, while Limbu et al. (1845–57) documented Yakthung cultural traditions, they used the Old Sirijanga script/writing system. Because of the Khas Aryan oppression in Nepal and Bhutia oppression in Sikkim, Yakthungs gradually lost the Old Sirijanga script, histories, and Mundhum rhetorics. Unlike today's Sirijanga script, the Old Sirijanga script, until the 19th century, used to be an /a/-based syllabary.

As I stated earlier, Yakthung language or phonology, in practice, is still an /a/-based one. Meaning, when Singthebe redesigned the Sirijanga syllabary, it was /a/-based (see figures 5 & 8), and when Limbu et al. (1845–57) documented Yakthung customary rhetorical traditions, they also followed the /a/-based writing system that Singthebe re/introduced and popularized in the early 18th century. The Old Sirijanga syllabaries were written in the following order:

/ka, ba, a, ma, ta, ya, dha, na, sha, nga, sa, wa, ha, la, ja, pha, kha, ra, cha, yan/

or

/का, बा, आ, मा, ता, या, धा, ना, शा, ङ, सा, वा, हा, ला, जा, फा, खा, रा, जा, जा/

European colonial agents and sites of Yakthung langauge and literacies

During the East India British colonial era, the colonial agents collected all available data from the Himalayan Indigenous communities; then, they classified, labelled, and interpreted them for colonial purposes (not for the purpose of Indigenous peoples). In this process, A. Campbell collected many books from Ilamsing Limbu in the early 1840s, and he revisited the Limbu family and collected several books after Limbu's death as well (Sprigg, 1959). After he had collected dozen of Yakthungs books, Campbell (1855) wrote an article on theoretical and practical aspects of the Sirijanga script and writing system. Campbell's research article also demonstrates that Yakthungs' writing system or Sirijanga script was an /a/-based one. Campbell, however, excluded "a" (/a/) from the syllabary and affirmed that Yakthungs had only 19 syllabaries in the script (see figure 13.1 in Chapter 5). For instance, R. K. Sprigg (1998) states:

> In Limbu too the position as regards 'a is very much like that of 'a Lepcha. In the three (Hodgson—Collected books vol. 87 *(Limbu haru ko kakhaharu)* 'a has been included in the syllabary, but in the third place, after *ka* and *pa*, in a syllabary of 20 symbols, not in the first place as in Lepcha. Campbell 1855, however, has only 19 symbols in the syllabary ... he has removed 'a from the syllabary and associated it with a vowel series: 'a, e, ei, i, u, o, o, ai'. (p. 1)

Campbell's research discussion was/is not a cutting-edge one for Yakthung communities, but I do not understand why Yakthungs romanticize Campbell's documentation on Yakthungs' writing system. Yakthungs had always been literate; they had documented their culture, history, and Mundhum rhetorics in their own script and language (Hodgson collection and the 18th century Yakthung language and literacy implied). Campbell collected some important Yakthung manuscripts and never returned them to the Limbu family, and he transported or dumped them in unknown places, and we do not know the whereabouts of the books that he took from Ilamsing Limbu and his family from Sikkim.

The colonial agents like Campbell, Vansittart, and Hodgson, to mention a few, portrayed Yakthungs as though they would not speak for themselves. The colonial agents constantly constructed Yakthung knowledge as though they had to speak for them, more often than not, showing them as inferior beings. The colonial construction of knowledge was consistently supported by the Khas Aryan ideology and politics in Nepal. As a result, *Yakthung phu-ne-nusa* (brothers and sisters) still believe in the colonial narratives. This is how Yakthungs, including Indigenous people's knowledge, has been constructed; this is how Yakthung knowledge has been imprisoned in European and Khas Aryan social and academic institutions. The Europeans used the Western colonial logic to make Yakthungs see their culture, language, bodies, and space through the colonial lenses. Similarly, Khas Aryans coerced Yakthungs to see their culture, language or themselves from the Khas Aryan lens. They blinded Yakthungs with the Khas Aryan and European colonial logic; their colonial logic paralyzed Yakthungs; and their ideology petrified Sawa Yet Hang and Susuwa Lilim epistemologies. The Khas Aryan coloniality of political, economic, and military power and ideological discourse stun/ ned Yakthung Suhang epistemologies for centuries. As Yakthungs have/had been blindfolded in Khas Aryan popular culture, or as Yakthungs have/had been imprisoned in Khas Aryan social institutions, they neglected their own culture, language, body, religion, and costume. Even in Yakthung academic culture, Yakthung scholars, historians, and writers disregard to quote their own *Yakthung phu-ne-nusa* scholars when they write or talk about their own culture, history, language, and literacy. Instead, they feel so content to quote Western and Khas Aryan theories, philosophies, or knowledge in academic and popular culture settings.

Yakthungs believe that they elevate their academic standard when they disregard their own Yakthung scholars, including Mundhum theories, and regard Western/Khas Aryan theories. During my research, I attended several Yakthung workshops and conferences where I met Yakthung scholars feeling proud for not knowing Yakthung language and culture, but English language and Western cultures. Overall, it feels as if their identity, space, and history will remain incomplete if they do not reference Khas Aryans and Europeans in the debates and discussions in communal Yakthung discussions, including in Yakthung Indigenous studies. Yakthung cultural and academic spaces suggest how their knowledge has been trapped in Khas Aryan and European popular spaces and academic institutions. Now is the time, Yakthungs must delink para-colonial logic to discover who they were, are, and should be because the foundation of delinking, relinking, and linking methodology will be Yakthungs' intellectual struggle to liberate our imprisoned Yet Hang and Thibong Yakthung knowledge, language, and literacy.

R. K. Sprigg was an emerging linguist, and his research focused on Tibeto-Burman language (primarily Lepcha). Again, we have to critically question and comprehend that his study was absolutely interconnected to "orientalism." Sprigg's purpose was to study the orients or native Indigenous peoples in South Asia for the European colonial purpose. In the pursuit of his study, he went to Darjeeling to study the Lepcha language. While he was doing research, he found some Yakthung manuscripts in the British Library (in London), written by Jobhansing Limbu, Chyangresing Phedangba, Ranadhoj, and Jit Mohan in 1845–1857 (this collection is popularly known as Hodgson collection). Concerning Yakthung research and writing, unlike many other European scholars, Sprigg not only collected information from Indigenous communities and transported them to the European libraries, but he also brought back some historical documents (manuscripts) to Indigenous peoples' home countries. In other words, Sprigg made copies of some books (volumes) from the Hodgson collection, and he brought them to Yakthung laje, Nepal. Among many other Yakthungs, he met with Imansing Chemjong, Kajiman Kandangwa, and Ranadhoj Nembang, etc. in 1955. Before Sprigg brought some copies of the Hodgson collection, the Yakthungs, including Yakthung scholars, from Nepal, India, and Sikkim, did not know anything about the Old Sirijanga script and/or the Hodgson collection (that had been written by their ancestors).

Unfortunately, the Yakthung writers, such as Bajbir Subba, Imansing Chemjong, and other Yakthungs created a New Sirijanga script. I call this script the Bajbirian Sirijanga script, for Bajbir Subba wrote *Tum Yakthung Ningwaphu Sapla* (1928) in this script. Subba, in this book, mimicked the Devanagari script or Devanagari writing system. The Yakthung writers of the early 20th century also followed the script that Bajbir Subba introduced (see

Chapter 7). The prominent Yakthung scholars of the early 20th century were Bajbir Subba, Kalusing Papo, Buddhiraj Phago, Jasman Sangwa, Harkajang Makhim, E. K. Bahadur Sereng, Sher Bahadur Neyonghang, Nirmal Limbu, Mohan Lal Hangam, Buddhi Raj Phago, Jash Man Sangwa, Tiloksing Nugo, and Imansing Chemjong. As they did not know about the Old Sirijanga script, they shifted the Sirijanga writing system from an /a/-based to an /ə/-based one. In conclusion, due the Khas Aryan and European colonization, Yakthungs lost the Old Sirijanga script and writing system, and due to unfamiliarity of the Old Sirijanga script, the Yakthung scholars of the early 20th century mimicked the Devanagari script. In the late 20th century, though Yakthungs knew about the Old Sirijanga script, they continued to practice the New Sirijanga script.

Part III
Local and Global Para-Colonization

Intervention in writing and rhetorics
in Yakthung laje

4 Khas Aryan invasion in Yakthung laje

Site of Yakthung language and literacies

Encroachment of Khas Aryans in Yakthung laje: site of Yakthung writing and rhetorics in Para-Colonial context

After the rise of the Gorkha Empire in the late 18th century, Gorkhali (Khas Aryan) soldiers attacked the Malla kingdoms and eventually conquered them. The denigration of the Malla reign, culture, and civilization became the proliferation of Gorkhas (not of Magars and Gurungs, though they were the ones who fought the battles). The Mallas would have never lost the battle to the Gorkhas if the British East India Company had not betrayed the Malla Kings. The British East India Company's conspiracy against the Malla Kings led to the downfall of the Malla Kingdoms. In other words, the British East India Company had promised that they would fight for the Mallas against the Gorkhas, and the Mallas did not prepare for the war trusting that the British East India Company would come to fight for them against the Gorkhas. The Malla history demonstrates that it was the British East India Company that was accountable for the downfall of the Malla reign (Giuseppe, 1790; Kirkpatrick, 1818). Similarly, the British East India Company is also responsible for the downfall of Khambu and Yakthung reigns. The British East India Company feared the Mallas, Yakthungs, and Khambus; so, they secretly supported the Gorkhas, for the Gorkhas seemed to be weak militarily and economically. Based on the background information, this chapter discusses the Khas Aryan encroachment into Yakthung laje via the Nun-Paani Sandhi (1774), and later, why and how they overlooked the Nun-Paani Sandhi. The chapter further exposes why Khas Aryans divided Yakthungs, and how they gradually displaced Yakthungs, Yakthung cultural traditions, the Sirijanga script/writing system, language, and literacy in Yakthung laje.

After the Khas Aryans had entered Yakthung laje, they banned the teaching of the Sirijanga script and writing system. The Khas Aryans banned the promotion of their script, writing, culture, and Mundhum rhetorics like they did in other communities, such as Magar, Gurung, and Thakali, etc. in Nepal. As Wallo Kirats (Kõiches/Kõits) and Majha Kirats (Khambus) were adjacent to Kathmandu (the capital city), it was easier for the Khas Aryan-centric government to militarily suppress them and impose the Nepali language, culture, and Hindu religion (see also Limbu et al., 1845, vol. 85). Though it was against the Nun-Paani Sandhi (1774), the Khas Aryans banned Yakthungs from learning and teaching of their script and writing system until 1990. It was also one of the pertinent reasons why Kirats from Wallo Kirat and Majha Kirat stopped using the Sirijanga script and writing system. It is also believed that when Majha Kirats were conquered by the Khas Aryans, they handed over their important books and other documents to Yakthungs (Limbu, et al., 1845; "Pallo Kirat Limbuwan," 2066 BS, p. 6; Mabuhang & Tunghang, 2070 BS). The Khas Aryans practiced the same suppression, execution, or expulsion theories over Yakthungs. As *samariti* Yakthungs (Gorkha/Khas Aryan statutory law supporters) reinforced the Khas Aryans, they, Khas Aryans in the presence of *samariti* Yakthungs, became able to torture, execute, or banish *niti* Yakthungs (pro-Yakthung customary institutional law and practice supporters) for their teaching and learning of the Sirijanga script and writing system. Thereafter, the Khas Aryans forced Yakthungs to follow Hindu religion, Hindu caste system, Nepali language, and writing system to displace Yakthung Suhang culture, religion, language, and literacy. In this regard, Chaitanya Subba (1995) states:

> When [Yakthung laje] came under the rule of Gorkha dynasty, Nepalization, a process of integration of different communities into an organized single structure, introduction of vertical hierarchical caste system and syncretization of diverse and variegated folk culture, languages and lifestyle … became the political priority of the [Khas Aryan] government and such temerarious process accelerated pace of cultural change which placed the heritage of Limbu in peril. (p. 294)

Gradually, Yakthungs were oriented to see their Yakthung Suhang culture from the Khas Aryan ideals, norms, and values. They were programmed to believe *"Sirijanga saksak ni?ma, pa?ma menlo, hangle ase?tlo"* (let's not study the Sirijanga script, and let's not speak Yakthung language, the Khas Aryan King kills us) (Pallo Kirat Limbuwan, 2066 BS, p. 5). The Khas Aryans constantly programmed the Indigenous peoples from Wallo Kirat, Majha Kirat, and Pallo Kirat (Yakthung laje) that their languages were *"jangali bhasha"* (savage language). The Khas Aryans persuaded them to learn the superior language, the Khas language. For instance, Krishna Chandra Aryan and Baidhya Joshi-Sedhai (1974 BS) mentioned that Newar, Bhote, Magar, Gurung, Limbu (Yakthung), Sunuwar (Kõich), Danuwar, and Tharu spoke the "savage" language; and these savage people had to be persuaded to speak the civilized language, the Khas language (as cited in Mabuhang, 2063 BS, p. 66). By abusing the political and military powers, the Khas Aryans distorted the discourse as they wanted. Eventually, they forced Yakthungs to follow Hindu culture, religion, language, and their writing system (it has created a blazing issue in Yakthung community in terms of language, literacy, politics, and religion).

The Yakthungs did not have the privilege in the Khas Aryan controlled state; the privilege was on the side of the Khas Aryans. They also became able to divide Yakthungs into *niti* and *samariti* and create enmity among Yakthungs. The Khas Aryans enflamed Yakthung aggressions among themselves and made them destroy each other. Yakthung Suhangs did not even realize that the Khas Aryans created such hostility among themselves for the para-colonial purposes (see also Limbu et al., 1845; Mabuhang & Tunghang, 2070 BS). As the Khas Aryans were able to divide and rule Yakthungs, after the Nun-Paani Sandhi, they (Khas Aryans) were able to capture, torture, execute, or banish Yakthungs if they did not follow the Khas Aryan executive orders. Jobhansing Limbu, Chyangresing Phedangba, Ranadhoj Limbu, and Jit Mohan (1845) state that, in terms of general characteristics, Yakthungs are good people; they are honest, trustworthy, and hardworking. In fact, this is how Yakthung society based on Mundhum is constructed, and that is how Yakthungs are oriented to be. On the other hand, based on Limbu et al.'s (1845) decades of experience after the Nun-Paani Sandhi, they found that the Khas Aryans were dishonest, deceitful, and fraudulent. They also claimed that Yakthungs became homeless due to their own *samariti Yakthung* leaders because Yakthung leaders never learned anything from the Khas Aryans' treacheries on Yakthungs (see Hodgson collection, vol. 85), and the conditions of Yakthung leaders have not changed yet in the context of the 21st century in Nepal.

In relation to the 19th century Yakthung language and literacy, Limbu et al. (1845–1857) re/documented dozens of books (manuscripts) on various cultural, academic, political, religious, agricultural, and historical traits of Yakthung laje from 1845 to 1857. They also wrote books in diverse topic areas, such as Yakthung syllabary, alphabets, and grammar books. Most of their writings were based on the *kuhiyeko pustak* (old, damaged book) found in Sikkim (see figure 9).

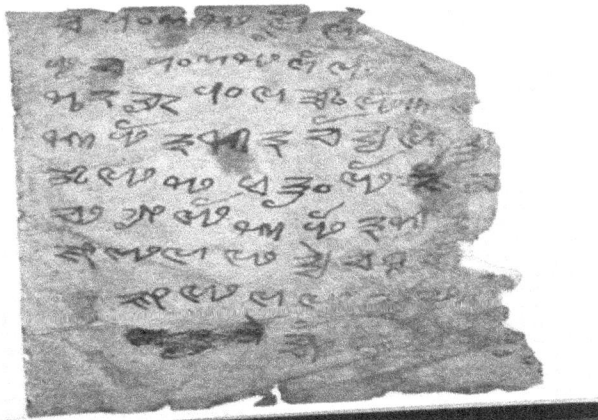

Figure 9 The Tye Angsian Sirijanga script book found in damaged condition in Sikkim, and Yakthungs learned to read and write from it (Source: The British Library, London).

Based on the manuscripts they wrote, some of them learned to read and write after they had found the *kuhiyeko pustak* (old, damaged book/s in Sikkim). In the manuscripts that they documented, Limbu et al. (1845–57) addressed diverse Yakthung cultural traditions like Mundhum, agriculture, *Limbu boli* (Yakthung language), religion, and culture (will discuss them in detail in Chapter 5).

As Khas Aryans banned Yakthungs from the teaching and learning of the Sirijanga script and writing, Yakthung intellectuals, scholars, researchers, and writers had to settle in newer place/s to escape execution. However, they still wanted to read, write, and share Yakthung histories, narratives, and Mundhums. For the restoration of Yakthung language and literacy, the native Yakthungs of Darjeeling, Kalimpong, and Sikkim played a great role in the development of Yakthung language and literacy. Historically, Yakthungs had to go through turmoil ever since the collapse of the Kirat reign and the Khas Aryan invasions in the Wallo Kirat, Majh Kirat, and Pallo Kirat regions (Bista, 1991; Mabohang, 2061 BS, pp. 1–5). For instance, Lichchhavis, Sens, and Shahs distorted and displaced their identities, and Yakthungs, including other Kirats, lost their cultural, linguistic, and political identities since the emergence of the Lichchhavi reign (Bista, 1991). Similarly, in the 18th century, Tye Angsi Singthebe was executed for his teaching of Yakthung language, writing, and Mundhum rhetorics in Sikkim. The Yakthung history demonstrates that thousands of Yakthungs, who advocated for their linguistic, cultural, and political identities after the Nun-Paani Sandhi, had been executed or banished from Nepal. Due to these innumerable ordeals, Yakthungs were hesitant to read, write, and/or promote their language, writing, and rhetorics.

Figure 10 Yakthungs learned to read and write based on the book they found in Sikkim (Source: The British Library, London).

To make a connection to the 19th century Yakthung language and literacy, after Yakthungs found the *kuhiyeko pustak* (old damaged book/s), Jobhansing Limbu, Chyangresing Phedangba, Ranadhoj Limbu, and Jit Mohan or at least a few of them learned to read and write in the Old Sirijanga script. For instance, as shown in figure 10, you can see the scribbles in the Sirijanga script that evidently suggest that they learned to read and write in the Tye Angsian Sirijanga script. Then, they redocumented Yakthung history, syllabary, and Mundhum narratives (based on the old, damaged book/s they found in Sikkim). Based on my research findings, they wrote more than a dozen books, which are still available in the British Library in London. The manuscripts, I found in the British Library, indicate that Jobhansing Limbu, Chyangresing Phedangba, Ranadhoj Limbu, and Jit Mohan were literate in Sirijanga, Devanagari (Nepali/Hindi), and Roman (English) scripts.

The Nun-Paani Sandhi and Khas Aryan politics of knowledge construction in Yakthung laje

Historically, after the Gorkhas had defeated Wallo Kirat and Majha Kirat, the Gorkha soldiers attacked Yakthung laje 17 times, but they lost all 17 wars to Yakthungs (Limbu, 2017; Limbu, et al., 1845; Pallo Kirat Limbuwan, 2066 BS, p. 6; Mabuhang & Tunghang, 2070 BS). As Yakthung laje was unconquered territory, the Gorkha kingdom had requested the Yakthung chieftains for the Nun-Paani Sandhi (see figure 11). In the following sections, I discuss the Nun-Paani Sandhi, such as what it was, what it meant to the Yakthungs, what it meant to the Khas Aryans, how the treaty did function or did not function, and how it intersected or did not intersect the cultural and political relationships between Yakthung laje and the Gorkha Kingdom based on the Nun-Paani Sandhi.

The Nun-Paani Sandhi was the treaty between King Prithvi Narayan Shan (king of Gorkha Kingdom) and Yakthung Hangs (Yakthung chieftains) from Yakthung laje. However, all Thibong Yakthung Suhangs (ten chieftains) did not approve the treaty. The Gorkha never had a treaty with Wallo Kirat and Majha Kirat, for the Gorkha Kingdom was able to conquer them in the war. As the Khas Aryans were very cunning, they fraudulently persuaded Yakthung chieftains that they had to merge into one nation for the peace, progress, and prosperity of both Yakthung laje and the Gorkha kingdom. King Prithvi Narayan Shah assured the Yakthung chieftains that Yakthung laje would always remain an "independent state," and Yakthungs would always have their rights to their ancestral land, property, culture, and language.

The Gorkhas and some Yakthung chieftains agreed upon the Nun-Paani Sandhi (the Treaty of Salt-Water, literal translation in English); the treaty took place on Sombar (Monday), Shrawan 22, 1831 BS. In the treaty (Lal Mohar), King Prithvi Narayan Shah promised that Gorkhas and Yakthungs would perpetually coexist without violating the treaty and without hurting each other (see figure 11). Prithvi Narayan Shah took the oath and swore on "nun" and

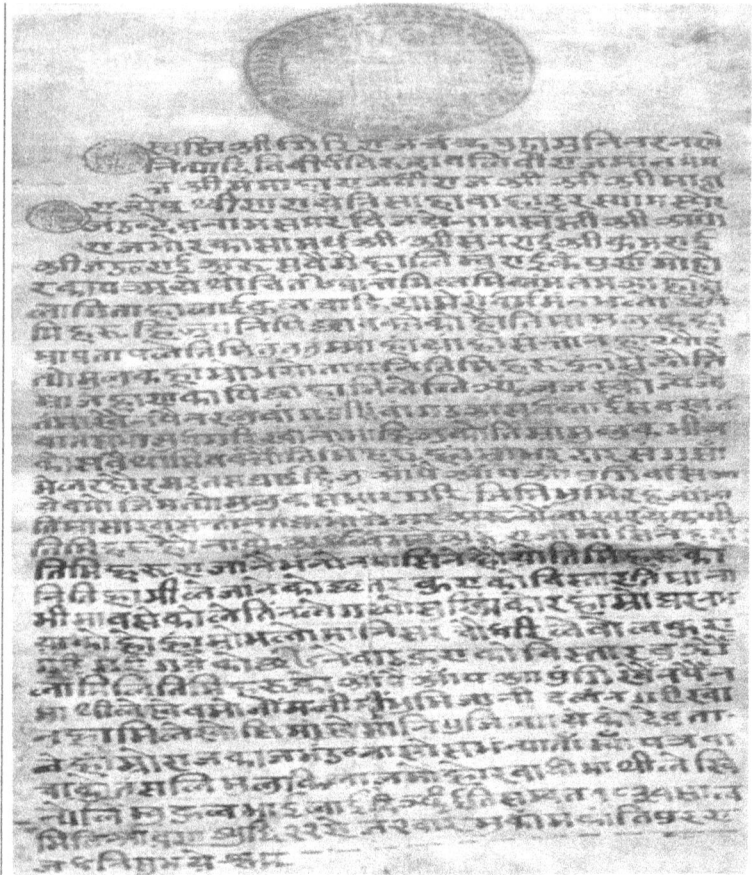

Figure 11 Lal Mohar offered to Yakthung Suhangs by King Prithvi Narayan Shah.

"paani" (salt and water) promising that the Gorkha Raja (Gorkha King) would never confiscate Yakthungs' ancestral lands nor would he destroy Yakthungs' customary cultural traditions, their *khambong-lungbong* identity, language, and their right to land (see Chemjong, 2003; Mabohang & Dhungel, 2047 BS, p. 244; Laksamba, 2016; Mabuhang & Tunghang, 2070 BS, p. 119). If Prithvi Narayan Shah or his descendants either confiscated the Yakthungs' rights to ancestral land or destroyed Yakthung cultural traditions, language, and literacies, the God upon which King Prithvi Narayan Shah (Gorkha Raja) sworn upon, would destroy him, his descendants, and his kingdom and would perish them from this world. In the treaty, a big *khadkuda* (copper pot) was brought in front of the Gorkha ministers and Yakthung Suhang ministers, and one *pathi* (a unit of capacity, approximately 4.546 liters) of salt was put into it. Then, water was poured into the pot and was stirred properly to mix the salt with water (Chemjong, 2003, p. 205; Pallo Kirat Limbuwan, 2066 BS, pp. 6–8). By quoting the Nun-Paani Sandhi, Chemjong (2003) states:

> The Gorkha Bhardars, on behalf of Gorkha Raja, took handful of salt water in their hands and swore that the Gorkha Raja would never betray [the Yakthungs] by forgetting the Kipat land. If [King Prithvi Narayan Shah] did so, his descendants would melt like the salt and disappear from the world. The Gorkha Bhardars, then questioned the Kirat ministers, saying if they will betray the Gorkh Raja by violating the "Nun Paani" agreement what oath would they take for never violating such agreement. The Kirat minsters also took a handful of salt water and swore that they would never go against their King. If they did so, their descendants would also melt like salt and disappear from the world. (p. 206)

As soon as the treaty took place, the Khas Aryans divided the Yakthungs into two groups: *niti* (pro-Yakthung leaders and activists) and *samariti* (Gorkha/Khas Aryan statutory law supporters). The Khas Aryans supported *samariti* over the *niti* Yakthungs (see also Ingnam & Ingnam, p. 31; Lumphungwa Limbu, 2075 BS, p. 57). They, once again, promised the *samariti* Yakthungs that the Khas Aryans would offer them land, high official titles, and administrative powers not only within Yakthung laje, but also beyond Yakthung laje. Thereafter, Yakthungs started fighting among themselves; they started hurting each other, and they supported the Khas Aryans to execute or banish their own *phu-ne-nusa* from Yakthung laje (Limbu, 2017; Limbu, et al., 1845; Mabuhang & Tunghang, 2070 BS).

The original inhabitants of Yakthung laje include/d Yakthungs, Yakkhas, Athphariyas, Yamphus, Meche, and Dhimals, etc., and these communities coexisted since the establishment of Yakthung laje. After the Nun-Paani Sandhi, the Khas Aryans classified them, and they gave them different sub-group titles. In addition, no sooner the Nun-Paani Sandhi contract was signed, a huge number of Bahuns, Chhetris, including Kami, Damai, Chamar, and Newar encroached the Yakthung laje in 1780s (Nembang, 1987). This encroachment was much more ideological and political, for the purpose of the migration was to subjugate the Yakthungs and Yakthung culture. These new groups of people also migrated to Yakthung laje as missionaries of Hindu religion and para-colonial agents. The new immigrants' obligation was not only to watch the daily activities of Yakthungs, but their duty was also to displace Yakthung culture, language, script, and writing. The Khas Aryans banned the teaching of Yakthung language, writing, and Mundhum rhetorics by ignoring the Nun-Paani Sandhi. This was the first intervention in the Yakthung language, rhetorics, and writing practices in the history of Yakthung civilization.

In addition, by abusing the political and military power, Khas Aryans started to suppress Yakthung language and writing. For instance, Govinda

Tumbahang (2007) states, "During the reign of king Rana Bahadur Shah, a royal order was issued forbidding the use of Limbu language in any official letter" (p. 74). Yakthungs were controlled at the hands of armed forces. The Khas Aryan-centric government paid Bahun-Chhetris or armed forces bounties, such as *birta* (land) and title, for the extermination of Yakthungs from Yakthung laje. For instance, Rana Bahadur Shah (grandson of Prithvi Narayan Shah) ordered General Abhiman Basnet to capture and execute all Yakthungs who were promoting the Sirijanga script and writing system. Fearing the Khas Aryan's torture and execution, thousands of Yakthungs fled to West Sikkim and beyond. Whereas, many Yakthungs (mostly old Yakthungs and children), who were not able to join in the arduous journey, were captured, tortured, and executed by the Khas Aryan armed forces (Laoti, 2005, p. 142; see also Chemjong, 2003; Limbu et al., 1845).

The Khas Aryan suppression on Yakthung language and literacy was ideological and political. Tumbahang (2007) states that "[t]he area of [Yakthung language] use further shrank when Chandra Shumser Rana declared that any document recorded in Limbu would have no authentic recognition" and "if money was lent by a creditor to a debtor preparing a document in Limbu, the complaint resulting from the failure of paying the amount would not be heard in any court" (p. 74). The Khas Aryans continuously abolished the practice of Yakthung language, writing, and rhetorics in Yakthung laje. The Khas Aryans created dichotomy between Khas Aryans and Yakthungs to introduce a newer identity and knowledge in Yakthung laje. They forced Limbus (they called Yakthungs as Limbu; they forced Yakthungs to accept this identity) to accept the Hindu caste system. Once the culture was introduced in Yakthung laje, Yakthungs were labelled as inferior to Khas Aryans. Then, the Khas Aryans started labelling Yakthungs as uneducated, uncivilized, and savage. In the Hindu caste system, Khas Aryans, especially Bahuns and Chhetris, recognized themselves as higher caste people. After they imposed Nepali language and the Hindu caste system in Yakthung laje, the Khas Aryans created knowledge that Yakthung language was inferior to Khas (Nepali) language, and Yakthung culture was inferior to Khas Aryan culture.

The Khas Aryan ideological architecture of knowledge construction and dissemination of the knowledge in Yakthung communities deteriorated the Thibong Yakthung customary cultural traditions. In terms of the para-colonial politics of knowledge production (Powell, 2002; Vinezor, 1978), Yakthungs and their children, including Nepali Indigenous peoples, were/are persistently taught through the Khas Aryan-centric social and academic institutions. Such Khas Aryan, Indian, and Western epistemological and ontological orientations became convincing elements that petrified Yakthung culture for centuries. The Khas Aryan architecture of knowledge construction was so well engrained in Yakthungs' mind, body, and soul that Yakthungs ignored their own cultural rhetorical traditions. Therefore, we need a decolonial approach or delinking orientations at schools and Yakthung social spaces for which we need to critically question how we can orient our children to see themselves from the Thibong Yakthung Suhangs' perspectives. We need to question how we can orient our children to delink the para-colonial epistemological and ontological colonization from the 21st century Yakthung Suhangs' perspective, and how we can orient Yakthung children to link their Yakthung cultural experiences and language to classroom activities so that they do not get alienated in local, regional, and global cultural and academic settings.

Para-Colonial politics of knowledge construction in academic institutions

Teaching of the Khas Aryan language, culture, and religion was very systematic, political, and ideological at schools in Yakthung communities. We (Yakthungs) spoke *Yakthung pa:n* at home, but when we went to school, we were programmed to believe that our language was inferior. We were oriented to believe that we were savage, and that our culture was lesser. The main purveyors of the Khas Aryan knowledge were teachers, professors, Hindu pandits, and the media. I did not know that my culture was lesser, and that our language was lesser until I went to the Khas Aryan-centric Nepali school. Similarly, Ganga Kimdang Limbu (originally from Athpahariya community) always told me that they did not want to wear their costumes, and they did not want to talk in their Athpahariya language (one of the Indigenous languages) at schools and social spaces. They also did not want to talk to their teachers and non-Athpahariya friends because they (Athpahariya children) believed that they were inferior in relation to culture and language. Ganga Kimdang mentioned that they had/have different Athpahariya accents, and their teachers and friends used to deride them on their Athpahariya race, language, and culture. As many of her friends (Athpahariya children) could not bear the humiliation, they stopped pursuing their academic journeys. Hence, the Khas Aryan-centric social and academic institutions always excluded Indigenous peoples in Nepal. The Khas Aryan social and academic institutions never validated Indigenous students' prior or lived experiences. They never respected the students' cultural norms and values; they never valued their language. As a result, the majority of Yakthung children, including linguistic minority children, do not even want to go to school as they do not find schools as welcoming places for them. This discrimination is ideological, political, and systemic, and it will not stop until Yakthungs and Indigenous peoples unite and fight for their linguistic and cultural rights.

In terms of my own experiences, while I was pursuing my PhD in the department of English (Rhetoric and Composition Studies) at the University of Texas at El Paso, I happened to meet Chandan (not a real name), a new PhD student (a Bahun male student) from Nepal who was in his mid-50s. When the student met me in the teaching assistant (TA) office the first day, one of the questions he asked me was "Do Limbus and Rais also study?" and "Do Limbus and Rais also go to university to study?" and these questions were followed by other demeaning and humiliating remarks. Chandan had been a lecturer at Tribhuvan University, Nepal for more than two decades (before he came to the US to pursue the PhD degree), but the Khas Aryan orientation in Nepali academic institutions made him believe that the universities are established for Only Khas Aryans. Chandan's Khas Aryan-centric mindset also did not navigate how racist his remarks were. Chandan, more often than not, used the Nepali Khas Aryan discourse to humiliate, dominate, and embarrass Yakthungs, other Indigenous peoples, and minorities during our social gatherings. It was not Chandan who was uttering the insensitive remarks, but the Khas Aryan-centric Nepali government that orient the Khas Aryans to believe that they are superior, and that they can say whatever they want to humiliate Nepali Indigenous peoples in Nepal.

Although we live in a multicultural setting in Nepal and encounter people from different cultural and linguistic backgrounds every day because of the discriminatory Khas Aryan government, institutional racism exists in multiple ways. There are dominant and dominated cultures and languages that were created and have been maintained by the discriminatory Khas Aryan dominant culture in Nepal. Here, I want to share a story of my Bahun friend named Ratna. I gave Ratna a ride from college to school (college to workplace) on my motorcycle for several years (in Kathmandu). Ratna always said that *Limbuharuko culture nai hunna* (Limbus do not have any good culture), and I did not even understand what he was implying. Furthermore, Ratna used to usually gather ignorant Yakthung college students and got them to fight with other students at Tribhuvan University (Kirtipur, Tahachal, and Trichandra colleges) for his purpose (or for Khas Aryan student leaders' purposes). Similarly, when I went to Nepal in 2015 for the research purposes, I met an elderly Bahun English teacher, and during our conversation, the Bahun English teacher was mimicking his Yakthung students the way they (Yakthung students) spoke Nepali language in Yakthung tone. As I am a Yakthung, the teacher, implicitly, was humiliating me, too; he was dominating my culture, language, and tradition. He did not say anything about how he spoke in English as an English teacher, or how good or bad his English was. The Bahun English teacher believed that his Yakthung students were weak in Nepali, but he never saw himself as weak in English (as an English teacher, his English was obviously worse than his Limbu students' Nepali). These examples justify that Khas Aryan social institutions depict the Khas Aryans as superior beings, and they have been oriented to believe that they are superior to Yakthungs, Khambus (Rais), Tamangs, Magars, Gurungs, and Kõiches, etc. The Khas Aryans like Chandan, Ratna, and Bahun English teacher are uncritical individuals. They have been programmed in the Khas Aryan social institutions to hurt and humiliate Yakthungs and Indigenous peoples.

Currently, the colonial atrocities do not necessarily come as they used to be; the colonial wounds are not in the physical forms, such as torturing, executing, and/or banishing Indigenous people, but the colonial wounds are much more psychological and emotional ones. They are constantly inflicted by words, implications, and insinuations after the restoration of democracy in 1990 in Nepal. The Khas Aryans use language as weapons to imply racism, sexism, and castism (that implies Limbuwan, Khambuwan, Tamuwan, Magarat, Newa, and Tharuhat, etc.). They demonstrate how Khas Aryan supremacy perpetuates the Khas Aryan ideology and politics in which the Khas Aryan ruling class creates an invisible norm to dominate Yakthungs and other Indigenous peoples. These are a few examples of how the Khas Aryan-centric culture creates dichotomies between Khas Aryans and Yakthungs.

The above-mentioned problems not only exist in certain spaces or regions of Nepal, but are spread and maintained through the Khas Aryan-centric social institutions. There are innumerable instances where Khas Aryans psychologically, emotionally, and physically tortured minorities in Nepal. There was not a caste system or a castic hierarchy in Nepal before the Khas Aryan invasion; once they invaded, from northern India, they introduced their caste system that they had practiced in India for centuries (Bista, 1991; Limbu, et al., 1845; Subba, 1995). The Khas Aryan hierarchy, based on caste, race, language, religion, and culture, does not only exist in Nepal alone, but it also exists in India as a cancer. Despite the fact that such horrifying religious, political, and cultural inequalities exist in South Asia, our South Asian scholars, such as among many others, Homi Bhabha, Gayatri Spivak, and Salman Rushdie do not address the Indigenous and minority issues because most of them always claim that they belong to the highest caste in the Khas Aryan Hindu caste system (I heard a few of them romanticizing their Brahman race). Though Indigenous peoples know that the Hindu cultural practice is cancerous to the development of global communities, the Khas Aryan scholars brag about their own Hindu Bahun identity. The caste system is a systematic colonial organization of Khas Aryan politics of knowledge construction in India and Nepal, and it is strongly supported by both political leaders and scholars from the Khas Aryan communities. They strongly perpetuate and practice such cancerous caste hierarchies in the name of the Hindu religion and caste system. Many people argue that caste-politics is not ingrained in Hinduism; however, when people say Hindu/Hinduism or Brahman, the caste system is already implied there. Whether we live in the globalized world, or we live in the digitally networked civilized world, such issues always exist due to the interest of Hindu Khas Aryan oppressors in Nepal and India.

Indira Mishra, one of my colleagues from a Bahun community, told me that, as a child, she was continually told that Rais and Limbus were inferior and savage. As the Khas Aryan orientation continued to persist in Khas Aryan communities, Mishra believed that that schooling was true. She, for a long time, believed that Limbus (Yakthungs) and Rais (Khambus) were uneducated, inferior, savage, and alcoholics. She further mentioned that due to the Khas Aryan socio-cultural, religious orientation, she feared to be around Yakthungs and Khambus. Later, when Mishra became a professor at Mahendra Multiple Campus, Dharan, Nepal, she met Yakthung and Khambu students who were equally bright and talented students or were better than

Bahun and Chhetri students. Professor Mishra's experience demonstrates how the Khas Aryans' politics of knowledge construction is ideological and hegemonic. As Khas Aryans retain political, economic, and military power, they still can construct any knowledge to humiliate, dominate, and destroy them, their cultures, religions, and languages. More importantly, as long as the Indigenous peoples are fragmented, the Khas Aryans will continue to suppress Indigenous peoples in Nepal.

In the context of Nepal, knowledge, discourse, and power are always created and used in unequal power relations. For example, the Khas Aryans control all economic, political, and military powers; whereas, Yakthungs, including other Indigenous peoples, do not have any state resources and power. As Khas Aryans have military power, economic power, political power, including bureaucratic power, they have created discourse to meet their purposes for more than two centuries (since the mid-18th century). And since the Khas Aryans are the ones who wrote the Nepali constitution, it does not advocate for the Nepali Indigenous people's issues. As Khas Aryans have the power to control people, they still create discourse through different Khas Aryan-centric social institutions (culture, community, and social practices), academic institutions (schools, colleges, formal, informal, and non-formal educational spaces), and mainstream media (state newspapers, TV, and radio). On the other hand, as Yakthungs, Khambus, and Yakkhas, including other Indigenous peoples, did/do not have power, they could not/cannot fight against the discriminations. As Yakthungs have only a voice to resist the Khas Aryan oppression (that is also only after 1990) and Khas Aryans have a gun,

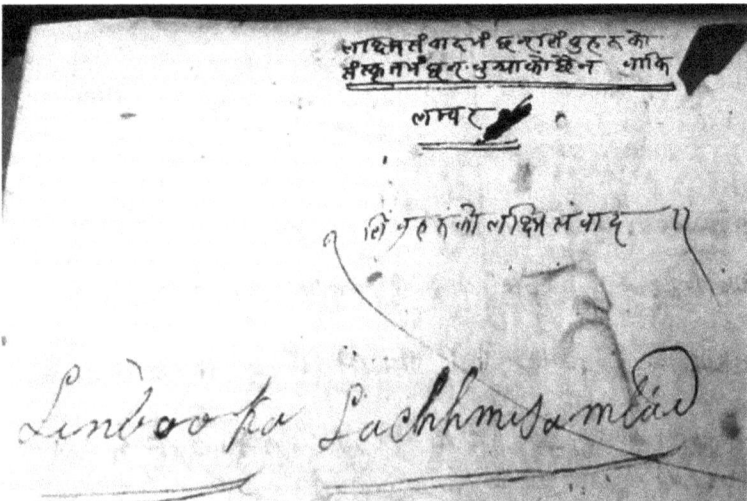

Figure 12 The Khas Aryans forced Yakthung to believe that Sanskrit was their language (Source: The British Library, London).

including political power and economic power, to suppress Yakthung's voice, the Khas Aryan way of knowledge production has been monolithic. Due to the unequal power relations, the Yakthungs, including other Indigenous peoples and places, have been marked as savage, uneducated, and untrustworthy. If Yakthungs, including other Indigenous peoples, advocated for their rights, they label/led them (Indigenous peoples) as separatists and rebels; consequently, they were either executed or were banished from Nepal.

As I mentioned above, the Khas Aryan-centric knowledge is deeply rooted in the minds of educators, political leaders, and common people, and the Khas Aryan people use the Khas Aryan discourse to humiliate and embarrass Yakthungs and other Indigenous peoples. The Khas Aryans can say anything to psychologically and emotionally hurt Yakthungs, other Indigenous peoples, and minorities in Nepal. On the other hand, Khas Aryans are protected by the state laws (Rai, Ghale, Limbu, Rai, & Thami, 2016). In 2015, the Khas Aryans, by abusing military, political, and economic powers, wrote Nepal's Constitution which favors only Khas Aryans and ignores Indigenous peoples, their identities, voices, rights, autonomies, and spaces (see also Rai, Ghale, Limbu, Rai, & Thami, 2016). As implied earlier, there was not any cultural binaries and linguistic hierarchies based on caste, religion, and race during the Himalayan Indigenous (Kirat) reign in Nepal before Sen and Khas Aryan reigns; and there was not any sign of castic binaries or castic hierarchies in Yakthung laje Limbuwan until the Nun-Paani Sandhi (1774). After the Nun-Paani Sandhi, the Gorkha soldiers and Yakthung soldiers fought collectively for the foundation of the greater Nepal. In this campaign, Yakthung soldiers were instrumental allies of the Gorkhas to win the Tanahu and Lamjung battles, including other battles, in the western region of Nepal. One day when Yakthung soldiers were exhausted and hungry, they asked "*Kaminis*" and "*Sarkinis*" (derogatory terms that refer to untouchable women in the Hindu caste system) to cook food for them (Yakthung soldiers), but they (*Kamini* and *Sarkini*) ignored their order; then, the Yakthung soldiers told them that "*Bahunis*" (highest caste women in Hindu caste system) and "*Khasinis*" (second highest caste women in Hindu caste system) "would cook and feed us, but you would pretend to be queens." In this regard, Imansing Chemjong (2003) adds:

> After [the Nun-Paani Sandhi], the Gorkha Raja made a regiment of the Limbus and led them to Lamjong and Tanahun to fight against his enemies. The Limbu force fought very bravely in the battles of Lamjong and Tanahun and conquered the land for the Gorkha Raja. They captured many people there as war prisoners. They were the Sarki, Damai, Kami, and Brahmin peoples. The Limbu officers ordered the Sarki women to cook food for the war prisoners. But the Sarki women refused insisting that they could not do so as they belong to the low caste. This annoyed the Limbus and they beat the women saying that Brahmin women and Khas women cook but that these Sarki women wanted to be queens and did not work. (p. 203)

The Yakthung soldiers smacked them (*Kaminis* and *Sarkinis*) because they (the Yakthung soldiers) were ignorant of the Hindu caste system (Limbu, et al., 1845, p. 137; Mabuhang & Tunghang, 2070 BS, pp. 35, 37, 39, 130). As the introduction of the caste system was much more political, ideological, and hegemonic, the Hindu caste system was one of the Khas Aryan practices that fragmented the Nepali communities. Meaning, the Khas Aryan castic hegemony compartmentalizes people based on the Hindu caste system, such as Bahuns as educators, Chhetris as warriors, Baishyas as traders/workers, and Sudras as untouchables. The Hindu caste system is a Khas Aryan hegemonic epistemic gauge through which Nepali Indigenous peoples, including minorities, have been measured. These norms and values are created and maintained in the Khas Aryan social, cultural, and religious institutions, such as schools, temples, media, and so on. The well-established social institutions make Khas Aryans invisible, subjective, and neutral. In other words, Khas Aryan ideology is so much imbricated in the Khas Aryan social institutions as well as in the Indigenous communities that Yakthungs could not and still cannot see it because the Hindu caste system has become a relational concept rather than something residing in individual Bahun or Chhetri. Khas-Bahun identity is related in complex and powerful ways to perceive phenomenon of Bahun-Chhetri in Nepali and South Asian cultures. In a nutshell, in Nepal, if you are Bahun-Chhetri, there is nothing to mark you as something wicked or inhumane, for Bahun-Chhetri in a Hindu community has constructed norms that defined them as humane and superior.

Encroachment of new immigrants in Yakthung laje: politics of spatial, cultural, and linguistic identities

After the Nun-Paani Sandhi in 1774, as I mentioned earlier, the Khas Aryans divided Yakthungs into two groups: *samariti* (Gorkha/Khas Aryan statutory law supporters) and *niti* (traditional Yakthung customary institutional law and practice supporters) and became able to rule the fragmented Yakthungs. Meaning, immediately after the Khas Aryans divided Yakthungs into *niti* Yakthungs and *samariti* Yakthungs, they (Khas Aryans) banished thousands of Yakthungs from Yakthung laje (Hodgson collection, vol. 85). The Khas Aryans not only captured, tortured, executed, or banished Yakthungs, but they also confiscated Yakthung ancestral lands in Yakthung laje; then, the Khas Aryans, including other Hindus, migrated to Yakthung laje (Limbu, et al., 1845). As soon as they invaded Yakthung laje, they started displacing and destroying Yakthung cultural practices, language, writing practices, Thibong Yakthung customary cultural traditions, and Mundhum literacies. Since the new Khas Aryan immigrants had strong support from the Nepali government, they started controlling us (Yakthungs) in our own homeland. Then, the Khas Aryans became able to dismantle Sawa Yet Hang Mundhumic cultural traditions; they became able to destroy Yet

Hang and Thibong Yakthung cultural traditions, and they became able to displace our *khambong-lungbong* (land-based) identities. We (Yakthungs) were labelled as Subbas and Limbus, and they converted our ancestral land into *kipat* then *raikar* (Limbu, 2019). Yakthungs gradually lost their rights to land and became homeless in their own homeland (Limbu, 2019; Lumphungwa Limbu, 2075 BS). We became homeless in our own home; we (landowners) became landless in our own land. The Khas Aryans destroyed not only our script, writing, and books, but also our tangible and intangible cultural heritages, economic conditions, political systems, and Mundhum traditions. The Khas Aryans targeted Yakthung children to linguistically, culturally, and religiously colonize at school; they colonized our minds, bodies, and souls in Khas Aryan social and academic institutions. They, by force and coercion, made us hate our own culture, language, and Yakthung Indigenous wisdoms. By the 19th century, we (Yakthungs) almost lost our culture, writing system, and Mundhum rhetorics (Limbu, 2017; Limbu et al., 1845 or Hodgson collection).

Our relationship with the ancestral land (Yakthung laje) was like a single body, an inseparable entity like nail and flesh, and Yakthungs (like other Indigenous peoples) treat/ed Yakthung laje as their Mother and mentor (see also Smith, Tuck, & Yang, 2018). We (Yakthungs) consider ourselves as *khambongsa-lungbongsa* of Yakthung laje. Meaning, Yakthungs were born, lived, and died on it since time immemorial (Khajum Limbu, 2069 BS, pp. 313–316). According to Limbu et al. (1845), having observed the Khas Aryans atrocities in Yakthung laje for decades (over 70 years), our Yakthung Indigenous scholars like Limbu et al. (1845–1857) at one point prophesied that Yakthungs and Khas Aryans would never be able to coexist in Yakthung laje. They claimed that Yakthungs were/are very friendly, trustworthy, and welcoming; whereas, Khas Aryans were/are deceitful, cunning, and devious (Limbu et al. 1845; see also Mabuhang & Tunghang, 2070 BS). Limbu et al. (1845) further stated that Yakthungs were/are not mean people; they culturally were/are not programmed to act like Khas Aryans; they could not or can never deceive like Khas Aryans. They also mentioned that Khas Aryan neighbors' betrayal and treachery were some pertinent reasons why thousands of Yakthungs could not co-exist with Khas Aryans and left Yakthung laje. When they left Yakthung laje, they promised that they would never come back to Yakthung laje as long as Khas Aryans would occupy their homeland (Limbu et al. 1845, vol., p. 149; Mabuhang & Tunghang, 2070 BS, p. 133; Pallo Kirat Limbuwan, 2066 BS, pp. 6–8). And these Yakthungs still live in India, Bhutan, Bangladesh, Burma, and Thailand.

In Yakthung laje, as in the past, there were Yakthungs who had inter-marriage relationships, including cultural and linguistic relationships with the Yakthungs, Bhutias, and Lepchas of Sikkim. The Sikkimi King Tensong Namgyal (1644–1700) (second Chogyal—monarch of Sikkim) married Princess Thungwamukma, a daughter of the Yakthung King Yo-yo Hang in 1670 (Chemjong, 2003, p. 164; Risley, 1894, p. 11).

Yakthungs, as the one of the major Indigenous residents of Sikkim, had strong social, cultural, and political relationships with the people of Sikkim (Limboo, Lepcha, and Bhutia). Therefore, many Yakthungs were also supporters of Sikkimi culture, the king, and Sikkimi *Yakthung phu-ne-nusa*, and they also had been the natives of Sukhim Thum, Yakthung laje. The Khas Aryan authorities feared the close relationship with the Sikkimi king and Sikkimi people. So, by accusing Yakthungs of plotting against the Gorkha kingdom, the Khas Aryan armed forces executed hundreds of Yakthungs and banished more than 32,000 Yakthungs from Yakthung laje immediately after the Nun-Paani Sandhi (Laksamba, 2016; Limbu, 2016, 2017; Limbu et al., 1845; Mabuhang & Tunghang, 2070 BS; Nembang, 1987, p. 8). Similarly, India and Britain also played one of the filthiest political strategies to divide us (Yakthungs) and destroy our collective power. The Khas Aryans, Indians, and British divided us (Yakthungs of Yakthung laje, Darjeeling, Kalimpong, and Sikkim) into three different countries in the Treaty of Sugauli (Sugauli Sandhi) in 1816; they divided, displaced us, and destroyed our culture, Mundhum rhetorics, and collective power (see also Laoti, 2069 BS, p. 357).

When the 32,000 Yakthungs were banished from Yakthung laje, one group of Yakthungs went to Sikkim and settled in Rung, Rhino, and Mangnesia villages; the second group moved to Bhutan and settled in Kuching, Tendu, and Jumsa villages; and the third group migrated to Assam (India) and settled in Beni, Kalchini, and Meche/Koch villages (Chemjong, 2003; Mabuhang & Tunghang, 2070 BS; see also Hodgson collection, vol. 85). The banished Yakthungs kept on seeking better places to live in where they would get a safer settlement for themselves and for their children. Currently, they (Yakthungs) live in India, Bhutan, Burma, and Thailand, and they might have migrated as far as Laos and Vietnam during political turmoil in Burma. The Khas Aryan's systemic expulsion of Yakthungs from Yakthung laje must be deeply studied, recorded, and archived for the Yakthung studies or a part of Indigenous studies.

In relation to the Khas Aryan politics of divide and rule in Yakthung laje, the Khas Aryans lured *samariti* Yakthungs with titles, properties, and lands, and some Yakthungs supported the Khas Aryans. As a result, they (Khas Aryans) were able to divide Yakthungs, abolish them, and ban them from the teaching of Yakthung language, script, writing, and Mundhum rhetoric for centuries (over 240 years). The Khas Aryans' dismissal of the Nun-Paani Sandhi and their century-long conspiracy paralyzed Yakthung culture. The Khas Aryan dismissal of the Nun-Paani Sandhi impaired Yakthung language, rhetoric, and writing; it petrified Yakthung Suhang epistemologies and Mundhum traditions. As I just mentioned after 1774, the *niti* Yakthungs supported their traditional Thibong Yakthung customary norms and values, including their *khambong-lungbong* identities; whereas, the *samariti* Yakthungs betrayed their own Yakthung *phu-ne-nusa* (brothers and sisters) and supported Khas Aryans (Ingnam & Ingnam, 2017 BS, p. 31; Lumphungwa Limbu, 2075 BS, p. 57).

While the Treaty of Nun-Paani took place in 1774, there were ten Yakthung chieftains or Yakthung kings, they included:

1 Srijang Raya (Aathrai),
2 Sri Phung (Kum) Raya (Panchathar),
3 Jamun (Sun) Raya (Chaubis),
4 Aitahang Raya (Phedap),
5 Sri Deb Raya (Maiyakhola),
6 Shubhawatta Raya (Tamorkhola-Chainpur),
7 Rainsing Raya (Mewakhola),
8 Sunuhang Raya (Chhathar),
9 Ashdeb Raya (Phakphok), and
10 Jasmukhi (Jaikarna) Raya (Chainpur).

The Khas Aryans provided all their rights to Yakthung Rayas of Athrai, Panchthar, Chaubis, Phedap, and Maiyakhola according to the Treaty of Nun-Paani. The Khas Aryans with the assistance of the *samariti* Yakthung chieftains, accused the rest Yakthung chiefs and their subjects of treason, and they banished them from Yakthung laje. The Khas Aryans politics of divide and rule was effective, for the *samariti* Yakthung chiefs supported the Khas Aryans. Gradually, the Khas Aryans could destroy the other Yakthung chiefs and Yakthungs, and finally, they destroyed Yakthung culture, language, social institutions, and Mundhum-based rhetorical traditions. The Khas Aryan-centric nation remains discriminatory based on caste, religion, and gender until today.

Limbu et al. (1845) state that Khas Aryans were never able to control Yakthungs (for decades as they lost all 17 battles to the Yakthung soldiers). The Khas Aryans knew that the united Yakthungs could never be defeated; therefore, once they had the Nun-Paani Sandhi in 1774, they divided Yakthungs first into two groups: *niti* and *samariti*; then, into three countries—Nepal, India, and Sikkim (the Treaty of Sugauli implied). Similarly, our *Yakthung phu-ne-nusa* always remained weak as they were divided, such as Rana Yakthungs and non-Rana Yakthungs; *nirdal* (one party system) Yakthungs and *bahudal* (multi-party system) Yakthungs during the Panchayat system; and Maoist Yakthungs and non-Maoist Yakthungs after 1990 to mention a few. Historically, the Khas Aryans always favored a group of Yakthungs over the other ones. The Khas Aryans consistently tempted them (Yakthungs) with high posts, property, and titles (Lumphungwa Limbu, 2075 BS). By observing the *samariti* Yakthungs' characteristics, Limbu et al. (1845 57) expressed their resentment over Yakthung leaders that we (Yakthungs) were not bad, but our Yakthung leaders were selfish; they did not support us; they rather wanted to destroy us, our culture, and *khambong-lungbong* identities. This narrative evidently demonstrates that the Khas Aryans fragmented Yakthungs. Due to the Khas Aryans divide and rule ideology, Yakthungs have been hating and hurting each other for centuries (Limbu, et al., 1845; Mabuhang & Tunghang, 2070 BS).

Race, gender, and identity are cultural and political constructs, and such false identities and dichotomies have been created and supported for centuries in Khas Aryan-centric social institutions), and due to the consistent Khas Aryan orientation, Khas Aryan folks also believe that they are superior and Indigenous peoples are inferior. They (Khas Aryans) have been cocooned in the traditional and conservative Khas Aryan ideology, and they have a blind spot of Khas Aryan ideological thinking. I call this ideological blind spot a *kaatakwa mik teptep*; the *kaatakwa mik teptep* is a situation in which the para-colonizers clearly see the Indigenous peoples, but pretend as if they have never seen because they do not want to recognize the Indigenous Yakthung customary cultural norms, values, and ideals. The main reason why the *kaatakwa mik teptep* situation exists is that, according to my Khas Aryan friends who are professors, leaders, and social workers, their parents invariably taught them that Yakthungs, including other Indigenous peoples, are lesser, danger, and savage. The Khas Aryan children have been oriented to believe that Yakthungs, including other Indigenous peoples, are inferior. Such kind of ideological pedagogy has been strongly supported by the Khas Aryan-centric Nepali social institutions, academic institutions, media, and film industries. For instance, the Hindu Lord Krishna killed his mama (maternal uncle); Krishna stole yoghurt (implies that "stealing" is acceptable); Krishna owned 1600 gopinees (implies that it's culturally accepted to have multiple women partners/wives; favors man over woman). Similarly, the Hindu Lord Ram burned Sita to test her chastity (implies that man has all rights, but a woman doesn't), and *sati* system. During the *sati* system, old Hindu Khas Aryans used to marry young wives, and when the old husband died, Khas Aryans used to burn their young wives alive in the name of *sati* (Hindu *sati* system was in practice until early 1920s). In the male dominant Khas Aryan culture, women's voices and spaces are ignored, but their bodies are under constant attack. Hence, after the Khas Aryan invasion, Yakthung including Indigenous women bodies were/are also defined in relation to Khas-Hindu man's perspectives and women bodies and spaces were/are ranked from the Khas Aryan man's benefits.

The Nepali Khas Aryan-centric ideologies are much more body-graphic, geographic, and caste-centric, and as I stated several times in this book, in the duration of 240 years, the Khas Aryans programmed Yakthungs the way they wanted; Khas Aryans also became able to label and distort Yakthung identities. For instance, when I was in elementary, lower secondary, and high schools, the Khas Aryan teachers and Khas Aryan friends used to ridicule our culture, language, and customary institutional practices. Our Khas Aryan teachers used to punish us for speaking *Yakthung pa:n* in the classrooms or at school/s; they used to accuse us of speaking against Bahun-Chhetri teachers and students when we spoke in *Yakthung pa:n*. Due to Khas Aryan peers' humiliation and teachers' domination at schools, we (Yakthung students), always felt that schools were not safe places for us. We could not express our Yakthung lived experiences, including our feelings; we could not share our Mundhum narratives at schools. Our Khas Aryan teachers and Khas

Aryan-centric government disregarded our Yakthung Suhang history, stories, narrative, and Mundhum rhetorics at schools and colleges.

The Khas Aryan politics of knowledge construction was dominant in Yakthung culture for centuries. I still remember that there were majority of Yakthung children, who along with their parents, thought that *Yakthung pa:n* was inferior, and they never spoke *Yakthung pa:n* at their homes and schools. There were many Yakthung students who did not write their last name as "Limbu" or "Yakthung"; they also did not prefer to speak *Yakthung pa:n* because they did not want to get embarrassed and punished at schools. They chose to write "Subba" as their last names; however, neither Limbu nor Subba is their real identity; these identities were given to Yakthung Suhangs by the Khas Aryans after the Nun-Paani Sandhi (1774). Many Yakthung parents discouraged their children to speak in *Yakthung pa:n* both at homes and schools because the parents were also oriented to trust that Yakthung culture, language, customary practices, and Mundhums were inferior. As the Khas Aryans coerced this discourse in Yakthung communities for centuries, they succeeded in eliminating our language and culture; they became successful in exterminating our writing system and Yakthung customary practices. Hence, they robbed us culturally, linguistically, and religiously. The Khas Aryans knew that our destruction was (and still is) their proliferation; our catastrophe was their success; our sorrow was their delight. The Khas Aryans did anything against Yakthungs as much as they could and have been doing until now. This is one of the dire situations why Yakthungs, including other Himalayan Indigenous peoples, need their own Himalayan Indigenous research theories, philosophies, and methodologies to delink, relink, and link their identities for themselves and for their future generations (see also Limbu, 2017; Mignolo, 2007; Smith, 1999, 2012; Wilson, 2008).

The Khas Aryan's teaching of language and culture dichotomy was successful in Yakthung communities, for they have been able to bribe our own Yakthung political and community leaders (see also Limbu et al., 1845). They used and have been using the corrupt Yakthung leaders to program us the way the Khas Aryans want/ed. Via this Khas Aryan politics of knowledge construction, they programmed Yakthungs to hate their own body, language, writing system, culture, and Mundhum rhetorics. Therefore, when we (Yakthungs) meet at Yakthung social spaces, we do not speak in our own language because we believe that our language is inferior. Similarly, when we (Yakthung activists and progressive intellectuals) meet at Yakthung workshops, conferences, and meetings, we do not speak in *Yakthung pa:n* (Gloria Anzaldua also mentions similar situation in Hispanic communities in the USA). For instance, once, Kirat Yakthung Chumlung, USA hosted a conference call. In the meeting, we were strictly instructed not to communicate in *Yakthung pa:n*. For instance, Limbu (2017) states:

> ... Kirat Yakthung Chumlung (KYC), USA (a globally popular Limbu organization) hosted [a telephone conference call] in 2016. We had four

major agenda to discuss over the conference call …. The invitees were only Kirat-Yakthungs and all of them were males except the General Secretary. I was the fourth or fifth invitee to join the conference call, and there were almost 30–40 invitees altogether. As we were waiting for other progressive Kirat-Yakthung intellectuals, I and one of the invitees (who I recognized for a long time) started conversing in Yakthung pa:n (Limbu language). In the meantime, another Yakthung from the group strongly forbade us to communicate in Yakthung pa:n (that I never expected in my life). (p. 562)

The Khas Aryan ideology of knowledge construction has become too prevalent that the Khas Aryan ideology flows through the veins of intellectual Yakthungs, activists, and leaders. Hence, the Khas Aryan's ideology controls us in our own Yakthung homes, communities, and Yakthung social institutions.

Because of the monolithic hegemony of the Khas Aryan government, Yakthung students never feel/felt homely in schools because the state, teachers, and peers (Khas Aryans) never created hospitable spaces for us where we could bring our Yakthung linguistic assets, cultural experiences, and Mundhum literacies. Instead of creating democratic and inclusive environment at schools, our Khas Aryan teachers constantly educated us that Yakthung language was a savage language, and we spoke *maanchhe khane kura* (man eater's language). In relation to Yakthung food culture, Khas Aryans used to tell us that our foods: *chemkhik/chemghik, chaamre,* and *yangben,* etc. were lesser. We hid our Yakthung foods in the presence of the Khas Aryans (for centuries); as a result, our Yakthung food culture is also on the verge of extinction. Based on my own lived academic experience, the Khas Aryan teachers never tried to create a safer environment for us at schools; they made us feel that we went to school to distrust and disbelieve our Yakthung Suhang customary cultural traditions. Our Khas Aryan folks, including our teachers, persistently created a discourse that Yakthung students were lesser and would not succeed academically. The Khas Aryan-centric culture and academic culture never portrayed me as a creative human being. This was one of the reasons why I was always reluctant to talk to my Khas Aryan teachers from elementary school to university-level. When I moved to the Western academic culture as a graduate student, I was still reluctant to express my thoughts and ideas, for I did not find it different from that of the Khas Aryan academic culture. The Khas Aryan and Western cultural and linguistic domination, such as the Khas Aryan-Only and Western Culture-Only ideology paralyzed my lived cultural experiences. The Khas Aryan and Western pedagogical practices petrified my Yakthung cultural traditions, and they impaired my Yakthung learning abilities.

Currently, the Yakthung ways of seeking to explore their space and identity is a newer way of paving the pathway for themselves and for their future generations. For this reason, the Yakthungs from across the world should network, collaborate, and succeed in creating their own spaces that will provide them better shelter, such as better political, linguistic, and Mundhum rhetorical spaces. This journey is possible through "delinking, relinking, and linking methodology" in the context of the 21st century and beyond (Limbu, 2017). The delinking, relinking, and linking methodology offers them opportunities to delink oppressive para-colonial, cultural, and political practices (wherever they reside); delinking helps them delearn the way Yakthungs, including Indigenous peoples, have been oriented for centuries; delinking facilitates them to denaturalize the way they have been programmed to see from the Khas Aryan lenses, including Indian and Western lenses for centuries. Similarly, the relinking approach provides them opportunity to relink their Susuwa Lilim epistemologies, Sawa Yet Hang wisdom, Yet Hang insights, and Thibong Yakthung customary rhetorical traditions. The relinking approach helps them digitally and physically network with other Yakthungs and other Indigenous and minority communities from around the world. Via this methodological approach, Yakthungs can inquire and discover what their culture was/is, where their culture was/is situated, and how/where their cultures intersect/ed with other Indigenous cultures. One of the relevant rationalities to remember is that across the world, the para-colonizers have invariably acted as if they have been rescuing Yakthungs, including Indigenous peoples, from cultural, linguistic, economic, and political colonization. This theory is nothing other than a myth; this is a lie. They lie because the para-colonizers feel unsafe in the stolen Yakthung land. Their forefathers lied and looted the Yakthungs' ancestral land and property, and their predecessors taught them to lie (Limbu et al., 1845; Lumphungwa Limbu, 2075; Mabuhang & Tunghang, 2070 BS). This could be one of the reasons why the Khas Aryan political leaders continually lie to Yakthungs, and they use Yakthung political leaders for their benefits (to hide their lies). Without lying to Indigenous peoples, they cannot establish a Khas Aryan-centric government in Nepal. This is one of the reasons why the Khas Aryans will never create an inclusive and democratic government in Nepal.

Cultural and linguistic colonization: resistance as power

Despite the Khas Aryan's politics of linguistic and cultural colonization, we (Yakthungs) spoke only *Yakthung pa:n* in Yakthung communities. My mother never spoke in Nepali with us (my siblings and me); we did not speak a single Nepali word at home and in our Yakthung community. Our community was culturally and linguistically homogenous, and we were monolingual *Yakthung pa:n* speakers. There was a Magar community adjacent to Yakthung community; we (Magar and Yakthung) used to speak Magar and Yakthung languages. Or some Yakthungs and Magars also spoke Nepali to communicate; Magars spoke Nepali in a Magar accent, and Yakthungs spoke Nepali in a Yakthung accent. Because of the cultural and linguistic make up, we did not speak Nepali well at schools like our Khas Aryan counterparts did. We, Yakthung students from the Yakthung community, had a very thick Yakthung accent. Our Khas Aryan teachers and peers used to humiliate us for having our thick Yakthung accents. When we (Yakthungs) spoke in *Yakthung pa:n* at school, the Khas Aryan teachers used to punish us. Due to Khas Aryan Nepali-only linguistic policy at schools, we (Yakthung, including other Indigenous students) never felt homely at school. As mentioned earlier, when we spoke in *Yakthung pa:n*, the Khas Aryans peers used to accuse us of speaking against them and teachers, and we used to get corporal punishment. Due to the Khas Aryan politics of Nepali-only linguistic policy, I found schools as alien spaces. As a child, I thought that school was not for Yakthung children, but only for Khas Aryan children. And I was also too scared to talk to the Khas Aryan teachers, and if I had to, I used to shake like a leaf.

As Nepali academic social institutions have been predominantly Nepali-only spaces (only for Khas Aryan students), many Yakthung, Magar, Gurung, and Rai students could not even graduate from the elementary schools for not accomplishing Nepali language competence. Since we were from a monolingual Yakthung language speaking community, we never got the opportunity to speak in Nepali at home. Therefore, we did not know how to speak and write in the Standard Nepali. In relation to English language skills: listening, speaking, reading, and writing, our Khas Aryan teachers were generous to students. The Khas Aryan English teachers themselves were not good at English, and they did not expect students to do better in English. This setting helped Khas Aryan students succeed at schools (because Nepali was their home language unlike other linguistic minority students). The Khas Aryans knew that it was/is difficult to learn a second language; nonetheless, the Khas Aryan teachers continued to give failing grades to Yakthung, Magar, Gurung, and Rai students. Hence, Yakthung and Indigenous students are deprived of their rights to bilingual or multilingual education system in Nepal, and the Indigenous children will not succeed at the Khas Aryan-centric schools (especially elementary school and junior high school) as long as bilingual or multilingual education is not introduced at schools in Nepal. ILO 169 declares that Indigenous students have the same right to benefit from the national education system as everyone else in the country (pp. 62–67). ILO Convention 169 further states:

> Education programmes and services for the peoples concerned shall be developed and implemented in co-operation with them to address their special needs, and shall incorporate their histories, their knowledge and technologies, their value systems and their further social, economic and cultural aspirations. (p. 62)

Currently, instead of introducing multilingual education system, the Khas Aryans are planning to impose Sanskrit from elementary to high school levels in Nepal. The Khas Aryan's linguistic and cultural colonization is systemic and structural, and it will always exist as long as Yakthungs and Indigenous peoples do not collectively advocate and combat against the systemic and structural discrimination to introduce multilingual education in Nepal.

There is an utmost need of Indigenous peoples' search for their linguistic and cultural identities, for the Indigenous peoples will not be able to compete with Khas Aryans, and Khas Aryans also will never create culturally and linguistically inclusive spaces for Indigenous peoples in Nepal. On the other hand, despite the Khas Aryan's suppression, Yakthungs, including other Indigenous people will never stop speaking their languages. For instance, Webster (2001) states:

> Limbu will remain in use as a mother tongue for foreseeable future. In fact, some of the trend toward more use of Nepali may slow down, stop, or even reverse, given the strongly favorable attitude toward the use of Limbu and the efforts being made to promote its development. (p. 67)

Due to the Khas Aryan's hegemonic linguistic policy, Yakthung students, including language minority students, have been trapped in the Khas Aryan discriminatory academic institutions. In my own case, although my mother was a monolingual Yakthung language speaker, she used to encourage us to speak in Nepali, partly because she didn't want us to get punished at school and partly because the Khas Aryan social institutions taught her that Yakthungs were/are lesser linguistically and culturally. As I always communicated in *Yakthung pa:n* with her, my siblings, and friends, my mother had a fear that I might not succeed academically. So, she got my cousin (Mandire Kanchha) to catch a *thanglekwa pu* (bird), kill the bird, and feed me its tongue. The *thanglekwa pu* are fast, sharply chirping birds, and my mother heard a narrative that eating the tongue of the *thanglekwa* would help me (children) speak Nepali better. My mother and many Yakthungs believe/d that Yakthung tongue is dull or slow. This cultural setting demonstrates how Khas Aryan's para-colonial ideology worked effectively in Yakthung communities in Yakthung laje. It evidently justifies how Khas Aryans by force and coercion programmed Yakthungs to see through the Khas Aryan lens. This story illustrates how the Khas Aryan politics of knowledge construction worked effectively to make us hate our own language, Yakthung culture, and Mundhum rhetorics.

Similarly, my father, Ganga Lal Limbu (a retired Subedar Major), used to always encourage me to learn English, for he always thought that English is the best language in the world. He bought an English grammar book and made me read it while I was in middle school. As it was written both in English and Hindi, I would be able to understand some words in Hindi, or as English words and sentences were translated in Hindi, I could process them in Nepali and *Yakthung pa:n*. Furthermore, when I attended wedding ceremonies and bajars in Yakthung community, I used to hear our uncles (retired Indian and British army veterans) speak in English. We (Yakthung kids) were frequently told that English was the "Raja" (king) language. We used to memorize a few words like "good morning," "yes," "no," and "good." Our uncles (retired army veterans) used to tell us that Nepali was a good language, Hindi was better, and English was the best of all. To demonstrate their retired army status in Yakthung communities, they tried not to converse in *Yakthung pa:n*, but in broken English, and we used to mimic them.

It is difficult to rebel against a colonially set system where Yakthungs and Indigenous peoples have been programmed over several generations to consider that the colonizer is superior and colonized is inferior. This discourse has been successful in para-colonial contexts, and/or in colonies and in minority communities across the world (see also Tyson, 1999). So, in terms of Khas Aryan colonial politics of language and literacy in Yakthung laje, Yakthungs were programmed in such a way that they (Yakthung parents) did not allow their own children to read and write in their own language. Yakthungs started observing themselves from the Khas Aryan lenses. For instance, when I was 4–5 years old, I was not allowed to read books or write on floors/slates (with charcoal/chalk). As I mentioned above, Yakthung knowledge was trapped in the Khas Aryan social institutions; and it supports/ed the theory that knowledge is a social construct (see also Bruffee, 1996; Brummett, 1979; Scott, 1967), and those who have the power construct knowledge in societies. In the case of Nepal, the Khas Aryans have the power to subvert and construct knowledge, and the Khas Aryans or Khas Aryan-centric government created knowledge that education is only for Bahuns (Brahmans), and our ignorant parents practiced the Khas Aryan norms on us (see Chandan's narrative in the beginning of this chapter). This setting sparks series of compelling questions, such as how did the Khas Aryan way of observing culture, people, and language. become a norm? Or why do even Yakthungs and other Indigenous peoples see themselves from the Khas Aryan lenses?

It is obvious that we (Yakthungs) see from the Khas Aryan terministic screen as we have been, by force or coercion, programmed in the Khas Aryan social institutions for centuries. In this process, if Yakthungs ignored the Khas Aryan ideals, or if they taught their children to read and write in *Yakthung pa:n*, or if they encouraged their children to promote their language, writing, and Mundhum rhetorics, the Khas Aryans captured, tortured, executed or banished Yakthungs from Yakthung laje. The Yakthung community went through such hardships, and Yakthung guardians/parents did not want to see their children tortured. Therefore, they did not allow Yakthung kids to read and write in *Yakthung pa:n*. After the centuries of orientations, Yakthungs, like my mother and sister, did not know the real Khas Aryan ideology and politics of knowledge construction, or how the Khas Aryans by force or coercion got Yakthungs and other Indigenous peoples to see from the Khas Aryan terministic screens. For instance, when I was a child, I used to, more often than not, play with my sister; when I wanted to read, she did not allow me to read the engraved letters on the epitaphs (at *chautaras*). If I attempted to read, she would cry because my mother and sister thought that if I read the carved epitaphs and did not know how to read them well, I would die. Gradually, I was also scared of reading the inscriptions on epitaphs; if my eyes accidently caught the carved inscriptions on epitaphs, I used to have goosebumps all over my body with fear. Because of the constant para-colonial teaching, I was programmed in the Khas Aryan institutions and felt scared to read old Yakthung documents. The Khas Aryan politics of knowledge construction suggests that pedagogy is where knowledge is, and knowledge is where pedagogy is, and this is how the Khas Aryan politics of knowledge construction has worked effectively in Yakthung communities.

Limbu et al. (1946–57) state that we (Yakthungs) considered, still consider, and will consider Khas Aryans as our brothers and sisters. Yakthungs not only ideally romanticize their relationship with new settlers (Khas Aryans), but Yakthungs helped them settle in Yakthung laje that is known as *rasti-chalaune* or *basti-basaune;* meaning, resettlement policy (Limbu, 2019, p. 865). Yakthungs gave them their (Yakthung) lands; Yakthung took care of them; they protected them from any kind of adversaries and natural disasters. Eventually, the Khas Aryans, in return, looted their lands, properties, and assets; they systematically tortured, banished, or executed Yakthungs (Nembang, 1987). The Khas Aryans came to Limbuwan with *mukhama ram-ram, bagalima chhura* (in theory they said virtuous things, but in practice they were back-stabbers). Since the Khas Aryans had military power and political support, they did whatever they wanted to humiliate and dominate Yakthungs. So, as they had political and military power, they invaded Yakthung homeland, Yakthung laje. They banished Yakthungs; they dismantled Yakthung laje beyond recognition. They displaced and destroyed Yakthung laje beyond recognition within 7–8 decades (in Hodgson collection, Yakthungs mentioned that they forgot about their culture and religion). Currently, Yakthung laje is irreparable culturally, economically, linguistically, spiritually, and religiously. To repair Yakthung laje, we need to understand delinking, relinking, and relinking methodology and apply it into practice. We must perform and restore intellectual *mangena* so that Yakthungs can get to their *cho:tlung* (destination).

Concerning the cultural colonization, during the reign of King Girvana Juddha Bikram Shah (1799–1816), celebrating Dashain (Hindu festival) was boycotted in Dhankuta since it eroded Yakthung culture and religion. The revolt broke out in Dhankuta and rapidly spread all across Yakthung laje (Limbuwan). The Khas Aryans forced Limbuwani people, such as Yakthungs, Yakkhas, Athpahariyas, and Khambus, to celebrate Dashain or face the consequences, such as a death sentence or expulsion from their homeland. Athpahariyas resisted the Khas Aryan oppression, and Khas Aryans captured and executed their community leaders, such as Ridama Athpahariya and Ramlihang Athpahariya. Ridama and Ramlihang were from the suburb of the Dhankuta bajar. The Khas Aryans executed them by hanging in Dhankuta, and the place they were hung is still known as *jhunda gairee.*

In relation to Athpahariya resistance as a power, Ganga Kimdang Limbu more often than not argues that Athpahariyas were one of the Limbuwani peoples who neither mimicked the oppressors (Khas Aryans) nor were afraid of the Khas Aryan (Rana) oppression. Ganga Kimdang Limbu states that the Rana (Khas Aryans) resided in their hometown Dhankuta Bajar, and they tried to impose the Hindu culture, religion, and practices, but Athpahariyas always resisted. For instance, when Buddiswori Rai (Ganga's mom) bought and wore a *cholo* (Hindu woman costume), her Athpahariya neighbors came to her home and tore her *cholo* into pieces. This action strongly supports Ganga's claim that the Athpahariyas condemned the Khas Aryans' cultural and religious imposition on Athpahariyas in Dhankuta. The Athpahariyas always lived in Dhankuta adjacent to the Khas Aryan Rana oppressors, but they resisted their cultural, linguistic, and religious oppression. According to Ganga Kimdang Limbu, the Athpahariyas always communicated and still communicate in their own language, and there are still monolingual Athpahariya language speakers. Athpahariyas still wear their own costume, such as *mekhli* and *chhita-sim* (*chhit sari*), *rangchhi* (necklace), *tariwan* (earrings), *bijkini* (earrings), *takhumbi* (scarf), *puwaalo* (necklace), and *kalli* (worn around ankle). To connect the Dashain and execution of Ridama Athpahariya and Ramlihang Athpahariya in Dhankuta, although Ridama and Ramlihang were executed publicly for resisting the Khas Aryan's executive order to celebrate the Dashain festival in 1867, the Athpahariyas strongly kept on opposing the Khas Aryan oppressions. In a nutshell, the Athpahariyas resisted the Khas Aryan cultural domination; they resisted linguistic repression; and they resisted Khas Aryan political subjugation, but their neighbor Yakthungs did not learn from Athpahariyas (G. Kimdang Limbu, personal communication, August 23, 2018). Yakthungs rather observed Athpahariya culture and people from the Khas Aryan lenses; Yakthungs thought that Athpahariyas were inferior (for they looked dissimilar culturally). Yakthungs used to call them "aathapre," a demeaning term for Athpahariyas. This setting suggests that due to the Khas Aryan's century-long systemic oppression, Yakthungs seemed to accept the structural inequalities unlike Athpahariya did. For the cultural, linguistic, and religious reclamation, we (Yakthungs), including other Indigenous peoples, must resist the traditional trajectory of Khas Aryan, Indian, and Western way of knowledge construction and maintenance; we must resist the traditional way of the Khas Aryan, Indian, and Western para-colonial way of knowledge production and maintenance. More importantly, we must be not only the consumer of knowledge, but also the prosumer (producer and consumer) of knowledge to protect our traditional customary institutional laws and practices for our and future generation's benefits.

Athpahariya's resistance to the Khas Aryan oppression was for their cultural existence—existence of themselves, their culture, traditional customary institutional laws and practices, and Mundhum rhetorics. When I married Ganga Kimdang, we (Yakthungs from Tehrathum) went to Ganga's parents' house to receive *tika* (Hindus wear it on their forehead); Khas Aryans forced Yakthungs or Subbas to practice it during Dashain, but Athpahariyas did not practice it (*tika*) in their community. The practice of receiving *tika* from elders in the Yakthung community suggests that the Khas Aryans forced Yakthungs (predominantly Subbas) to celebrate Dashain. Now, I understand that we (Yakthungs) supported the Khas Aryan, and we used to control our ancestral land in our village; therefore, we were forced to celebrate the Hindu festival Dashain in our community. Despite the fact that we put on *tika*, it used to be white *tika*, (not red one). Our (Subba Yakthung's) putting on white *tika* signifies that we still opposed the Hindu *tika* system; nonetheless, it was difficult to entirely reject the Khas Aryan oppression because immediately after Dashain and Tihar, the Khas Aryans used to come to Yakthung villages as *sadhus* (saints) and *jogis* (beggars) to spy if Subbas celebrated the Dashain (by sacrificing goat and buffalos). The *sadhus* and *jogis* would report if Subbas did not celebrate the Hindu Dashain festival; then, the Khas Aryans not only used to confiscate the Subba title, but also used to capture and punish the Subbas (Limbu, 2019). Even though the Khas Aryans used to punish Indigenous peoples for not celebrating the Dashain festival, the Athpahariyas resisted it. The Athpahariyas inherited their traditional customary traditions from their ancestors; they maintained their traditional Athpahariya customary cultural traditions. Athpahariyas knew that resistance was a form of power; power to protect their customary institutional theories and practices and deny the Khas Aryan hegemony.

As implied above, Athpahariyas sowed the seed of resistance as a power; resistance as their cultural and linguistic emancipation, or resistance as an Athpahariya Indigenous peoples' path to preserve their cultural traditions; their resistance was for their self-existence. Via resistance, Athpahariyas, including Indigenous peoples, relink their traditional Yet Hang and Thibong Yakthung epistemologies and create their own Athpahariya communal norms and values upon the foundation of Yet Hang and Thibong Yakthung philosophies. Together, we (Indigenous peoples) must reject the cultural violence, structural violence, and structural inequalities now. We must resist the Khas Aryan, Indian, and Western ideological business of knowledge construction in our Indigenous and minority communities and spaces (spaces, where we belong). In the local context, we must resist how new settlers are weaponizing Hindu philosophies and practices to destroy Yakthung culture, writing, and Mundhum rhetorics. We have to advocate and fight for our pre-existing rights to our ancestral land, traditional customary institutional law and practices, Mundhum rhetorics, and self-determination for our and our future generations' benefits. Overall, we must resist the practice of para-colonial Khas Aryan or Western discourse to reframe and reformulate Yet Hang and Thibong Yakthung epistemologies, and finally, we must delink the practice of Khas Aryan, Indian, and Western logo-centric discourse to change local as well as global Indigenous rhetorical traditions.

5 Yakthung language and literacies in para-colonial contexts

Khas Aryan Para-Colonial politics and presence of European colonial agents in Yakthung laje

Yakthungs have different Sawa Yet Hang, Susuwa Lilim Yakthung, Yet Hang, and Thibong Yakthung epistemological traditions that reframe the way they perceive the world, and the way they practice and observe the world. Under the para-colonial oppression, the Khas Aryan dictatorship suppressed Yakthungs in Yakthung laje after 1774, and they continue to oppress Yakthungs even after the advent of democracy in 1990 in Nepal. The para-colonial oppression impaired Yakthung wisdom; Khas Aryan and Western colonial wounds paralyzed their learning abilities. Currently, Yakthungs, including Indigenous peoples of Nepal and India, are seeking for a healing space; a healing space where they can soothe the wounds inflicted by the Khas Aryan para-colonizers, Indian para-colonizers (in relation to Indian Yakthungs), and Western colonizers (Limbu, 2017, p. 587). Yakthungs need to perform both physical and psychological *mangena* (a ritual, performed in Yakthung culture to raise one's self-esteem) to safeguard Yakthung Suhang culture in order to get to their *cho:tlung* (destination) because the *cho:tlung* offers them their Indigenous way of being, becoming, and belonging to Yakthung laje (as Yakthungs). In this chapter, I, based on the background information, examine how the Khas Aryans, Indians, and British colonizers divided Yakthungs into three different countries: India, Sikkim, and Nepal in the Treaty of Sugauli in 1816, and how they displaced Yakthungs and destroyed their cultural, linguistic, and *khambong-lungbong* (land-based) identities. This chapter also evidently exhibits how the Khas Aryan-centric Nepali government destroyed Yakthung books, official documents, cultural artifacts, archival materials, and how European colonial activities hurt the development of Yakthung language and literacies.

Limbu et al. (1845–57) contend that Khas Aryans were/are selfish and self-centered. Once they entered Yakthung laje after the Nun-Paani Sandhi (1774), they constantly sought opportunities to rob Yakthungs; they sought opportunities to confiscate their properties. They not only confiscated their ancestral land, but they also, by abusing political and military power, became able to eliminate traditional Yakthung customary institutions, language, culture, and Mundhum rhetorics (Caplan, 1970; Mabuhang, 2069

BS; Nembang, 1987). Limbu et al. (1845) state that Khas Aryans invariably accused Yakthungs of being anti-nationalists, traitors, and separatists; then, they tortured, executed, or banished Yakthungs from Yakthung laje. Similarly, the Khas Aryan-centric Nepali government engaged Yakthungs in futile wars, such as the Indian Rebellion of 1857, Tibet-Nepal war, Nepal-Sikkim war, Lamjung war, Tanahu war, WWI, and WWII. Though most of the wars were not beneficial for Nepal and Yakthungs, the Khas Aryans compelled Yakthungs (including other Indigenous peoples) to join the battles in order to exterminate them in the wars. While the young Yakthungs were in the battlefields, the Khas Aryans took the opportunity to capture, torture, execute, and banish (old) *niti* (Yakthung customary institution supporters) Yakthungs from Yakthung laje. This is one of the reasons why the current Yakthung population is not larger than it used to be in 1774 in Yakthung laje, Nepal.

After the Nun-Paani Sandhi 1774, the Khas Aryan-centric Nepali government suppressed the teaching of the Yakthung language, writing, and rhetorics. The Khas Aryans labelled the teaching and learning of the Yakthung language, writing, literature, and Mundhum rhetorics as an anti-nationalistic act in Yakthung laje in Nepal. This setting suggests that the Khas Aryan suppression was very systematic, political, and ideological. In addition, by giving various political and military protection, the Khas Aryan-centric government sent a huge number of Khas Aryans to reside in Yakthung laje, and the government also coerced the Yakthungs to take care of them (new settlers) (A. J. Limbu, personal communication, May 10, 2017). Having been empowered with political and military powers, the new Khas Aryan settlers migrated to Yakthung laje with the purpose to displace Yakthungs, Yakthung culture, and civilization by the end of the 18th century. Later, "The Prime Minister Junga Bahadur Rana introduced *Muluki Ain* (Civil Code) in 1854 based on the basis of castism to enforce Hindu culture, religion, and values through statutory provisions in the society" (Mabuhang, 2014, p. 174). After the enforcement of the *Muluki Ain,* the Khas Aryans further classified, labelled, and created hierarchies in Yakthung laje. For instance, they forced Yakthungs to follow the Hindu caste system, Hindu religion, and Hindu cultural practices that Yakthungs did not understand at all (Limbu et al., 1845; see also Mabuhang & Tunghang, 2070 BS).

Limbu et al. (1845–57) contend that the Khas Aryans destroyed Sawa Yet Hang, Susuwa Lilim Yakthung, Yet Hang, and Thibong Yakthung Suhang cultural traditions after the Nun-Paani Sandhi. As a result, Yakthungs, by the mid-19th century, had forgotten customary cultural ideals, histories, language, and writing system (Limbu et al. 1845; Mabuhang, 2014, p. 174). After the encroachment of Khas Aryans, including non-Yakthungs in Yakthung laje, the teaching of the *Yakthung pa:n* (Yakthung language) and writing practice was banned until the restoration of democracy in 1990 in Nepal. If Yakthungs attempted to teach, or if they were found teaching and learning the Sirijanga script and writing system, they were either executed or were banished from Yakthung laje, Nepal. For instance, Rana Bahadur Shah ordered the

Commander-in-Chief Abhiman Basnet to capture, torture, execute or banish Yakthungs who wanted to read, write, or promote their language and literacy (Tumbahang, 2007, p. 74).

After Yakthung laje was annexed to Gorkha, Yakthung and Gorkha armies fought the war against Sikkim and were able to annex Sikkim to Nepal. In this battle, the Yakthung and Gorkha soldiers fought, bled, and died together; their collective purpose, as Nepali warriors, was to create a greater Nepal. Though Yakthungs contributed to the expansion of greater Nepal (i.e. to defeat Sikkimi King), the Khas Aryans still continued plotting against Yakthungs. The Khas Aryans divided the Yakthung soldiers into two groups: *niti* (traditional Yakthung customary institutional theory and practice supporters) and *samariti* (Gorkha/Khas Aryan statutory law supporters). Once the Sikkim and Gorkha battle was over, the Gorkha and Yakthung soldiers congregated at the bank of the Tista River to clean their swords, shields, and cannons. The Gorkha soldiers put *tarusung* (water) in the ears of Yakthung soldiers, and if they shook their heads, the Khas Aryans falsely blamed them that since they could not bear the water in their ears, they also would not tolerate the Gorkha King. Then, Khas Aryans beheaded the Yakthung soldiers who shook their heads (Limbu, 2016; Limbu et al., 1845, vol. 85; Mabuhang & Tunghang, 2070 BS).

Historically, Sikkim, Darjeeling, Kalimpong, Siliguri, Dooars, and Jalpaiguri were a part of Yakthung laje. Meaning, many Yakthungs lived in Sikkim from the time immemorial. During the Gorkha and Sikkim war, Yakthungs either sided with Gorkha or Sikkim, or they remained neutral. When Yakthungs remained neutral, or they sided with Sikkimi *phu-ne-nusa* (brother and sisters), they were accused of betraying the Gorkha King; then, with the help of *samariti* Yakthungs, the Khas Aryans were not only able to execute Yakthung soldiers, but they were also able to banish more than 32,000 Yakthungs from Yakthung laje (see Limbu et al., 1845, p. 147 or Volume 85). In this regard, Chemjong (2003) further states:

> When the Sikkim-Gorkha war stopped at Limbuwan, some backbiters gave an ill report of some of the Limbus who sided with the Sikkimi force during the war. The Gorkha officers began to trace out the people who had … sided with the Sikkimi party and began to give them death punishment. Seeing this, all the Limbus who had fought against the Gorkhas by siding [with] the Sikkimi King, assembled at a place called Ambe Pojoma, consulted one another and decided to quit Limbuwan forever and migrate to other countries. They were all together 32,000 in number and migrated to Sikkim and settled in the Rungpo, Rhinok and Mangsila villages. The second group, who migrated to Bhutan, settled in the Kuching, Tendu and Jumsa villages. The third batch who migrated to Assam, settled in Beni, Kalchini and other Mech and Koch villages and mingled with the Mech and Koch races. (pp. 218–219)

Furthermore, as soon as 32,000 Yakthungs were banished from Yakthung laje, the Khas Aryans assembled thousands of elderly men, women, and children (who were the fathers, mothers, and children of the banished Yakthungs). Limbu et al. (1845) claimed that after the Khas Aryans had gathered them (elderly Yakthung men, women, and children), they ruthlessly executed them the same day in two different places in Phedap, Yakthung laje (see Hodgson collection, vol. 85).

When the 32,000 Yakthungs left Yakthung laje, they took some Yakthung books with them. However, they were not interested in the teaching and learning of the script and writing, for they had to struggle for their survival in their new homes. It might be one of the reasons why we do not find any Yakthung books written between the late 18th century and mid-19th century (the Treaty of Nun-Paani and Hodgson collection implied). Later, the European colonial agents such as Manwaring, Campbell, and Hodgson procured the Yakthung books that Yakthungs took with them when they left Yakthung laje (Sprigg, 1959). Later, the colonial agents transported the books, manuscripts, and other documents to Europe for colonial purposes. This suggests that the Khas Aryans and Europeans, including Bhutias (in Sikkim), were responsible for the deterioration of Yakthung language and literacy. Similarly, the Khas Aryans and Europeans (the East India Company) ideologically and politically divided the Yakthung collective power into three countries—Nepal, Sikkim, and India—in the Treaty of Sugauli in 1816 (Laoti, 2069 BS, p. 357). The Khas Aryan and East India Company's treaty was very ideological and political; they became successful to destroy Yakthungs' unity and collective power via the Treaty of Sugauli. The Khas Aryans and East India Company not only displaced Yakthungs in three different countries, but they also destroyed Yakthung Suhangs' culture, writing system, and collective power. The destruction of Yakthungs, since the late 18th century, became the proliferation of the Khas Aryans, Indians, and British people (Europeans). After the Nun-Paani Sandhi and the Treaty of Sugauli, Yakthungs became the puppets of Khas Aryans, Indians, and Europeans. Our Gorkha (Indigenous) soldiers became cheap soldiers of the Indians and British, and the Yakthung soldiers had/have never been treated equally in their workplaces.

In relation to Yakthung language and literacy, as Yakthung identities have been displaced and destroyed for centuries (after 1774), Yakthungs have disconnected identities, fragmented histories, and Mundhum epistemologies. As I mentioned several times, both Europeans and Khas Aryans played appalling roles to displace Yakthungs in multiple ways. For instance, the British colonizers assisted the Khas Aryans to destroy, enslave, and displace Yakthungs, their culture, language, and literacy. Since the Khas Aryans displaced and destroyed Yakthung cultural, linguistic, and *khambong-lungbong* identities, it is difficult for Yakthungs to distinguish their true Sawa Yet Hang, Susuwa Lilim Yakthung, Yet Hang, and Thibong Yakthung Suhang identities. The problem is that Yakthungs have been programmed to perceive from the Khas Aryan and European lenses. Although some European colonial agents documented Yakthung culture, language, and literacy for colonial purposes, the documentation was done entirely from the colonial perspectives. For instance, Kirkpatrick (1754–1812) wrote *Account of the Kingdom of Nepaul* (1793) as a colonel in the East India Company. Hamilton (1762–1829) was an East India Company surgeon, botanist, and studied local culture, religion, and history. Similarly, Campbell (1805–1874) was a superintendent of the Darjeeling district, and Brian Hodgson (1800–1894) was a diplomat and scientist and became a resident of Nepal in 1833 and left Nepal in 1845. During his stay in Nepal, Hodgson knew that Yakthungs had played a major role in the construction of the greater Nepal. He also learned that despite their rich culture, language, and Mundhum epistemologies, Yakthungs did not have any books, including Mundhum books in Yakthung laje, for the Khas Aryans had destroyed most of them. Therefore, Hodgson had Yakthung history, language, and Mundhums documented in Darjeeling from 1845–1857. Eden Vansittart, who knew little about Yakthungs, was a colonel in the 2/5th Gurkha Rifles. Similarly, we can also take some other names like Senior, G. A. Frierson, R. K. Sprigg, Boyd Michailovsky, A. Weidert, and George van Driem to mention a few. In this book, I briefly discuss Campbell and Hodgson (European colonial agents) who were colonial agents with the purpose to subvert and construct Yakthung histories, cultural traditions, Mundhum rhetorics, and *khambong-lungbong* identities. I will also talk about R. K. Sprigg who helped Yakthungs explore their history, script, and writing practices in the 20th century.

Arthur Campbell lived in Darjeeling as a civil servant of the East India Company who studied Yakthung language and writing. However, "Campbell was not in fact the first European colonial agent to call attention to the existence of a script among the Kirat script tribes; for Francis Hamilton (Buchanan) has already done so in 1819" (Sprigg, 1959, p. 591). As the East India Company was expanding its colony in that part of the world (South Asia and East Asia), the British colonizers wanted to expand their colony up to Tibet and China (Chakrabarti, 2012; Risley, 1928; also war digital documentation from the Gurkha Museum, UK). Before they wanted to invade Tibet and China, the Europeans conducted substantial research on Yakthung, Lepcha, and Newari cultures, histories, languages, and writing systems (see also Tumbahang, 2013, pp. 7–8; Tumbahang, 2007, p. 25). While A. Campbell was conducting research on Yakthung language, he met with Ilamsing Limbu (Yakthung) who, in Campbell's language, was the "Dewan of the Sikkim Raja" in the early 1840s. It is believed that Ilamsing Limbu had Yakthung books and other important Yakthung documents. According to Sprigg (1959), Campbell procured books from Ilamsing Limbu in Sikkim, and Campbell found the books to have been very useful for a colonial purpose; so, he wanted to acquire more books from Ilamsing Limbu again, and when Campbell revisited Sikkim, Ilamsing had already passed away. In terms of his second visit, Campbell states, "Ilam Singh, the late Dewan of the Sikkim Raja, who made me the promise [to give more information on Limboo books] and who was himself a Limboo, and well qualified to do so, died soon after" (p. 203). I read Campbell's short article on Yakthung writing system in which he discussed the Old Sirijanga script (see figure 13.1), and he even mentioned that "[t]he Limboo language is now practically extinct as a written one. The character is not used now—or very rarely indeed" (p. 203).

As shown in figure 13.1, Campbell omits /a/ from the syllabary and discusses only 19 syllabaries in the Old Sirijanga script. Yakthungs believe/d that Campbell collected more than a dozen of Yakthung books and other important documents from Ilamsing Limbu and his family members in the early 1840s (Sprigg, 1959, 1998). Sadly, during my research (2014–2020), I did not find any information about the Campbell's Yakthung book collection, and I also could not figure out where these books and documents had been archived. I have heard that there are many Yakthung books in Germany (see also Sprigg, 1959, p. 591), but I have not yet met any scholars who read the books in any German libraries. We (Yakthungs) are so hopeful that we will be able to find the books, including manuscripts, in the near future.

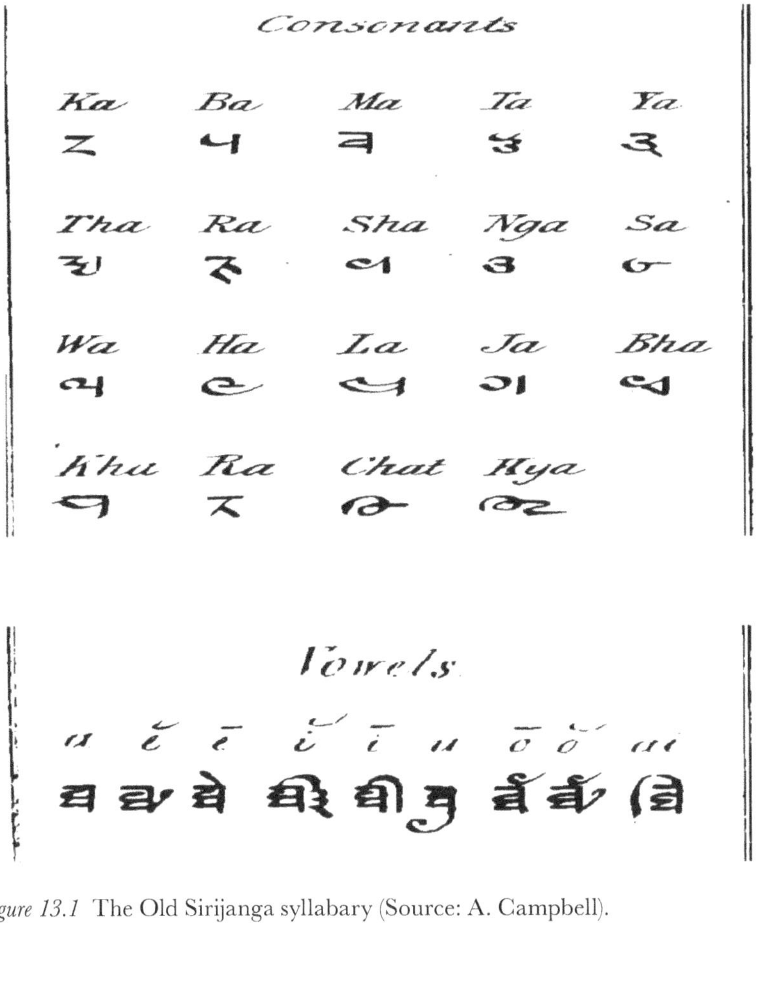

Figure 13.1 The Old Sirijanga syllabary (Source: A. Campbell).

When Brian Hodgson went to Darjeeling, A. Campbell and Francis Hamilton had already been there, and Campbell and Hamilton's presence in Darjeeling before Hodgson's arrival made it easier to undertake the imperial missions. Hodgson, like Campbell, collected old Yakthung books, documents, and other manuscripts from Sikkim, including Darjeeling and Kalimpong. Most of the books Hodgson collected were written in the Tye Angsian Sirijanga script, i.e. the Old Sirijanga script. It is believed that some of the manuscripts that Hodgson collected were written by Tye Angsi Singthebe in the early 18th century. Similarly, Hodgson also requested Jobhansing Limbu, Chyangresing Phedangba, Ranadhoj Limbu, and Jit Mohan (Jit Mohan is believed to have been a Newar; based on the manuscripts I found in the British Library, I believe Jit Mohan was primarily hired to document Newar culture) to document Yakthung histories, narratives, cultural practices, and Mundhums in Darjeeling from 1845 to 1857. The writers, who documented dozens of Yakthung books and manuscripts in the Old Sirijanga script, were multilingual and multi-literate scholars. They wrote the books and manuscripts in the Old Sirijanga script and Devanagari script (Nepali and Hindi), including in the Roman script (English). As the European colonizers had Khas Aryans (our para-colonizers) as counterparts, they wanted to take as much Yakthung information as they needed (see also Tumbahang, 2013, p. 7; Tumbahang, 2007, p. 25). Sprigg (1959) states:

> During his retirement in Darjeeling (1845–1857), Brian Hodgson acquired the fourteen Limbu books that since 1864 have formed part of the Hodgson Collection at the India-Office Library. Several Yakthungs knew that there were Yakthung books in the United Kingdom; they also believe that there are some in Germany. (p. 591)

Hodgson permanently moved to Britain in 1958 with the Yakthung books and manuscripts that he collected and had them documented during his stay (1845–1857) in Darjeeling. When I went to the British Library in London in 2016 and 2019, I also found a Yakthung book, written in 1967 that was also a part of the Hodgson collection.

In term of the Hodgson collection, the writers, such as Jobhansing Limbu, Chyangresing Phedangba, Ranadhoj Limbu, and Jit Mohan address "Shri Hodgson Saheb" or "Sri Saheb" (meaning, Sir Hodgson). The European colonizers and Khas Aryan para-colonizers created binaries that they were superior; therefore, they used "sir" to address Hodgson. The manuscripts also demonstrate that among Jobhansing Limbu, Chyangresing Phedangba, Ranadhoj Limbu, and Jit Mohan, some of them were highly literate in the Old Sirijanga script, writing system, and *Yakthung pa:n*; whereas, some of them just learned to read and write in the Old Sirijanga script. The reason I make this contention is that I found many errors and inconsistencies in the manuscripts (see the manuscript *Limbuharuko ka, kha, ...,* etc.); these writers also detected the errors and attempted to correct them in these manuscripts.

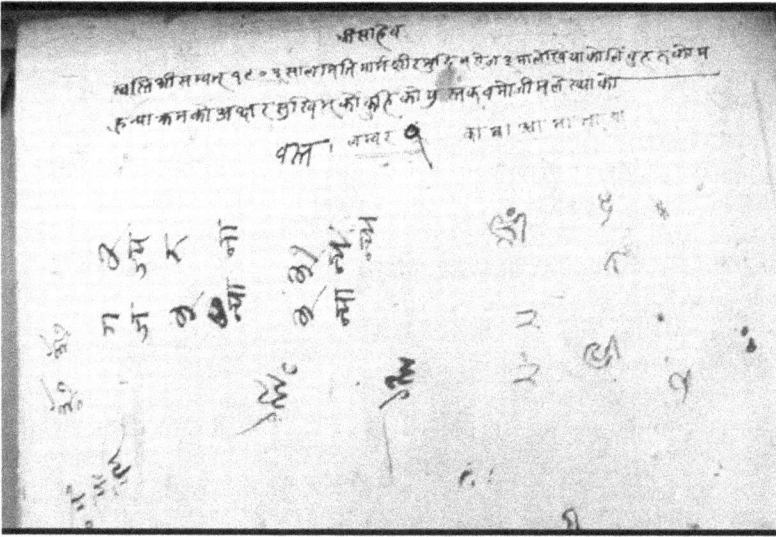

Figure 13.2 Yakthungs documented Yakthung history and Mundhum rhetorics, based on the old, damaged books found in Sukkim (Source: The British Library, London).

In the manuscripts, Limbu et al. (1845–57) contend that Yakthungs found *kuhiyeko pustak* (old, damaged book/s) in Sukhim. The scribbles on some pages of manuscripts suggest that they learned to read and write from the old book/s (see figure 13.2). Limbu et al. (1845–57) documented Yakthung histories, stories, war narratives, Mundhums, and Yakthung cultural practices based on the (damaged) book/s that they (Yakthungs) found in Sukhim. Concerning the Yakthung writers of the 19th century, we know only four major writers: Jobhansing Limbu, Chyangresing Phedangba, Ranadhoj Limbu, and Jit Mohan. Ganga Kimdang Limbu, Harkajang Kurumbang Limbu, Bhima Khapung, and I went to the British Library in London and took pictures of the manuscripts in 2016. Ganga Kimdang Limbu and I, including Harkajang Kurumbang Limbu revisited the library in 2019 to re-explore Yakthung history, language, and literacies, and in my second visit I found some documents that demonstrate that Yakthung writers sent their manuscripts to Brian Hodgson until 1867.

European colonial agents and sites of Yakthung language and literacies in the 19th century

When Hamilton, Manwaring, Campbell, and Hodgson collected books from Yakthungs from Sikkim, Darjeeling, and Kalimpong, they assured Yakthungs that their books would be preserved safely in the UK and other

European (German) libraries. As Yakthung writers and other Yakthungs were not able to travel to the UK and Germany, they just had faiths in them that their precious books had been safely preserved at European libraries. During my research, I also met many Yakthungs who always claimed that Yakthungs books were/have been safely preserved in the UK and German libraries. In my first visit to the British Library in London, I got the opportunity to read only the hardcopies (manuscripts) and made digital copies of them as well. However, in my second visit, the librarians and library curators preferred to give the readers the microfilms. As I wanted to read the original hardcopy manuscripts and wanted to make some digital copies, I had to make a special written request and wait for a couple of days. After reading the original Yakthung manuscripts I found out that the volumes (manuscripts) are not well organized; many pages are placed in wrong volumes and the pages or contents are scattered all around. It happened as the people who bounded the manuscripts did not know Yakthung language and the Old Sirijanga script. I found the following manuscripts at the British Library in London:

Volume 58:

- Limbu-in Nepali
- Ethnographical, topographical linguistic notes
- Route to China

Volume 73: Sirijanga and his execution
Volume 74: Yakthung (ritka kuraharu)
Volume 78: pp. 315–322
Volume 79: Limboo letter-Limbu akchhar
Volume 80: Lepche book
Volume 84: LIMBU I

- Limbooharuko bahrakhari
- … Limbuharuko barnakram akchhar, Sukhimko kuhiyeko pustak bamojim lekhyako …
- Yakthung Munthum
- Limbooharuko paidasaya

Volume 85: Hodgson Saheb, (writers: Jobhansing Limbu, Chyangresing Phedangba, Hawaldar Ranadhoj Limbu, and Khardar Jit Mohan)

- Limboo dharma au chalanko behora
- Limboo upadeshko pustak
- Limbu bibah au kheti-paati garnya barnyako lambhar
- Limbuharuko Laxmi sambad
- No title (Gorkha-Khambuwan-Limbuwan Yuddha??)
- Yakthungbahang Mundhum (Limbuharuko dantya katha)
- Sabako bolne miyasa huwa

Volume 86: Limbu original (1)
Volume 87: Limbuko ka, kha haru—(Limbu Alphabet)
Volume 88: Limbu Alphabets
Volume 89: Writing book

(see also Kainla, 2049, pp. 35–36; Limbu, 2017;
Mabuhang & Tunghang, 2070 BS, p. 9)

In this chapter, I have listed cover pages of some manuscripts from the Hodgson collection (see figures 14). The cover pages of the manuscripts exhibit that Limbu et al. (1845–57) documented diverse Yakthung histories, Mundhums, narratives, cultural practices, Yakthung lifestyles, language, religion, and culture of the 18th century and before to mention a few. Their documentation of Yakthung history, culture, language, and literacy was the first site of relinking Sawa Yet Hang wisdoms, Susuwa Lilim Yakthung epistemologies, Yet Hang insights, and Thibong Yakthung Suhang customary law traditions. They did not only re-articulate what they had found in the old damaged Yakthung book/s in Sukhim, but they also researched, collected information, revisited history, and rearticulated cultural practices from the 19th century's Yakthung Suhang perspectives. They recollected oral-performance or oral history, and oral Mundhumic narratives and updated them from the 19th century Yakthung viewpoints. Their redocumentation and relinking Sawa Yet Hang, Yet Hang, and Thibong Yakthung Suhang customary traditions embody how Yakthungs were colonized, how our para-colonizers imprisoned Sawa Yet Hang knowledge, Susuwa Lilim Yakthung wisdom, Yet Hang insights, and Thibong Yakthung Suhang ingenuities in the colonial discourse, and how colonial logics and ideologies paralyzed our culture.

Figure 14 Some cover (title) pages that Jobhansing Limbu, Chyangresing Phedangba, Ranadhoj Limbu, and Jit Mohan wrote from 1845–1857 (below) (Source: The British Library, London).

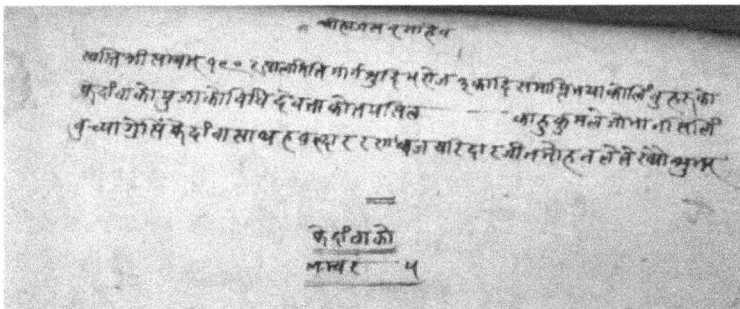

Figure 14.1 Limbu writers: Jobhansing Limbu, Chyangresing Phedangba, Ranadhoj Limbu, and Jit Mohan.

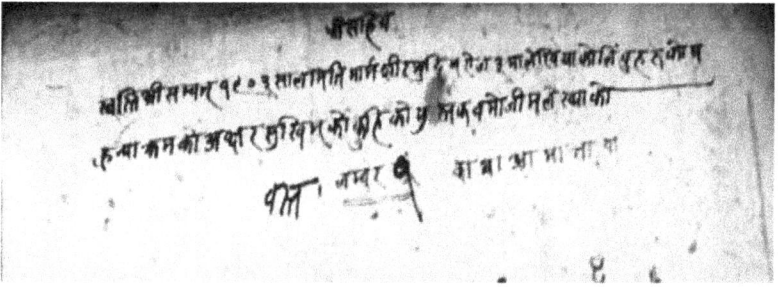

Figure 14.2 Limbu stories written based on the damaged book/s found in Sukhim.

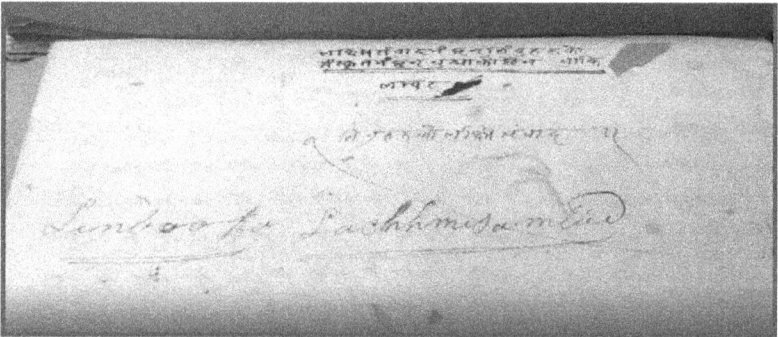

Figure 14.3 Limbu's Laxmi Sambad.

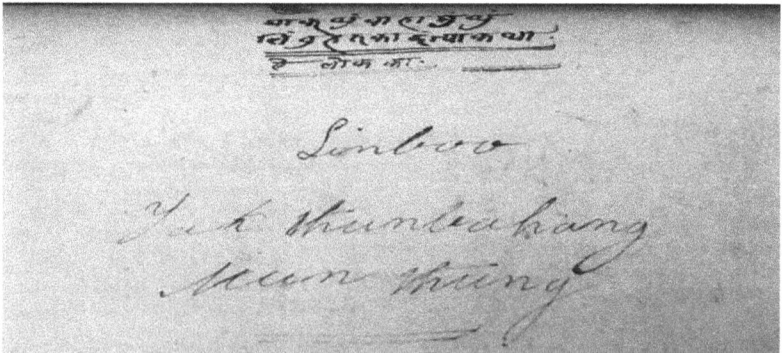

Figure 14.4 Folktales of Limbu.

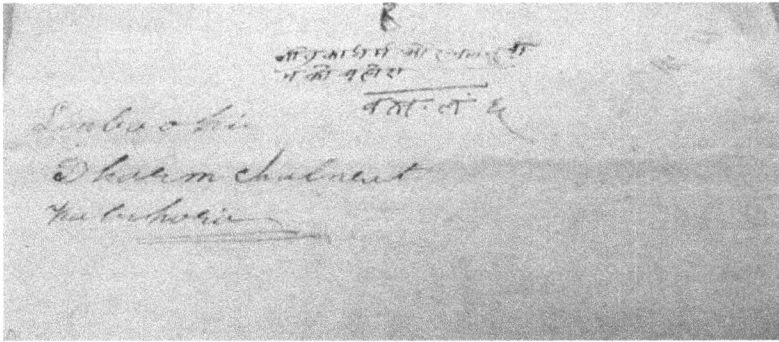

Figure 14.5 Religion of Limbu.

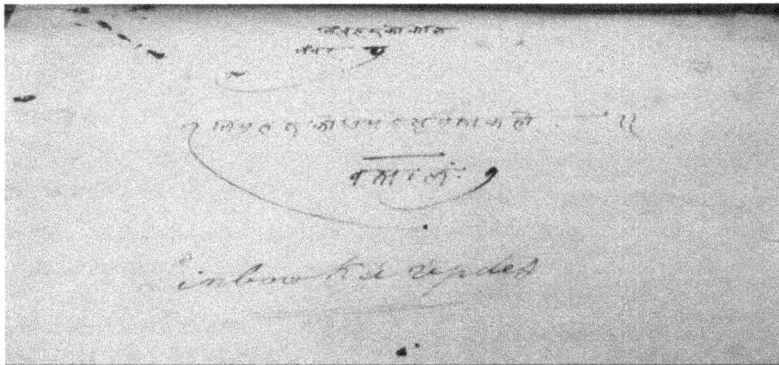

Figure 14.6 Limbu language and preaching of Limbus.

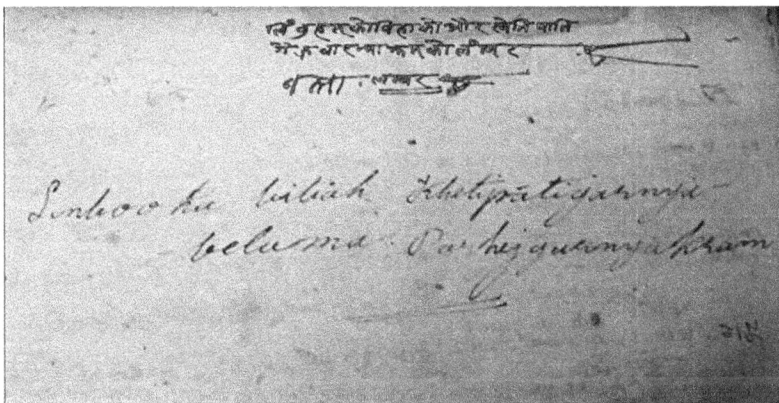

Figure 14.7 Marriage system and farming system of Limbus.

The manuscripts of this period (1845–57 or up to 1867) embodies a power of delinking cultural and linguistic colonization, relinking our Sawa Yet Hang, Susuwa Lilim Yakthung, Yet Hang, Thibong Yakthung Suhang, and Yakthung Suhang wisdoms. From this perspective, Jobhansing Limbu, Chyangresing Phedangba, Ranadhoj Limbu, and Jit Mohan were the historians of the 19th century who delinked the Khas Aryan and European cultural, linguistic, and religious colonization; they were the 19th century scholars who denaturized Khas Aryan, Indian, and Western colonial epistemologies and relinked Yet Hang wisdom and Thibong Yakthung epistemologies. They were the 19th century Yakthung scholars who linked both then and now Yakthung cultural theories, philosophies, and practices. They were the ones who flourished Yakthung Suhang knowledge of being, becoming, and belonging to the Yakthung Suhang space as *khambongsa-lungbongsa* (wherever we were and/or are). They sowed the seed of Sawa Yet Hang wisdoms, Susuwa Lilim Yakthung epistemologies, Yet Hang insights, and Thibong Yakthung Suhang insights in the context of the 19th century Yakthung perspectives. Their writing did not just convey the contents as I mentioned above and below, but they were the representation of Thibong Yakthung culture, histories, pains, and sufferings from the 19th century. If they did not re/landscape Yakthung culture, Thibong Yakthung Suhang tradition, and Mundhum rhetorics, we (Yakthungs) would have been absolutely imprisoned into the Khas Aryan para-colonial cage. Because of the 19th century writers, we can perceive and critically imagine the horizon of Sawa Yet Hang, Susuwa Lilim Yakthung, Yet Hang, and Thibong Yakthung epistemologies. Therefore, Yakthungs, including other minorities, have to understand that traditions and histories do not exist by themselves; they have to be reconstructed and reinvented for the social transformations.

As the teaching and learning of Yakthung writing, language, and literacy was banned, there was a Yakthung language, literacy, and knowledge gap from the 1850s up to early 1920s. It does not mean that Yakthungs did not read and write during that period; they did, but due to the Khas Aryan suppression in Nepal and Bhutia oppression in Sikkim, Yakthungs did not get the opportunity to read and write in the Sirijanga script in Yakthung language. Because of the Khas Aryan and Bhutia tyrannies, Yakthungs could not document their histories, narratives, culture, language, and Mundhum rhetorics. The Khas Aryans continued to banish Yakthung activists from Yakthung laje. For instance, they banished Lalshor Sendang, including other Yakthungs. When the Khas Aryans banished Lalshor Sendang, he was already 74 years-old (Limbu, 2017, p. 571; Kandangwa, 1999, p. 49; Nembang, 1987, p. 12). Although Lalshor Sendang was 74 when he was banished, he continued to advocate and fight for the promotion and preservation of Yakthung language, script, Mundhum rhetorics, and *khambongsa-lungbongsa* Yakthung identities from Kalimpong, Sikkim, and Assam. Lalshor Sendang also encouraged Yakthungs in Sikkim to study Yakthung writing system, culture, history, literature, and Mundhum rhetorics. As soon as Shree Yakthung Hang Chumlung was founded in Dungrabasti, Kalimpong in 1925, Yakthung community leaders and activists invited Lalshor Sendang to teach Yakthung language, script, and Mundhum rhetorics. Lalshor Sendang taught Yakthung language and Mundhum rhetorics in Dungrabasti (Kalimpong) for about a year (K. B. Sambahamphe, personal communication, May 23, 2018). This suggests that Lalshor Sendang was a Yakthung language, literacy, and Mundhum philosophy guru who played a substantial role in the restoration of Yakthung language and literacy (see Chapter 6).

In terms of Yakthung language and literacy in Nepal, not only was the teaching and learning of the Yakthung script, writing, and Mundhum rhetorics banned, but Yakthungs were persistently taught to disregard their own language through Khas Aryan social institutions (Limbu, 2017, p. 73). Yakthungs were programmed to see through Khas Aryan perspectives. For instance, Marohang Limbu (2017) states:

> As Khas Aryan colonized Yakthungs for centuries, Sawa Yet Hang epistemology has been paralyzed; Susuwa Lilim knowledge has been petrified; Yakthung knowledge has been impaired for centuries. As the result, Yakthungs started viewing themselves from Khas Aryan, Indian, and Western lenses; they started viewing their language and writing from Khas Aryan terministic screens. (p. 573)

Ever since the Nun-Paani Sandhi, there had been an intellectual power struggle between Khas Aryan rulers and Yakthungs. Despite the Khas Aryan's tyranny, Yakthungs to some extent resisted the oppression; they overtly or covertly delinked the Khas Aryan colonization. By delinking Khas Aryan para-colonization, Limbu et al. (1845–57) re-landscaped Yakthung culture, history, and Mundhum rhetorics; they relinked Yakthung culture, writing, and Mundhum rhetorics. Limbu (2017) further states:

> The relinking process explores historical and philosophical dimension of Indigenous knowledge, i.e. Sawa Yet Hang and Susuwa Lilim rhetoric, writing, and Mundhum rhetorics. The delinking and relinking process seeks to re-articulate Sawa Yet Hang Indigenous knowledge; it seeks the processes and practices of de-naturalizing Khas-Hindu, Indian, and/or Western cultural and linguistic colonization. Then, it seeks to perpetuate and practice the process of naturalizing, adapting, and solacing Sawa Yet Hang and Susuwa Lilim epistemologies. (pp. 573–74)

Yakthungs delinked the Khas Aryan logic of colonialism; they preserved Yakthung artifacts in order to empower Yakthung histories, chains of memories, and Mundhum rhetorics. They documented Yakthung cultural, linguistic, and historical artifacts to immortalize Sawa Yet Hang, Susuwa Lilim Yakthung, Yet Hang, and Thibong Yakthung Suhang memories.

They demonstrated that "traditions do not exist by themselves; they have to be communicated, contested, challenged, processed, constructed, and re/invented for our purposes" (Limbu, 2017, p. 574).

Currently, the Hodgson collection offers us the space of our existence as Yakthungs in Yakthung laje, India, Bangladesh, Burma, Bhutan, Thailand, and beyond. Limbu et al.'s (1845–57) manuscripts are the only legitimate written credentials that link (a part of delinking, relinking, and linking approach) Sawa Yet Hang, Susuwa Lilim, Yet Hang, Thibong Yakthung, and Yakthung Suhangs' epistemologies. The 19th century's Yakthung manuscripts play an immense role to link the historical conditions of Thibong Yakthungs' with that of our future Yakthung Suhangs' epistemic activities. More importantly, the manuscripts documented in the 19th century reveal the pressing issues of Yakthung studies of the past, present, and future, or they became tools to critically study, imagine, and interpret Yakthung histories, cultures, and Mundhum rhetorics. The Hodgson collection became one of the indicators of the Yakthung Suhang civilization, Thibong Yakthung voices, and Mundhum rhetorics; whereas, Yakthung Mundhums became one of the gauges of Yakthung Suhang histories and civilizations.

Part IV

The first Yakthung literacy wave

Delinking, relinking, and linking the Sirijanga script, writing, and rhetorics

6 Restoration of the Sirijanga script, writing, and rhetorics

Language is our identity; writing is a power, and our language and writing reveal a multiple way of being Yakthung Suhang, becoming Yakthung Suhang, and belonging to Yakthung laje. We (Yakthungs) understand the power of writing and rhetorics in local and global contexts. Despite the Khas Aryans' oppression of the teaching of Yakthung language, literacy, and Mundhum rhetorics, Yakthungs, from Nepal, India, Bhutan, Burma, and beyond, never gave up their hope of restoring their cultural identity, linguistic identity, writing, and Mundhum rhetorics. In the age of technology and globalization, although Yakthungs live in different parts of the world, their collective endeavor delinks Khas Aryan, Indian, and European colonization and relinks their Sawa Yet Hang, Susuwa Lilim Yakthung, Yet Hang, and Thibong Yakthung social, cultural, linguistic, and Mundhum epistemologies. In doing so, *Yakthung phu-ne-nusa* have been linking their Susuwa Lilim Yakthung epistemologies and Thibong Yakthung wisdoms, including current Yakthung cultural, linguistic, and political identities from the local to global levels (Limbu, 2017, pp. 573–575). Based on the information, this chapter discusses the first Yakthung literacy wave in the modern Yakthung history. This chapter focuses on why Yakthungs established Shree Yakthung Hang Chumlung in Kalimpong, how Yakthungs utilized Shree Yakthung Hang Chumlung, and how Shree Yakthung Hang Chumlung facilitated Yakthungs' campaign to delink the Khas Aryan, Indian, and European cultural and linguistic colonization, to relink Yet Hang and Thibong Yakthung Suhang civilization, and link Yakthung language and literacy in local and regional contexts in the early 20th century.

The Khas Aryan and Bhutia logic of para-colonization suppressed the development of Yakthung language, writing, and Mundhum rhetorics. Meaning, the Khas Aryans, including Bhutias, attempted to displace and destroy the Yakthung writing systems, rich cultural traditions, and Mundhum rhetorics for centuries. As soon as some Yakthung chieftains accepted the Nun-Paani Sandhi with Gorkhas, the Khas Aryans strategically divided Yakthungs into *niti* (traditional Yakthung customary institutional law and practice supporters) and *samariti* (Gorkha/Khas Aryan statutory law supporters) and ruled over them. Then, in the Treaty of Sugauli in 1816, they dispersed Yakthungs into three countries: Nepal, India, and Sikkim (independent country then). Similarly, the Khas Aryans also used World War I (WWI) as an opportunity to displace Yakthungs and to weaken their collective power in Yakthung laje (Lumphungwa Limbu, 2075 BS, pp. 55–60; Mabuhang & Tunghang, 2070 BS; see also Limbu, Phedangba, Limbu, and Mohan, 1845).

The Khas Aryan-centric government forced Yakthungs from ages 18–50 (from each family) to compulsorily join WWI, which deteriorated Yakthungs' collective struggle and power (Lalshor Sendang's campaign implied). While the young Yakthungs were fighting in the battlefields for global peace, progress, and prosperity during WWI, instead of taking care of their families, the Khas Aryan-centric Nepali government tortured, executed, or banished them from Yakthung laje. Similarly, the Khas Aryans forced Yakthungs to hand over their books and important documents; then, the Khas Aryans destroyed all Yakthung books, manuscripts, and other important documents during WWI. During the Nepali Prime Minister Chandra Shamser's reign or while the young Yakthungs were fighting for the global peace, progress, and prosperity, the Nepali armed forces collected more than 60,000 books, archival materials, Lal Mohars (treaty documents from Shah Kings), Yakthung genealogies, and Mundhum books from Yakthung laje and burned all of them in Chainpur, Yakthung laje (see Mabuhang & Tunghang, 2070 BS; Nembang, 1987, p. 12; "Pallo Kirat Limbuwan" 2066 BS, p. 5). If Yakthungs were reluctant to hand over the books and documents, the Gorkha armed forces tortured, executed, or banished them (men, women, and children). Hence, by torturing, executing or banishing Yakthungs from Yakthung laje, Nepal, the Khas Aryans compelled all Yakthungs to destroy their books, documents, archival materials, and Mundhum books.

Bir Nembang (1987) describes how Khas Aryans forced the Yakthungs to mandatorily join the East India Company. Yakthungs from the age of 18–50 joined WWI and fought, bled, and died together with other global brothers for the peace, progress, and prosperity of the local and global communities. While the young Yakthungs were in the war zones, the Khas Aryans destroyed Yakthung books, Royal seals, the treaty documents from the Sen and Gorkha rulers, and other precious Yakthung archival materials. The Khas Aryans used WWI not only to destroy Yakthung cultural culture, history, and rhetorical traditions, but also to displace Yakthungs from Yakthung laje. To weaken Yakthung collective power, the Khas Aryans banished Lalshor Sendang and his followers from Yakthung laje during WWI (Mabuhang & Tunghang, 2070 BS; Nembang, 1987, p. 12; "Pallo Kirat Limbuwan" 2066 BS, p. 5; Y. Laoti, personal communication, May 23, 2017). Similarly, the Khas Aryans continued to torture, execute, or banish progressive Yakthung intellectuals from Yakthung laje until 1990. For instance, the Khas Aryan armed forces captured Prem Kandangwa (Limbu), Jasoda Kandangwa (Limbu) from Tehrathum, and Raj Kumar Angdemgbe (Limbu) from Kerkha, Jhapa and 300 other people, and they also executed Yakthungs for their campaign of teaching and learning of Yakthung language, writing, and Mundhum literacies (see Baral & Tigela-Limbu, 2008, p. 45; Nembang, 1987). The Yakthung Mundhums and Yakthung history demonstrate that though Yakthungs were divided and displaced innumerable times after the Nun-Paani Sandhi (1774), Yakthungs never gave up their hope of relinking Yet Hang and Thibong Yakthung customary traditions, the Sirijanga writing system, and Mundhum rhetorics.

Yakthungs invariably supported and contributed as local and global citizens for the peace, progress, and prosperity of global communities. Yakthungs fought, bled, and died together with their global allies, and they also learned the importance of reading and writing from their European allies in the battlefields. Upon the arrival of Yakthung soldiers to their homeland, after WWI was over, instead of appreciating them for their service, bravery, and sacrifice, the Khas Aryans did not allow many Yakthung soldiers to reenter Yakthung laje. The Khas Aryan-centric Nepali government accused them of revolting against the Nepali government. This suggests that the Khas Aryans' main mission was to exterminate Yakthungs and their culture, language, and literacy in Yakthung laje, Nepal. Due to the inhumane Khas Aryan aggression, the majority of Yakthungs who fought in WWI decided to settle in India, Sikkim, and Burma (see Chemjong, 2003). In relation to Yakthung history, language, and literacy, Gregoire Schlemmer (2003/2004) states:

> … Aryans [Khas Aryans] invaded the country [Yakthung laje], destroyed their society, burnt their books, occupied their land, divided the Kirants, and marginalized them. These outsiders [Khas Aryans] are the cause of Kirant disunity and of the perversion of the Kirants' traditions. This finally led to the disintegration of the mundhum and the loss of harmony between the Kirant, their land and their ancestors, and was moreover the cause of their current poverty, backwardness, and low political representation. (p. 138)

These are some of the reasons why Yakthungs have lost the Sirijanga script, writing system, and Yakthung cultural traditions, including Yakthung collective power in Nepal. By the early 20th century, Yakthungs created a new Sirijanga script and writing system. The New Sirijanga script resembled the "Devanagari script" because due to the Khas Aryan oppression over Yakthung language and literacy, they forgot the Old Sirijanga script and writing system. Immediately after Yakthung scholars created the New Sirijanga script, they started documenting Yakthung history, grammar books, cultural practices, and Mundhum rhetorics.

Establishment of Shree Yakthung Hang Chumlung: sites of Yakthung language and literacies in South Asian contexts

The Yakthungs of Kalimpong established a Yakthung social institution known as Shree Yakthung Hang Chumlung on July 26, 1925 in Dungrabasti, Kalimpong (India). Then, Shree Yakthung Hang Chumlung became the center of Yakthung language and literacy development in the context of the 20th century. Shree Yakthung Chumlung became Yakthungs' heart, body, mind, and soul in terms of the development of Yakthung language, literacy, writing, and Mundhum rhetorics. In other words, Shree Yakthung Hang Chumlung became a Yakthung home; it provided every opportunity to Yakthungs that Khas Aryan and European colonizers had taken away from them for centuries. After the foundation of Shree Yakthung Hang Chumlung, Yakthungs, for the first time in a long time, grasped the meaning of being Yakthungs, becoming Yakthung Suhangs, and belonging to Yakthung laje in Yakthung Suhang way. For the reader's information, Kalimpong has always been a Yakthung home, and it was under Yakthung laje during the Yakthung reign. Among many others, the main purpose of Shree Yakthung Hang Chumlung (1925) was to promote the teaching, learning, and documentation of *Yakthung pa:n*, Yakthung histories, and Mundhum rhetorics. After the foundation of Shree Yakthung Hang Chumlung, Yakthungs delinked the Khas Aryan, Indian, and Western cultural and linguistic colonization. Shree Yakthung Hang Chumlung named the script the "Sirijanga" script. After the foundation of Shree Yakthung Hang Chumlung, Yakthungs wrote more than 14 books within a decade (see Chapter 7). So, Shree Yakthung Hang Chumlung provided Yakthungs a safe *chumlung* through which they could delink the Khas Aryan and Indian cultural and linguistic colonization and could relink their Yet Hang and Thibong Yakthung Suhang cultural traditions.

In relation to language, writing, and rhetorics, Shree Yakthung Hang Chumlung not only gave a voice to the voiceless Yakthungs, but it also woke Yakthungs up from their centuries-long trance. As I stated earlier, Shree Yakthung Hang Chumlung energized Yakthungs; they felt like Yakthung Suhangs, like their Yet Hang and Thibong Yakthung ancestors, for the first time after a long time. Shree Yakthung Hang Chumlung became a Yakthung Suhang network space that facilitated Yakthungs link distant past, present, and future. It oriented them, the ways of reconstructing the contemporary Yakthungness through which they could both envision their past, present, and future; especially, the future for the Yakthung cultural, linguistic, and political identities. So, via Shree Yakthung Hang Chumlung, Yakthungs started linking Yakthung rhetorics and writing; they revived Susuwa Lilim Yakthung history, Thibong Yakthung Suhang narratives, and Yakthung Suhang stories—the stories of tears and turmoil because "[s]tories not only convey information, but they have the power to change" and "[t]he exchange of stories from teller to listener is a form of relational knowledge" (Morris & Eldridge, 2020, p. 283). Hence, the stories reinvigorated the Sawa Yet Hang epistemologies, revived the Susuwa Lilim Yakthung histories, and revitalized Yakthung Suhang Indigenous wisdoms. Via the local and global Yakthung *phu-ne-nusa* network, Yakthungs relinked Yet Hang and Thibong Yakthung histories and traditional Yakthung Suhang wisdoms, and they updated them from the 20th century's Yakthung Suhang perspectives.

To always remember and cherish their Motherland, Yakthung Suhang culture, and Thibong Yakthung history, the Yakthungs of the early 20th century established *phu-ne-nusa* network spaces in South Asian and Southeast Asian regions. Meaning, as soon as they founded Shree Yakthung Hang Chumlung, they started networking with *Yakthung phu-ne-nusa* (brothers and sisters) from Nepal, Darjeeling, Kalimpong, Sikkim, Assam, Bhutan, Bangladesh, Burma, and Thailand. They established *Yakthung chumlungs* in Darjeeling, Bhutan, Bangladesh, and Burma. *Yakthung chumlungs* energized *Yakthung phu-ne-nusa* in local and regional contexts in Yakthung communities. Via *chumlungs* (as social spaces), they collectively explored Yakthung histories, relinked their Yet Hang and Thibong Yakthung epistemologies, and shared them locally and regionally with Yakthung and non-Yakthung *phu-ne-nusa*. After the foundation of Shree Yakthung Hang Chumlung, Yakthungs learned to read and write in the Sirijanga script and in *Yakthung pa:n*. Henceforward, *Yakthung phu-ne-nusa*, from different geo-political locations, collaborated to document, disseminate, institutionalize, and preserve their language, script/writing, histories, and Mundhum rhetorics. This collaboration and documentation were the early signs of delinking, relinking, and linking Yakthung epistemic activities in Yakthung communities in the context of the 20th century.

As I mentioned above, the *Yakthung phu-ne-nusa* who migrated to new places established Yakthung organizations in their communities so that they could network with other Yakthungs in order to document, preserve, promote, or disseminate their cultural heritages. The banished Yakthungs networked with their families, relatives, and friends from Yakthung laje, Limbuwan to maintain and perpetuate their Thibong Yakthung cultural traditions, writing, and rhetorics. Today, in the context of the 21st century globalized world, these displaced Yakthungs' children constantly network with other Yakthungs from Nepal and other countries via social networking spaces, interactive Web 2.0 tools, and cloud technologies. Via social media or crowd and cloud spaces, they learn *Yakthung pa:n*, culture, history, writing, and Mundhum rhetorics. For instance, I have never been to Yakthung communities, such as Bhutan, Hong Kong, and Burma to mention a few, but I learned how Yakthungs have been practicing, perpetuating, and disseminating Yakthung rituals, Mundhums, and other Yakthung traditions in these places.

The advent of the digital technologies helped Yakthungs delink Khas Aryan, Indian, and Western colonization; it helped them relink Yet Hang and Thibong Yakthung Suhang cultural traditions, Yakthung Suhang rituals, and practices. Yakthungs have regularly been organizing local, national, and international conferences, including webinars on Yakthung cultural practices, Mundhum literacies, language and literacies. By sharing their conceptual, theoretical, and practical Yakthung Suhang epistemic activities and emerging pressing issues in both virtual and physical spaces, they are delinking Khas Aryan, Indian, and Western cultural colonization and relinking Yet Hang and Thibong Yakthung rhetorical traditions and linking them to current Yakthung cultural practices in the context of the 21st century digital age.

Based on the above discussion, Yakthung Indigenous social and academic institutions should support digital networks with the building of diverse network capacities, such as digital media technologies, media journalism, multimodal production, advocacy skills, communication abilities, local and global networking skills, and multimodal production. The reason why we should engage Yakthung youths in digital literacies is that the digital network is immune to physical borders and oppressive political borders. Currently, Yakthungs reside across the world, and their digital engagement have diverse potential to shape their culture, language, and literacies. By engaging in crowd and cloud spaces, they are shaping and reshaping their community the way they want it to be. Similarly, they will create knowledge, content, manage, disseminate, and institutionalize them for their benefit. In short, digital literacy facilitates Yakthungs to create their digital and physical identities. Finally, they will create their own network paths to meet their needs and expectations, such as their cultural needs, economic demands, and political expectations; then they will make their voices, identities, and agencies visible both in local and global contexts.

Although Khas Aryans suppressed Yakthungs in Nepal, King Mahendra Shah, including his Khas Aryan cronies, is considered as one of the cancerous rulers to Yakthungs and Yakthung laje. He destroyed Yakthungs' Yet Hang and Thibong Yakthung cultural norms, values, rights to their ancestral land, language, and literacy. Before the Nun-Paani Sandhi, Yakthungs were the owners of their land (Yakthung laje), and in Yakthung laje, no one was allowed to sell the ancestral Yakthung land (to non-Yakthungs), but the land was rented to people for certain periods of time (until Mahendra Shah confiscated the ancestral Yakthung land). When Khas Aryans encroached into Yakthung laje, Yakthungs welcomed them as *phu-ne-nusa* (brothers and sisters); they shared their land with Khas Aryans. The Khas Aryan-centric Nepali government displaced Yakthungs from Yakthung laje and encouraged Khas Aryans or non-Yakthungs to migrate to Yakthung laje, and the vulnerable Yakthungs were forced to share their properties with new immigrants (Limbu, 2016, p. 865; see Caplan, 1970). The Yakthungs were politically forced to even take care of Khas Aryans and their children in Yakthung laje when Khas Aryans beguiled the *rasti-basaune, basti-basaune* campaign. Since the new Khas Aryan settlers and the rulers (Khas Aryan rulers) had a mission to destroy Yakthungs and their cultural, educational, and economic prosperities, they secretly conspired against Yakthungs to confiscate their ancestral lands, to displace them, and to destroy their history and identities. In this regard, Lionel Caplan (1970) states, "The political hierarchy created two centuries ago by Brahman dependence on Yakthung land grants gradually collapsed and was replaced by one in which the Brahmans have become the most powerful group" (p. 9). King Mahendra Shah and his cronies not only illegally confiscated the Yakthung lands, but they also officially supported Bahuns and Chhetris (Khas

Aryans) to seize the Yakthung lands and properties in Yakthung laje (see also Lumphungwa Limbu, 2075 BS, pp. 67–97). For instance, from the late 18th century, Bahuns and Chhetris wrote *tamasuks* (paper bonds) in Nepali. Since Yakthungs were not able to read and write in Nepali, Khas Aryans wrote whatever they wanted on the paper and got the Yakthungs to sign it; later, the Khas Aryans confiscated the ancestral Yakthung lands and properties. The Khas Aryan-centric government and armed forces helped the Bahuns and Chhetris confiscate the land and properties (Caplan, 1970; Khajum-Limbu, 2017, pp. 1–21; Lumphungwa Limbu, 2075 BS, pp. 67–97).

In terms of Yakthung language and literacy, "[d]uring the reign of King Rana Bahadur Shah, a royal order was issued forbidding the use of Limbu (Yakthung) language in any official letter," and Rana Bahadur Shah ordered Abhiman Basnet to capture and execute all Yakthungs who were reading, writing, and promoting their script, writing, language, and literacy (Tumbahang, 2007, p. 74). Tumbahang (2007) further states that "[t]he area of [Yakthung language] use further shrank when Chandra Shumser Rana declared that any document recorded in Yakthung language would have no authentic recognition"; and "if money was lent by a creditor to a debtor preparing a document in Limbu, the complaint resulting from the failure of paying the amount would not be heard in any court" (p. 74). Hence, by abusing the political and military power, the Khas Aryan rulers attempted to eliminate the Yakthung language, writing system, and Mundhum rhetorics for centuries in Yakthung laje (Limbuwan), Nepal.

Lalshor Sendang: his teaching in Yakthung laje (Limbuwan), Sukkhim, and Kalimpong

In this section, I introduce Lalshor Sendang and discuss his contribution to the development of Yakthung language and literacy. Lalshor Sendang (1840–1926) was born and brought up in Athrai Yakthung laje, Nepal. As Hangbir Sendang (father of Lalshor) was a culturally and linguistically conscious Yakthung Suhang, he hid some old Yakthung books when Khas Aryans were destroying Yakthung books in Yakthung laje. Hangbir Sendang dreamed of educating Yakthungs in *Yakthung pa:n* to resist the Khas Aryan oppression and to preserve Yakthung language and literacy. Later, his own son, Lalshor Sendang had an earnest passion to learn Thibong Yakthung history and Mundhum rhetorics (Kainla, 2049 BS, pp. 39–41; Yakthumba, 2062 BS, pp. 80–86). As soon as Sendang knew how to read and write in the Sirijanga script, writing system, and Yakthung Mundhums, he started studying Yakthung books, such as *Mundhum Sapla, Khahun Sapla*, Yakthung histories, and Mundhums. Soon after he had studied Yakthung books, his understanding of Yakthung Mundhum rhetorics sparked a series of inquiries. These inquiries facilitated him to explore Yakthung language and literacies, Yet Hang and Thibong Yakthung historical traditions, and Mundhum pedagogies. Sendang's heuristic and hermeneutic approaches on

Yakthung histories, philosophies, and Mundhum pedagogies added another milestone in the development of Yakthung language and literacies in the modern Yakthung history. For instance, among many scholars, Sendang is believed to have written *Sirijanga Parichaya, Sirijanga Sapla, Kirat Itihasko Lipi,* and *Shiwa Khaun.* Sendang not only wrote about the Sirijanga script, writing system, and Yakthung historical traditions, but he also preached the value of Yakthung Mundhum theories and philosophies. As the Khas Aryan-centric Nepali government banned Yakthungs from the teaching and learning of the Yakthung language, literacies, and Mundhum rhetorics, Sendang organized a group of young Yakthungs, and the young Yakthungs supported his campaign. He taught them the Sirijanga script, writing system, Thibong Yakthung history, and Mundhum rhetorics in Yakthung laje.

According to Bir Nembang (1987), during World War I, the Khas Aryans banished Lalshor Sendang and dozens of his followers who were campaigning the teaching and learning of the Yakthung language, script, and writing. The Khas Aryan political ideology of recruiting Yakthungs to East Indian Army weakened Sendang's campaign of delinking Khas Aryan colonization and relinking of Yakthung Suhang histories, writing system, and Mundhum rhetorics, including Yakthung Suhangs' customary institutional laws and practices. As Sendang's supporters joined WWI, the Khas Aryans were able to suppress Yakthungs' campaign of teaching of the Yakthung language, writing, and Mundhum rhetorics in Yakthung laje. Kajiman Kandangwa (1999) states that Lalshor Sendang was one of the Yakthung scholars, who like Tye Angsi Singthebe, promoted the Sirijanga script, Yakthung language and literacies, and Mundhum rhetorics (p. 49). Sendang advocated for the rights of Yakthungs for traditional customary institutional laws and practices, their mother-tongue education, and rights to their ancestral land; he encouraged Yakthungs to learn their language, Mundhum, and Sawa Yet Hang, Susuwa Lilim Yakthung, Yet Hang, and Thibong Yakthung histories, and how the Khas Aryans imposed their culture and confiscated the ancestral Yakthung lands. Meaning, Sendang waged a campaign in Yakthung communities to delink the Khas Aryan cultural, linguistic, political, and religious colonization. Sendang appealed Yakthungs to relink their Sawa Yet Hang, Susuwa Lilim Yakthung, Yet Hang, and Thibong Yakthung histories and cultural practices and to restore their *khambong-lungbong* (land-based) rights. As I mentioned earlier, Sendang and his cronies went from village-to-village and door-to-door to promote the Yakthung customary institutions, teaching of Yakthung language, writing, and Mundhum literacies literacy (Kandangwa, 1999; Nembang, 1987, p. 12; Tumbahang, 2013, pp. 9–10).

The Khas Aryans detested Lalshor Sendang and his colleagues' campaign of promoting Yakthung language and literacy. To weaken the campaign, the Khas Aryan-centric Nepali government forced Yakthungs from ages 18–50 to join WWI. The shocking reality about Yakthungs' joining WWI was that the Khas Aryan-centric government did not enlist Yakthungs to the official Nepali Army (like other Nepali soldiers were enlisted), but the Khas Aryan government forced Yakthungs to join WWI only as volunteers. After the Khas Aryans dispersed the young Yakthungs in the battlefields during WWI, the Khas Aryan-centric Nepali government banished Lalshor Sendang at the age of 74 from Yakthung laje, Nepal. After the expulsion, Lalshor Sendang stayed in West Sikkim where he continued to promote the Sirijanga script, writing, Mundhum rhetorics (Kandangwa, 1999; Limbu, 2017; Subba, 2015). After a decade of his expulsion, Yakthungs of Kalimpong heard of Sendang, and they requested Sendang to teach them the Sirijanga script, writing system, Mundhum philosophies, and Yakthung histories at Shree Yakthung Hang Chumlung in Dungrabasti. He taught Yakthungs for about a year in Dungrabasti, Kalimpong. Unfortunately, because of his old age and depression due to the Khas Aryan inhumane coercion on him and Yakthungs, he looked and acted very strange. So, in the eyes of Kalimponge Yakthungs, he looked insane and called him *kenangba* (stupid man). Although he taught them on various disciplines, they did not treat him well (K. B. Sambahamphe, personal communication, May 23, 2018).

After Lalshor Sendang had taught at Shree Yakthung Hang Chumlung, he went to Tinkhuti, Assam (India) to visit his daughter, and Sendang passed away there in 1926 at the age of 86. When I went to Assam in May 2018, I asked Assame Yakthungs if they knew about Sendang and his daughter. Sadly, they did not know anything about them. After his banishment, Sendang always wanted to go back to Yakthung laje and wanted to die where he was born. However, the Khas Aryan-centric Nepali government did not allow him to reenter Yakthung laje, Nepal. Despite Sendang's interest to go back and die in the lap of his motherland, the Khas Aryans never accepted his solemn requests (Kandangwa, 1999, p. 49; Nembang, 1987, pp. 11–12). In summation, despite the Khas Aryan, Indian, and British suppression and political ideologies, Yakthungs advocated and fought for their language and literacy. To challenge the Khas Aryan oppression, Yakthungs established Shree Yakthung Hang Chumlung in Kalimpong in 1925 in Dungrabasti, Kalimpong, and they utilized Shree Yakthung Hang Chumlung to delink the Khas Aryan, Indian, and European cultural and linguistic colonization, to relink Yet Hang and Thibong Yakthung Suhang civilization, and link Yakthung language and literacy in local and regional contexts in the early 20th century. The next chapter further exposes how progressive Yakthung intellectuals and activists delinked the Khas Aryan para-colonization; how they relinked Yet Hang and Thing Yakthung cultural traditions; and how they linked Yakthung language, literacy, and Mundhum literacies in local, regional, and global contexts from the early 20th century perspective.

7 Relinking the Sirijanga script/s and writing system

Influence of WWI on Yakthungs, writing, and rhetorics

As I mentioned in the previous chapter, during World War I (WWI), most of the Yakthungs (ages 18 to 50) joined the British East India Company. During the war, Yakthung soldiers got the opportunity to meet European soldiers in the battlefields, where they (Yakthung soldiers) saw the European soldiers writing about war narratives, cultures, people, and events. By seeing the Western counterparts, Yakthung soldiers learned the importance of reading and writing or the importance of being literate; so, they also learned to read and write in Nepali, Hindi, and English. Based on the information, this chapter exhibits how fellow European soldiers influenced Yakthung soldiers, how Yakthung soldiers restored their script and writing system (Khas Aryans banned them from teaching and learning of Yakthung language), and how they (Yakthungs) documented Yakthung cultural traditions and disseminated them in local and regional contexts. Overall, this chapter exposes how Yakthungs of the early 20th century collectively promoted writing and rhetorics to subvert Khas Aryan, Indian, and British colonial discourse and reconstruct Yakthung history, narratives, and Mundhum literacies.

During WWI, when young Yakthungs were in the battlefields, the Khas Aryans not only tortured and/or executed their parents, siblings, and children, they also banished Yakthungs from Yakthung laje. Later, the Khas Aryans did not allow many WWI Yakthung veterans to reenter to Yakthung laje upon their return from the battlefields. The reason WWI veterans were not allowed to reenter to Yakthung laje, for Yakthung soldiers not only had become literate, but also the Khas Aryans' main purpose was to displace Yakthungs as much as they could from Yakthung laje. The Khas Aryan-centric Nepali government forced Yakthungs to either get tortured, executed or to abandon Yakthung laje (Nepal). Due to Khas Aryan's systemic and structural conspiracy, many WWI Yakthung veterans and their families abandoned Yakthung laje. The Khas Aryan's forcing Yakthungs to join WWI, including other wars, was to send them not only to the war zones, but primarily to the death zones, or the Khas Aryans main purpose was to exterminate Yakthungs. During WWI, more than 20,000 Yakthungs, Rais, Magars, and other Indigenous peoples (ages 18–50) were killed (Parker, 2005). These 20,000 soldiers were not the Gorkha soldiers representing Nepal Army, but they were forced to join WWI as volunteers. Meaning, the Khas Aryans forced them (Yakthungs and other Indigenous peoples) to join the British East India Company with the purpose to implicitly eliminate them in the war zones. In fact, WWI, including other wars, was an absolutely futile war for the Yakthungs, including other Nepali Indigenous peoples, but WWI served the Khas Aryan discriminatory government's purpose to displace and destroy Yakthungs from Nepal.

The Khas Aryans purposefully wanted to displace and destroy Yakthungs because they (Yakthungs), like Lalshor Sendang and his cronies, were fighting for their rights based on the Nun-Paani Sandhi (1774). Yakthungs were not only killed and wounded in the battlefields, but they were also psychologically and physically wounded by the Khas Aryans in Nepal. Such Khas Aryan atrocities did not happen only once or twice or thrice in Yakthung laje, but the Khas Aryan brutalities had become a pattern from 1774 to 1990, and the Khas Aryan's discrimination against Yakthungs still exists in multiple forms in Nepal. After the Nun-Paani Sandhi (1774), the Khas Aryan oppressive government both continued to bring a massive number of Khas Aryans to Yakthung laje and constantly banished Yakthungs from Yakthung laje until 1990 (Lumphungwa Limbu, 2075 BS). This is one of the reasons why a huge number of Yakthungs live in Sikkim, India, Bhutan, Burma, Bangladesh, and beyond. The Khas Aryan brutality and abuse of power will not diminish as long as Yakthungs and Indigenous peoples unite and fight for their rights (Limbu et al., 1845; Limbu, 2017).

The Khas Aryan's WWI policy on Yakthung was very ideological, political, and systemic, which forced Yakthungs to leave Yakthung laje and settle in alien places. After the banished Yakthungs had settled in new places, they continued to network with other Yakthungs. They, including the native Yakthungs of Sikkim, Darjeeling, and Kalimpong, taught the Sirijanga script, writing, and Mundhum rhetorics in informal setting (not in Nepal), for the Yakthungs of Darjeeling and Kalimpong were not banned to teach the Sirijanga script, writing system, and Mundhum rhetorics. Though it was sad for Yakthungs to abandon their homeland (Yakthung laje), it was also an opportunity for them, for they could delink Khas Aryan's cultural, political, and linguistic oppression from their new homeland, and they could relink their Sawa Yet Hang, Yet Hang, and Thibong Yakthung social, cultural, linguistic, and Mundhumic epistemologies. This setting suggests that Yakthungs who lived outside Nepal became culturally and linguistically conscious and were also free to learn their language and writing system unlike Nepal. As I already mentioned, Yakthungs of Sikkim were still hesitant to teach and learn the Sirijanga script, writing system, and Mundhum rhetorics after the execution of Singthebe (1741) until 1968.

The banished Yakthungs and native Yakthungs of Kalimpong founded Shree Yakthung Hang Chumlung on July 26, 1925 in Dungrabasti, Kalimpong.

Immediately after the foundation of Shree Yakthung Hang Chumlung, Yakthungs founded other social institutions in Yakthung communities as well. Through the Yakthung social institutions, they collectively challenged the Khas Aryan cultural and linguistic colonization, or they started delinking the Nepali, Indian, and European cultural and linguistic colonization and relinking traditional Yakthung Suhang customary laws, writing, and Mundhum rhetorics. Similarly, Phalgunanda and his followers also popularized the Sirijanga script, Yakthung language, and Mundhum literacies in the name of Satya Hangma Pantha to some extent in some places in Yakthung laje. Satya Hangma Panthi Yakthungs taught Yakthungs to read and write the Sirijanga script; they documented and taught Yakthung Mundhums in the name of religious preaching (Kandangwa, 1999; Nembang, 1987, p. 13). The Satya Hangma Pantha followers played a significant role to delink Khas Aryan cultural, linguistic, and religious colonization and to relink traditional Yakthung Suhang language, literacy, and rhetorical traditions in Nepal. Similarly, the Yakthungs, in the early 20th century, collectively reintroduced the Sirijanga script both in Kalimpong, including Nepal, for the first time in the modern Yakthung history. Historically, during 1845–1857, Hodgson requested Jobhansing Limbu, Chyangresing Phedangba, Ranadhoj, and Jit Mohan to document the Sirijanga script, writing system, Yakthung Suhang histories, Mundhum narratives, and Yakthung cultural practices. As Limbu et al. (1845–57) documented Yakthung history, Mundhum, language and literacy, I call them the documentarians of Yakthung culture of the 19th century.

As I mentioned above, in terms of the early 20th century Yakthung language and literacy, the Yakthungs of Kalimpong waged a campaign to reintroduce Yakthung Suhang language, literacy, and Mundhum literacies. I call them, the "First-Generation Yakthung Scholars" of the modern Yakthung history. Among many other scholars, some of the prominent Yakthung scholars were:

1   Harka Prasad Limbu
2   Bajbir Subba (Thalang)
3   Kalusing Papo
4   Tilaksing Nugo
5   Harkajang Makhim
6   Dr. I. K. Bahadur Sereng
7   C. B. Rai Sangma
8   Maitasing Thegim
9   Jit Bahadur Thebe
10   Daroga Dhanraj Phenduwa
11   Buddhiraj Phago
12   Jibandas Rai
13   Lalsing Subba
14   Narbir Ijam

15   Ashman Subba
16   Manbahadur Limbu (from Burma)
17   Imansing Chemjong
(see also Kainla, 2049 BS, pp. 49–50)

As Yakthungs knew the power and prestige of collective Yakthung intellectual power, they also founded other Yakthung organizations, such as Akhil Sikkim Kirat Limbu Chumlung, Yakthung Sapsak Sakchumbho (Sikkim), Akhil Bharatiya Kirat Chumlung Sabha (Darjeeling), Sarba Kirat Chumlung (Kalimpong), Kirat Dharma Tatha Sahitya Utthan Sanga (Damak and Kathmandu), and Akhil Burma Chumlung (Burma). Yakthungs knew that the founding of Yakthung-centric social institutions would foster Yakthung collaborative initiatives to delink the Khas Aryan oppression and to relink the Yet Hang and Thibong Yakthung cultural traditions.

The Yakthung collaborative initiatives and Yakthung social institutions, not only created space for the teaching and learning of Yakthung writing and rhetorics, but they also united Yakthungs from India, Sikkim, Bhutan, and Burma to network, collaborate, and document Yakthung histories, Mundhum narratives, and Yet Hang, Thibong Yakthung, and Yakthung Suhang rhetorical traditions. Within a decade of the foundation of Shree Yakthung Hang Chumlung, Yakthungs wrote and published more than a dozen books on Yakthung culture, history, cultural practices, and Mundhums rhetorics. Some noteworthy books/booklets they published during this period were:

1   Tum Yakthung Ningwaphu Sapla (1928) by Bajbir Subba
2   Nisigek Yakthung Sapla (1931) by Imansing Chemjong and Bajbir Tholong (Subba)
3   Yakthung Sewa Samlo (1930) by Kalusing Papo
4   Kirat Yakthung Mundhum (1931) by Buddhiraj Phago and Jasman Sangwa
5   Mad-pan Nisedh (1930) by Harkajang Makhim
6   Sabda Sangrah (1930) by Harkajang Makhim
7   Kirat Barnamala (1931) by Ser Bahadur Neyonghang and Mohan Lal Hangam (the medium of print of lithography and was published from Mewakhola, Taplejung, Limbuwan).
8   Yakthung Hisab Hapla (?)
9   Sirijanga Mundhum Sapla (?)
10   Sumsigek Mundhum Sapla (?)
11   Tum Yakthung Sapla (1931) by E. K. Bahadur Sereng
12   Tum Yakthung Sapla (?) by Nirmal Limbu
13   Kirat Barnamala (?) by Sher Bahadur Meyohang and Mohan Lal Hangam
14   Kirat Mundhum (?) by Tilaksing Nugo
(see Kainla, 2049 BS, pp. 43–44; Limbu, 2017, pp. 577–578)

The medium of publication during this period was lithography. Lithography is a process of printing from a metal surface on which the printing areas are not raised, but are made in-receptive while the non-image areas are made in-repellent. Through this printing process, Yakthung books and pamphlets were published during the early 20th century.

After the foundation of Shree Yakthung Hang Chumlung, Yakthungs not only became consumers of Khas Aryan, Indian, and European knowledge, they also became prosumers (producer and consumer) of knowledge in their own Yakthung language and Sirijanga script. Through various Yakthung social institutions and networks, Yakthungs reformulated Sawa Yet Hang, Yet Hang, and Thibong Yakthung-centric epistemologies that, for the first time, valued their language, validated their writing, and respected their Yakthung rhetorical traditions. The first-generation Yakthung scholars utilized writing as a powerful tool not only to network, collaborate, and document Yakthung language and literacy, but also to disseminate and preserve Yakthung knowledge, history, and Mundhum rhetorics. The first-generation Yakthung scholars' writing and rhetorics embodied the ethos of their reflexivity that emphasized delinking para-colonization and relinking Yakthung Suhang rhetorical traditions rather than just an inclusion in pre-existing Yakthung language and literacies. The delinking local colonization redirected a deep commitment of Yakthungs to their exploration of Thibong Yakthung cultural traditions. The first-generation Yakthungs' documentation of Yakthung culture, language, and literacy echoed Yakthungs of who they had been, who they are now, who they should be, and how they can delink cultural colonization and relink their own Yet Hang and Thibong Yakthung cultural traditions. From this perspective, the first generation Yakthung scholars shaped Yakthung knowledge, language, writing system, and Mundhum literacies. This age was one of the prominent periods for Yakthungs in relation to delinking cultural colonization, relinking Yet Hang and Thibong Yakthung traditional epistemologies, and linking Yakthung Suhang cultural practices in local and regional contexts. However, the first-generation Yakthung scholars were not familiar with the Old Sirijanga script due to the Khas Aryan oppression in Yakthung laje, Nepal, and Bhutia suppression in Sikkim. As a result, they unintentionally shifted the /a/-based Sirijanga script to the /∂/-based one (will discuss later).

Bajbir Subba (Thalang): sites of the Sirijanga script/s, writing, and rhetorics

Bajbir Subba (Thalang) served for the Indian Imperial Police in Burma and was promoted up to "Subedar" (Kainla, 2049 BS, pp. 90–91; Yakthumba, 2062 BS). While Subba was in the service, a globally well-known author, George Orwell, also joined the same Indian Imperial Police in Burma as a policeman in 1922. As Subba was promoted up to "Subedar," we find his name written as "Subedar Bajbir Subba" in his books. After he retired from the Burma Police Force, he settled in Kharsang, West Bengal, India (Kainla, 2049, pp. 90–91; B. Kirati, personal communication, May 10, 2018). We find Subba's name as Bajbir Subba in his book *Tum Yakthung Ningwaphu Sapla* (1928), Bajbir "Tholong" in *Nisigek Yakthung Sapla* (1931), and Bajbir Thalang in *Yakthung Nisigek Sapla* in 1951. Subba's *Tum Yakthung Ningwaphu Sapla* (see figure 15) was the first Yakthung grammar book published after the foundation of Shree Yakthung Hang Chumlung in 1925 in Kalimpong. Subba's *Tum Yakthung Ningwaphu Sapla* (1928) became popular in Yakthung communities; the book was reprinted many times and was widely distributed in Yakthung communities, such as in Nepal, Darjeeling, Kalimpong, Sikkim, Assam, Bhutan, Burma, and Thailand. As I stated earlier, the script that Bajbir Subba reintroduced did not resemble the Tye Angsian Sirijanga script or the Old Sirijanga script; it rather resembled the Devanagari script. Therefore, I call it, the "Bajbirian Sirijanga script," and Yakthungs started following the Bajbirian Sirijanga script. Bajbir Tholong (he wrote "Tholong" in this book) co-authored *Nisigek Yakthung Sapla* (a small booklet) with Imansing Chemjong in 1931 (see figure 17). Since Subba was exposed to Hindi, Nepali, and English, we can see the heavy influence of the Hindi and Nepali writing system in his books.

Because of Bajbir Subba's personal and professional background, or as he was familiar with Devanagari script, he shifted the old Yakthung /a/-based syllabary, the Old Sirijanga script to the New Sirijanga /∂/-based syllabary. Because Bajbir Subba was literate in Hindi and Nepali, I believed that the

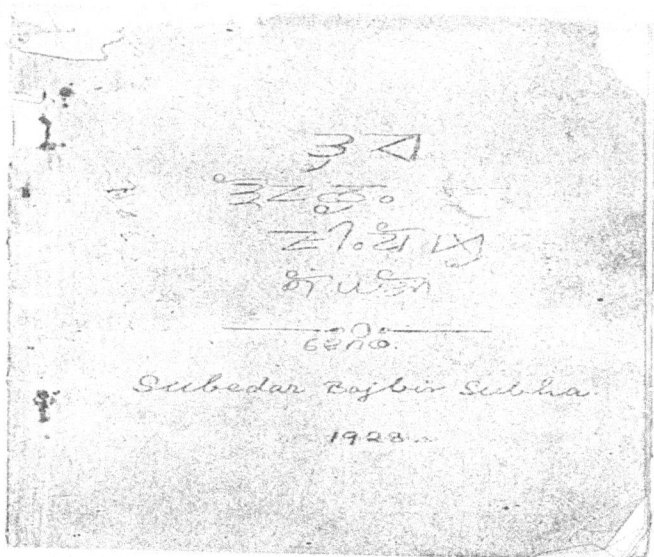

Figure 15 Bajbir Subba's *Tum Yakthung Ningwaphu Sapla* published in 1928 (Source: Ambar Jang Limbu).

Sirijanga script would look like the Devanagari script because he saw many writing systems looked like the Devanagari script in this region (implying the influence of the Brahmi script). Subba also did not know the phonological differences between Nepali, Hindi, and Yakthung, and Imansing Chemjong did not see the differences either. As Bajbir Subba, including Imansing Chemjong, did not see the Old Sirijanga script, Subba was content with his new redesign.

When Lalshor Sendang taught Yakthungs the Sirijanga script, writing system, and Mundhum philosophies, Yakthungs, including Bajbir Subba and Imansing Chemjong, also disregarded his old Yakthung knowledge, for many Yakthungs called him (Sendang) insane and stupid. Bajbir Subba (Thalang) and Imansing Chemjong's choice of writing style was not who they actually were (they ignored Yakthungness), but they valued the Khas Aryan, Indian, and European knowledge. Therefore, they mimicked the Devanagari script (Hindi and Nepali) and Roman script (English) rather than the Old Sirijanga script (see figure 5). They did not write the Yakthung words the way they were/are pronounced in *Yakthung pa:n*, they rather followed European style. For instance, they wrote "Sirij**u**nga" for "Sirijanga," "Zamb**u**k" for "Jambak," and "Dungrab**u**sti" for "Dungrabasti." They ignored Lalshor Sendang and were also unaware of Yakthungness or Yakthung phonology. Therefore, they mimicked Hindi, English, and Nepali; Subba and Chemjong did not know that mimicry was a menace. Honestly, there are still many *Yakthung phu-ne-nusa* who tend to mimic Nepali, Hindi, and English in the 21st century; they still believe that their mimicry elevates their social and academic standards. Due to the lack of Yakthungs' critical thinking, their

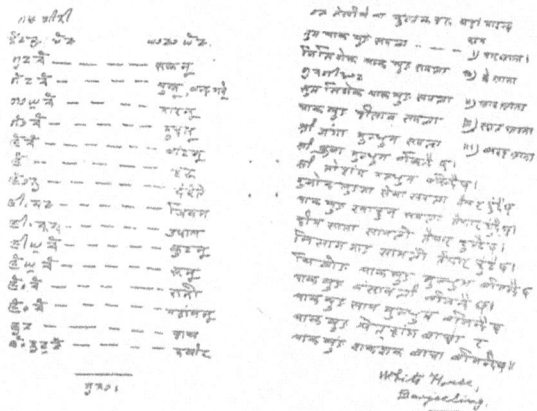

Figure 16 List of books Yakthungs published, but mysteriously most of them are not available now (from *Tum Yakthung Ningwaphu Sapla* 1928) (Source: Ambar Jang Limbu).

mimicry is hurting Yakthung Suhang cultural studies. Yakthungs mimic because they have been programmed to believe that their language is inferior to Nepali, Hindi, and English (I mentioned with evidence in this book). The British colonial epistemology made us observe our culture and language via the colonial lenses, and they made us disregard our own Yakthung language, culture, and writing. The British colonizers made us believe that English is the most prestigious language in the world. Currently, though Yakthungs seem to preserve their language and writing, they still believe that Anglicizing Yakthung words would elevate their academic ethos.

As I stated earlier, Bajbir Subba was the first Yakthung writer who wrote *Tum Yakthung Ningwaphu Sapla* (1928) in the New Sirijanga script after the foundation of Shree Yakthung Hang Chumlung in 1925. Lalshor Sendang (who was banished by the Khas Aryans from Nepal) taught the Sirijanga writing system and Mundhum rhetorics to Yakthungs at Shree Yakthung Hang Chumlung in Dungrabasti, Kalimpong. However, I did not find any written Yakthung grammar books that he wrote, and I did not find any books that he used to teach his students in Nepal, Sikkim, and Kalimpong. I went to Yakthoong Shong Chombho (a Yakthung social institution) in Dungrabasti, Kalimpong in 2018 and asked Yakthungs the same questions, and they did not know anything either. In his *Tum Yakthung Ningwaphu Sapla* (1928), Bajbir Subba states, "according to Guru"; he perhaps called Lalshor Sendang a "Guru," for I have not heard of any other Gurus (teachers) in Yakthung communities from the early 20th century except Lalshor Sendang (obviously, he did not imply Phalgunanda as Guru, for Phalgunanda was a "Hawaldar," and he (Bajbir) was a "Subedar" in the Armed force), and if Bajbir Subba implied Tye Angsi Singthebe as a Guru, his writing system and script would have been in the original Old Sirijanga script.

As I stated earlier, Yakthungs published Yakthung books (booklets) in varied genres after the foundation of Shree Yakthung Hang Chumlung. As you see in figure 16, they advertised a series of their publications to promote and disseminate Yakthung language and literacy. However, the list does not include Lalshor Sendang's books. Figure 16 suggests that he did not write any books during his stay in Kalimpong. Perhaps, Sendang had written books before the Khas Aryans banished him from Nepal and during his stay in West Sukhim, and the Khas Aryans also collected almost all Yakthung books and documents during WWI and burned more than 60,000 books in Chainpur, Limbuwan (Nembang, 1987, p. 12; Pallo Kirat Limbuwan, 2066 BS, p. 5). When he taught at Shree Yakthung Hang Chumlung, he was already 85 years old. Additionally, as shown in figure 16, I found only *Tum Yakthung Ningwaphu Sapla* (Subba, 1928) and *Nisigek Yakthung Sapla* (Chemjong & Tholong, 1931). Other than these two books, I neither found any other books nor met any individual who could talk about the books during my research (see figure 16). During my research, I also did not find any written document in the Sirijanga script published (documented) between the era of Jobhansing Limbu, Chyangresing Phedangba, Ranadhoj Limbu, and Jit Mohan and Lalshor

Sendang. I also did not find any Yakthung grammar books or Mundhum books written between 1857 or 1867 and 1928, or before Bajbir Subba's *Tum Yakthung Ningwaphu Sapla* (1928) and after Hodgson's last collection (1867).

Bajbir Subba profoundly shifted the Old Sirijanga writing system to the New Sirijanga script. Subba's contemporary Yakthung scholars, such as Imansing Chemjong, Kalusing Papo, Buddhiraj Phago, Jasman Sangwa, Harkajang Makhim, E. K. Bahadur Sereng, Sher Bahadur Neyonghang, Nirmal Limbu, Mohan Lal Hangam, Buddhi Raj Phago, Jash Man Sangwa, and Tiloksing Nugo, also followed the Bajbirian writing system. Though Bajbir Tholong (Subba) and Imansing Chemjong collaborated to write Yakthung books, they could not detect the shift in the script and writing system. The reason was because neither of them were linguists, grammarians, or fluent Yakthung language speakers; meaning, neither of them had an advanced Yakthung language competence. Perhaps, when Lalshor Sendang taught Yakthungs the Sirijanga script, they did not quite understand the /a/-based Yakthung phonology and the /a/-based Old Sirijanga script. Bajbir Subba and Imansing Chemjong's not knowing the Yakthung phonology and the Old Sirijanga script adversely affected the development of the Sirijanga syllabary from the early 20th century. So, whatever script or writing system, Bajbir Subba introduced in his *Tum Yakthung Ningwaphu Sapla* (1928), Imansing Chemjong did not amend any syllabary and writing system when Bajbir Subba and Imansing Chemjong wrote *Nisigek Yakthung Sapla* in 1931 (see figure 17). Hence, Imansing Chemjong, including Kalusing Papo, Buddhiraj Phago, Jasman Sangwa, Harkajang Makhim, E. K. Bahadur Sereng, Sher Bahadur Neyonghang, Nirmal Limbu, Mohan Lal Hangam, Buddhi Raj Phago, Jash

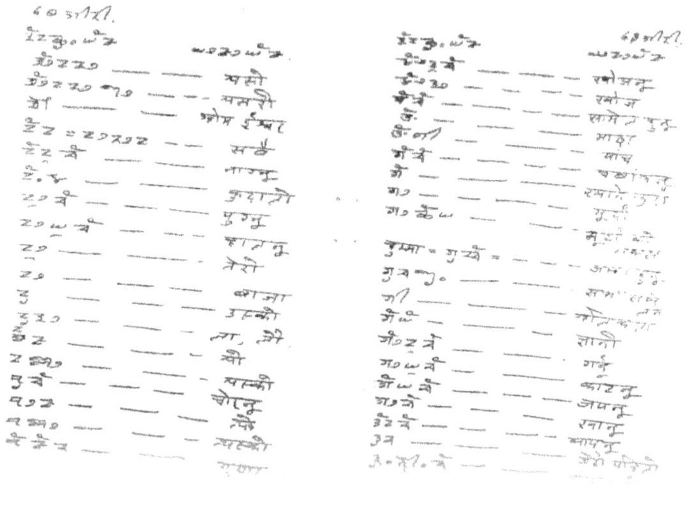

Figure 17 Nisigek Yakthung Sapla by Imansing Chemjong and Bajbir Tholong (1931) (Source: Ambar Jang Limbu).

Man Sangwa, and Tiloksing Nugo, continued to follow the Bajbirian Sirijanga writing system without any questions. Meaning, the Yakthungs of the early 20th century approved the Bajbirian Sirijanga script, for neither of them was literate in the Old Tye Angsian Sirijanga syllabary. Moreover, they had never even seen the Hodgson collection (Yakthung books and manuscripts) until R. K. Sprigg brought some copies of the manuscripts (Hodgson collection implied) to Nepal in 1955 from the British Library, London.

In terms of the naming of the script, Yakthungs of the early 20th century were the ones who entitled the script, the "Sirijanga script" for the first time in 1925 at Shree Yakthung Hang Chumlung. Henceforth, Yakthungs started calling it, the "Sirijanga script." Although Yakthungs unanimously decided to name the script, the Sirijanga script, Bajbir Subba in his *Tum-Yakthung Ningwaphu Sapla* 1928) called the script, "Kirat Yakthung akchhar." In a nutshell, the Yakthungs of the early 20th century were the ones who campaigned the decolonial movement. They were the first Yakthung scholars who collectively denaturalized the Khas Aryan, Indian, and Western cultural and linguistic colonization. They were the ones who relinked traditional Yakthung Suhang cultural epistemologies from the early 20st century Yakthungs' perspective. They were the ones who sowed the seed of Yakthung Suhang emancipation from the Khas Aryan, Indian, and European cultural and linguistic colonization.

During my research tour in 2018, when I went to Dungrabasti, Kalimpong, I had the opportunity to converse with Lalit Thegim, a grandson of Maita Thegim. Thegim mentioned that Man Bahadur Sereng helped Bajbir Subba to the production of his Yakthung books, and Sereng was originally from Assam, India. In terms of Imansing Chemjong's role at Shree Yakthung Hang Chumlung, both Thegim (2018) and K. B. Sambahamphe (2018) stated that the Yakthungs of Kalimpong were reluctant to allow Chemjong to participate in the Chumlung activities as much as he wanted due to his Christian religious faith. Thegim (2018) and Sambahamphe (2018) mentioned that, in the early 20th century, Yakthungs did not quite value Christianity in Yakthung communities and Kalimponge Yakthungs were hesitant to approve Chemjong's active participation in most of the Yakthung activities.

Phalgunanda Lingden's Satya Hangma Pantha: sites of Yakthung language and literacies

Phalgunanda (Phalamsing) Lingden (1942–2005 BS) is also known as "Mahaguru Phalgunanda." While Phalgunanda was in the army (WW I implied), he saw the deaths, disasters, and destructions caused by the war. In the battlefields, Phalgunanda vividly experienced the demeaning and debasing traits of human beings. So, after the war was over, he returned to his homeland and founded Satya Dharma Muchulka in 1988 BS (1931). Phalgunanda not only experienced human devastations caused by the war in the global context, but he also vividly experienced the Khas Aryan brutalities over Yakthungs in a local context. He saw the culturally, linguistically, and politically fragmented Yakthungs and hopeless Yakthung communities in Nepal and beyond. He detested the way the Khas Aryans divided Yakthungs as *niti* (traditional Yakthung customary institutional law and practice supporters) and *samariti* (Gorkha/Khas Aryan statutory law supporters) and constructed Yakthung knowledge, souls, and minds. Phalgunanda, including other Yakthungs, experienced the deteriorating Yakthung cultural traditions due to the Khas Aryan oppressions over them. At the same time, Yakthungs, due to the depression and frustration, developed the habit of drinking and spending too much wealth on feasts, festivals, and other Yakthung rituals. It was mainly due to depression, humiliation, and oppression, Yakthungs and Yakthung culture broke into pieces (see also Limbu, 2019). Having seen the deteriorated Yakthung circumstances, Phalgunanda was determined to reform Yakthung communities in local or regional contexts, such as Nepal, India, Bhutan, Sikkim, and Burma implied. Phalgunanda wanted to denaturalize the Khas Aryan politics of knowledge construction in Yakthung laje, for after the Nun-Paani Sandhi, the Khas Aryans divided Yakthungs into two groups: *niti* (traditional Yakthung customary institutional law and practice supporters) and *samariti* (Gorkha/Khas Aryan statutory law supporters). It was an ongoing disgusting disunity among Yakthungs as *niti* and *samariti* Yakthungs (Limbu, et al., 1845–57; Lumphungwa Limbu, 2075 BS, pp. 55–60; Schlemmer, 2003/2004, p. 138). Hence, Phalgunanda founded Satya Dharma Muchulka in 1988 BS (1931) to unite Yakthungs and reform Yakthungs' deteriorated cultural practices, and Mundhum practices. As I implied, Phalgunanda was mainly a socio-cultural reformist, educator, and activist. This was one of the reasons why he introduced Satya Dharma Muchulka, both to bring social changes in Yakthung laje and to restore Yakthung language, script, and writing (B. Kainla, personal communication, January 3, 2015; Laoti, 2069 BS, pp. 357–60). By introducing Satya Dharma Muchulka in Yakthung laje, Phalgunanda overtly or covertly challenged the systemic and structural Khas Arya hegemony. While Khas Aryans were suppressing the teaching of Yakthung language, writing, and literacy, he restored the Yakthung language, writing, and Mundhum rhetorics as a challenge to Khas Aryan authorities in Nepal. I gathered many documents from Satya Hangma Muchulka and old Satya Hangma Mundhum, and based on the documents, I can state that Phalgunanda pursued what Kalimponge Yakthungs initiated in Kalimpong and Darjeeling. I am not arguing that Yakthungs did not read and write in the Sirijanga script in Yakthung laje, Nepal, but Satya Hangma Mundhum documents seem to follow the Bajbirian Sirijanga writing system, not the Old Sirijanga script. If Satya Hangma Panth developed the Sirijanga script and writing system independent to Kalimponge Yakthung language and literacy movement, they would have used the Old Sirijanga script (because the Old Sirijanga script was used until the late 1860s according to the documents I found).

Among many others, the purpose of the Satya Dharma Muchulka was to establish peace, harmony, humility, and unity of Yakthungs within Yakthung laje, Limbuwan and beyond because Phalgunanda saw the demeaning practices of Khas Aryans, and how they were robbing Yakthungs, torturing Yakthung, and displacing Yakthungs from Yakthung laje and were confiscating their lands and other properties (Khajum-Limbu, 2017; Limbu, 2016, 2017; Limbu, 2019; Nembang, 1987, p. 11). Phalgunanda not only saw how the Khas Aryans coerced Yakthungs to disregard their own culture, language, writing, and Mundhum rhetorics, but also vividly saw how Khas Aryan ideologies petrified Thibong Yakthung knowledge and Yakthung Suhang customary cultural traditions. For instance, Phalgunanda, including Yakthung activists and community leaders, saw how the Khas Aryans petrified the Yakthung body, mind, and soul, and how Khas Aryan politics impaired their *phu-ne-nusa* relationships in Yakthung laje (Limbu, 2016, 2017; Limbu, 2019). Therefore, as I implied earlier, Phalgunanda founded Satya Dharma Muchulka to relink Sawa Yet Hang, Susuwa Lilim Yakthung, Yet Hang, and Thibong Yakthung Mundhum rhetorics and *khambong-lungbong* identities. Through Satya Dharma Muchulka, Phalgunanda and his cronies attempted to heal Yakthungs and Yakthung communities that were torn apart for centuries.

Gregoire Schlemmer (2003/2004) states that Khas Aryans invaded Yakthung laje; they divided, displaced, and destroyed Yakthungs' unity in Yakthung laje. Schlemmer (2003/2004) claims that the Khas Aryans were the main cause of Kirat and/or Yakthung disunity. The Khas Aryan oppression "led to the disintegration of the [M]undhum and the loss of harmony between the Kirant, their land and their ancestors, and was moreover the cause of their current poverty, backwardness, and low political representation" (p. 138). Phalgunanda was shocked to see the impaired Yakthung culture, shattered Yakthung unity, and loss of the Yakthung language and writing system. Therefore, to educate Yakthungs and to address impaired Yakthung Suhang culture, language, and literacy, Phalgunanda travelled some parts of the Yakthung laje region and preached Yakthungs on their social, cultural, political, and linguistic issues (I did not see any Satya Hangma Pathi Yakthungs in my region—I am from Sungnam, Phedap region). Phalgunanda is believed to have travelled some parts of Yakthung laje and Sikkim to help Yakthungs to reform Yakthung social and cultural practices. Phalgunanda and his followers established many *Mang-hims* (temples) in Yakthung laje, such as:

1   Charkhola, Chukinamba, 1986 BS: Priest Badrinanda Tumbapo
2   Panchathar, Lalikharka, 1988 BS: Priest Baijanaath Tumbapo
3   Yangrup, Kabeli, 1992 BS: Gangadil Tumbapo
4   Panchathar, Silouti, 1985 BS: Siddhananda Phejong
5   Athrai, Nigraden, Chilingse: 1997 BS: Bisonanda Yonghang
6   Charkhola, Jitpur, 1999 BS: Nardil Lingden
7   West Sikkim, Khamdong

These social and religious institutions greatly contributed to the development of Yakthung language, the Sirijanga script, and Mundhum rhetorics. Satya

Dharma Muchulka promoted the mother-tongue education in the informal context (Angbunghang, 2069 BS; Kandangwa, 1999, p. 49; Tumbahang, 2013, pp. 10–11).

Satya Hangma Pantha quickly became popular after the Chukinamba Temple was built in 1988 BS, and they (Satya Hangma Panthis) became successful in documenting, preserving, and disseminating the Sirijanga script, writing, and *Yakthung pa:n*. As the Chukinamba temple had a positive impact on Yakthungs and Yakthung communities, they built several other temples, such as Charkhola, Chukinamba (1988 BS), Panchathar, Lalikharka (1988 BS), Yangrup, Kabeli (1992 BS), Panchathar, Silauti (1985 BS), Athrai, Nigraden, Chilingse (1997 BS), Charkhola, Jitpur (1999 BS), and West Sikkim, Khamdong. Satya Dharma Muchulka priests wrote Yakthung Mundhums and hymns, such as *Hangsam Sak Sap*, *Thakthuk Sewa Sak Sap*, *Sikkum Ningwabhu Manglak Sap*, *Hang Sam Samyo Sak Sak*, and *Siwa Khahun*. The establishment of Satya Hangma temples and documentation of Mundhums in the Sirijanga script in Yakthung language intersected religion, Sirijanga syllabary, Mundhums, and Yakthung Suhang cultural traditions. The intersectionality of Satya Dharma Muchulka, the Sirijanga script, Mundhum texts, and *Yakthung pa:n* promoted as well as prompted the teaching and learning of Yakthung language, Mundhum, writing, and rhetorics.

Phalgunanda's theoretical, philosophical, and conceptual idea of Satya Hangma was political and ideological. His religious theory and philosophy facilitated the teaching of Yakthung language and writing; meaning, Satya Hangma Panth required the followers to be literate in the Sirijanga script, writing system, and Yakthung Mundhum. Since the number of *sewa-sabas* (priests) gradually increased in Yakthung communities, the number of priests also increased. For the Satya Hangma Pantha priests and followers had to perform rituals in Yakthung Mundhum, they were/are required to have basic knowledge of reading and writing in the Sirijanga script and Yakthung language. The Satya Hangma priests were compulsorily required to chant Mundhums in *Yakthung pa:n* (Limbu language) in other words, the Satya Hangma Pantha priests were obligated to be literate in the Sirijanga script (Laoti, 2069 BS, pp. 357–60). The Satya Hangma followers not only became literate in *Yakthung pa:n* and writing (in the Sirijanga script) to perform the religious hymns and mantras, but they (Satya Hangma followers) had to write Satya Hangma hymns, mantras, and Mundhums.

As the new settlers, especially Khas Aryans, saw the increasing number of Phalgunandian followers, Kanchan Giri, a Khas-Arya, was against the Yakthung literacy movement, and he reported to the Khas Aryan administrators that Phalgunanda and his cronies were revolting against the Nepali government. Phalgunanda was immediately arrested and was brought to Dhankuta. The Khas Aryan authorities, however, did not find him guilty as Phalgunanda could justify that they had been promoting religion in Yakthung communities (Gurung & Dahal, 2064 BS, pp. 47–48; Kainla, 2049 BS, pp. 44–48; Nembang, 1987, p. 13). It is quite clear to us that the Khas Aryan authorities did not allow him to promote the Sirijanga writing system, Yakthung language and literacy, and Yakthung religion in the traditional Yakthung way in Yakthung communities during the Rana regime. For instance, the Khas Aryans banished Lalshor Sendang and his cronies for their teaching and learning of Yakthung language, script, and writing, and they also burned more than 60,000 books during WWI (Nembang, 1987, p. 12; "Pallo Kirat Limbuwan" 2066 BS, p. 5). The Khas Aryans forced Yakthungs to convert to Hinduism during the Janga Bahadur Rana's regime, and Rana raised the Yakthung land taxes when Yakthungs rejected his order. The Khas Aryans tortured, executed, or banished if Yakthungs resisted the Khas Aryans law and order after their invasion in Yakthung laje. So, we can speculate that there had been a negotiation between Phalgunanda Linden and the Khas Aryan authorities to promote the Hinduism or a Hindu-like religion in Yakthung communities (Limbu, 2017, p. 583) because the Khas Aryan authorities had been coercing Yakthungs to convert to Chhetri or Hindu and wear *janai* (thread, Khas Aryans wear round the shoulder) from the 19th century (Janga Bahadur Rana's religious policy implied).

In the late 1970s, Satya Hangma Panthis changed their religious identity from Satya Hangma religion to Kirat religion. Since the Kirat religion (Kirat Guru and followers) mimics Hindu religious practices, other Yakthungs who are known as Yuma Samyo are advocating for fundamental Yakthung cultural practices and are revolting against the Hindu-like practices. Therefore, lately, there are many Yakthungs who tend to condemn the Satya Hangmaism (P. Pomo, personal communication, May 21, 2018). Based on my research findings, I believe that as Satya Hang Panthi religious practices were formulated during the oppressive Rana regime, and Phalgunanda also suggested his followers to reform the Hindu like practices later. Despite the reformation of the Hindu like practices, the Mangsebunge Kirat religious folks have capitalized the "Kirat" terminology for their benefits, and it is not promoting the Yakthung customary tradition, but polluting it; it is helping to reform Yakthung culture that Phalgunanda saw, but it is hurting. Though there was/is a harsh criticism over his introduction of Hindu-like Satya Hangma cultural and religious practices, Phalgunanda, without doubt, strategically popularized the Sirijanga script, writing system, and Mundhum in Nepal. Currently, we live in the 21st century's democratic society; we (*Yakthung phu-ne-nusa*) ought to delink the Khas Aryan oppression and relink our Sawa Yet Hang, Yet Hang, and Thibong Yakthung cultural traditions and practices. Despite the fact that the teaching of Yakthung language and writing was banned during the Phalgunandian era, in the name of Satya Hangma Pantha, Satya Hangma Pantha followers delinked Khas Aryan linguistic and cultural colonization, and the language and literacy; for instance, they learned to read, write, and chant Mundhums in *Yakthung pa:n* in the Sirijanga script. The Satya Hangma Pantha followers paved the early sites of delinking the Khas Aryan politics of knowledge construction, and they relinked Sawa Yet Hang, Susuwa Lilim Yakthung, and Thibong Yakthung customary cultural traditions.

8 The influence of other scripts and emergence of delinking, relinking, and linking approach

King Sirijanga redesigned the (Sirijanga) script upon the foundation of the Himalayan Indigenous peoples' writing system that had been designed and practiced during the King Maarang, and King Sirijanga's reigns (Kandangwa, 1999, pp. 44–55; Laoti, 2005, p. 143; Subba, 1995, p. 294, Subba, 1989, pp. 41–42). The Kirat kings, including King Maarang, had used the script to document Yakthung Mundhums, oral histories, and Royal chronicles and to communicate within Yakthung laje and other neighboring nations. The construction and design of the Sirijanga script is different from many South Asian, Southeast Asian, and East Asian scripts. Based on the construction and design of the script, we can state that the Sirijanga script developed independently to other scripts. However, I have not yet found any document written in this script during the King Sirijangian era. In the 18th century, Tye Angsi Singthebe (1704–1741) once again redesigned and popularized the Sirijanga script in Yakthung laje. We still find many books and manuscripts written by Singthebe and his followers in this script. Later, in the mid-19th century (1845–1857), Yakthungs continued to use this script to document Yakthung histories, narratives, stories, cultural practices, and Mundhum rhetorics (Hodgson collection implied). After the Khas Aryan invasion in Yakthung laje, Khas Aryans destroyed all Yakthung books, documents, and other archival materials and banned the teaching and learning of *Yakthung pa:n* (Yakthung language). Based on the background information, this chapter discusses the influence of Nepali and Hindi on the Sirijanga script and writing system, and how the Old Sirijanga script and old Yakthung writing system shifted to the new Bajbirian Sirijanga writing system. This chapter stresses how the Khas Aryan's banning the teaching of Yakthung language and writing adversely impacted the development of Yakthung language and literacy. Furthermore, this chapter demonstrates my critical understanding, interpretation, and analysis of Yakthung language and literacy in relation to transcultural, transborder, and political terrains on how cultures both adopt and reject culture, writing, and rhetorics.

Historically, after Yakthung laje (Limbuwan) was annexed to the Gurkha kingdom (see Chapter 4), we can detect the influence of Khas Aryan culture in many aspects, such as language, culture, politics, religion, and writing. The Khas Aryans forced the Wallo Kiratis (Kõits/Kõiches), Majha Kiratis

(Khambus), and Pallo Kiratis (Yakthungs) to learn and speak Nepali (Khas) language and to follow the Hindu religion. In relation to Yakthungs and Yakthung laje, by violating the Nun-Paani Sandhi between Prithvi Narayan Shah (Gorkha) and Yakthung chiefs (see Lumphungwa Limbu, 2075 BS, pp. 57–59), the Khas Aryans forced Yakthungs to give up the teaching and learning of the Sirijanga script, writing, and *Yakthung pa:n*. The Khas Aryans politically and militarily coerced Yakthungs to embrace their culture, language, writing, and religion (1774 to 1990). As Khas Aryans imposed Yakthungs to learn Nepali language to pursue Hindu cultural traditions, and to follow Hindu religious practices, Yakthungs, to some extent, forgot their Thibong Yakthung history and cultural traditions. For instance, when Jobhansing Limbu, Chyangresing Phedangba, Ranadhoj Limbu, and Jit Mohan documented Yakthung rhetorical traditions from 1845–57, they mentioned that they did not know what their religion was. Meaning, within the first century after their encroachment to Yakthung laje, the Khas Aryans were able to displace and destroy Yakthung cultural traditions and were able to orient Yakthungs to see Thibong Yakthung rhetorical traditions and Yakthung Suhang cultural practices from the Khas Aryan lenses. When Imansing Chemjong, Bajbir Subba, and other Yakthungs campaigned for the development of Yakthung Suhang culture, they also looked through the Khas Aryan and Indian cultural and linguistic lenses. Meaning, since Imansing Chemjong and Bajbir Thalang (Subba) grew up in Kalimpong and other parts of India, they were heavily influenced by Indian cultural traditions, including the Devanagari writing system.

As implied above, Yakthungs used the Old Sirijanga script until the mid-19th century, and Jobhansing Limbu, Chyangresing Phedangba, Ranadhoj Limbu, and Jit Mohan documented Yakthung cultural conditions and Mundhum rhetorics in the Old Sirijanga script. Based on the manuscripts I found in the British Library, they wrote on Yakthung histories, narratives, Yakthung syllabaries, Yakthung cultural practices, and Mundhum rhetorics from 1845–1857 (I also found one manuscript from 1867). Currently, Yakthungs believe that Brian Hodgson requested Jobhansing Limbu, Chyangresing Phedangba, Ranadhoj Limbu, and Jit Mohan, to document Yakthung cultural traditions, and they wrote more than a dozen Yakthung books (volumes). Brian Hodgson also procured some other Yakthung books and transported them to the UK for colonial purposes in 1857. When I went to the British Library in London in 2016 and 2019, I found most of them. The books and manuscripts are still in decent and/or readable condition and are available to the general public (however, one has to issue a library membership card to enter the library, but it is easy to acquire).

Lalshor Sendang was five years old when Brian Hodgson hired Jobhansing Limbu, Chyangresing Phedangba, Ranadhoj Limbu, and Jit Mohan to document Yakthung histories, narratives, cultural traditions, social conditions, and Mundhum rhetorics. When they stopped writing for Brian Hodgson, Lalshor Sendang was 17 years old. Before Lalshor Sendang was born, the

Khas Aryan and British colonizers had dispersed Yakthungs in three different countries, such as Nepal, India, and Sukhim in the Treaty of Sugauli in 1816. When Limbu et al. (1845–57) documented Yakthung histories, narratives, and Mundhum rhetorics in Darjeeling, Yakthungs were not allowed to read and write in Yakthung laje, Nepal, and Sikkimi Yakthungs were also hesitant to read and write in the Sirijanga script and in *Yakthung pa:n*. In their manuscripts, Limbu et al. (1845–57) mentioned that they wrote histories, narratives, stories, and Mundhum rhetorics in Darjeeling based on the book/s they found in Sukkim; for instance, they say, *"Sukhim ko kuhiyeko pustak bamojim lekhyako"* (books/manuscripts written based on the old and damaged book/s found in Sikkim). After Jobhansing Limbu, Chyangresing Phedangba, Ranadhoj Limbu, and Jit Mohan had stopped writing for Brian Hodgson, no books and manuscripts were written in the Old Sirijanga script until now.

Lalshor Sendang grew up learning Yakthung history, politics, culture, and Mundhum rhetorics. Later, he waged a campaign to delink Khas Aryan, Indian, and Western cultural and linguistic colonization, to relink Yet Hang and Thibong Yakthung Suhang language, literacy, history, and Mundhum literacies and to link them from local and regional contexts. Sendang, including other Yakthung activists, and his supporters collectively started advocating and fighting for their *khambong-lungbong* rights (rights to land), mother-tongue education, and the freedom to promote religion and Mundhum rhetorics based on the treaty of the Nun-Paani Sandhi (1774). The Khas Aryan-centric-Nepali government abhorred the Lalshorian and other progressive Yakthung intellectuals' campaign. When Lalshor Sendang was 74 years old, the Khas Aryan-centric Nepali government banished him from Yakthung laje for his unshakable advocacy for Yakthungs' rights to ancestral land, customary institutional law and practice, language, literacy, religion, and Mundhum rhetorics. After the banishment, Lalshor Sendang lived in West Sukhim; it is widely believed that he lived in a *phukku* (cave) in Sukhim for 10 years until Yakthungs from Kalimpong knew about him. During his isolated stay in Sikkim, he was not able to develop a congenial network with other Yakthungs. During the banishment in Sikkim, Sendang could barely manage food and clothing for his survival; Sendang used to go hungry for weeks since he could barely manage food in all seasons, and he barely had rags to cover his loin. Therefore, Sikkimi Yakthungs called him *Naga* (naked man) and his dwelling place *Naga Phukku* (naked man's cave). Currently, the cave, where Sendang lived, is popularly known as *Naga Phukku* or *Sendang Phukku* (Sendang cave) in West Sikkim, India.

After the foundation of Shree Yakthung Hang Chumlung in Kalimpong in 1925, Kalimponge Yakthungs heard of Lalshor Sendang about his expertise in Yakthung language, literacy, Mundhum rhetorics, Sirijanga script, and writing system. Kalimponge Yakthungs invited him to teach the Sirijanga script, writing system, Mundhums, and Yakthung histories. When Sendang taught Yakthung language and literacy in Dungrabasti, Kalimpong, he was 85 years old. While Sendang taught in Dungrabasti, he affirmed the

Kalimponge Yakthungs that King Maarang ($6^{th}/7^{th}$ century) and Sirijanga ($9^{th}/10^{th}$ century) re/designed the script (Limbu, 1928), and later, Tye Angsi Singthebe re-introduced the script in the 18th century and was executed by Thachhang Lamas and the Bhutia King (see Chapter 3). Lalshor Sendang taught at Shree Yakthung Hang Chumlung for about a year; then, he went to Tinkhuti, Assam to visit his daughter, and he passed away in Assam at the age of 86.

When Lalshor Sendang lectured on the Sirijanga script and writing system at Shree Yakthung Hang Chumlung in Kalimpong, the Kalimponge Yakthungs unanimously decided to call the script, "Sirijanga script." Hence, the Kalimponge Yakthungs named the script, the Sirijanga script for the first time in the history of Yakthung civilization. Among many other Yakthungs, Imansing Chemjong was one of Sendang's students at Shree Yakthung Hang Chumlung. Chemjong was in his early 20s when Sendang taught Yakthung writing system, history, and Mundhum rhetorics in Shree Yakthung Hang Chumlung, Dungrabasti, Kalimpong. In relation to Yakthung language and literacy, Tye Angsi Singthebe linked old Yakthung language and literacy from the 18th century Yakthung Suhang cultural perspectives. Jobhansing Limbu, Chyangresing Phedangba, Ranadhoj Limbu, and Jit Mohan bridged the old Yakthung writing tradition and Tye Angsian era with the 19th century Yakthung language and literacy. Similarly, Lalshor Sendang is one of the Yakthung scholars and activists who bridged the 19th century and the 20th century Yakthung language and literacy.

The Old Sirijanga vs. New Sirijanga scripts and epistemic gaps: relinking Yakthung language and literacy

During my research, I came to know that there is a great Yakthung writing and literacy gap between the Old Sirijanga script and the New Sirijanga script (Bajbirian Sirijanga writing system). I persistently raised questions, such as why is there a Yakthung literacy gap, why is there disconnected literacy knowledge between the Old Sirijanga and New Sirijanga scripts, and what was the pertinent reason/s behind it? Was it due to spatial and temporal reasons? The spatial and temporal settings even force/d me to raise a series of questions, such as in what script did Lalshor Sendang teach in Yakthung laje, Sikkim, and Kalimpong? Did Sendang know the Tye Angsian Sirijanga script, for Limbu et al. (1845–1857) state that they wrote books and manuscripts based on the old, damaged book/s that they (Yakthungs) found in Sukhim (Sikkim)? If Imansing Chemjong and Bajbir Subba (Thalang) were Lalshor Sendang's students, why did they shift the Old Sirijanga script to the Devanagari writing system (the Devanagari-based Sirijanga script)? Or when Lalshor Sendang learned to read and write, did his father teach him the way Subedar Bajbir Subba wrote *Tum Yakthung Ningwaphu Sapla* in 1928? I asked these questions, for *Tum Yakthung Ningwaphu Sapla* is the first

Yakthung *saksak sapla* (book) written after 1857 or 1867 (I also found a Yakthung book written in 1867 in the British Library, but it was collected after Hodgson had left Darjeeling). So, the Yakthung literacy gap has been very mysterious, ideological, and political. I never stopped raising questions, such as was the Sirijanga script that Lalshor Sendang learned influenced by the Devanagari script? Did Yakthungs have any *Yakthung saksak* (books) to learn from in Yakthung laje, Nepal during the late 19th century and the early 20th century? (We all know that Khas Aryans destroyed all Yakthung books). Or did the Yakthungs of Kalimpong and Darjeeling (mainly the members of Shree Yakthung Hang Chumlung) just ignore the Old Sirijanga writing system, for they did not trust Lalshor Sendang? Similarly, the Mundhum texts I got from Satya Hangma Panthis that was written in 1931 (or 1988 BS) was also written in the New Sirijanga script. These settings further both ease and complicate the study of the historical development of the Sirijanga script and writing system.

Yakthungs during World War I joined the East India Company and had opportunities to read and write in Devanagari and Roman scripts. Meaning, many Yakthungs became literate for the first time. This could be one of the reasons why we find the influence of the Hindi and Nepali writing system in the New Sirijanga script. As I mentioned above, Yakthungs did not have a uniformed writing system, i.e., syllabaries; syllabaries differed place-to-place and person-to-person throughout the Yakthung communities in Nepal, Sikkim, India, Bhutan, and Burma, etc. Mainly, the teaching of the Sirijanga script, Yakthung language, and culture was banned in Nepal, and the situation was not favorable in Sikkim, including other places where Yakthungs resided. Based on the background information, I will primarily focus on some lines of inquiry, such as when did the major shift occur in the process of writing system (in the Sirijanga script or Sirijanga writing system)? Why did the writing system become more important over the orality or performative rhetorics? What characters (syllabaries) changed in the writing system in the early 20th century? What caused the shift in the Sirijanga writing system?

Based on my five-year long research though the Sirijanga script and writing system shifted in Nepal and beyond, we do not have any strong evidence to exhibit why the Sirijanga syllabary shifted, and why it shifted when it shifted. Though Yakthung scholars attempted to answer the questions in multiple ways, the main reason was that the teaching of the Sirijanga script was banned in Yakthung laje (Nepal), and Yakthungs were reluctant to learn the Sirijanga script in Sukhim (Sikkim) as well after the execution of Tye Angsi Singthebe in 1741. The other strong reason why the Sirijanga writing system shifted was because the Yakthungs (of the early 20th century) who wrote in the Sirijanga script were heavily influenced by the Devanagari script (Nepali and Hindi writing system). Therefore, in the New Sirijanga script, we find a heavy influence of the Devanagari script (Nepali and Hindi). After the foundation of Shree Yakthung Hang Chumlung in 1925, Yakthungs shifted Yakthung syllabary to the Devanagari script (Nepali and Hindi). R. K. Sprigg (1959) states:

> [Chemjong's] efforts to preserve his people's script have resulted in the establishment of a Limbu society for this purpose during the early [1920s]; the founding of a Limbu-Language school, the Zambak-Memorial School, near Kalimpong, [1938]; the publication of several Limbu primers and readers in the Kiranti script at Kalimpong, Darjeeling, and Gangtok; and the use of the script in Limbuan [Limbuwan] for dedicating *chautaras*.
>   In the course of reviving it the Kirant script has however been much modified under the influence of Devanagari, with the result that Limbus who can read and write the modern-style script fluently can make little or nothing of the old books. (p. 591)

Although Yakthung scholars, including the foreigners, give credit to Imansing Chemjong in relation to the Sirijanga script and writing, in reality it was Subedar Bajbir Subba (Thalang) who was the first Yakthungs to introduce the new version of the Sirijanga script in his *Tum Yakthung Ningwaphu Sapla* in 1928. Then, other Yakthungs, such as Imansing Chemjong, Kalusing Papo, Buddhiraj Phago, Jasman Sangwa, Harkajang Makhim, E. K. Bahadur Sereng, Sher Bahadur Neyonghang, Nirmal Limbu, Mohan Lal Hangam, Buddhi Raj Phago, Jash Man Sangwa, and Tiloksing Nugo started following whatever Bajbir Subba introduced in 1928.

As I mentioned above, I always wondered why there was a knowledge gap between the Old Sirijanga and New Sirijanga scripts. Lalshor Sendang was born in 1840, and when Jobhansing Limbu, Chyangresing Phedangba, Ranadhoj Limbu, and Jit Mohan were writing Limbu (Yakthung) books from 1845–1857, Sendang was growing from a child to a teenager. This setting, more often than not, makes me raise compelling questions, such as which Sirijanga script (Old or New Sirijanga) did Lalshor Sendang learn? Did he not know the Tye Angsian Sirijanga script? Or what did he learn, and what did he teach to Yakthungs at Shree Yakthung Hang Chumlung in 1925? Did Yakthungs ignore him as he looked like a *kenangba*? The reason I raised these questions is that Shree Yakthung Hang Chumlung produced so many Yakthung activists, community leaders, and writers. They were the ones who first delinked the Khas Aryan, Indian, and European cultural and linguistic colonization. They were the ones who denaturalized para-colonization and relinked the Sirijanga writing system. If they had not reintroduced the writing system, we would have forgotten our script and writing system. Due to Yakthung activists and leaders, whether the Old Sirijanga and New Sirijanga scripts, we are in the process of being Yakthung, becoming Yakthung, and belonging in physical and spiritual Yakthung laje. Additionally, there are a few major fundamental Yakthung Suhang accomplishments that contributed to the development of Yakthung language and literacy. If Hodgson did not archive the Yakthung manuscripts in the British Library (now popular as

Hodgson collection) in the 19th century, or if R. K. Sprigg did not bring some copies of the Hodgson collection (Yakthung manuscripts) to Yakthung laje in 1955, or if Shree Yakthung Hang Chumlung was not founded in Kalimpong in 1925, and if Yakthungs did not collaborate, write, and disseminate the Sirijanga script, writing system, and Mundhum rhetorics, the Khas Aryans would have been successful in wiping out Yakthung history writing system, and Yakthung cultural traditions.

After Yakthungs had written several books in the Sirijanga script and *Yakthung pa:n*, they established Zambuk Junior Basic School in Dungra Basti Kalimpong in 1938 (see figure 18). This was the first school where Yakthung language and writing was introduced after the Khas Aryans, including Bhutias, banned Yakthungs the teaching of their language, writing, and Mundhum rhetorics. Zambuk Junior Basic School became the first site of Yakthung academic space in the modern history (I also got an opportunity to visit this school in 2018). Through the teaching of Yakthung language and literacy, the foundation of Zambuk Junior Basic School delinked the Khas Aryan and Indian structural language and literacy colonization; it delinked the para-colonial logic of knowledge construction (Nepali, Hindi, and English as superior languages to Yakthung language) in Yakthung communities. In other words, the foundation of Zambuk Junior Basic School denaturalized the Khas Aryan, Indian, and Western colonial logic that Yakthung language was/is inferior to Nepali, Hindi, and English. The foundation of Zambuk Junior Basic School delinked the para-colonizer's way of weaponizing Khas Aryan hegemony to construct cultural, linguistic, and academic hierarchies in Yakthung communities.

Before the foundation of Shree Yakthung Hang Chumlung and Zambuk Junior Basic School, *Yakthung pa:n* was labeled as an uncivilized and savage

Figure 18 Zambuk Junior Basic School, established 1938.

language. The foundation of Zambuk Junior Basic School ensured Yakthungs and Yakthung children that knowledge and space are ideologically and politically constructed entities, and Yakthungs can also re/construct Yakthung knowledges, histories, and identities. The foundation of Shree Yakthung Hang Chumlung and Zambuk Junior Basic School challenged the way the Khas Aryans, Indians, and Europeans displaced and destroyed Yakthung Suhang (and Indigenous) cultural, linguistic, and spatial identities.

As I stated earlier, after the foundation of Shree Yakthung Hang Chumlung in 1925, Yakthungs continued to network, collaborate, research, and document Yakthung histories, Mundhum rhetorics, Yakthung grammar books, and Yakthung lived narratives. Before the foundation of Shree Yakthung Hang Chumlung (1925), Yakthungs also attempted to resist the Khas Aryan domination and oppression, and they, based on the Nun-Paani Sandhi agreement (see Lumphungwa Limbu, 2075 BS, pp. 57–59), advocated for their rights to ancestral land, customary institutional law and practice, script, writing, history, and Mundhum rhetorics. However, Khas Aryans ignored their demands and misinterpreted their creative and constructive petitions. Instead of addressing their creative demands based on the Nun-Paani Sandhi, they captured, tortured, executed or banished Yakthungs from Yakthung laje. Therefore, the foundation of Shree Yakthung Hang Chumlung became the first *Yakthung Chumlungden* (contact zone) to discuss, collaborate, and disseminate their voice in order to relink Thibong Yakthung Suhang histories, culture, writing, and Mundhum rhetorics. It was the first *Yakthung Chumlungden* where Yakthungs had a collective voice to delink Khas Aryan and Bhutia colonization and to denaturalize European cultural and linguistic colonization (after the Nun-Paani Sandhi in 1774). As Yakthungs from Yakthung laje were under the Khas Aryan oppression, they had to secretly establish Yakthung communal social institutions in Yakthung laje to support other *Yakthung phu-ne-nusa*'s (brothers and sisters') movements.

After the foundation of Shree Yakthung Hang Chumlung, Yakthungs popularized the Sirijanga script, writing system, and Mundhum literacy in Yakthung communities in Nepal, India, Bhutan, Burma, and Thailand. They researched, wrote, and published more than a dozen Yakthung books in *Yakthung pa:n* (see Chapter 7). The medium of publication during this period was chirography (handwritten books) and lithography; they used carbon papers and could produce up to 3–5 carbonated copies at a time. Later, Yakthungs used an advanced method of printing that was lithography, i. e. a water and oil-based printing. In other words, Yakthung writers wrote books, pamphlets, and Mundhums by hand on carbon and stencils, and they printed materials, such as books and pamphlets, manually, which is known as carbon print and lithography.

Concerning the development of Yakthung language and literacy, Yakthungs who lived outside Nepal were culturally and linguistically conscious, and they also consistently advocated for the development of Yakthung writing, language, and Mundhum rhetorics. I am not implying that Yakthungs from Yakthung laje (Nepal) ignored their language, writing, and Mundhum rhetorics; they implicitly cherished, preached, and practiced Yakthung writing, language, and Mundhum literacy. Despite their utmost interest and advocacy for Yakthung language and literacy, the Khas Aryans captured, executed, or banished Yakthungs for their teaching or learning of their language, writing, and Mundhum rhetorics. The Yakthungs, who lived in Yakthung laje (Nepal), could not read and write openly, for the new immigrants (Khas Aryan neighbors) would report to the Khas Aryan authorities. Therefore, when foreign scholars (Hamilton, Mainwaring, Campbell, Hodgson, and Sprigg) wanted to study the Yakthung language, writing, and culture, they used to consult the Yakthungs who lived in Kalimpong, Sikkim, and Darjeeling (including the Yakthung soldiers who worked for the British East India Company). For instance, Campbell went to Sikkim and collected Yakthung books and/or manuscripts from Ilamsing Limbu. Similarly, Hodgson lived in Kathmandu for decades (1824–1844) as a postmaster, assistant resident, and resident. Later, Hodgson moved to Darjeeling and stayed there from 1845–1857 where he collected Yakthung books and old Yakthung manuscripts, including non-Yakthung books, and also requested writers, that included Yakthungs and non-Yakthungs, to document Yakthung culture, histories, narratives, and Mundhums (according to the manuscripts I found in the British Library). Likewise, Sprigg went to Darjeeling to study Lepcha language and culture, a Tibeto-Burman language. During his research, he made copies of the Old Yakthung manuscripts from the British Library and brought them with him. He met with Yakthung scholars in Nepal, including in India, and shared the Yakthung manuscripts with them.

When Sprigg brought the copies of the 19th century Yakthung documents from the British Library (London), Yakthung scholars realized that they involuntarily shifted the Sirijanga script from its original form, such as its phonology and character (writing system). As I mentioned above, since the foundation of Shree Yakthung Hang Chumlung (1925), Yakthung writers introduced a newer version of the Sirijanga script because they did not know that Tye Angsi Singthebe redesigned the script in the 19th century. The newer Sirijanga script, as discussed above, was influenced by the Devanagari (Nepali and Hindi) writing system. The Yakthung activists and scholars, mainly, Bajbir Subba and Imansing Chemjong, who introduced the script were not literate in the Old Sirijanga script (Chemjong learned about the Old Sirijanga script only after R. K. Sprigg brought some copies of the Old Sirijanga script from the British Library in 1955).

The Yakthungs who lived in the foreign countries networked and collaborated for the development of Yakthung language and writing. During the early 20th century, Yakthungs, such as Subedar Bajbir Subba (Thalang), Subedar Harkadal Makkhim, Mandal Jitbahadur Thebe, Daronga Dhanraj Phenduwa, Mandal Hangsaraj Thegim, Buddhiman Chemjong, Kulahang Chemjong, Imansing Chemjong, Nirmal Ongling, and Jasbahadur Songbangphe constantly networked and collaborated to reestablish the Sirijanga script, writing, and Mundhum rhetorics, or they spent most of their time in the development of Yakthung language, writing, and Mundhum rhetorics (Kainla, 2049 BS, pp. 40–41). For your information, most of the early 20th century Yakthung scholars did not see the Old Sirijanga script, for Sprigg brought the copies of the Hodgson (Yakthung) manuscripts only in 1955. Despite the fact that Yakthungs came to know the Old Sirijanga script through R. K. Sprigg (meaning, Hodgson collection), they, perhaps, were not able to navigate how the Old Sirijanga script could be used in practice.

In relation to Yakthung language and literacy, Yakthungs understood that writing is a rhetorical tool; a rhetorical tool not only to create Yakthung cultural, linguistic, and *khambong-lungbong* identities, but also to remap physical and symbolic Yakthung laje. The first-generation Yakthung realized that writing, in Sirijanga script and *Yakthung pa:n*, was a physical, psychological, and spiritual struggle that linked them and Yakthung ancestors; Yakthung writing and rhetoric solaced the tormented colonial wounds. Yakthungs gradually learned that writing delinked the Khas Aryan, Indian, and European cultural, linguistic, and academic colonization. They knew that Yakthungs and their children could delearn and denaturalize local para-colonial and European colonial knowledge making business. Through their writing, Yakthungs learned that they, including their children, could relink their Yet Hang insights, Thibong Yakthung wisdoms, and Sawa Yet Hang epistemologies. They practically could grasp that writing was a tool that gave them their meaningful Yakthung Suhang existence—existence for their being and becoming Yakthung and belonging to Thibong Yakthung epistemic spaces. They felt that their voice flew like a river that touched the desires and expectations of theirs and their ancestors. Hence, for Yakthungs, writing became a tool to delink the colonization and relink Yet Hang and Thibong Yakthung cultural epistemologies; it became a means to subvert the Khas Aryan, Indian, and European colonization and to construct Yakthung space, identity, and power.

After 1990, we (Yakthungs) understand that we can use our language and writing to resist the Khas Aryan para-colonial power because resistance is a form of power, expression, and creative action. Writing is a sign of struggle and creative action. We can position ourselves at the center with it; we can decenter the center by deconstructing the well-established discourse. Having understood the power of language and writing, Yakthungs established Kirat Yakthung Chumlung in Nepal during the Shah oppressive regime in 1989 (see in Chapter 11). Before 1990, the Khas Aryan-centric government did not allow any Indigenous peoples to establish organization like Kirat Yakthung Chumlung. Despite the Khas Aryan oppression, Yakthungs resisted; they risked their lives for Yakthungs and Yakthung community (in Nepal). They were prepared to get tortured, executed or banished for the sake of their children, culture, language, writing, and Mundhum rhetorics. Such Yakthung people's resistance demonstrates they had the Thibong Yakthung

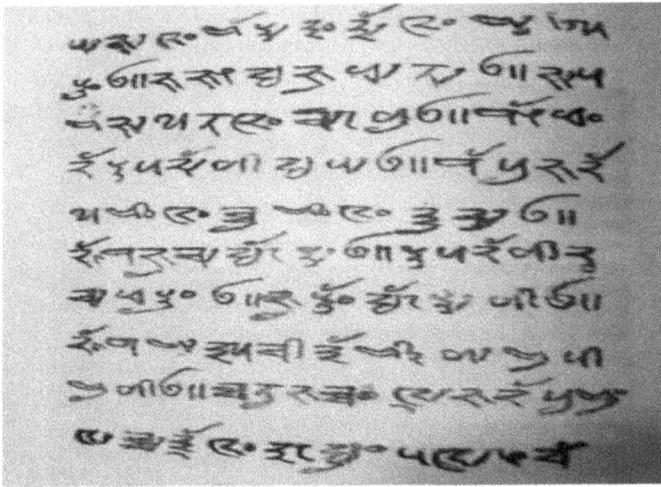

Figure 19 The Sirijanga script, written by Jobhansing Limbu, Chyangresing Phedangba, Ranadhoj Limbu, and Jit Mohan (Source: The British Library, London).

thirst for centuries—thirst for their script, writing, language, ancestral land, and customary institutional law and practice. They revolted to delink Khas Aryan para-colonialism to relink Sawa Yet Hang, Susuwa Lilim Yakthung, Yet Hang, and Thibong Yakthung civilization and link them in local, regional, and global contexts from the late 20th and 21st century perspectives. These were some Yakthung Suhang sites of early delinking Khas Aryan oppression and relinking Yet Hang and Thibong Yakthung cultural traditions during the heyday of the Khas Aryan oppression in Nepal.

Even before the restoration of democracy in Nepal (1990), we (Yakthungs) knew that Limbuwan (Yakthung laje) was a sleeping lion. Our action, documentation and/or writing woke us up from a long trance. Then and now, Yakthungs knew/know that writing serves us from what we fear, and writing compensates what the Khas Aryan government has not given to us for centuries. From this perspective, Limbus et al.'s (1845) documentation of Yakthung history, Yakthung syllabaries, narratives, Mundhums, and Yakthung grammar were the early sites of delinking Khas Aryan para-colonization and relinking Yet Hang and Thibong Yakthung epistemologies in Yakthung communities (see figure 19). Limbu et al.'s documentations demonstrate that Yakthung historians, grammarians, scholars, and writers had written Yakthung histories, genealogies, cultural practices, and Mundhums before the Khas Aryans banished Yakthungs from Yakthung laje. Yakthungs continued to learn the Sirijanga script and writing system and wrote books, syllabaries, and Mundhums after they had settled in Darjeeling, Kalimpong, and Sikkim.

Delinking, relinking, and linking the Sirijanga script, writing, and rhetorics

In the early 1840s, Arthur Campbell took many books from Ilamsing Limbu in Sikkim. After Limbu passed away, Campbell again visited the Limbu family and took books from them. We (Yakthungs) do not know the whereabouts of these books until today (discussed in detail elsewhere in this book). The Khas Aryans and European colonizers systematically destroyed Yakthung knowledge in multiple ways. The Yakthungs were banned from the researching, documenting, and disseminating of Yakthung culture, language, and literacy in Nepal, and Yakthungs were also discouraged to read and write in their language, *Yakthung pa:n* after the execution of Tye Angsi Singthebe (1741) in Sikkim. These were some of the reasons why Yakthungs lost their writing system and Mundhum rhetorics. By the early 20th century, Yakthungs felt the urgency of Yakthung unity, research, and writing. Therefore, they founded Shree Yakthung Hang Chumlung in 1925 to research, document, preserve, and institutionalize Yakthung language, writing, and rhetorics.

In the Yakthung's writing system, we can observe a heavy influence of the Devanagari script on the Sirijanga script after the foundation of Shree Yakthung Hang Chumlung. The influence of other scripts and writing systems on Yakthung writing system made it both easy and complex to read and write in the Sirijanga writing system. It was easy in the sense that the Old Sirijanga script was a complicated writing system, for it was not practiced for centuries. Yakthungs lost the original script and writing system, for Khas Aryans banned them from reading and writing in the Yakthung language and script. As a result, they were alienated with their own Sirijanga script and writing system and became familiar with the Devanagari script (Nepali and Hindi writing system). The familiarity of the Devanagari script or Nepali and Hindi writing system shifted the concept of the Old Sirijanga script and writing system. Meaning, the influence of Devanagari script and writing system made the reading and writing in the Sirijanga script easier, for Yakthung knowledge was caged in the Khas Aryan and Indian cultural and academic institutions.

Although Bairagi Kainla (Til Bikram Nembang) stated that Tibetan and Lepcha script, including the Devanagari script influenced the Sirijanga script. Based on my research findings, I am hesitant to admit Kainla's claim that the Tibetan and Lepcha scripts influenced the Old Sirijanga script because it (Old Sirijanga script) developed independent of other scripts, such as the Devanagari, Ranjana, and Brahmi scripts, including the Tibetan and Lepcha scripts (see Chapter 1). The Old Sirijanga script rather influenced many local scripts (see Gaur, 1987; Brown & Yule, 1983; Limbu, 2016, 2017; Scharfe, 2002). The Old Sirijanga writing system has, however, some similarities with that of the Tibetan and Lepcha writing systems. For instance, in terms of the Sirijanga or Kiranti script, Sprigg (1959) states:

> A comparison of the Kiranti with the Devnagari, Tibetan, and Lepcha scripts establishes that the Kiranti is the same in principle as they in that it

makes use of vowel signs as modifiers, and of *zero*, the absence of a writing sign, as itself a vowel sign. There are respects in which the Kiranti script resembles any one of these three scripts more than the other two; but in general the resemblance seems closest to a Tibetan cursive, 'khyugyig, and Lepcha. In particular the Kiranti script shares with these two the features of having a special series of letters for syllable-final consonants. (p. 591)

On the other hand, after the Bajbirian script was introduced, the influence of other scripts (Lepcha, Tibetan, and Devanagari) also complicated the Sirijanga writing system because some of the Sirijanga characters or sound system did not accurately represent the Yakthung phonology. It did not represent Yakthung phonology as in many languages, we do not write as they are pronounced, and we do not pronounce as they are written. In other words, characters and sound images are signifiers; signifiers are a jumble of letters through which meanings are created. Hence, meanings, concepts, and objects are signified. Signifiers are more stable, whereas, signified differs person-to-person and context-to-context. Therefore, signifiers and signified are more often than not slippery because we communicate via arbitrary signs, and no inherent meaning is communicated.

Since the Yakthungs redesigned and revised the New Sirijanga script with specific purposes, this script has represented Yakthung sound systems more accurately than other Kõiches and Khambu linguistic groups because the scholars and linguists who were involved in the development of the Sirijanga script and writing system were mostly Yakthungs, and they designed and redesigned for Yakthung purpose (I, based on my research, believe that the Old Sirijanga script was the script of all the Himalayan Indigenous communities who have /a/-based phonologies like that of Tibetan). For instance, R. K. Sprigg (1998) argues that some of the reformed Yakthung characters tend to represent the entire Kirat sound system (p. 1). Based on my research, I claim that the study of the Old Sirijanga script is a compelling research area, which needs to be further inquired, studied, and discovered as it not only bridges all Himalayan Indigenous communities, but also eases the readership in relation to one writing system (but different Tibeto-Burman languages).

There are many instances that justify that the Tibetan script and writing system influenced the Sirijanga script and vice versa (the Old Sirijanga writing system implied). For instance, in terms of writing, though there are words that are written as "a" (/∂/), they are pronounced as "aa" (/a/). This does not mean that Tibetan's do not have the "∂" sound; they do, but it is both written as "a" (/∂/) and is pronounced "/a/." Yakthungs also have the similar linguistic features and characteristics that we find in fluent Yakthung language speakers, and we find these linguistic features in the Old Sirijanga script or writing system (as we, Yakthungs, have such linguistic or phonological features in our *Yakthung pa:n*, my Khas Aryan friends used to tease and laugh at me in school). In a nutshell, /a/ phonological feature for /∂/ is one of the strong features in

Figure 20 Sprigg used this writing system to study Sirijanga syllabary (Source: R. K. Sprigg).

Yakthung language, including other Indigenous languages (Athpahariya, Rai, Tamang, Sherpa, and Gurung languages implied), and Tibetans also have similar type of linguistic features like that of Yakthungs. Similarly, R. K. Sprigg also found similar linguistic features in Lepcha. For instance, Sprigg states that the Limbu (Yakthung) "a" is very much like that of "a" in Lepcha. By quoting the Hodgson collection books vol. 87, *Limbu haru ko kakhahara*, Sprigg (1959) states that "a" has been included in the syllabary, which includes 20 Limbu (Yakthung) symbols; whereas, Campbell excluded /a/ from the syllabary, and he claimed that there are only 19 symbols in Yakthung syllabary (see figures 13.1).

In the early 20th century, Bajbir Subba shifted the Old Sirijanga script to the New Sirijanga writing system. Though it was Bajbir Subba who wrote or introduced the first New Sirijanga writing system (*Tum Yakthung Ningwaphu Sapla*, 1928 implied), our local, regional, and global scholars tend to give the credit to Imansing Chemjong in the development of the Sirijanga writing system. In terms of Imansing Chemjong's Yakthung language and writing skills, Yehang Laoti (2016), Bairagi Kainla (2017), and Ambar Jang Limbu (2017) state that neither was Imansing Chemjong a fluent Yakthung language speaker nor was he a linguist by training (personal communication). Because of Chemjong's inability to critically study and analyze the Yakthung phonology and writing system, he admitted what Bajbir Subba introduced in 1928 (*Tum Yakthung Ningwaphu Sapla* implied). The shift in the Sirijanga script happened because Imansing and Bajbir Subba were familiar with the Devanagari script (Hindi and Nepali). Though some first-generation Yakthung scholars were fluent in Yakthung language, they did not know about the Old Sirijanga script. Therefore, Yakthungs had to follow the Bajbirian Sirijanga script (as the valid Sirijanga script). In terms of the development of the Sirijanga script and writing system, Bajbir Subba, Iman Singh Chemjong, and Amiran Chemjong (Chemjong's wife) tried to give a historical shape in terms of the development of the Sirijanga writing system. As they did not know the Old Sirijanga script, they even might have thought that the Yakthung script did not represent the Yakthung sound system; therefore, Chemjong and his cronies "followed the Devanagari script by beginning with the ten *swara-barna* '*a* to '*e:* except that *i*, *u*, and *r* have been omitted and '*a:* and '*e:* have been added; he continues with the 30 *byanjana-barna* from *ka* to *ha*, with *tra* and [*gya*] added" (Sprigg, 1998, p. 4; see figures 20, 22, & 23). In the process of mimicking the Devanagari script (Hindi and Nepali), they distorted the originality of the Sirijanga script and writing system because they did not know about the Old Sirijanga script, and they were not well versed in Yakthung phonology. Despite the heavy influence of the Devanagari script on the modern Sirijanga script, there are some similarities in the Sirijanga, Tibetan, and Lepcha scripts and writing systems (see figures 5 & 6). For instance, it looks like the Old Sirijanga script influenced all of them in relation to modern Sirijanga, Tibetan, and Lepcha scripts and writing systems (see Chapter 1). It is also believed that during the 17th, 18th or 19th centuries, the Lepcha script was designed based on the Tibetan script, and the purpose of the teaching Sikkimi Ron and its fast development was to disseminate the Buddhism in Sikkim.

As I mentioned earlier, the Sirijanga script seems to be different from the Devanagari script; however, due to Bajbir Subba, Imansing Chemjong, and their cronies, there is much more influence of the Devanagari script. When we

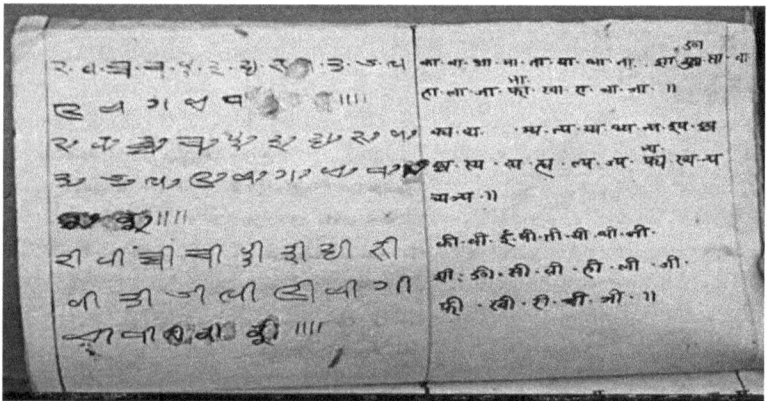

Figure 21 The Sirijanga script documented by Yakthung scholars in the 19th century (Source: The British Library, London).

say the Devanagari script, it refers to the influence of both Nepali and Hindi (Indian) writing systems. Sprigg (1998) also states:

> ...the Limbu script is probably known only in the form in which it appears in Chemjong 2018 (1962 A.D.); but there are earlier versions of both scripts to be found in handwritten books collected in Darjeeling in the 40s [1840s] of the last century by B. Hodgson. These earlier books have an original, and strikingly different, picture of the two scripts from the later .... (p. 1)

Imansing Chemjong, Padamsing Muringla, Kajiman Kandangwa, and Ranadhoj Nembang attempted to modify the Sirijanga script after they met with Sprigg in 1955. However, due to the lack of Yakthung linguistic command, both in linguistic theories and practices, they could not address the issues. Later, Birkh Bahadur (B. B.) Muringla addressed or redesigned most of the issues. Muringla is one of the Yakthung individuals who shaped the development of the Sirijanga script and Sirijanga writing system because he is a fluent Yakthung language speaker. He is also linguistically well-versed in relation to the Sirijanga writing system and Yakthung phonological system. However, Muringla was not a linguist (by training), he also did not know about the Old Sirijanga script, and he could not shift the /∂/-based Sirijanga syllabary back to the /a/-based Old Sirijanga writing system again (as the new Sirijanga script became already popular in the Yakthung communities). In our long personal conversation at his home in Lingchom in 2017 and 2018, I asked B. B. Muringla the reason for not shifting the Bajbirian Sirijanga script or writing system to the Old Sirijanga script again. Muringla was very displeased with Imansing Chemjong, for he (Chemjong) did not inform him of the Old Sirijanga script.

   In the following section, you can see the differences between the Tye Angsian Sirijanga (Old Sirijanga) and Bajbirian Sirijanga scripts. The Bajbirian Sirijanga script or the Sirijanga script we use today is an /∂/-based one; whereas, the 18th and 19th century Sirijanga script (based on the Yakthung books I found in the British Library) was an /a/-based one (see figures 21, 5). For instance:

> /ka, ba, a, ma, ta, ya, dha, na, sha, nga, sa, wa, ha, la, ja, pha, kha, ra, cha, yan/
>   or
> /का, बा, आ, मा, ता, या, धा, ना, शा, ङ्‌, सा, बा, हा, ला, जा, फा, खा, रा, जा, अा/

As I mentioned earlier, Subedar Bajbir Subba published a primer book entitled *Tum Yakthung Ningwaphu Sapla* in 1928, and he called this script, the "Kirat Yakthung Akchhar." The Sirijanga script (or the script he used) in that particular book was much more influenced by the "Devanagari script" (Hindi and Nepali writing system). For example, Bajbir Subba added almost all the

Devanagari syllabaries (*kudhak sak*) to the Sirijanga script/writing system; there were 30 consonants in Bajbirian "Kirat Yakthung akchhar" (see figures 20, 22, & 23). Bajbir Subba introduced them in this order:

/ka, kha, ga, gha, nga, cha, chha, ja, jha, yan, ta, tha, da, dha, na, pa, pha, ba, bha, ma, ya, ra, la, wa, yan, sha, sa, sh, ha, gya/

Similarly, Bajbir Subba (1928) also introduced the Devanagari vowels to the Sirijanga script. However, both consonants and vowels were not written in this pattern in the Old Sirijanga script. Bajbir Subba was literate both in Hindi and Nepali language; therefore, based on his Devanagari syllabary knowledge, he also developed the Sirijanga script dependent (similar) to the Devanagari script. Bajbir Subba's *Tum Yakthung Ningwaphu Sapla* (1928) clearly demonstrates that he was not literate in the Old Sirijanga script. Bajbir Subba shifted the Sirijanga script, and many Yakthung writers, activists, and scholars also started following the Sirijanga script and writing style that he introduced. In a nutshell, the Bajbirian Sirijanga script (1928) changed the landscape of the Yakthung writing system because Imansing Chemjong and other Yakthung scholars followed the Bajbirian Sirijanga script as a face value (Limbu, 2017, p. 580).

In the early 20th century, Yakthung scholars, like Lalshor Sendang, taught Yakthung language, philosophy, script, and Mundhum rhetorics. Sadly, the teaching of the Yakthung language, script, literature, and Mundhum rhetorics digressed due to the Khas Aryan subjugation in Yakthung laje. Due to the disconnection of the Old Sirijanga script and writing system, the early 20th century's Yakthung scholars and writers, such as Bajbir Subba (Thalang), Subedar Harkadal Makkhim, Mandal Jitbahadur Thebe, Daronga Dhanraj Phenduwa, Mandal Hangsaraj Thegim, Buddhiman Chemjong, Kaluhang

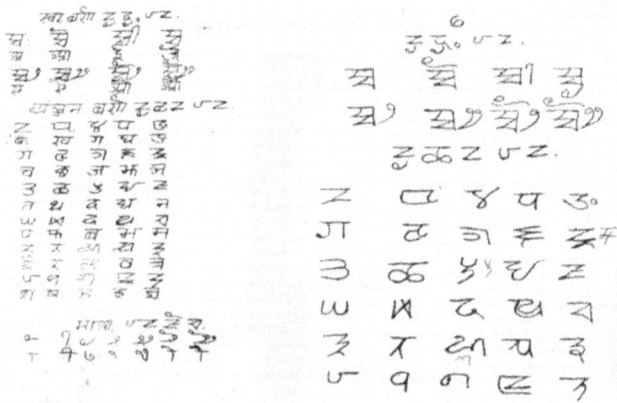

Figure 22 The Bajbirian Sirijanga script from *Tum Yakthung Ningwaphu Sapla* 1928 (Source: Ambar Jang Limbu).

Chemjong, Nirmal Ongling, Jasbahadur Songbangphe, Imansing Chemjong, and Ranadhoj Nembang unconsciously shifted the Sirijanga script (from the Old Sirijanga script to the new Sirijanga script). The shift of the Sirijanga writing system was due to the Khas Aryan's ban over the continuation of the Yakthung writing system and the Sirijanga script in Yakthung laje, Limbuwan, and due to the execution of Tye Angsi Singthebe in Sikkim in 1741. Since the teaching of *Yakthung pa:n* was banned, Yakthungs had to memorize the Sirijanga script and writing system, and in the long run, they forgot the Old Sirijanga writing system.

Bajbir Subba wrote the first Yakthung book, *Tum Yakthung Ningwaphu Sapla* (1928), but he was not a linguist by training. Later, Imansing Chemjong and Bajbir Subba (Tholong) co-wrote *Nisigek Yakthung Sapla* in 1931; however, both of them were not well-versed in *Yakthung pa:n* (Yakthung language), but in Hindi and Nepali. It is obvious that both Bajbir Subba and Imansing Chemjong were not familiar with the Old Sirijanga script, and they were not able to make a connection between the Yakthung phonology and writing system. Similarly, after the death of Bajbir Subba though Chemjong consistently contributed to the development of the Sirijanga script and writing system, he was not able to distinguish between the Old Sirijanga script and Bajbirian script (1928), or though he could distinguish them later in his life, he was not able to reintroduce the Old Sirijanga script. Or due to Chemjong and other early and mid-20th century Yakthung scholars' linguistic inability to distinguish the Yakthung phonological system and writing practice, Chemjong and other Yakthungs followed the Bajbirian Sirijanga writing system.

Sprigg: sites of Yakthung language and literacies in the mid-20th century

In relation to the development of Yakthung language and literacy, R. K. Sprigg played a great role. Sprigg was a British linguist who earned his BA degree (1944) and MA degree (1947) on war tactics or war strategies. After Sprigg received his MA degree, he started working at the School of Oriental and African Studies as a lecturer in Phonetics in London in 1948. Sprigg studied Tibetan culture and language during 1949–1950 in Kalimpong and Gyante, which demonstrates that he showed a great interest in language and linguistics as soon as he worked as a lecturer at the School of Oriental and African Studies. When Sprigg studied Tibetan language, David MacDonald was his mentor. Sprigg worked with Karphoo Tamsang from 1951–1952 in Kalimpong (from Sprigg's Obituary, written by Heleen Plaisier, 2011). After Sprigg studied Tibetan for a few years, he went to Yakthung laje, Limbuwan and Kathmandu for fieldwork for six months. When Sprigg went to Limbuwan, he met with Yakthung scholars, such as Imansing Chemjong, Kajiman Kandangwa, B. B. Subba, and Ranadhoj Nembang. During his six months' fieldwork, Sprigg collected abundant archival materials in Limbu, Newar, Bantawa, Sherpa, and Tamang (from Obituary by Heleen Plaisier,

2011). Sprigg continued doing research and writing in the field of Tibeto-Burman languages, such as Tibetan, Lepcha, Limbu, Newari, Burmese, and so on.

As I mentioned above, Sprigg started learning Tibetan and Tibeto-Burman languages in 1949 and learned Yakthung (Limbu) language over a couple of years (his mentor MacDonald did not know anything about Yakthung language and culture). Before R. K. Sprigg met with Yakthung scholars, the Sirijanga script had already been redesigned or shifted to the Devanagari like Bajbirian Sirijanga script due to the disconnected knowledge of the Old Sirijanga script and Yakthung writing system. In other words, in the 18th century, Tye Angsi Singthebe redesigned and reintroduced the Sirijanga script, and in the 19th century, Yakthung scholars, such as Jobhansing Limbu, Chyangresing Phedangba, Ranadhoj, and Jit Mohan wrote dozens of Yakthung histories, Yakthung narratives, language and grammar books, and Mundhum rhetorics in the Old Sirijanga script. Brian Hodgson procured the books and manuscripts and transported them to the UK. Currently, though the collected manuscripts are not well managed or organized (due to several reasons), they are still available to the public in the British Library in London (I have shared some of the title pages, including other important contents/pages of the books/manuscripts in this book).

In December 1955, R. K. Sprigg brought Yakthungs manuscripts written by Jobhansing Limbu, Chyangresing Phedangba, Ranadhoj Limbu, and Jit Mohan (which is now popularly known as Hodgson collection). Sprigg met with Imansing Chemjong, Kajiman Kandangwa, and Ranadhoj Nembang

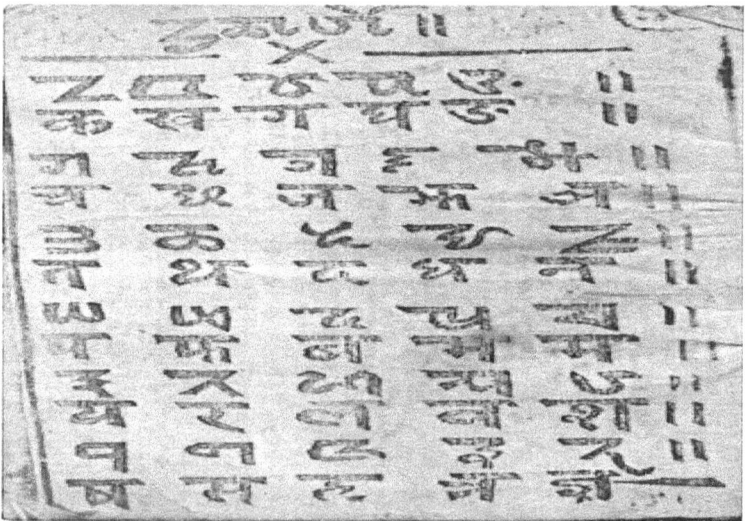

Figure 23 Ranadhoj Nembang's wooden block design follows the Bajbirian Sirijanga writing style (Source: Ambar Jang Limbu).

(who designed Sirijanga script wooden blocks; see figure 23) in Sartap, Panchathar (Limbuwan). As Yakthungs found the Old Sirijanga script from Sprigg, they knew that they already had misinformed Yakthungs about the Sirijanga script. Meaning, they totally shifted the script, for instance, the /a/-based script became an /ə/-based Sirijanga script like the Devanagari script. Sprigg stayed in Panthar until 1956; during his stay in Limbuwan, many Yakthung scholars, historians, and writers who were interested in Yakthung language congregated there; they discussed the development of Sirijanga script and writing system; they discussed the shift of the Sirijanga script. Sprigg and Yakthungs discussed the Old Sirijanga and New Sirijanga scripts, Yakthung language, writing systems, and phonological system (in 1955–1956), and we can see the reflection of the discussions on Sprigg's journal articles.

As Sprigg was a Tibeto-Burman researcher and writer, he theoretically (not practically—he did not speak Yakthung language) knew about some Tibeto-Burman languages; therefore, Sprigg and Ray Sprigg (his wife), along with Yakthung scholars, observed and studied Yakthung language from the practical point of view of how Yakthungs speak, what kind of sounds Yakthungs produce, and how the Yakthung sounds are similar or dissimilar with other Tibeto-Burman languages. Sprigg, including other Yakthung scholars theoretically and practically, realized that Yakthung phonology sounded like Tibetan and Lepcha phonology; meaning, "a" (/a/)-based phonology, but their writing (Sirijanga characters they designed) resembled the Devanagari script in practice. So, the research and observation also proved that there was a great influence of the Devanagari (Nepali and Hindi) writing system to the New Sirijanga script, and they also realized that the newer Sirijanga script did not reflect the Yakthung phonology. As the reformed characters did not reflect the Yakthung language and/or Yakthung phonology, they again, to some extent, reformed the Sirijanga script. The reformation of the script was not really a reformation. They found out that the Tye Angsian script or the Old Sirijanga was /a/-based syllabary that also portrayed that linguistically, the Yakthung syllabary or language system belongs to Tibeto-Burman language family. This research study on the Sirijanga script and writing system was one of the sites of delinking Nepali and Indian colonization from the perspective of the Sirijanga writing system. As the Tye Angsian Sirijanga script was much more scientific and practical in relation to Yakthung language and phonological system, Sprigg called Tye Angsi Sirijanga one of the greatest linguists of the 18th century (Sprigg, 1959, 1998).

R. K. Sprigg wrote several research-based journal articles on Yakthung (Limbu) language in which he discussed the shift, or variation, of the Sirijanga scripts and/or writing system. In his research articles, Sprigg demonstrated the phonological system of Yakthung language. For example, /a/, /a:/; when these sounds are produced, how they are pronounced, how they sound, and how they change meanings. Sprigg introduced the study of Yakthung language from a scientific, theoretical, and practical point of view, and Bairagi Kainla (2015), in the interview, claimed that the scientific study of Yakthung language, particularly on the sound system, did not exist before Sprigg's study. Among many foreign scholars, Sprigg's study on Yakthung language, especially the writing system, greatly facilitated the development of Yakthung (Limbu) language, writing, and phonological system. However, Sprigg was not an expert in Yakthung language; he was only a linguist in Tibeto-Burman language families. Sprigg found the Tye Angsian script, or the Old Sirijanga script (the Yakthung manuscripts of the 19th century in the British Library, London) while he was searching for the archived materials for his research. The Old Sirijanga script drew Sprigg's attention; therefore, he brought some copies of Yakthung documents written in the Old Sirijanga script with him and shared them with Yakthung scholars. Imansing Chemjong would not be able to do what Sprigg did according to Bairagi Kainla, for Chemjong was not linguistic by training. This is one of the reasons why Kainla, including many Yakthung scholars, refers to Chemjong as a cultural historian only. However, Chemjong's followers who had Limbu (Yakthung) linguistic knowledge (not academic degree) and also spoke *Yakthung pa:n* could do better research and writing, one of the Chemjong's disciples is Birkha Bahadur (B. B.) Muringla. B. B. Muringla is one of the calligraphic writers, who redesigned the Sirijanga script, wrote Yakthung textbooks from Kindergarten to college level by his own hand from the early 1970s in Sikkim. This particular age (meeting of Limbu scholars and Sprigg) helped young Yakthung scholars study phonology and morphology of Yakthung language.

Limbu et al.'s (1845–57) documentation of Yakthung history, narrative, cultural practices, and politics was the first site of delinking, relinking, and linking approaches in relation to the development of Yakthung language, writing, and literacy. Similarly, the foundation of Shree Yakthung Hang Chumlung in Kalimpong in 1925 and Yakthung Chumlung in Darjeeling in 1928 played significant roles to delink, relink, and link the Yakthung rhetorical traditions. Despite the Khas Aryan oppression in Nepal, Yakthungs were able to delink the Khas Aryan colonization; they were able to relink the Yet Hang and Thibong Yakthung cultural rhetorical traditions. Therefore, these sites, such as the documentation of Yakthung history, writing, language, literacy in the 19th century, and the foundation of Chumlungs were the early sites of delinking and denaturalizing the Khas Aryan, Indian, and Western cultural, linguistic, and political colonization. The Yakthungs' collective act of seeking their cultural and linguistic identities served as the early sites of delinking, relinking, and linking approaches. It woke Yakthungs up from the colonial trance. For instance, they could see what they had not seen for centuries; they could feel what they had not felt for centuries. Gradually, Yakthungs relinked Sawa Yet Hang epistemologies, or they relinked Yet Hang and Thibong Yakthung cultural rhetorical traditions. The early delinking and relinking sites further facilitated Yakthungs to link their history, narrative, and language in local and regional contexts, such as Yakthung laje (Limbuwan), Sikkim, Darjeeling, Kalimpong, Bhutan, Assam, Manipur, Burma, Thailand, and beyond.

Part V

The second Yakthung literacy wave

Delinking, relinking, and linking the Sirijanga script, writing, and rhetorics

9 The second-generation Yakthung activists and rhetors

It is apparent that the first-generation Yakthung scholars, writers, and historians influenced the second-generation Yakthung scholars, activists, and rhetors (in the 20th century). The second-generation Yakthung scholars practiced what the first-generation Yakthungs conceptualized, imagined, and envisioned. The second-generation Yakthung activists, historians, and writers predominantly continued to write on similar topic areas as that the first-generation Yakthungs initiated. This chapter focuses on how the second-generation Yakthung activist writers contributed to the development of Yakthung language, writing system, and Yakthung rhetorics. It demonstrates how they networked through the "Patra-mitrata" or "Patra-mitre" campaign, and how the Patra-mitre campaign supported the publication of Yakthung journals and pamphlets. It reveals some pressing issues and challenges in relation to Yakthung local and regional network, Yakthung knowledge construction, and dissemination in Nepal and beyond. Overall, this chapter examines how the second-generation Yakthung scholars networked with other *Yakthung-phu-ne-nusa* to delink the Khas Aryan, Indian, and European colonization, relink Yet Hang and Thibong Yakthung customary cultural traditions, and link Yakthung Suhang culture, writing, and rhetorics within Yakthung laje (Nepal) and beyond.

The second-generation Yakthungs, like the first-generation Yakthung rhetors, addressed the contemporary social, cultural, linguistic, *khambong-lungbong* (land-based) identities, and political issues. The targeted audiences of the second-generation Yakthungs were their cotemporary fellow Yakthungs, and their purpose was to delink Khas Aryan, Indian, and European cultural and linguistic colonization, for which they strategically oriented Yakthungs to delearn Khas Aryan cultural and linguistic colonization and relink Yet Hang and Thibong Yakthung Suhang cultures, Yakthung language, writing system, and Mundhum rhetorics. With the objectives to relink Yet Hang and Thibong Yakthung customary cultural traditions, they solemnly requested their fellow Yakthungs to read and write in the Sirijanga script in *Yakthung pa:n* and share their lived experiences, narratives, and stories on Yakthung Mundhums, writing system, and Yakthung histories. The second-generation Yakthung scholars primarily focused on:

1   Yakthung Barnamala (Limbu alphabets),
2   Short Yakthung prayers,

3   Yakthung sewa samlo (Yakthung hymns),
4   Yakthung song of praises,
5   Yakthung psalms,
6   Yakthung narratives, stories, and history,
7   Yakthung folktales or folklores,
8   Mundhum Khahun (moral education), and
9   Yakthung cultural practices, etc.

The second-generation Yakthung scholars, activists, historians, and writers were intermediately literate in the Sirijanga script and writing system. They did not know the Old Sirijanga script that had been popular until the mid-19th century (Hodgson collection, 1845–57 or 1967 implied). Since the second-generation Yakthung scholars did not know the Old Sirijanga script, they mimicked the Devanagari (Nepali and Hindi) script. The second-generation Yakthung writers, like the first-generation Yakthung rhetors, added many characters to the Sirijanga script (mimicked the Devanagari writing system). Like the first-generation Yakthung writers, the second-generation Yakthung writers were not consistent in relation to the Sirijanga writing system; their use of the Sirijanga script differed from place-to-place and person-to-person. Some of the major reasons for the variations in the Sirijanga script or writing system were due to the heavy influence of the Devanagari writing system, slow means of communication (traditional post office-based network), oppressive government/s, and the Sirijangian literacy gap. The second-generation Yakthungs waged a campaign called the Patra-mitrata campaign to educate Yakthungs in the Sirijanga script, Yakthung language, and writing system. The major issue they encountered was that they had to rely on the slow *hulak* (traditional post office) service. Due to the lack of a fast means of communication as we have the Internet-based communication now, when the first-generation Yakthungs redesign the Sirijanga script and writing system, they, perhaps, had to depend upon their parents and grandparents who could barely remember the Sirijanga writing system.

Once the second-generation Yakthung writers gradually learned the Sirijanga script, writing system, and Yakthung phonology, they realized that the Sirijanga characters that they used did not actually represent Yakthung language and phonology. So, the second-generation Yakthung scholars omitted some characters from the Sirijanga syllabaries. During my research, I had opportunities to talk to Yehang Laoti and B. B. Muringla (both were Patra-mitre campaign representatives and writers), including Pratap Pomo from Golaghat Assam, and in the interviews, they mentioned that they, including other Yakthungs, added as well as omitted many syllabaries, and sadly, they did not know the Old Sirijanga script at all. Until the late 20th century, the teaching and learning of Yakthung language and script was banned for which Yakthungs were very closely watched in Nepal. For instance, the Khas Aryans used to disguise as *sadhus* (Hindu religious saints) and frequently wandered around the Yakthung communities until the restoration of democracy in

1990. The duty of the *sadhus* was to secretly watch Yakthungs, and their social, cultural, and political activities and to report to the Khas Aryans (Tumbahang, 2017). Similarly, the Khas Aryan neighbors used to also watch Yakthungs' language, literacy, and cultural activities in Yakthung laje. In this manner, the Khas Aryans suppressed the teaching and learning of Yakthung language, writing, and Mundhum rhetorics for over 240 years in Nepal.

Despite the Khas Aryan suppression, the second-generation Yakthungs played a great role to the restoration of the Sirijanga script and writing system. Beginning from the first-generation, Yakthungs started sowing the seed of Yakthung spiritual, psychological, and intellectual emancipation. They started relinking Sawa Yet Hang epistemologies, Susuwa Lilim Yakthung sagacity, traditional Yet Hang and Thibong Yakthung customary laws and practices in the context of the 20th century. It was obvious that their lifestyle was not who they actually were; their way of life and tradition were constructed in the Khas Aryan, Indian, and European social and academic institutions. Despite the Khas Aryan suppression, Yakthungs knew that their minds, bodies, and souls were imprisoned in Khas Aryan and Indian social institutions. Therefore, they collectively struggled to decolonize their knowledge; decolonizing their mind liberated them from perpetuating the Khas Aryan, Indian, and Western politics of knowledge construction. Hence, the first-generation and second-generation Yakthung scholars campaigned to liberate their minds, bodies, and souls in multiple ways from the Khas Aryan, Indian, and British colonial cage. Their collective endeavor via Shree Yakthung Hang Chumlung, Yakthung Chumlungs, and Patra-mitrata campaign challenged the Khas Aryan para-colonization and relinked Susuwa Lilim Yakthung, Yet Hang, and Thibong Yakthung Suhang epistemologies.

Contribution of the Patra-mitrata campaign to the development of Yakthung language and literacies

Yehang Laoti (2069 BS) states that due to Khas Aryan oppression, Yakthungs almost forgot the Sirijanga script and writing system, including their cultural and linguistic identities, and many people did not want to read and write in the Sirijanga script because the Khas Aryans forced Yakthungs to observe their Yakthung culture through the Khas Aryans lenses. As I stated earlier, Khas Aryan suppression, such as torture and/or execution frequently caused fear and anxiety in Yakthung communities. Due to the constant Khas Aryan oppression, Yakthung knowledge was (still is) caged in Khas Aryan norms in visible forms, or Sawa Yet Hang and Susuwa Lilim wisdom was (still is) trapped in the Khas Aryan social, cultural, academic, and religious institutions. The Yakthung Suhangs' knowledge was cocooned in the Khas Aryan social, religious, political, and academic institutions. Therefore, according to Yehang Laoti (2069 BS), even during the Patra-mitrata campaign, many ignorant Yakthungs suggested them (Patra-mitrata progressive intellectuals) not to waste their time and energy to read and write in Yakthung language and script; they suggested their *Yakthung phu-ne-nusa* (brothers and sisters) to rather learn Nepali and English or Hindi (pp. 357–60). However, progressive Yakthung intellectuals did not give up the Patra-mitrata campaign; they constantly networked and learned to read and write in the Sirijanga script in *Yakthung pa:n* (Yakthung language).

Yakthung scholars and activists, who were culturally, linguistically, and academically conscious, initiated the Patra-mitrata campaign in Yakthung communities in the mid-20th century. The Patra-mitrata campaign was a resistance against the Khas Aryan oppression over the teaching and learning of the Yakthung language and literacy in Nepal. This campaign fought against the Khas Aryan colonization of mind, body, and soul; it fought against the Khas Aryan ideological construction of the para-colonial difference based on body, geography, space, and caste (Yakthungs never understood the meaning of the Hindu caste system). The Patra-mitrata campaign was a process of healing Yakthung wounds inflicted by para-colonizers (Bahuns) for centuries. It was a process of decolonizing the Yakthung mind, body, and wisdom. As majority of Yakthungs lived in Yakthung laje, Nepal, Yakthungs, who lived in India, Burma, Bhutan, Bangladesh, Assam, and other places, were not able to independently restore, document, and disseminate Yakthung language, literacy, and Mundhum rhetorics. Therefore, Yakthungs, from Nepal, India, Bhutan, Assam, and Burma, networked and learned to read and write in the Sirijanga script in *Yakthung pa:n*. According to Yehang Laoti, the Yakthungs, who networked with other Yakthungs through Patra-mitrata, were required to read and write in the Sirijanga script (see figure 24). Through the Patra-mitrata network, Yakthungs requested other Yakthungs folks, from Nepal, India, Bhutan, Bangladesh, Burma, and Thailand, to teach the Sirijanga script and writing system in their communities. So, the purpose of Patra-mitrata campaign was to repair the displaced Yakthung linguistic and cultural identities, to relink Yet Hang and Thibong Yakthung rhetorical traditions, and to heal the tortured Yakthungs' physical and spiritual wounds. Among many other Yakthung community leaders and activists, some Yakthungs who consistently communicated in the Patra-mitrata campaigns were:

1   Imansing Chemjong, Nepal
2   Yehang Laoti, Biratnagar, Nepal
3   Atmananda Lingden, Chukchinamba, Ilam, Nepal
4   Gyanodaya Laoti, Ilam, Nepal
5   Purna Bahadur Hangshrong, Tehrathum, Nepal
6   Bijaya Subba, Tehrathum, Nepal
7   Bijuli Prasad Anchhangbo, Taplejung, Nepal
8   Harkajang Yakso, Taplejung, Nepal
9   Chandra Kumar Sherma, Panthar, Nepal
10 Purnajang Chemjong, Panthar, Nepal
11 Subedar Dhan Bahadur Anglabang, Mirik, Darjeeling
12 Subedar Bikram Sangbangphe, Kalimpong

13 Pratap Subba, Assam, India
14 Padam Muringla, Sikkim
15 B. B. Muringla, Sikkim
16 Akbar Tamling, Higaun, Sikkim
17 Yam Prasad Yakwa, Sikkim
18 Chandra Mangyung, Sikkim,
19 T. D. Phedaphang, Sikkim, etc.

(Laoti, 2069 BS, pp. 359–60)

The second-generation Yakthung progressive intellectuals/activists regularly networked, collaborated, and developed a basic level of Yakthung language and literacy. As you see above, the Patra-mitrata network was not only local, but was transnational. For instance, Sikkimi Yakthungs like B. B. Muringla and Chandra Mangyung regularly communicated with Imansing Chemjong and Yehang Laoti from Nepal. The Yakthungs who were engaged in the campaign and whoever were interested in the promotion of Yakthung language and literacy expanded the Patra-mitrata network up to Burma and beyond (see figure 24, the piles of letters, written during Patra-mitrata campaign). The Yakthungs who realized the dire situation of their language, writing, literacy, and identity wrote letters to even unacquainted Yakthung folks (Laoti, 2069 BS, pp. 357–60). Through Patra-mitrata network, they (Yakthungs) requested Yakthung Suhangs to encourage other Yakthungs to read and write in the Sirijanga script in *Yakthung pa:n*. In our different interviews, Yehang Laoti mentioned that he used to buy hundreds of Yakthung grammar booklets and mailed them to his Patra-mitre colleagues during the Patra-mitrata campaign.

According to Chandra Mangyung from Sikkim, in the Patra-mitrata campaign, he corresponded with several Yakthungs, including Imansing

Figure 24 Patra-mitrata letters compiled by Yehang Laoti (Source: Yehang Laoti).

Chemjong and Yehang Laoti. Both Imansing Chemjong and Yehang Laoti were from Nepal. Imansing Chemjong used to live in Naradevi, Kathmandu and Yehang (Dhan Prasad) Laoti used to live in Biratnagar. Through Facebook messages, Chandra Mangyung mentioned that he first networked with Imansing Chemjong; then, he corresponded with Yehang Laoti, including many other Yakthungs from Sikkim, Darjeeling, Kalimpong, Bhutan, Assam, and Burma with the purpose to restore the Sirijanga script and writing system, including Thibong Yakthung rhetorical traditions.

The second-generation Yakthung scholars not only popularized the Sirijanga script and writing system, but they also advocated for their rights to ancestral land, customary institutional practices, language, literacy, and Mundhum rhetorics in Yakthung laje. They knew that Yakthungs still spoke *Yakthung pa:n*, but the Sirijanga script, writing, and rhetorics were almost obsolete in Yakthung communities (Nepal, Sikkim, India, Bhutan, Bangladesh, and Burma, etc.). The Patra-mitrata campaign relinked Yet Hang and Thibong Yakthung Suhang language and literacy; it reshaped the Sirijanga script, writing, and Yakthung literacy in the modern Yakthung history. Among many other Yakthungs, the easy part of Patra-mitrata for Sikkimi Yakthungs was that the Sikkimi government approved the teaching of Yakthung language at schools in 1968. Hence, during the Patra-mitrata campaign, Chandra Mangyung was already a *Yakthung pa:n* teacher, and B. B. Muringla was still

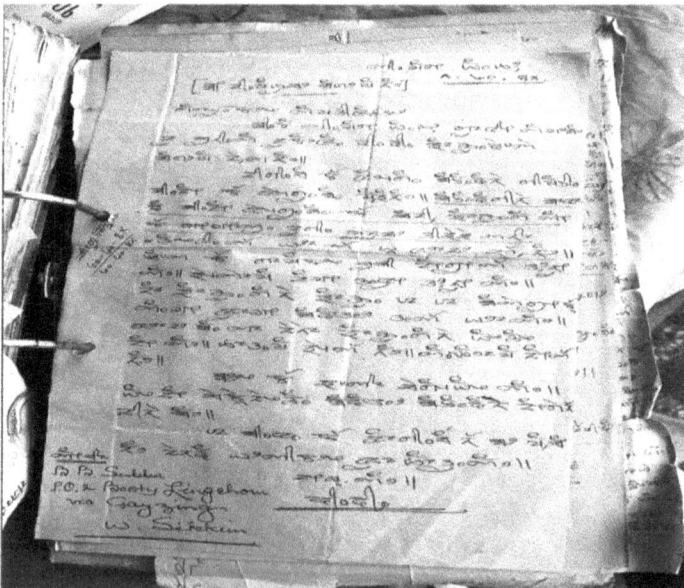

Figure 25 B. B. Muringla's letter to Yehang Laoti (Source: Yehang Laoti).

teaching his villagers the Sirijanga script and writing system in Lingchom, Sikkim (see Muringla's letter to Yehang Laoti in figure 25).

Chandra Mangyung mentioned that he communicated with Imansing Chemjong and Yehang Laoti from Nepal and with many Yakthungs from Sikkim, Darjeeling, Kalimpong, Bhutan, Assam, and Burma. He further mentioned that due to the regular Patra-mitrata network, they collectively could shape the Sirijanga script and writing system even though they lived in different countries, had different political values, and never met in face-to-face situations. The Patra-mitrata campaign further prompted Yakthungs to collaboration, writing, editing, and publishing various journals and magazines to promote Yakthung language and literacy. Later, the Patra-mitrata network profoundly facilitated the teaching of Yakthung language after the Sikkimi government officially approved the Limboo (Yakthung) language teaching at schools.

The collective campaign of Yakthungs rearticulated Yakthung history, Sawa Yet Hang, and Susuwa Lilim Mundhum narratives. The first-generation and second-generation Yakthung progressive intellectuals knew that traditions do not exist by themselves, but they must be constructed and be invented (by Yakthung themselves). In Nepal, even though Yakthungs were not allowed to read and write, they promoted Yakthung language,

Figure 26 Chemjong's letter to Yehang Laoti (Source: Yehang Laoti).

writing, and literacy, and they printed Yakthung books (grammar books) and secretly distributed in Yakthung communities. According to Yehang Laoti, during the Patra-mitrata campaign, he worked for the Nepali government; however, he resisted the Khas Aryan coercion. Laoti mentioned that he wrote letters even in his office and sent them (he called them "airmails") to other Yakthungs. Laoti also mentioned that during the Patra-mitrata campaign, many Yakthungs were captured, tortured, and banished from Nepal, but he was one of the luckiest Yakthung progressive intellectuals who never got arrested.

The Patra-mitrata campaign (promotion of Yakthung language and literacy) paved the way to Yakthung Suhang's discovery of self. Via the Patra-mitrata campaign, their way of probing self was a way to search their existence as the descendants of Yet Hang and Thibong Yakthung Suhangs. The Patra-mitrata campaign was a collective struggle to relink Yet Hang and Thibong Yakthung social, Mundhumic, cultural traditions and link the Thibong Yakthung Suhang customary traditions to current and future Yakthung Suhang traditions. The campaign led Yakthungs' ontological identities, such as discovery of their being Yakthung, becoming Yakthung, and belonging in physical and spiritual Yakthung laje in Yakthung Suhang way. Their struggle gradually paved the Yakthung's critical path to their *cho:tlung* (destination). In this journey, Yakthungs denaturalized the Khas Aryan and Western cultural and linguistic colonization. In this critical Yakthung Suhang journey, Yakthungs relinked their Yet Hang and Thibong Yakthung epistemologies and reconstructed their own Yakthung Suhang communal epistemological, ontological, and axiological customary rhetorical traditions. The first-generation and second-generation Yakthung scholars of the 20th century helped Yakthung communities (within Nepal and beyond) reframe Yakthung epistemologies, Susuwa Lilim Yakthung epistemologies, and Thibong Yakthung histories from the 20th century's contexts. They oriented Yakthungs and Yakthung communities, in such a way that they would link both the distant Yakthung past to the distant Yakthung future in the context of the 20th century. The 19th century scholars, such as Jobhansing Limbu, Chyangresing Phedangba, Ranadhoj Limbu, and Jit Mohan relinked Yet Hang and Thibong Yakthung Suhang histories, narratives, cultural practices, and Mundhum rhetorics and updated them from the 19th century perspectives; they handed them down to the 20th century the first and second-generation Yakthung activists, community leaders, and scholars. Now, we, the Yakthungs of the 21st century, have become not only the keepers of the traditional Yakthung Suhang knowledge, but we also have become the balancers of the distant past, present, and distant future Yakthung Suhang wisdoms. So, we collectively have to relink traditional Yakthung Mundhum theories, philosophies, and practices; we have to remap Yakthung Mundhum philosophies that will tap into higher Yakthung Suhang wisdom to create an inclusion, equity, dignity, and representation in multiple aspects in Yakthung laje.

Sites of Yakthung journals and pamphlets in Nepal and beyond

The first-generation Yakthung scholars shifted the original Sirijanga script an /a/-based syllabary to an /ə̂/-based syllabary (Bajbir Subba's *Tum Yakthung Ningwaphu Sapla* 1928 implied). The first-generation Yakthungs were not familiar with the Old Sirijanga script, for Yakthungs did not have any books written in the Old Sirijanga script. The Khas Aryans destroyed all Yakthung books and documents in Yakthung laje, Nepal, and European colonial agents procured all Yakthung books and manuscripts from Sikkim, Darjeeling, and Kalimpong. Therefore, the first-generation Yakthungs ignorantly shifted the /a/-based syllabary to an /ə̂/-based one in the early 20th century. Then, Yakthungs collectively followed the Bajbirian Sirijanga script (Nepali and Hindi Devanagari writing style). They wrote Yakthung Barnamala (Yakthung grammar books), Yakthung syllabaries, Yakthung hymns, and Mundhums (in the new Bajbirian Sirijanga writing system). Hence, the second-generation Yakthungs mostly pursued what the first-generation Yakthung progressive intellectuals initiated because it was easier for them to read and write, and they also did not know about the Old Sirijanga script and writing system.

Through the Patra-mitrata campaign, the second-generation Yakthungs documented and disseminated the Sirijanga script, writing, and rhetorics in South Asia, such as Nepal, India, Burma, Bhutan, Bangladesh, and Thailand. They were, to some extent, able to standardize the Sirijanga syllabary; then, the Sirijanga syllabary came up to the point of publishing popular journals and pamphlets. The second-generation Yakthungs could foresee and exploit more than just introducing the Sirijanga syllabary, Yakthung Barnamala (grammar), history, and Yakthung hymns. The second-generation Yakthungs also started collecting Yakthung narratives, stories, and Mundhums, and they edited and published innumerable Yakthung journals in the Sirijanga script in *Yakthung pa:n*. This period was one of greatest sites of delinking cultural and linguistic para-colonization (both in India and Nepal), relinking Sawa Yet Hang, Susuwa Lilim Yakthung, Yet Hang, and Thibong Yakthung Suhang epistemologies, and linking Yakthung Suhang cultural traditions in local and global context from the 20th century Yakthung perspectives.

In terms of the development of Yakthung language and literacy, B. B. Muringla and Chandra Mangyung edited and published *Tum-Tum Tunhena*. *Tum-Tum Tunhena*'s major audiences were all basic, intermediate, and advanced level Yakthung readers, and the medium of publication was a carbon copy. According to B. B. Muringla (2017), they could produce three copies or print three carbon copies at a time, and in carbonated print, four or five copies can be printed if the right tools are used. Back to the subject matter, even though Khas Aryans politically and militarily suppressed Yakthung language and literacy, Yakthungs resisted the Khas Aryan oppression. Similarly, they published journals and popular magazines; the publication of Yakthung journals and magazines highly contributed to the restoration of the Sirijanga script, writing, and Mundhum rhetorics. For instance, Birahi Kainla published *Kom* (a handwritten journal) in 1967 (2024 BS), which is/ was regarded as the first Yakthung journal, or it was one of the first journals in the development of Yakthung language and literacy. Later, Ashman Subba edited and published *Sak-ingkhang* journal in Kathmandu from 2026 BS (1969), and Puspa Thamsohang edited and published *Sirijanga* journal since 1972 from Darjeeling. Puspa Thamsohang was a Yakthung activist, community leader, and writer, and as he advocated for Yakthungs' rights to their language, writing, and ancestral land, the Khas Aryan discriminatory government considered him as a threat to the Khas Aryan regime. So, by convicting him of the political treason, the Khas Aryan-centric government banished him, including his colleague Bir Nembang from Yakthung laje, Nepal. After the expulsion from Limbuwan, Puspa Thamsohang lived in Darjeeling from where he edited and published the journal called *Sirijanga* up to 12 issues (Y. Laoti, personal communication, May 23, 2017, 2018; B. B. Muringla, personal communication, May 28; May 25, 2017). During this period, some of the notable journals and pamphlets published (from Sikkim) were:

Thokla (1973 or 2030 BS)
Nowa Inghang (1978)   Sekmari (1980)
Pe?li (1981)   Lingnaamphung (1981)
Sirijanga (1982)   Aani Lakkhum (1982)
Saakthimsung (1983)   Marotiphung (1983)
Phung.ik (1983)   To:ji (1983)
Sumbugen Hukwa (1984)   Tijo (1983)
Chuksadin Sewa (1984)   Tijo (1984)
Naadang (1986)   Taanaam (1985)
Muinaam (1987)   Ime:tnasung (1986)
Tummui (1987)   Ningsang (1987)
Uwa unning (1988)   Mering (1988)
Phungwaanaambaa (1988)   Laamdhaan (1988)
Phung.ik (1988)   Naamsaang (1988)
Sikkim Herald (1989)   Aani Phung.ik (1988)
Sangsemi (1991), etc.   Yakthung Sakpewa (1990)
                             (Amar J. Limbu, 2017; G. M. Subba 2018;
                                            Yehang Laoti, 2018)

Though the journals were the emerging site of delinking, relinking, and linking approach, the second-generation Yakthung activists and scholars denaturalized the Khas Aryan, Indian, and European logic of knowledge construction. The journals as evidence portrayed that we (Yakthungs) have our own language, script, writing system, *khambong-lungbong* (land-based) identities, and Mundhum rhetorics. The Patra-mitrata and Yakthung language-based journal and pamphlets, first, delinked colonially constructed knowledge that the Yakthung language is inferior; second, they constructed

Yakthung knowledge of self-respect. Meaning, Yakthungs constructed the knowledge that we have our language, history, and writing that are valued, validated, and respected both in popular and academic cultures (formal, non-formal, and information spaces implied). The Patra-mitrata campaign and Yakthung journals embodied the Yakthung Suhang ethos of their reflexivity that emphasized delinking Khas Aryan, Indian, and Western colonial logic of knowledge construction. It paved the Yakthung Suhang literacy path of commitment of relinking Yet Hang and Thibong Yakthung Suhang customary institutional epistemologies. They paved the path that linked their own identities in the context of the 20th century Yakthung Suhang cultural and political conditions. The second-generation Yakthung *tutu-tumyahangs'* campaign was the intersection of Yakthungs self-respect and silenced Yakthung communities for centuries. Via the Patra-mitrata campaign and Yakthung language-based journals and pamphlets, Yakthung writers helped other Yakthungs and their children delink and/or delearn what they had been taught at Khas Aryan-centric, Indian, and European social and academic institutions.

After the advent of so-called democracy in Nepal in 1990, Yakthungs started the teaching and learning in Yakthung language. Once Yakthungs became literate in their own culture, language, and writing, they started writing essays, articles, stories, and Mundhums in the Sirijanga script in *Yakthung pa:n*. They understood the meaning of collective power; they understood the meaning of networking, creating, and succeeding within Yakthung community and beyond; a huge number of Yakthungs for the first time realized how it felt to be literate in their own language and writing system. Most of the journals, as implied above, were chirographic and lithographic (in relation to publishing process). As a result, many popular journals appeared in the market for time being and disappeared right away without gaining any popularity in public (usually due to the Khas Aryan-centric oppressive government). Some of the notable Yakthung journals published from Nepal were:

Naamsange (2032 BS)
Sirijanga (2051 BS)   Yakthung Sapsak nu Sakthim (2049 BS)
Tanchhoppa (2052 BS)   Sumhaatlung (2056 BS)
Laam (2057 BS)   Sehonaamlaang (2057)
Laraangseri (2057 BS)   Kirat Cheli (2058 BS)
Chumlung Bulletin (2059 BS) Semi Phaktaanglung (2060 BS)
Yakthungba (2051 BS)   Thaangsaang (?)
Hinja (?)   Mundhum (?)
Tangsing (?)   Lungwaa (?)

Sekmaari/Sekmuri (?) was published from Kirat Yakthung Chumlung, Hong Kong in Nepali language.

(Ambar J. Limbu, 2017; G. M. Subba 2018;
Yehang Laoti, 2018)

Before the advent of democracy, Yakthungs knew that their body, soul, and knowledge were trapped in the Khas Aryan social and academic institutions, and after the advent of the democracy in 1990, the urgent task for Yakthungs was to decolonize their own mind, body, and soul.

Via the Patra-mitrata campaign and Yakthung journals, Yakthungs denaturalized Khas Aryan and Western cultural and linguistic colonization; the Patra-mitrata campaign and Yakthung journals were the first site of the decolonial shift. Mignolo (2007) contends that the decolonial shift is a project of delinking, denaturalizing, and unlearning colonial logic of knowledge construction (p. 547). In terms of Nepal, Yakthung activists and scholars risked their lives for the emancipation of Yakthung culture, Yakthung Suhang wisdom, and Sawa Yet Hang sagacity before the advent of democracy. Their collective struggle enabled the delinking (decolonial) era that greatly offered Yakthungs a sense of their being and becoming Yakthung Suhang in the context of the 21st century Yakthung civilization.

The Yakthung journals and pamphlets gradually contributed to the development of Yakthung language and literacy in the Yakthung formal education system. Despite the Khas Aryan-centric Nepali government's ban to establish any social institution, Yakthungs felt the urgency of delinking the Khas Aryan politics of knowledge construction; they felt the urgency of delearning the Khas Aryan para-colonization of the Yakthung body, soul, and mind. They felt the urgency to challenge the Khas Aryans politics of divide and rule in Yakthung laje. Via the Patra-mitre campaign and journals and pamphlets, Yakthungs delinked Khas Aryan cultural colonization and relinked their traditional Yet Hang and Thibong Yakthung epistemologies. The journals and pamphlets, including Yakthung social institutions and the Patra-mitrata campaign, provided Yakthungs what the Khas Aryan-centric discriminatory Nepali government didn't provide for centuries. It gave voice to voiceless Yakthungs; it provided hope for hopeless Yakthungs; it provided Yakthung Suhang identity for the first time after a long time (the Treaty of Salt-Water implied). For Yakthungs, their writing was physically and spiritually becoming Yakthung Suhang; becoming Yakthung Suhang in the writing mean relinking traditional Yakthung Suhang customary institutions, practices, and civilization once again; being Yakthung Suhang in writing meant, belonging in Yakthung laje. For us (Yakthungs), writing is our soul; it is our heart; it is our *khambong-lungbongsa* space; they flow between our ancestors and descendants, by linking our Yet Hang and Thibong Yakthung historical traditions and distant future Yakthung Suhang cultural rhetorics.

Khas Aryan political ideologies and Yakthung language and literacy movement

The second-generation Yakthungs, like the first-generation Yakthungs, encountered Khas Aryan structural brutalities and systemic oppressions. In 1956, Yakthungs demanded their rights to mother-tongue education, politics, and *kipat* or rights to ancestral land based on the Nun-Paani Sandhi in Nepal. However, Surya Bahadur Thapa, Badriprasad Thapaliya, Tilbikram Maske,

Ganga Prasad Sitaula, and Ganga Dahal disputed against the Yakthung demands. Yakthung demands were misinterpreted and were never addressed (Nembang, 1987). In 1961, King Mahendra Shah and his cronies (Khas Aryans) rather than addressing the demands of Yakthungs, confiscated their (Yakthung) rights to their ancestral land, customary institutional laws and practices, mother-tongue education, and religion. The Khas Aryans disregarded the treaty—Nun-Paani Sandhi. Mahendra Shah and his cronies imposed the Khas Aryan only ideology, such as *eutai bhasha, eutai bhesh, eutai dharma, eutai raja*, and *eutai desh* (one language, one costume, one religion, one King, and one country), etc. The Khas Aryan-centric Nepali government continued to prohibit Yakthungs from the teaching and learning of their language, script, and writing; they also forbade Yakthungs to promote their culture, religion, language, and writing. The Khas Aryans ignored the demands of Limbus; those who revolted against the Khas Aryan *eutai bhasha, eutai bhesh, eutai dharma, eutai raja*, and *eutai desh* campaign were captured, jailed, humiliated, executed or banished from Nepal (Lumphungwa Limbu, 2075 BS; Nembang, 1987). The Khas Aryans started the lethal campaign—one country, one culture, one language to eliminate Yakthungs, including other Indigenous cultures, languages, religions, and other traditional epistemologies in Nepal.

The *Pallo Kirat Limbuwanka Magharu* (2002 BS?) suggests that the Yakthungs appealed many times for the Yakthung rights to inclusion, dignity, and equity, such as Yakthung *kipat*, administrative positions, politics, and mother-tongue education, etc., but the Khas Aryans misinterpreted the Yakthung demands. Instead of negotiating with Yakthungs, Yakthungs received only hostile responses. For instance, Chaitanya Subba (1995) states:

> There is no doubt that sense of insecurity and fear of being disenfranchised from any stake of future progress and prosperity, feeling of humiliation, disgrace, domination, disfavor and social degradation, arrogant attitude as well as culturally incompatible even often hostile responses of the ruling elites are in fact some of the responsible factors that have been generating and promoting misunderstanding, hostility and rivalry among culturally diverse groups of people, particularly between traditionally dominant ruling classes and the newly emerging social (Indigenous ethnic) forces. (p. 306)

Even though Yakthungs, along with other Indigenous peoples are in majority in Nepal, have been systematically minoritized, they have already been systematically manacled by the Khas Aryan cultural, academic, ideological, and political institutions. The Khas Aryan-centric Nepali government abused political, economic, and military power to humiliate, disgrace, and demean Yakthungs, including other Indigenous peoples.

As Yakthungs learned why their demands were important for them as well as for their children and future descendants, they revolted against the subjugation of Mahendra Shah. As the revolt was against the Khas Aryan political and ideological campaign, the Khas Aryan-centric government sent the Royal Nepali Army and other Nepali armed forces to the villages of Yakthung laje, Limbuwan. The Armies inhumanely shot innocent Yakthungs and killed who were herding their cattle in Yakthung villages; they killed Yakthungs who were strolling around in Yakthung laje; they captured, tortured, and killed hundreds of innocent Yakthungs who were working in their own farms in Yakthung laje (Lumphungwa Limbu, 2075 BS; Nembang, 1987, p. 16). As the Khas Aryan-centric government authorized the armies to exterminate Yakthungs, they did whatever they wanted to humiliate Yakthungs in their own homes, villages, and Yakthung laje. Nembang (1987) who was also banished from Yakthung laje, Nepal further states that the Khas Aryan armed forces got the Yakthungs to dig ditches; then, they shot and buried them in the ditches. Nembang further discloses the horrible incidents that the Khas Aryan armed forces shot innocent Yakthungs and buried many of them alive (p. 19). From the Nun-Paani Sandhi to current the Khas Aryan-centric Nepali government is castic-discriminatory; the Khas Aryans also abused power to exterminate Yakthungs, including other Indigenous peoples (vividly mentioned in this book); they engaged in the para-colonial difference based on caste, gender, religion, and language; this is one of the reasons why the Khas Aryan-centric Nepali government does not approve Yakthungs, including other Indigenous peoples, in the higher political, bureaucratic, and other policy making positions in Nepal.

It is quite common to hear that Khas Aryan political leaders, including diplomats and scholars, consider that the Khas Aryan-centric government is liberal, freedom-loving, and democratic. By labelling themselves as liberal, freedom-loving, and democratic, they label Yakthungs, including other Indigenous peoples as traitors and separatists. This ideological politics demonstrate that the Khas Aryan politics has been always discriminatory and reversal; meaning, they make Khas Aryan institutional castic racism invisible and systematic. The Khas Aryan political leaders, including diplomats, for instance, Mr. Ambassador Karki (who labelled Nepali Indigenous peoples as separatists in one of the informal gatherings in Michigan, USA) and Aryan folks claim/ed that they are not racist, and they use reversal rhetoric and label Yakthungs, including Indigenous peoples as racists, separatists, and traitors in Nepal. By using the reversal rhetoric, the Khas Aryan-centric Nepal government always distorts and misinterprets the demands of Yakthungs and Indigenous peoples. Even after the restoration of democracy in 1990, when we (Yakthungs) talk about our history and Khas Aryan brutalities, the Khas Aryans call us separatists; they call us terrorists. If any Khas Aryans do not like Yakthungs, they call us whatever they want; they punish us as they want, for the Khas Aryans retain all state powers and resources. The problems would not come only from Khas Aryans, but our own self-centered Yakthungs also take their side in the name of political parties, titles, business advantages, and properties, etc. They (self-centered Yakthungs) support them to create discriminatory state rules and regulations (let's say, constitution);

Nepali constitution never favored Yakthungs and will never favor Yakthungs as long as Yakthungs, other Indigenous peoples, and minorities are not united to fight for their rights. Due to the Khas Aryans politics of divide and rule, we (Yakthungs ourselves) have been hurting each other for centuries (Limbu et al., 1845; Nembang, 1987, p. 20), and we can still experience such suicidal activities emerging from our own Yakthung communities. The suicidal behaviors often happen in Yakthung communities, for the para-colonizers know how to label, divide, displace, and destroy Yakthungs, including other Indigenous peoples. My *Yakthung phu-ne-nusa* and other Indigenous peoples have better examples, and you definitely remember some incidents while you read this book and also imagine what labels, divides, displaces, and destroys us and other indigenous peoples and minorities in Nepal.

Again, despite all theoretical and practical issues that I mentioned in this book, the second-generation Yakthung scholars, activists, and writers, like that of the 19th century and the first-generation Yakthungs, created the Yakthung epistemological playing field upon which we can play our own Yakthung communal games; the games of Yakthung histories, Susuwa Lilim Yakthung narratives, Yakthung Suhang Mundhums, and Yakthung sufferings. This is our playing field; we have or have to create our own game and own rules; we will not use the Khas Aryan, Indian, and Western standards to play our Yakthung Suhang games, or we must not use the Khas Aryan, Indian, and Western standards to play our Yakthung Indigenous games. We may use their rules as a reference, but we must not let them control us and our game. We ought to be thoughtful, critical, and imaginative about the norms and values that Khas Aryans and Europeans created because their values invariably exhibit Yakthungs as inferior and savage ones; their racist, sexist, and discriminatory lenses label Indigenous peoples as lazy and savage (but uncritical Yakthung fellow scholars always romanticize them). This problem arises when theorists, rhetors, and scholars go through the etic approach since Yakthung culture is different from Khas Aryan and Western colonial culture. Meaning, Sawa Yet Hang, Susuwa Lilim, and Yakthung cultures cannot be evaluated from the Khas, Indian, and Western standards. Many Yakthung pre-emergent scholars do not understand that Khas Aryan and Western rhetoric often misconstrues Yakthung Suhang cultural ideals, Thibong Yakthung social structures, and Yakthung rhetorical patterns; it is always difficult for us to understand Sawa Yet Hang, Susuwa Lilim Yakthung, Yet Hang, and Thibong Yakthung Suhang cultures via Khas Aryan, Indian, and Western lenses.

Understanding Yakthung culture via other cultural lenses is one of the challenging issues because we cannot be able to understand Yakthung rhetorics; however, our own Yakthung scholars introduce and preach in Yakthung or non-Western social and academic institutions. Furthermore, when Yakthung rhetoric is judged from the traditional hegemonic Khas and Western theories, they cannot get to the Sawa Yet Hang, Susuwa Lilim Yakthung, Yet Hang, and Thibong Yakthung cultural, political, and social epistemologies, ontologies, and axiologies. The Khas Aryan and Western theories deteriorate and/or distort our Yakthung Suhang culture (in the name of research). This may not be intentional, but Khas Aryans and Europeans have been indoctrinated to believe Hindu ideal patriarchal realities (Aryans implied) and Platonic ideal truth (European traditional traditions implied). As the result, they see their culture, writing, and religion superior to Yakthung culture (in relation to other culture: see also Binkley, 2004; Lipson, 2004; Lyon, 2004; Xu, 2004).

We (Yakthungs) must change the traditional trajectory of knowledge construction; we must change the Yakthung Indigenous epistemic game to incubate a new rhetoric in which we (Yakthungs) do not devalue our Sawa Yet Hang, Susuwa Lilim, Yet Hang, and Thibong Yakthung values. We must cease to distrust our trusts; it is the time to trust ourselves that we have tremendous Yet Hang, Thibong Yakthung, and Mundhumic knowledge to heal and maintain the Yakthung Suhang cultural rhetorical traditions. Now, we must trust ourselves to heal our para-colonial wounds; then, we can create unity, peace, progress, and prosperity in Yakthung communities (Limbu, 2017, p. 587). I call this healing process a delinking, relinking, and linking process; for me, delinking, relinking, and linking approach is the quest of the Yakthung progressive intellectuals' struggle that leads us to our self-discovery and *cho:tlung* (destination). Additionally, as long as we do not collectively advocate and combat for Yakthung peace, progress, prosperity, and unity for our own Yakthung Suhang purpose, the Khas Aryans, Indians, and Westerners will always divide us. They will label us and fight for that label (title) with other fellow beings; for instance, how external factors are misleading Yakthungs from the major Limbuwan issues; how invisible powers are dividing Yakthung in the name of religions and politics. Sadly, due to the internal conflicts, our *Yakthung phu-ne-nusa* are derailing from their main agenda for their progress and prosperity; they are derailing from how they have to prepare themselves and their children for tomorrow. Hence, we must protect ourselves from further misrepresentation, fragmentation, mystification, and commodification. We all have to be links of a chain, and we do not want to be an unwanted link in the chain; we don't want to be the ignored link in the system; we must cling together as local and global citizens to get to our *cho:tlung*.

Part VI

The third Yakthung literacy wave

Institutionalizing the Sirijanga script, writing, and rhetorics

10 Establishment of Kirat Yakthung Chumlung and sites of Yakthung language and literacies in Nepal

The Nepali Yakthungs invariably advocated for their rights to mother-tongue education, *khambong-lungbong* (land-based) identity, and inclusion in politics despite the fact that Khas Aryans divided Yakthungs into *niti* and *samariti* and destroyed their collective power for centuries (Limbu, 2019; Limbu, 2016). In 1925, Yakthungs founded a Yakthung social institution, Shree Yakthung Hang Chumlung in Kalimpong to collectively create their spaces, identities, and social recognitions. Similarly, Sikkime Yakthungs founded Akhil Sikkim Kirat Limbu Chumlung in 1973. Likewise, although the Khas Aryan-centric Nepali government did not permit Indigenous peoples to establish any ethnicity-related social institutions until 1990, Yakthung community leaders, scholars, activists, and students founded a Yakthung social institution, Kirat Yakthung Chumlung (KYC) in 1989 in Kathmandu (Limbu Lumphungwa, 2019, pp. 154–64; Singak-Limbu, 2018). As this book focuses on the development of the Sirijanga script, writing, and rhetorics, it discusses how KYC facilitated the development of Yakthung language and literacy. Hence, this chapter briefly discusses the establishment of Kirat Yakthung Chumlung (KYC) in Nepal, and how Yakthungs have utilized KYC as a *chumlungden* (contact zone) to promote Yakthung language and literacy and to facilitate the Yakthung network to collaborate and advocate for their cultural, linguistic, and academic identities. The chapter succinctly focuses on why KYC established other specialized organization, such as Limbuwan Studies Center, Limbu Bhasha Sahitya Pratisthan, Limbu Saskritik Parisad, Yakthung Sahayog Kosh, and Kirat Yakthung Chumlung-Punarjeevan Kendra (will discuss Limbuwan Study Center only in the next chapter). This chapter also depicts how KYC created spaces through which Yakthungs could delink Khas Aryan, Indian, and European cultural and linguistic colonization and relink Yet Hang and Thibong Yakthung cultural traditions from the 21st century perspective.

The progressive Yakthung activists established Kirat Yakthung Chumlung on September 2, 1989 in Nepal, which was another form of Shree Yakthung Hang Chumlung (Kalimpong) and Akhil Sikkim Kirat Limbu Chumlung. After the establishment of Shree Yakthung Hang Chumlung in Kalimpong, Yakthungs understood the influence of collaboration, creation, and success as a collective Yakthung Suhang power. The Yakthung Chumlungs were effective to unite Yakthungs from across the world and collectively promote Yakthung writing and rhetorics, Yakthung language and literacies, and Mundhum epistemologies. After the foundation of KYC, it linked Yakthungs from across the world, and they collectively relinked Yet Hang and Thibong Yakthung Suhang cultural rhetorical traditions. It delinked the Khas Aryan, Indian, and Western cultural colonization and relinked Sawa Yet Hang epistemologies, Yet Hang and Thibong Yakthung epistemic traditions. KYC gave what the Khas Aryan-centric oppressive culture did not give to Yakthung Suhangs for centuries. To strategically and tactfully address Yakthung and Limbuwani issues, they (Yakthungs) established several other Yakthung organizations across the world (will discuss later). When Yakthungs founded the first Kirat Yakthung Chumlung in Nepal, the following personnel were the founding executive officers:

> Chairperson/President: Nanda Kandangwa
> Vice Chairperson/Vice President: Rakam Chemjong
> Secretary: Tej Bahadur Yakso
> Assistant Secretary: Uttamsing Thangden
> Treasurer: Laxmi Labung Limbu
> Member: Nar Prasad Lumphungwa (Sunsari district representative)
> Member: Tika Sambamphe (Morang district representative)
> Member: Chhabi Subba (Jhapa district representative)
> Member: Dipak Thebe (Ilam district representative)
> Member: Omraj Sambamphe (Panthar district representative)
> Member: Bhim Chongbang (Taplejung district representative)
> Member: Gopal Sanhita (Shangkhuwasabha district representative)
>   (Source: Nar Prasad Lumphungwa)

Yakthungs of the late 20th century understood that their priority ought to be the reintroduction of the Sirijanga script and writing, for writing was a tool to reclaim their Thibong Yakthung Suhang and *khambong-lungbong* (land-based) identities. They knew that writing is a sign of struggle; a struggle to delink (para) colonization and to relink Yet Hang (eight chieftains) and Thibong Yakthung Suhang epistemologies; a struggle to create Yakthung space and challenge the dominant Khas Aryan hegemony. They weaponized Yakthung language and writing as signs of Yakthung struggle; writing as a struggle of memorizing Sawa Yet Hang (refers to Yakthung Mundhum), Susuwa Lilim Yakthung, Yet Hang, and Thibong Yakthung Suhang, for our present Yakthung situation cannot be recognized without relinking our Yet Hang and Thibong Yakthung cultural traditions in Yakthung laje, including their sufferings, betrayals, executions, and expulsions. Our writings should reflect how the Khas Aryans betrayed and still have been betraying us, how they deprived us of our rights and liberties, and how they consistently attempted to exterminate us (Yakthungs), our culture, language, and Yet Hang and Thibong Yakthung history. Our writing should vividly reflect how they wanted to make us the people without history, language, and culture. From this theoretical point of view, the establishment of KYC was one of the most instrumental Yakthung social institutions that delinked para-colonization, relinked Yakthung Suhang histories, and linked them in local and regional setting in the context of the modern Yakthung history in Nepal. We (Yakthungs) understand that KYC is a healing place; it heals the wounds inflicted by the Khas Aryans for centuries. Similarly, it provides voice to voiceless Yakthungs; it also provides a communal space to network, collaborate, and succeed as Yakthung Suhangs in the context of the 21st century (Limbu, 2017, p. 587). Conclusively, KYC became a collective *Yakthung Chumlungden* from where we (Yakthungs) have grown like Thibong Yakthung Suhangs once again in the context of the 21st century globalized world.

Yakthungs embraced writing as a place and sign of intellectual struggle. Our writing, during the (Thibong) Yakthung Suhang age, was a sign of our pride and identity; our writing (Patra-mitre campaign implied) during the Khas Aryan oppression until 1990 was a sign of resistance; and now our writing has become a sign of global visibility. So, our writing as a struggle is a movement against the oppressive boundaries, structural inequalities, and class/caste dominations in Nepal, including other Yakthung communities. Yakthungs have realized that they ought to seek alternative Indigenous-centric theories and ways of articulating our *khambong-lungbong* identities. We are in the urgency of theorizing Yakthung, including local and global Indigenous research methodologies that both solace our century-long inflicted wounds and provide our *khambong-lungbong* identities from where we can relink Yet Hang and Thibong Yakthung epistemologies, Yet Hang insights, Thibong Yakthung customary rhetorical traditions, and link them to our distant future Yakthung Suhang culture. From the newer delinking, relinking, and linking Yakthung Indigenous methodology, I, including my *phu-ne-nusa*, bridge both the past and future; and from this space, I/we can capture the epistemic activities of Sawa Yet Hangs, Yet Hang, and Thibong Yakthung Suhangs. From this place, I/we repair the displaced, distorted, and destroyed Yakthung Suhang histories, Yakthung epistemologies, and Mundhum rhetorics so that my/our distant future *phu-ne-nusa* can envision what Yakthung Suhang culture always had/has been. The alternative theories, principles, and methodologies we envision should be more ethno-relative to address the problems of Yakthung Suhangs, including Indigenous peoples within Yakthung communities and beyond.

As Yakthungs were culturally, linguistically, and politically colonized for centuries, they, immediately after the foundation of Kirat Yakthung Chumlung, realized that writing, rhetorics, and Mundhum literacies were spaces of struggle to re/landscape their physical, spiritual, and psychological spaces. They learned that these spaces were/are the signs of struggle to delink para-colonization, to relink Yakthung Suhang civilization, and to link them from the 21st century's context. Even before the restoration of democracy in Nepal (1990), Yakthungs researched and documented even during Rana regime (see Chapters 6 & 7) Yakthungs started sowing the seeds of delinking the colonization, and in the process of Yakthung delinking and relinking approaches, they resisted the Khas Aryan suppression; they understood that resistance was a power to create a critical Yakthung mass. Gradually, as the sites of delinking structural inequalities and hierarchical Khas Aryan hegemonic castic dominations, though in small number, Yakthungs started questioning and contesting the Khas Aryan hegemonic ideologies, Khas Aryan dominant values before the restoration of democracy in Nepal.

Ever since Yakthungs established Kirat Yakthung Chumlung in 1989, they also established non-government organization and Yakthung social institutions, and they collectively have advocated for their cultural, linguistic, political, and geo-political (Limbuwan) identities. After the foundation of KYC in Nepal, Yakthungs evidently felt the power of unity within the country and beyond. By knowing the significance of KYC, they established several KYCs in various districts of Yakthung laje, including some other districts of Nepal. These Kirat Yakthung Chumlungs include:

1 Kirat Yakthung Chumlung, Tehrathum,
2 Kirat Yakthung Chumlung, Sangkhuwasabha,
3 Kirat Yakthung Chumlung, Dhankuta,
4 Kirat Yakthung Chumlung, Sunsari,
5 Kirat Yakthung Chumlung, Morang,
6 Kirat Yakthung Chumlung, Taplejung,
7 Kirat Yakthung Chumlung, Panchathar,
8 Kirat Yakthung Chumlung, Ilam,
9 Kirat Yakthung Chumlung, Jhapa
10 Kirat Yakthung Chumlung, Kathmandu
11 Kirat Yakthung Chumlung, Lalitpur
12 Kirat Yakthung Chumlung, Bhaktapur
13 Kirat Yakthung Chumlung, Chitawan
14 Kirat Yakthung Chumlung, Okhaldhunga (proposed)
15 Kirat Yakthung Chumlung, Kaski (proposed)

The KYC branches collectively collaborate, network, and succeed in the context of the 21st century. Their active network initiation from a local to regional level has changed the landmarks of Yakthung Suhang spaces in relation to their linguistic identities, Yakthung Suhang subjectivities, Yakthung communal agencies, and Yakthung Mundhum theories and philosophies.

Networking with Yakthung *phu-ne-nusa* within Nepal and beyond

After the advent of Web 2.0 and social media, network communication became easier than in the past; communication, networks, collaboration, knowledge construction and sharing processes, and content circulation processes became easier than ever. In this digital age, information and knowledge are key determinants of social transformation in which language is a primary trajectory for information and knowledge. To create content and circulate the information, the Internet plays instrumental role to expose one's individual and collective identities. We have already experienced the multimodal discourse, especially video or YouTube video exponentially impacting the global communities in the last several years. For example, Marohang Limbu (2013) states:

> [Yakthungs] profoundly use social media (Facebook, blogs, Wikis, YouTube, Google Sites, Google Hangout, Twitter, podcasting, and Skype) across the [world], cloud-based communication considerably changed [Yakthungs'] personal and professional lifestyles. The cloud-based communication has not only changed the way [Yakthungs] network— communicate, collaborate, share, and co/create contents—in this digital village, but it has also changed the way [they] circulate information across global cultures. (p. 67)

Because of the prosumer-based engaged networked tools and cloud technologies, Yakthung (cultural, linguistic, and political) activists are connected with other activists in the cloud, such as social media, interactive cloud tools, zoom conference, YouTube videos, and webinars. The 21st century interactive technologies and smart handheld devices offer Yakthungs the opportunity where they network with other activists from different parts of the world who they have never met in their life. It explicitly encourages to observe para-colonial discourse the way they have never thought of; it facilitates them campaign, advocate, and fight for their rights. Via the local and global engaged digital or cloud networks, they discover strategic and tactical skills to delink Khas Aryan, including Indian cultural and linguistic colonization in local contexts. The cloud and crowd-based networks empower them to relink Sawa Yet Hang, Yet Hang, and Thibong Yakthung epistemologies and finally to establish harmonious, cooperative, and inclusive communities for themselves and for community members (Limbu, 2016; see also Limbu, 2013, p. 67).

Yakthungs (including other Indigenous peoples) from around the world utilize digital affordances that interconnect oral-based Mundhum rhetorics with digital story-telling approaches and oral-performance-based storytelling practices. These digital affordances not only facilitate our delinking and relinking methodologies, but they become a medium to heal or at least to solace the wounds inflicted by Khas Aryan, Indian, and Western colonizers. The digital affordances become tools to both collectively fight against the discrimination and to promote their effective participation in Yakthung Suhang rhetorical practices that concern them. In this process, Yakthungs relink Sawa Yet Hang epistemologies, Yet Hang insights, and Thibong Yakthung Suhang wisdoms. The digital affordances become tools to link the distant Yakthung past and distant future; the digital affordances facilitate Yakthung Suhangs network with other Indigenous communities. The digital network between Yakthungs and non-Yakthungs supports the conceptual, theoretical, and practical aspects of Yakthung culture, language, rhetorics, and Mundhum epistemologies. Such digital networks facilitate the promotion of Yakthung culture, including other local and global Indigenous cultures. For instance, KYCs, that are located in different countries, regularly network with other Yakthungs from across the world; they also frequently invite Yakthung political leaders, scholars, writers, and artists from Yakthung communities to globally network, interact, and inspire Yakthung culture and Mundhum rhetorics in the context of the 21st centuries.

Kirat Yakthung Chumlung's active network initiation, from a local to global level, has changed the landmarks of Yakthung Suhang epistemic spaces in relation to their linguistic identities, Yakthung Suhang subjectivities, and Yakthung Suhang communal agencies. In the context of the 21st century, Kirat Yakthung Chumlung, including Yakthungs, have utilized the power of cloud technologies (Web 2.0/3.0) not only to challenge the traditional para-colonialism, but also to relink their Yakthung Mundhum epistemologies. Yakthung cloud and crowd-based networks, in local and global contexts, have materialized the Yakthung Suhangs' compelling and pressing issues. Yakthungs' social institutions have been recalibrating, re-incubating, and reconnecting their ancestral Yet Hang histories and Thibong Yakthung Suhang epistemic activities via the 21st century's Yakthung Suhang epistemic lenses. Hence, Kirat Yakthung Chumlung has been relinking Sawa Yet Hang wisdom and Thibong Yakthung rhetorical traditions in multiple ways since its inception. Through the recalibrating and relinking processes, Yakthungs will link both Thibong Yakthung epistemologies and current Yakthung Suhang cultural traditions and practices. Our relinking process will also bridge Yet Hang knowledge, Thibong Yakthung wisdom, and current Yakthung Suhang subjectivities with that of distant future Yakthung Suhang *chumlung* spaces and subjectivities (Limbu, 2017, pp. 560–593).

Yakthungs (Indigenous people) always behave rationally with local and global *phu-ne-nusa*; we teach, learn, and share relationally. We always maintain a sense of family with both humans and non-humans relatively (Yakthung Mundhum implied). We also engage in communal relationships; we based on Mundhum discourse always act relationally in relation to nature-creature practices (see also Wilson, 2008). If we practice and perpetuate Yakthung Suhangs' relational and inter-relational Mundhum philosophy (performative philosophy) in social and academic institutions as (alternative) pedagogy, we will be able to create inclusive global institutions and cultures. In summation, our network with other global Indigenous, including non-Indigenous *phu-ne-nusa*, will promote our visibility; our network will facilitate Yakthungs' delinking, relinking, and linking approaches; our network and relational network will orient the descendants of Thibong Yakthungs. The orientation process will ultimately lead us to our Yakthung Suhang *cho:tlung* (destination). In other words, Yakthungs and Yakthung social institutions, such as KYC, are in the process of healing Yakthungs and Yakthung communities from the colonial wounds. To heal from the colonial wounds and to revive Indigenous language and literacy, every Indigenous person needs to rediscover himself or herself (Limbu, 2017, pp. 587, 589; see also Lambert, 2014, p. 10).

Currently, in the search of opportunities and careers, Yakthungs have migrated to different parts of the world, such as South Korea, Belgium, Israel, Portugal, Malaysia, Singapore, Saudi Arabia, Qatar, and beyond in the late 20th and 21st centuries. Similarly, due to the globalization, science, and technologies, immigration patterns in the late 20th and the early 21st centuries skyrocketed. Consequently, Yakthungs also immigrated and permanently settled in different parts of the world to seek better opportunities, such as for academic and economic prosperity. Though they immigrated to different parts of the world and achieved economic and academic prosperity, they have been contributing to the development of Yakthung language, writing, and Mundhum rhetorics in their new homes. To stay connected with other Yakthungs, they have established Kirat Yakthung Chumlungs (they have affiliation with KYC, Nepal) in their new home countries or workplaces. Among many other countries, Yakthung Suhangs founded Kirat Yakthung Chumlungs in the following countries:

1   Kirat Yakthung Chumlung, Hong Kong,
2   Kirat Yakthung Chumlung, USA,
3   Kirat Yakthung Chumlung, Canada,
4   Kirat Yakthung Chumlung, UK,
5   Kirat Yakthung Chumlung, Israel,
6   Kirat Yakthung Chumlung, Qatar,
7   Kirat Yakthung Chumlung, Malaysia,
8   Kirat Yakthung Chumlung, Portugal,
9   Kirat Yakthung Chumlung, Brunei,
10   Kirat Yakthung Chumlung, UAE,
11   Kirat Yakthung Chumlung, South Korea,
12   Kirat Yakthung Chumlung, Japan,
13   Kirat Yakthung Chumlung, Australia,
14   Kirat Yakthung Chumlung, Bahrain,
15   Kirat Yakthung Chumlung, Singapore,
16   Kirat Yakthung Chumlung, Kuwait,
17   Kirat Yakthung Chumlung, Germany, etc.

Through these social institutions, they not only constantly network to preserve, document, and disseminate their language, literature, culture, writing system, and Mundhum, but also collaborate to make their identities visible in local, regional, and global contexts. Kirat Yakthung Chumlungs, from across the world, have been helping the needy Yakthungs, including non-Yakthungs, in the new places (in their new homelands). They have been assisting the central Kirat Yakthung Chumlung, other Limbuwani (Yakthung and non-Yakthung) organizations, and Nepali people (in Nepal) in multiple ways.

Similarly, Yakthungs, both natives to their homelands and some new settlers in new places, have founded Yakthung social institutions in their countries and network with other Yakthungs from across the world. The Yakthung network is the strong evidence that Indigenous Yakthungs, like any global Indigenous peoples, do not believe in the modern political borders (the Treaty of Sugauli implied). For instance, the Khas Aryans and the British colonizers ideologically and politically dispersed Yakthungs in three countries—Nepal, India, and Sukhim via the Treaty of Sugauli in 1816 to weaken Yakthung collective power. Though the Khas Aryan, Indian, and British displaced *Yakthung phu-ne-nusa*; they remained *phu-ne-nusa* and will remain *phu-ne-nusa* forever. Based on the Yakthung relational and cultural border, Yakthungs have founded their Yakthung social institutions with the specific purpose to collectively document, disseminate, institutionalize, or preserve Yakthung culture, Mundhum rhetorics, cultural practices, and language. Among many others, some of the popular Yakthung Suhang social institutions in the native lands (other than Nepal) were/are:

1   Yakthung Shong Chumbho Dungrabasti, Kalimpong, India,
2   All India Limbu Tribal Association, Darjeeling Town,
3   Yakthung Tribal Youth Association, Mirik, Darjeeling,
4   Yuma Yakthung Tribal Youth Phojumbho, Darjeeling Town,
5   Yoktum Songsa Phojum, Ghoom,
6   West Bengal Limbu Development Board, West Bengal, India,
7   Kirat Community, Bhutan,
8   Limbu Mahashabha, Assam, India,
9   Kirat Chumlung, Bangkok, Thailand,
10   Myanmar Kirat-Yayokha Chumlung, Burma,
11   All India Limbu Mahasangha,
12   Sukhim Yakthung Sapsok Songjumbho, Sikkim,
13   Sirijanga Yakthung Sakthim Phojumbho.

The Yakthung social institutions network with other local and regional Yakthungs or Yakthung organizations; they organize local, regional, and international Yakthung-centric activities to communally share Yakthung Mundhum-based cultural theories and practices. In so doing, Yakthungs have been able to delink local and global colonization and to relink their Sawa Yet Hang or Susuwa Lilim Yakthung (Mundhum implied), Yet Hang, and Thibong Yakthung rhetorical traditions. Yakthungs have been exponentially documenting, preserving, and disseminating Yakthung history, Mundhum rhetorics, and Yakthung cultural lores in the recent years.

Similarly, by celebrating Yakthung festivals, such as *Chasok Tangnam, Sisekpa Tangnam,* and *Kakphekwa Tangnam* both in their new homes and native homelands, they document, disseminate, promote, and maintain Yakthung Suhang traditional cultural theories, philosophies, and practices. In this digital global village, Yakthungs communally have been relinking Sawa Yet

Hang, Yet Hang, and Thibong Yakthung Suhang cultural practices and have been linking Sawa Yet Hang, Susuwa Lilim Yakthung, and Thibong Yakthung Suhang cultural epistemologies in multiple ways. The Yakthung social institutions, such as KYC, are also establishing informal Yakthung language schools where they teach the Sirijanga script, Yakthung language, and Mundhum rhetorics to their children.

Teaching of *Anipa:n* in Nepal

Teaching of Yakthung language started in 2053 BS in Limbuwan, Nepal. Before the teaching of *Anipa:n* formally started in Yakthung laje, Kirat Yakthung Chumlung used to train Yakthungs as teachers to teach Yakthung language. Kirat Yakthung Chumlung organized informal Limbu (Yakthung) language centers in Kathmandu and Yakthung laje, Nepal. Later, the Khas Aryan-centric Nepali government approved the teaching of *Yakthung pa:n*; however, it has not provided any financial aid and did not provide any logistic support to the teaching of Yakthung language. Therefore, KYC managed and is still managing all resources for the teaching of *Yakthung pa:n*. In the beginning, the Yakthungs who were literate in Yakthung language, writing (script), and literacy volunteered to teach Yakthung language, script, and writing. When I was the High School Principal of National Orchid Boarding High School, Kathmandu, Nepal, I also attended some Yakthung meetings where Yakthungs discussed the approaches of teaching of Yakthung language. Although Yakthungs unanimously agreed to teach *Yakthung pa:n* in Yakthung laje, they lack/ed the financial resources and also did not or still do not have access to decision-making platforms to support the teaching of *Yakthung pa:n*. Therefore, to support the Yakthung language teachers, Yakthungs collected donations from the villagers; the donated amount from the villagers was very nominal, such as 10, 20, 30, or 50 Rupees (equivalent to US $0.10, $0.20, $0.30, or $0.50 cents); however, Yakthungs were excited and determined to teach *Yakthung pa:n*. Similarly, KYC facilitated to train Yakthung language teachers who were equally excited to teach Yakthung language and writing in remote Yakthung villages (N. P. Lumphungwa, personal communication, May 28, 2017).

According to Nar Prasad Lumphungwa (2017), Kirat Yakthung Chumlung also sent Bikram Subba to Dharan in 1994 to teach Yakthung language and writing in order to train Yakthung teachers (see figure 27). After Yakthungs received trainings, they went to the villages of Yakthung laje to teach Yakthung language and writing. KYC also published Yakthung textbooks, such as *Tarang* and *cho:tlung*, and the targeted audience of the books were both adult Yakthungs and Yakthung children. The purpose of the program was to introduce and/or bridge old Yakthung language, literacy, and cultural rhetorics to Yakthungs and Yakthung communities as in the late 20th century's perspective. Since Yakthungs have always been fluent Yakthung language speakers, or the trainees were fluent in *Yakthungpa:n*, their problem was only to learn the Sirijanga script and writing system, including Yakthung language grammar. In the process of introducing Yakthung language and literacy, "... Kirat Yakthung Chumlung, a registered ethnic NGO, has initiated four monthly non-formal education through Limbu language and [Sirijanga] script." Similarly, "[a]s a second pilot course, the same program being implemented in fiscal year 1994/95, with financial assistance of Canadian International Development Agency (CIDA)/Canadian fund" (Publisher's note). While KYC was supporting the Yakthung language development program, CIDA funded KYC's Yakthung language teaching initiatives for six months.

According to Arjun Limbu (2020), he was the coordinator of the program, and Nar Prasad Lumphungwa and Binod Pomo were the observers of the programs. As observers, Lumphungwa and Pomo went to Yakthung villages to both observe the teaching of Yakthung language and to pay the Yakthung teachers. During this period, as I mentioned above, Yakthungs wrote *Tarang* and *Cho:tlung* (with the technical and financial support of World Education) because the textbooks from Sikkim, India were not appropriate in Nepal due to the geo-political reasons. Although Kirat Yakthung Chumlung, including CIDA, was supporting this program, as Nar Prasad Lumphungwa mentioned, local Yakthungs also made donations to support the teaching of Yakthung language and literacy. According to Arjun Limbu and Nar P. Lumphungwa, the informal teaching of Yakthung language and literacy significantly contributed to the formal teaching of *Anipa:n* in formal setting in Nepal.

Figure 27   Yakthung language teachers trained by KYC (Source: Nar P. Lumphungwa

After the Nepali government approved the teaching of Yakthung language, *Anipa:n* has been taught in Taplejung, Panthar (Panchthar), Ilam, Tehrathum, Shangkhuwasabha, Dhankuta, Sunsari, and Morang districts. Currently, *Anipa:n* is taught approximately at 140 schools in Limbuwan region, and Kirat Yakthung Chumlung, local village development committees, and local Yakthung Suhangs have been supporting the program. Although the Central Kirat Yakthung Chumlung trained *Anipa:n* teachers in the beginning, the central Kirat Yakthung Chumlung later assigned district education offices and KYC district branches to locally train the *Anipa:n* teachers. Unfortunately, the central Nepali government (Khas Aryan-centric government) still has not played any role to produce well trained *Anipa:n* teachers and has not created any *Anipa:n* teacher positions at schools. Mahendra Lawoti (2013) mentions that "[the Khas Aryan] dominant group has control over discourse to perpetuate their group interests, maintain status quo of their dominant position or delayed changes as much as possible, resulting in delayed empowerment of multiple marginalized groups in Nepal" (p. xvii). This is one of the reasons why the village development committees and sometimes district offices are required to allocate the budget for the *Anipa:n* education. As the village development committees do not have an immense budget, the larger problem is that they (local village development committees) cannot allocate the budget in a regular basis. Similarly, since *Anipa:n* is taught as an optional subject, publishers do not want to publish the textbooks on time because the publishers give priority on bulky publications from which they can make larger profits.

Anipa:n has been taught at schools in Limbuwan, Nepal for more than a decade, and *Anipa:n* teachers have become experienced as well; they have produced many students. Furthermore, the upper level *Anipa:n* curriculum was designed in 2015 with the help of Yakthungs, KYC, and Yakthung scholars, including Yakthung language experts from Sikkim. Finally, the Nepali government approved it for implementation; however, what I am implying here is that the Khas Aryan-centric Nepali government does not provide any financial aid and resources. Hence, Yakthungs by themselves are steadily struggling to create their academic including social, cultural, and political spaces in Nepal. As my research informants, such as A. J. Limbu, Y. Lawoti, and A. Limbu mentioned, *Anipa:n* will be taught in the middle schools and high schools in the near future in Yakthung laje, Nepal. In Nepal, teaching of Yakthung language is in the making, and we must be constantly in the pursuit of relandscaping Yakthung Suhang wisdom, Sawa Yet Hang school of thoughts, and Yet Hang sagacity. Furthermore, we must continue to combat against the Khas Aryan castic or racial discrimination until we establish Mundhum-based and/or Sawa Yet Hang, Yet Hang, and Thibong Yakthung-based social and academic institutions in Yakthung laje because Yakthung, including Indigenous customary institutional epistemology is built upon the foundation of Mundhum practice and Mundhum knowledge system (that has been in existence from time immemorial). Hence, (Yakthungs) must change the para-colonial trajectory of knowledge construction or traditional

Khas Aryan and Western way of knowledge construction and dissemination. We collectively must deconstruct and reconstruct the existing traditional Khas Aryan-centric trajectory of knowledge building process for the sake of Yakthungs, including Indigenous peoples and minorities.

The contemporary world does not provide us a good shelter, or there is not a true world that gives us a good shelter; we do not have a safe place to live in. The mythical democratic nations, their rules and regulations, and their norms and values devalue themselves. Therefore, we (Yakthungs), including other Indigenous peoples, ought to mutually create communal theories, philosophies, norms, and values that transform the discriminatory social institutions and discriminatory foundations upon which the discriminatory governments stand. We, including global Indigenous peoples, collectively have to create a world in which Yakthung Suhang values do not devalue themselves. The world that we create will not only romanticize the inclusion and equity of both the natives and new settlers, but it should, ought to, or have to call on the practice that will value, validate, and respect all local and global communities, cultures, languages, religions, sexualities, and other differences.

Finally, although Kirat Yakthung Chumlung, as a Yakthung social institutions, played a significant role to the promotion of Yakthung language, literacy, writing system, and Yakthung identity, some KYC folks stopped invoking our Susuwa Lilim Yakthung and Thibong Yakthung identity. For instance, KYC's brutal decision to exclude "Yakthung" identity in language, race, and history in the upcoming census in 2021 in Nepal displaces and destroys our Yakthung identity. For instance, KYC appealed Yakthungs to write: race-Limbu, ancestor's language-Limbu, mother-tongue-Limbu, and religion-Kirat. Yakthungs (mostly, KYC folks) tend to lean toward Kirat (religion created in 2036 BS) and Limbu (race created after the Nun-Paani Sandhi, 1774), which is demeaning, ideological, and political, and their (KYC folks') ideology or ego and religious faith is displacing and destroying the Thibong Yakthung identity from the Yakthung history. The key conception we have to understand is that Kirat is an exonym (not native) identity; the Hindus (Aryans) called the Himalayan Indigenous peoples the Kirats (to refer to inferior race), which refers to not only Rai, Yakthung, Kõich, Athpahariya, Yakkha, and Dhimal, but all Himalayan Indigenous peoples other than Khas Aryans, and majority of the Himalayan Indigenous peoples do not approve the Kirat identity.

Pedagogical issues in para-colonial context (in Yakthung laje)

The Khas Aryan, including Indian and Western pedagogy, is sexist, racist, and discriminatory against Indigenous students, minority students, or non-Western students. The Khas Aryan and Western traditional pedagogical propaganda against the Indigenous students, including non-Western students, is always observed in new forms now. The Khas Aryan, including Western pedagogy, imposes local-centric or mono-centric education system, and it ignores the pursuit of inclusive and representational global education system. To be more specific in the local context, the Khas Aryan-centric government coerces Nepali-only policy, including Sanskrit, education systems in which monoculture, i.e. Khas Aryan culture is prioritized. The Nepali government ignores Yakthung culture, Yakthung language, and Yakthung education within Yakthung laje. Even though they allow Yakthungs and non-Yakthungs to study Yakthung language at Sanskrit college (in Dharan), they coerce students to take Sanskrit courses before they take their target *Yakthung pa:n* courses. Currently, the Khas Aryan-centric Nepali government is compulsorily imposing Sanskrit courses at schools. Hence, the Khas Aryan policy still colonizes Yakthungs, including Nepali Indigenous peoples' bodies, minds, and souls; Yakthung knowledge is caged in Khas Aryan, including Indian and Western, social and academic institutions. They attempt to orient Yakthung children (students) in Sanskrit language before they start introducing them to the target language, i. e. Yakthung language. Because of the Khas Aryan-centric Nepali government's language policy, many Indigenous students do not even complete Sanskrit courses to get the opportunity to study their target Yakthung language, writing, and Mundhum rhetorics. Hence, the Khas Aryan-centric government strategically petrifies Yakthung knowledge in the Khas Aryan social, academic, and religious institutions. They strategically program Yakthungs in Hindu culture before they are introduced to their own language and culture.

The Nepali education system, including the Western education system, has become a veil through which Yakthung students, including minority students, cannot distinguish their own culture, such as Sawa Yet Hang, Susuwa Lilim Yakthung, Yet Hang, and Thibong Yakthung cultural traditions. Yakthungs students are not given the opportunity to feel, see, and grasp their cultural and linguistic identities. For instance, I earned two BA degrees, two MA degrees, and a PhD in Khas Aryan and Western academic institutions, but none of the academic institutions introduced me to Sawa Yet Hang, Yet Hang, and Thibong Yakthung cultural traditions. During the process of receiving the degrees (and even later), education as space and time, teacher, student (myself), and my Yakthung community always contradicted. I never felt home in the Khas Aryan and Western academic institutions, and I also never felt safe in the Khas Aryan and Western academic institutions. As my cultural tradition did not have space in the Khas Aryan academic spaces, I (many students like me) had to distrust their cultural trusts; that was one of the hardest parts in my academic journey in my life. The more I engaged in Khas Aryan and Western academic cultures, the more I got misdirected and disoriented. I sat in the class/es and walked around college campuses as a dead man without soul, spirit, and empathy. Walter Mignolo (2007) rightly states "[t]he colonized do not have epistemic privilege…the only epistemic privilege is in the side of the colonizer" (p. 459). The Khas Aryan and Western social and academic institutions paralyzed my Yet Hang insights and Thibong Yakthung Suhang epistemologies; they impaired my Sawa Yet Hang-centric learning abilities; they petrified my Yakthung Suhang cultural and linguistic experiences. I was absolutely stunned by Khas Aryan, Indian, and Western academic and cultural ideals, ideologies, and hegemonies. My prior Sawa Yet Hang knowledge, Thibong Yakthung learning skills, and Yakthung Suhang scholarships were defined and ranked in relation to Khas Aryan, Indian, and Western academic and popular cultural ideals. Thus, Yakthung students', including other local and global Indigenous and language minority students', knowledges are constructed in the cocooned Khas Aryan, Indian, and Western academic institutions. The knowledge and ideals I received via the degrees had absolutely nothing to do with my body, soul, culture, and identity. I felt that my body, language, and culture were trapped in the Khas Aryan, Indian, and Western social and academic institutions. The Khas Aryan, including Western academic ideals, made me discredit my own language, my body, and/or my culture. They isolated me from my own Yet Hang and Thibong Yakthung history and Sawa Yet Hang or Yakthung Suhang Mundhum rhetorics (for ages).

As I mentioned earlier in this book, Yakthungs hated to speak their language, to talk about their culture, and to share their Mundhum rhetorics. As a global citizen, scholar, and educator, I always claimed that our education system was (and still) faulty and colonial, but now I realize that it was/is not faulty and colonial; it was/is strategically designed for the mainstream students only. Still, this is how the architecture of education is engineered to colonize Indigenous students, including minority students, in the context of the 21st century in para-colonial or colonial hegemonic cultures. I now realize that Khas Aryan and Western academic institution's purposes are to displace, distort, and destroy Indigenous and minority students' cultural and linguistic identities and colonize their mind, body, and soul in the name of globalization, so called inclusion, and global education systems. This, I felt, is not a democratic and inclusive pedagogy; this is a knowledge displacing, replacing colonial pedagogy.

In para-colonial spaces, many instructors, administrators, and mentors claim to be democratic; they pretend to create inclusive and representational pedagogical practices. However, though they believe that they create democratic, inclusive, and representational curricula, syllabi, and courses, they have been programmed in the Khas Aryan and Western hegemonic and ideological academic institutions for centuries. They have not been oriented to understand Yakthung or Indigenous students' culture, language, prior Indigenous cultural experiences. We, instructors and administrators, do not know what problems and issues our students have or bring to classrooms, what preferences our global students have, what needs and expectation they have, and how we can help them address these issues. In other words, in the Khas Aryan and Western academic institutions, we do not try and do not help students address their cultural issues; we rather impose what we know and what we have been practicing to Indigenous and minority students; we coerce them to follow the curricula, syllabi, and/or colonial pedagogy that have been prepared only for Khas Aryan and Anglo-American students. This setting suggests that academic institutions have been designed to colonize Indigenous students; and they obviously have become ideally a colonial space, including a colonial space of business and politics. In the business and political academic spaces, rather than imparting inclusive, representational and democratic education to better shape the global communities, they (academic institutions) have become the ideal places of colonization, for in this place, we, more often than not, are programmed (via mainstream institutions) to ignore diverse students' voices, their culture, language, geo-political locations, needs, and expectations. This is one of the reasons why I have proposed delinking, relinking, and linking methodology or delinking, relinking, and linking pedagogy in the context of the 21st century networked world. There is an urgent need that we ought to transform our academic institutions; we have to re/formulate research designs. We must recalibrate our human powers; then, we can serve the purpose, need, and expectation of our students and global communities. Therefore, first, we must change the traditional colonial mind set; then, we can decolonize administrators and educators' minds, bodies, and souls. They must unlearn the traditional concept of the universal knowledge or mono-centric pedagogy and accept pluriversal pedagogy. My pluriversal pedagogy is a global centric or student-centered pedagogy in which Indigenous as well as mainstream students contest, question, share, negotiate, and produce knowledge, circulate knowledge, and maintain knowledge for their purposes from the 21st century's perspective.

The delinking, relinking, and linking pedagogy by theory and practice does not treat students and cultures as predictable, mechanical, and objective. The delinking, relinking, and linking pedagogy also does not integrate Indigenous students and other cultural and linguistic minority students into the Khas Aryan-Only and Anglo-American-Only culture. They will be integrated into transformed global societies in which they can create their voice, space, and identity as global community members. In the process of integrating students, they must be counted as numbers, but as diverse human beings representing diverse culture, race, body, gender, and sexuality. Therefore, first, educators should learn to delink or denaturalize the way they had been programmed in social and academic institutions. Once they denaturalize and delearn Khas Aryan and/or Anglo-American cultural and academic colonization, they become able to understand who they are, who their students are, what needs and expectations they have, what pedagogical tools they have to share with them, what kind of approaches they have to negotiate so that they (students) can take those tools with them that better shapes our local, regional and global communities (I always praise both better hearts/souls and better grades, or I admire better hearts than grades; better hears make our global village a better place to live in).

The tools that they take with them are not coerced tools, but they are shared, negotiated, and recalibrated ones. Our now students and future partners and colleagues will use them to delink para-colonization in relation to academic cultures, social institutions, and political foundations. They, with the shared tools, will denaturalize colonization, delearn oppression, and disempower suppression. In so doing, they will relink their own traditional cultural ideals in order to create a better world for themselves. Finally, they will learn to link their cultures, histories, ideals, theories, and practices from the local to global levels in the context of the 21st century cloud-centered global village. The linking approach will allow everyone to create a safer place where everyone's culture is valued, language is validated, and identity is respected regardless of race, color, caste, creed, and geo-political locations. The delinking, relinking, and linking approach not only unveils pluri-versalities for the benefits of translingual and transcultural students, but it also challenges Khas Aryan discriminatory and Western colonial hegemonic practices. It will lead Yakthung Suhangs, including Indigenous peoples, towards a collective *chumlung* space in which they will both inquire and discover their subjectivities, agencies, and identities. As it is a negotiated and shared pedagogical space (pedagogy as a place to construct representational space), it neither serves the interest of oppressor, nor it supports a group of people over another one. It advocates for everyone's space, subjectivity, and identity. We know that when time changes, our needs and expectations also change, and we also have diverse needs and expectations. So, we must construct alternative pedagogies that value Indigenous and minority cultural norms, values, and ideals. To meet diverse needs and expectations, we must re/formulate newer pedagogical settings that validate everyone's linguistic and cultural ideals. We, Yakthungs, Indigenous peoples, and minorities, are the ones who have to re/construct delinking, relinking, and linking pedagogical approaches for our benefits because "traditions do not exist by themselves; they have to be contested, challenged, processed, constructed, and re/invented for our purposes" (Limbu, 2017, p. 574).

11 Delinking, relinking, and linking Yakthung language and literacy in glocal contexts

In the context of the 20th century, the first generation Yakthung scholars founded Shree Yakthung Hang Chumlung in Kalimpong and introduced the Sirijanga script (see Chapter 6). Despite the Khas Aryan suppression in Yakthung language teaching, Yakthungs, including Phalgunand's followers, facilitated the development of the Sirijanga script, writing system, and Mundhum rhetorics in Nepal (see Chapter 7). Similarly, Yakthung scholars, writers, and Mundhumists (oral text experts) from Nepal, Indian, Burma, and beyond campaigned to promote and preserve the Yakthung language and literacy via the Patra-mitrata campaign (see Chapter 9). Gradually, when Yakthungs conducted informal Yakthung language classes with the objectives of promoting the Sirijanga script and writing in Panchthar in 1983, Ram Swarup Sing (District Education Officer of Panchthar) ordered Yakthungs to immediately stop the teaching and learning of *Yakthung pa:n*, and the Yakthungs who conducted the classes and/or who supported the promotion of Yakthung language and literacy were convicted of treason. The Khas Aryan-centric Nepali government labelled them (Yakthungs) terrorists (see also Nembang, 1987, p. 21).

After the advent of democracy in 1990, Yakthungs were/are allowed to read and write in their languages as optional course/s up to an elementary level. However, the Khas Aryan-centric government did/does not provide any financial aid to support the teaching of Yakthung language in schools. Instead of supporting mother-tongue education at schools (specially in elementary and middle schools), currently, the Nepali government spends millions of dollars on Sanskrit education; and now, the Khas Aryan-centric Nepali government is imposing Sanskrit education at schools as compulsory courses. Hence, despite the advent of democracy in 1990, Yakthungs, other Indigenous peoples, or linguistic minorities still face discrimination in Nepal. For instance, during the Nepali civil war, the Khas Aryans promised that they would fight for the Nepali Indigenous people's rights, and the Indigenous peoples supported the Maoist movement for over 10 years. The Nepali people's war overthrew the monarchy in Nepal in 2007. In this war, Nepali people fought, bled, and died together not only to overthrow the monarchy, but also to change the traditional oppressive political and social conditions in Nepal, and although Nepalis collectively overthrew the king, the oppressive Khas Aryan ideology has not changed yet. Meaning, the Nepali Indigenous peoples did not benefit at all from the Nepali civil war in relation to the development of their cultural, linguistic, and political rights, etc. After the restoration of democracy in 1990 and the dethronement of the kingship in 2007, the political difference we witness is that the Chhetris (Shahs) used to have dominant power in the past, and currently, the Bahuns control state's power and resources. The Khas Aryans misuse the state's resources, and they abuse the state's power to mainly suppress Indigenous peoples and minorities. The Khas Aryan-centric Nepali government has never welcomed Yakthungs, including other Indigenous peoples, in the nation's political and bureaucratic spaces. Based on this information, this chapter discusses the foundation of Limbuwan Study Center (LSC) and the contemporary sites of Yakthung writing and rhetorics in Nepal, India, and beyond. This chapter exposes how LSC is establishing leading-edge Yakthung Suhang academic and popular cultures; how LSC is facilitating the research on diverse Yakthung studies or Limbuwani studies, such as Yakthung language, arts, literature, culture, music, history, politics, and Mundhum rhetorics; how LSC is aiming to pave strategic ways to succeed in academic and cultural avenues; and overall, how LSC is critically delinking, relinking, and linking the Yakthung language and literacies.

As mentioned above, when time changed, human needs and expectations also changed. In this process, Yakthungs needs and expectations also changed; they started demanding more and more to preserve and disseminate Yakthung Suhang epistemologies, and more importantly to institutionalize their culture, language, writing, and Mundhum rhetorics. Yakthungs founded Kirat Yakthung Chumlung (KYC), a Yakthung social institution, in 1989 (see Chapter 11). Although KYC advocated and fought for the Yakthungs' individual rights, collective rights, cultural rights, and rights to mother tongue education, it alone was not able to address diverse Yakthungs' needs and expectations. Therefore, KYC founded some specialized bodies in order to address the needs and expectations of Yakthungs of the 21st century. The specialized bodies (of Kirat Yakthung Chumlung) include:

- Limbu Bhasha Sahitya Pratisthan,
- Limbu Saskritik Parisad,
- Yakthung Sahayog Kosh,
- Kirat Yakthung Chumlung-Punarjeevan Kendra, and
- Limbuwan Study Center.

As Limbuwan Study Center was one of my major research sites, I focus only on Limbuwan Study Center, its mission, vision, and activities in this chapter, and I will discuss the other specialized bodies only in contexts.

Limbuwan Study Center: Yakthung writing and rhetorics in local and global contexts

LSC was founded in 2014 as one of the specialized bodies of KYC. After the foundation of LSC, it has invited innumerable national and international researchers, historians, activists, community leaders, and writers from diverse fields to share their research findings, oral performative experiences, lived experiences, and Mundhum rhetorics. As mentioned above, Yakthung Indigenous peoples (scholars, writers, musicians, community leaders, and activists) live around the world; they constantly network with other Yakthungs, Yakthung social institutions, and other global Indigenous peoples and institutions. The networking spaces, for instance, social media tools of the 21st century have empowered Yakthungs, including the local and global Indigenous peoples in the digital village. Since social networks, such as Internet-based communication and discourse, are immune to physical and political borders, Yakthung Indigenous peoples are collaborating, creating, and succeeding unlike the previous generations (the first and second-Yakthung generations implied). Because of the Internet-based network, they (Indigenous peoples) can locally and globally network in the cloud, collectively create their common voice, and challenge the local and global colonial or para-colonial powers. In terms of Yakthung studies, although they established several Yakthung organizations (see Chapter 12), they still felt the urgent need of their scholarly growth and intellectual global network. Having felt the Yakthung professional growth and intellectual global network, KYC, including Yakthungs founded Limbuwan Study Center as one of the specialized bodies of KYC. Since its inception, LSC has been able to demonstrate its impact from local and global context, and LSC has also established other LSCs in Limbuwan regions and beyond (UK, USA, Hong Kong, and Canada, etc.). Among many others, LSC has the following major objectives:

- To conduct extensive research in Limbuwan area on language, arts, culture, literature, music, history, oral tradition, and traditional skills of Indigenous peoples and document them,
- To carry out studies on the forest, land, and environment as well as a bio-diversity conservation and its sustainable development in the Limbuwan area,
- To critically cross-examine social, political, cultural, and socio-economic characteristics of Limbuwan area, and
- To study and contribute analytical thoughts and burning concerns related to Limbuwan.

(quoted from the LSC bylaw)

As mentioned above, LSC focuses on language, arts, philosophy, culture, Mundhum, literature, and music to mention a few. Similarly, it emphasizes on Yakthung Suhang history, Yakthung oral-performance-based tradition, performative rhetorics, Yakthung Mundhums, *khambong-lungbong* identities, language and literature to mention a few. It supports both Yakthung and non-Yakthung researchers to undertake advanced research in the areas of traditional Yakthung cultural assets and traditional Yakthung Suhang cultural traditions. It also closely studies the Limbuwan forest, land, bio-diversity conservation, and ecosystem.

During my research, I went to LSC at least twice if not once a year. I am indebted to LSC and/or executive members of LSC who unconditionally supported me by organizing conferences, seminars, workshops, and meetings. Among many other LSC executive officers, I interviewed Arjun Limbu on many occasions. Limbu, who is the Chair of LSC, was also one of the Ex. Presidents of KYC as well and has massive Yakthung and Limbuwani institutional and management knowledge on Yakthung Indigenous studies. Limbu (2015) mentioned that, LSC strongly encourages Yakthungs to research in Yakthung Suhag culture, writing, and Mundhum rhetorics. LSC's strategic plan is to significantly shift the Yakthung language, writing, and literacy or Yakthung studies. According to Limbu (2015), currently, LSC executes the following activities:

    i Documentation and archiving of published books, which are related to Limbuwan,
    ii Recording of oral traditions of Indigenous peoples and their oral history,
    iii Establishment of well-equipped resource center for Limbuwan study,
    iv Collaboration with national and international government, non-governmental organizations, and scholars for research and study in Limbuwan area,
    v Capacity enhancement activities for interested individuals in the areas of research methodology,
    vi Establishment of a research fellowship from donations to provide researchers to accomplish their studies,
    vii Publication of printed and electronic journals of research finding or papers related to Limbuwan area, and
    viii Convening of study related symposiums, workshops, and seminars etc.
                (see also Limbuwan Study Center's bylaw)

During our meetings, Arjun Limbu mentioned that there are various departments under LSC; so LSC, along with the different departments, can initiate diverse specialized programs and execute the objectives, missions, and visions. LSC's other departments include:

- History, oral tradition, and Yakthung Mundhum,
- Language, arts, culture, literature, and music,
- Traditional skill and Indigenous Peoples' specific expertise,
- Forest, land, bio-diversity conservation, and ecosystem, and
- Politics, education and socio-economic aspects.
                (quoted from the LSC bylaw)

To address diverse departmental programs, LSC has been inviting Yakthung and non-Yakthung scholars as guest speakers to discuss current Limbuwani or Yakthung issues, explore histories, traditional narratives, and share their current research findings. LSC has become a *chumlungden* (contact zone) for both Yakthungs and non-Yakthungs, such as a contact zone for local and global scholars, writers, professors, researchers, musicians, singers, artists, and actors. LSC, as a *Yakthung Chumlungden,* recognizes the value of supporting and nurturing emerging and pre-emergent Yakthung and non-Yakthung scholars who have been engaging in cutting-edge Limbuwan-centric research initiatives.

According to Arjun Limbu (2020), LSC not only has been funding emerging Yakthung scholars to undertake research, but also has been publishing books and journal articles on the issues that matter most to Yakthung and South Asian, including global Indigenous studies. For instance, it has not only supported Yakthung scholars to conduct research on the issues in Yakthung communities, but also has published a Yakthung dictionary and have a plan to publish peer-reviewed academic journal articles and peer reviewed books, etc. In terms of academic publications, it has been partnering with the US-based academic journal, *Journal of Global Literacies, Technologies, and Emerging Pedagogies* (JOGLTEP) that is housed in Writing, Rhetoric, and American Cultures (WRAC) at Michigan State University, East Lansing, USA. As the founding editor and editor-in-chief of JOGLTEP, I have been constantly and consistently networking and collaborating with LSC as well. As the editor-in-chief and activist writer, I have been bridging Eastern and Western academic cultures so that scholars from both cultures understand how they are interconnected from academic and popular cultural point of view. Meaning, both JOGLTEP and LSC have been strategically supporting emerging Indigenous and non-Indigenous researchers, scholars, students, and writers from Nepal, South Asia, the USA, and beyond. This network or collaboration has massively benefitted researchers, writer, professors, graduate students,

Figure 28 Bairagi Kainla giving a talk on Yakthung Mundhum at Limbuwan Study Center, Lalitpur.

and my interns to perceive, navigate, and project cross-cultural rhetorics in the context of the 21st century globalized world.

Arjun Limbu (2015) stated that LSC is a new Limbuwan-centric (not only Yakthung-centric) research organization; within a short span of time, it is definitely creating a constructive and representational contact zone in which both Yakthung and non-Yakthung scholars, researchers, leaders, professors, administrators, and graduate students are becoming familiar with local and global cultures, arts, and philosophy; they are developing a range of cross-cultural critical thinking, questioning, logical argument, and interpretation of varied kinds of culture-based information (Limbu et al., 2013). In other words, LSC encourages Yakthungs and Limbuwani (both Limbu and non-Limbu) scholars, historians, writers, and experts to share their leading-edge research and findings in local, regional, and global contexts. LSC has become an academic *chumlungden* for all Yakthungs and non-Yakthung scholars, researchers, writers, and historians to mention a few that is leading us towards our collective *cho:tlung* (fundamental destination) in the context of the 21st century networked global village. LSC is also developing a non-Yakthung and non-Indigenous allies to have a unified voice for the equal opportunity and positive change in Nepal. Through the collective *chumlungden*, LSC is facilitating research initiatives through which Yakthung and other Indigenous scholars can delink cultural, linguistic, and political colonization and relink their traditional cultural epistemologies and link their histories, language, literacies, and Mundhum rhetorics in local and global contexts. Hence, LSC is creating spaces where Yakthung and non-Yakthung voices, identities, and subjectivities are equally valued and validated.

As LSC helps Yakthungs and non-Yakthungs to delink local and global cultural, linguistic, and economic colonization, it creates spaces through which Yakthungs and non-Yakthungs can delearn the way they were colonized in multiple ways; it helps them relink their histories, oral traditions, Mundhum rhetorics, traditional arts, and literature. In other words, LSC is informing Yakthungs of their rights to self-determination, Limbuwani issues, and cultural and linguistic threats that have been affecting Yakthung and Indigenous communities for centuries. LSC creates environments through which Yakthungs and Indigenous peoples can distinguish what kind of relationships Yakthungs have with nature and nurture, such as people, forests, ancestral land, air, and water, and why people have to care about bio-diversity conservation in the context of the 21st century global village.

In doing so, LSC helps people to collaborate, create, share, and succeed within local and global contexts to make their voices heard and to make their identities visible in local and global contexts. It is also obvious that LSC has become a Limbuwani epistemological hub through which Yakthungs, Indigenous peoples, and minorities can grow from local to global levels. Meaning, LSC is informing Yakthungs and Indigenous peoples of rights to self-determination, their pre-existing Indigenous rights, freedom of expression, and their responsibility to protect, preserve, and institutionalize their culture, language, and Mundhum rhetorics. It also has become both Yakthung rhetorical and Limbuwan-centric research hub in the context of the 21st century through which we can discuss, debate, negotiate, and share local and global socio-political, academic, economic, and technological dynamics. From these settings, LSC has genuinely become one of the sites of delinking, relinking, and linking methodology. Basically, what I am foreseeing is whatever begins at LSC, it can shape Yakthung discourse, Yakthung studies, and Mundhum epistemologies, including regional and global Indigenous rhetorics. In summation, LSC creates a safe *chumlungden* (contact zones) where local and global scholars debate, discuss, and explore a wider range of Yakthung Suhang, including Indigenous sagacity, knowledge, and wisdoms. The discussions that happen in LSC have already ignited local and global research collaboration and engagement, and this book is one of the examples (see figures 28, 29, & 30).

LSC has distinct objectives to develop Yakthung social and academic culture, such as reading critically, writing analytically, understanding and interpreting a wide range of texts critically. LSC is also determined to create a culture of reading, writing, and publishing initiatives to foster Yakthung language and literacy. The Yakthung Indigenous-based critical and analytical understanding and interpreting oral, written, and performative rhetoric challenge the existing dominant para-colonial discourses (Eastern and Western cultures). LSC has significantly shifted the traditional colonial concept of knowledge construction, such as reading, writing, and understanding texts (not only in Yakthung culture, but also in South Asian cultures). LSC is significantly promoting the culture of collaboration, creation, and dissemination of history, arts, and narratives from both Sawa Yet Hang including Yet Hang, Thibong Yakthung, and Limbuwani

Figure 29 Limbuwan Study Center, Bijaypur, Dharan.

perspectives. It is also fostering the Mundhum-based culture of critical and analytical thinking, such as critiquing, commenting, analyzing, interpreting texts, and negotiating (Yakthung Mundhums implied). The footstep/s of LSC is becoming an alternative pedagogical conduit that updates ways of Yakthung Suhang knowledge construction within South Asian communities and beyond. Henceforth, LSC is also developing the culture of Yakthung Indigenous research methodology through which we (Yakthungs) will be able to delink Khas Aryan, Indian, and Western cultural and linguistic colonization; we will be able to relink our Susuwa Lilim epistemologies, Sawa Yet Hang knowledge, and Yakthung Suhang wisdom. Gradually, we will be able to establish an inclusive and representational society in which our voices will be valued, identities will be validated, and we will be once again respected like Yet Hangs and Thibong Yakthung Suhangs in the context of the 21st century and beyond. However, in terms of LSC's adventure, Arjun Limbu (2015) argues that LSC's introduction of newer academic culture and traditional Yakthung Indigenous rhetorical traditions seems like it is a fun project, but in actuality, it is strenuous adventure, for Yakthung Indigenous-based research, writing, and advocacy are still in the making.

As I mentioned before, through the pedagogical process of sharing, critiquing, commenting, analyzing, and negotiating, LSC is delinking the Khas Aryan-centric pedagogy (the orientation that was imposed on Yakthungs for centuries), is relinking the Yakthung Suhang cultural, linguistic, and religious identities (from critical and analytical perspectives), and is linking Yakthung culture (writing and rhetoric) to the global level in the context of the 21st century global village. As you see in the figures 28 and 29, national and international scholars (Laura Gonzales' presentation implied), linguists, historians, researchers, writers, oral-text experts, *tutu-tumyahangs* (scholars), students, professors, bureaucrats, and political leaders congregate to share their research findings, Mundhum performative rhetorics, Mundhum epistemologies, and other lived experiences. Based on my knowledge, LSC is one of the Yakthungs or the first Yakthung social institution that is cross-culturalizing academic culture of Mundhum-based critical thinking in Yakthung community in Nepal.

In relation to cross-cultural collaboration, although LSC is a new specialized body of Kirat Yakthung Chumlung, it has already conducted intercultural or cross-cultural interactions and collaboration with many local, regional, and global scholars. For instance, Catherine Jennings, Kenlea Pebbles, Arjun Limbu (Nugo), and I edited a special issue for *Journal of Global Literacies, Technologies, and Emerging Pedagogies* in 2019 for which contributing scholars were from Nepal, India, and the USA, and we are now in the process of editing a book on global Indigenous rhetorics in 2020 for which our contributors from Nepal, India, and USA. Similarly, LSC's peer-reviewed journal/s, books, and popular magazine/s will address diverse Limbuwani (Yakthung) rights, liberties, spaces, and identities. LSC, through various programs, is delinking the local and global cultural, linguistic, and academic colonization by inviting scholars from Yakthung communities and non-Yakthung communities, including non/Western academic and popular communities. LSC has been archiving the research presentations and discussions (both physical and online library implied) so that current and future Yakthung and non-Yakthung researchers will have the access to Yakthung studies related resources. The regular workshops and conference/s will facilitate Yakthung (non-Western) ways of delinking para-colonization in the context of the 21st century networked world. And LSC, since its inception, has been constantly seeking potential ways of relinking Yet Hang and Thibong Yakthung Suhang epistemologies to meet our needs and expectations in the context of the 21st century. By networking and collaborating with local and global scholars, LSC has a strategic move to expose Yakthung Suhang Indigenous knowledge on a global level. In so doing, LSC is sharing Yakthung, including other South Asian research findings, cultural lores, and Mundhum epistemologies with emerging Yakthung and non-Yakthung scholars to create current and future critical Yakthung and non-Yakthung study masses.

Arjun Limbu (2020) claims that since there are many Yakthung scholars, linguists, and writers who are engaged in the research and writing in the development of Yakthung language, writing, and rhetoric, LSC will be one of the first social institutions to expand the network in local and global contexts. To accomplish its mission, vision, and objectives, LSC has created awards, fellowships, and research grants, such as the Bishnu Datta-Saraswati Angbuhang Award, the Bishnu Datta-Saraswati Angbuhang fellowship, small research grants, and women empowerment research initiative grants. Bishnu Datta Angbuhang and Saraswati Angbuhang founded the Bishnu Datta-Saraswati Angbuhang Award and the Bishnu Datta-Saraswati Angbuhang fellowship. The former one is awarded biannually to a scholar. Whereas, the latter one is awarded annually to two emerging scholars. These awards are administered by LSC. As I stated earlier, LSC has a plan to create

Figure 30 Limbuwan Study Center, Basingstoke, UK.

small research grants to support emerging writers, and women empowerment research grants to encourage women scholars, researchers, and writers in research initiatives. The main purposes of this research awards, fellowships, and small research grants are to involve emerging scholars to explore Yakthung histories, traditional customary institutional laws and practices, Mundhum pedagogies, and oral-performance-based rhetorics. Likewise, LSC has also established physical and online libraries, and those whoever want to research on Yakthung studies and/or Limbuwani studies are profoundly benefiting from the LSC's e-library and other resources.

LSC is not limited within Nepal, and there are many other Limbuwan Study Centers (alliances) across the world (wherever Yakthung scholars, historians, activists, writers, and media personnel reside). For instance, in 2016, Tehrathum Samaj, UK invited me as the chief-guest to the United Kingdom. During the visit, LSC, Basingstoke, UK invited me to share my research findings (see figure 30). Yakthungs, including non-Yakthungs via LSC, network, collaborate, and create Yakthung spaces with other LSCs from across the world. We not only shared our collective critical thoughts on the issues of immigration, process of Yakthung knowledge construction, and understanding of Yakthung Suhang epistemologies, but we also discussed the significance of local and global Yakthung and Indigenous networks.

LSC is providing a safer *chumlungden* to all Yakthungs and non-Yakthungs where they share theoretical, conceptual, methodological concepts and findings. It undeniably understands that Yakthungs and non-Yakthung emerging scholars are the future of local, regional, and global communities and supports them with their research initiatives. From this perspective, LSC has not only become a space of innovation and opportunity, but also has become a critical *chumlungden* from where scholars, researchers, and writers delink the traditional Khas Aryan castic hegemony, relink traditional Yakthung rhetorical traditions and customary institutions, and link them in local, regional, and global contexts. In summation, LSC invariably encourages Yakthungs to stand in solidarity and constantly advocate for the development of Yakthung or Indigenous cultures, languages, and literacies and consistently fight for their inclusion in the mainstream institutions.

12 Yakthung writing and rhetorics in the late 20Th and the early 21St centuries (beyond Limbuwan)

As discussed in the previous chapters, the Sirijanga writing system has shifted many times since its inception. Based on the Yakthung historical archives, some major reasons that affected the Sirijanga script are cultural influences, political influences, and Yakthungs' epistemic gap on the Old Sirijanga script and writing system. The Yakthungs always had closer relationships with Tibetans, Bhutias, Khas Aryans, Newars, Indians, and English (British), and these cultures apparently affected the development of the Sirijanga script and writing practices. This scenario explains that Tibetan (Bhutia), Lepcha, and the Devanagari (Khas Aryan) writing systems influenced the Yakthung phonology and script as well (after the Khas Aryan colonization). One of the most explicit reasons that affected Yakthung language and literacies is that Yakthungs have been colonized for centuries (the Nun-Paani Sandhi in 1774 to 1990), and the Khas Aryans politically and ideologically brought Yakthungs and Yakthung laje under their control (Limbu, 2016, 2017; Limbu, 2019). The Khas Aryans controlled the teaching, writing, and dissemination of Yakthung epistemology, Yakthung Suhang pedagogies, and axiologies in Yakthung laje (see Ingnam & Ingnam, 2070 BS; Lumphungwa Limbu, 2075 BS; Nembang, 1987). Gradually, as I discussed in the previous chapters, the first-generation and second-generation Yakthung progressive intellectuals, including the 19th century Yakthung documentarians, not only contributed to the development of Yakthung language and literacy, but their collective endeavor also shaped the Yakthung academic culture in the context of the late 20th and 21st centuries. Based on the background information, this chapter discusses the historical development of Yakthung writing and rhetorics in Sikkim (independent country until 1975, now in India), and how writing and rhetoric fostered or did not foster in Sikkim? How did Yakthungs, in the late 1960s and early 1970s, not force the urgency of Yakthung language, literacy, and Mundhum rhetorics? This chapter also discusses how the teaching of Yakthung language got the official recognition at school in Sikkim in 1968, and currently, how Sikkimi (Sukhime) Yakthungs are introducing Yakthung studies up to MA level (soon to be PhD level) in Sikkim. Finally, this chapter uncovers how Yakthungs are in/formally teaching Yakthung language in West Bengal, such as Darjeeling, Kalimpong, and Dooars, Assam, Bhutan, Burma, and Thailand, and how Yakthungs across the world are relinking Yet Hang and Thibong Yakthung epistemologies and linking them in them in Yakthung rhetorical traditions in the context of the 21st century digitally networked global village.

When King Sirijanga redesigned the script upon the foundation of the Maarangian script (see Bhumika by Bajbir Subba, 1928; Subba, 2015, pp. 99–101; Vansittart, 1991, p. 105), it still used to be chirographic like any other scripts. The chirography is the study of penmanship and handwriting; the word "chirography" combines the Greek word for "hand" and "writing." As we know chirography beginning other writing in all cultures, the practices of chirography also revolutionized the writing and/or writing systems in the development of Yakthung language and literacy. When Tye Angsi Singthebe (1704–1741) redesigned and popularized the script and writing system during the early/mid-18th century, the medium of writing was chirography or paper-based writing. However, the Sirijanga syllabary did not change in relation to medium of printing until the late 20th century, for the Yakthungs of Yakthung laje (Limbuwan) did not have a favorable situation in Nepal and Sikkim. In the context of Nepal, the Khas Aryans not only banned from the teaching of the Sirijanga script, but they ideologically and politically planned to eliminate it, including Yakthung cultural, linguistic, and Mundhumic traditions from the face of human civilization, for they knew that to destroy Yakthungs, they had to destroy their culture, language, and Mundhum rhetorics. Similarly, Yakthung language and writing also did not foster in Sikkim due to the Bhutia autocratic monarchical system until the mid-1960s. Second, since the teaching of the Sirijanga script and Yakthung language did not get official recognition, Yakthungs did not force the urgency of developing modern ways of publishing Yakthung textbooks, books, and Mundhums.

Only after the advent of democracy in 1990, Yakthungs have been allowed to teach their language up to elementary level in Nepal. The oppressive Nepali (Khas Aryan-centric) government allowed Yakthungs to teach their language only up to an elementary level; however, the Sikkimi Government approved the teaching of Limboo (in Sikkim "Limbu" is written as "Limboo") language in 1968, and teaching of *Yakthung pa:n* commenced at school in 1969 as an optional subject (Khamdhak, 2019, pp. 901–902). Likewise, Yakthungs are also in the process of teaching their language, script, and culture in Assam, Manipur, and Nagaland in India in informal settings. Currently, Yakthung language, culture, and literature is taught up to MA level in Sikkim since 2016, and Yakthungs have a commitment to upgrade it up to PhD level soon. In the following section, I discuss the development of Limboo (Yakthung) language teaching in Sikkim, India.

Institutionalizing Yakthung writing and rhetorics in Sikkim

The Yakthungs, who live in Sikkim call themselves "Yakthungs" or "Limboos" or "Tsongs," are the natives of Sikkim. Many Yakthungs, from Yakthung laje, joined their brothers and sisters in Sikkim when Khas Aryans banished them from Yakthung laje after the Nun-Paani Sandhi. Sikkim was originally called Sukhim; Sukhim was known as Sukhim Thum, a part of Yakthung laje. The Sikkimi Yakthungs write their last name or family name as Limboo (also Tsong) whereas Nepali Yakthungs write their last name as Limbu. However, neither Limbu nor Limboo is their native language; their native (original) identity is Yakthung; Limboo or Limbu is a term given to them by the Khas Aryan rulers after the Nun-Paani Sandhi in 1774. Therefore, the term Limbu and Subba have nothing to do with Yakthungs who reside other than Nepal. As I mentioned earlier, Yakthungs were great warriors; so, both the Khas Aryans and British East India Company played shrewd roles to weaken Yakthung Suhang collective power. Later, they (the British and Khas Aryans) ideologically and politically divided Yakthung laje into three countries: Nepal, Sikkim, and India in the treaty of Sugauli in 1816 (see also Laoti, 2069 BS, p. 357). When we talk about collective Yakthung Suhang identity, they did not cross the borders, but borders crossed them. Hence, the British, Indian, and Khas Aryans politically deteriorated Yakthung unity and progressive intellectual campaigns.

In terms of Yakthung language and literacy, the Sikkimi Limboos (Yakthungs) got the official approval to teach Yakthung language during the reign of King Palden Thondup Namgyal and Queen Hope Cooke; the King P. T. Namgyal approved the proposal of minority communities to officially teach their languages at schools in Sikkim (Muringla, 2017). After King Palden Thondup Namgyal's government officially approved the teaching of Yakthung language in Sikkim (India), among many other Yakthungs, B. B. Muringla played a great role to shape Yakthung writing, script, language, and literacy. For instance, A. B. Subba (2016) states:

[B. B. Muringla] was the youngest son of Lal Man Nugo of Lingchom who happened to be the business man and financier when they were struggling for the inclusion of Limboo language education in the government schools and the reservation of Limboo seat in the council. Language was only a treasure that was left with the Limboos during the merger of Sikkim. He binds both the pre-merger period and post-merger period particularly in the linguistics and politics of Sikkim. He was the eye witness of all happenings of those days. (p. 61)

I went to Lingchom, Geyzing (Gyalshing), Sikkim to meet B. B. Muringla in 2017 and 2018 in order to further inquire the development of Yakthung writing and literacy. According to B. B. Muringla (2017, 2018) Sikkimi Yakthungs elected Harkadhoj Mandal (Limboo) as their councilor to represent them in 1966 (Khamdak, 2019, p. 901). In each council meeting, Harkadhoj Mandal (Limboo) proposed for the teaching of Yakthung language in Sikkim (West Sikkim). In the council meeting, they required him to present Yakthung (Limboo) books as evidence to demonstrate that Yakthungs had language, scripts, books, and/or enough materials for the teaching of *Yakthung pa:n* (Yakthung language) in Sikkim. Harkadhoj Mandal (Limboo) presented *Tum*

Yakthung Ningwaphu Sapla, *Nisigek Yakthung Sapla*, and *Yakthung Nisigek Sapla* as evidence that Yakthungs (Limboos) had their language, script, and books. According to Muringla (17, 2018), these books were written and re/written and published by P. S. Muringla, Man Bahadur Khamdak, and Imansing Chemjong in Gangtok, Sikkim in the early 1950s. For my audience's information, *Tum Yakthung Ningwaphu Sapla* was the first published in 1928 (by Bajbir Subba) and *Nisigek Yakthung Sapla* was first published in 1931 (by Imansing Chemjong and Bajbir Thalang); later, *Nisigek Yakthung Sapla* was published as *Yakthung Nisigek Sapla* in the early 1950s as Muringla stated.

According to B. B. Muringla, in the mid-1970s, P. S. Muringla designed Yakthung books for elementary schools; he formatted the books and included images/pictures to make the book reader friendly. The information suggests that P. S. Muringla was also one of the accountable persons to produce the Limboo textbooks in Sikkim. However, both Man Bahadur Khamdak and Imansing Chemjong could not contribute to the production of Yakthung books as much as Muringla could as they were engaged in the government jobs. The textbooks (mainly Muringla) prepared were easy to read as they were written in *Yakthung pa:n* and translated into Nepali as well.

After the Sikkimi Government approved the teaching of Yakthung (Limboo) language in 1968, and it was taught as an optional subject at school mostly in West Sikkim during the reign of King Palden Thondup Namgyal and Queen Hope Cooke up to grade II (see Subba, 2001). However, the teaching of *Yakthung pa:n* formally started only from 1969, and there were not many Yakthung (Limboo) teachers then. Harkadhoj Mandal (Limboo) first appointed Ichchha Purna Das (Limboo) his own uncle as a Limboo language teacher. In this regard, Buddhi L. Khamdhak states:

> A committee consisting of two members, Man Bahadur Khamdhak and Padam Singh Subba, under the Chairmanship of the Gyalmo Hope Cook to assess the need of Limbu textbooks in Sikkim in 1969 …. Ichha Purna Das (Limbu) was appointed as a Tsong (Limbu) teacher at Bara Samdong Primary School by the School Committee. Thereafter the committee voluntarily contributed money for Tsong texts at the schools. On 23 February 1970, Ichha Purna Das received official appointment order of Tsong (Limbu) teacher from the Government of Sikkim. (pp. 901–902)

Then, gradually, other eight (8) teachers were appointed as Limboo language teachers who were all Limboos from 1969–1972. In 1972, Chandra Mangyung was the last appointee as a Limboo teacher when Ichchha Purna Das (Limboo) got retired (during King Palden Thondup Namgyal's reign). According to B. B. Muringla (2017), most of the Yakthung (Limboo) language teachers did not choose to stay as a Limboo language teachers as the teaching of Limboo language was an optional subject and was disregarded position at schools in Sikkim. After 1972, the Sikkimi Government did not appoint any Yakthung language teachers until 1975. Additionally, according to B. B. Muringla,

Yakthungs had only two books; they were *Tum Yakthung Ningwaphu Sapla* and *Nisigek Yakthung Sapla* beginning at school from 1969 to 1972 in Sikkim.

According to B. B. Muringla, before he was appointed as a Yakthung textbook writer, he used to teach the Sirijanga script and writing system in his village, Lingchom in the 60s in an informal setting. In other words, he taught Limboo language to his villagers in the evenings because most of the Yakthung villagers were busy in the farming activities during the day and were free in the evenings. Muringla also mentioned that he used to collect negligible amount of money from the villagers who wanted to learn the Sirijanga script, Yakthung language, and literacy. With the money he collected, he used to buy kerosene to have enough *tuki* (kerosene lamp) to run the classes in the evenings. During the daytime, while Muringla used to herd cattle, he would prepare the reading materials for the evening classes. He, for instance, used to write short stories, essays, and songs, etc., and he used to print them in carbonated copies. Muringla mentioned that he could produce three copies at a time. In such type of printing, if people use the right technique and right materials, they could produce up to four to five copies at a time. Similarly, B. B. Muringla was also a popular musician; so, while he was teaching Limboo language in informal setting in Lingchom, N. K. Jagira, who was the Principal at Pelling High School, West Sikkim, came to know about his music knack, and Jagira hired Muringla as a music teacher. Muringla used to write songs, play musical instruments, and sing Nepali as well as Yakthung music. Some of his music were recorded and aired from the Radio Peking, Nepali Program from China. Because of the music, Muringla not only was a regionally popular singer, but his music knack also paved a praiseworthy network with N. K. Jagira. Muringla added that when Jagira became a Joint Director in Sikkim, he went to Gangtok, and he chose Muringla as a Limboo text-book writer in 1975, for Jagira knew that Muringla was an amazing teacher, writer, and musician.

Figure 31   Handwritten textbooks by B. B. Muringla (Source: Yehang Laoti).

B. B. Muringla mentioned that though the Sikkimi government approved the teaching of *Yakthung pa:n* in 1968, Yakthungs had very limited resources or books as I implied above. According to B. B. Muringla, in the process of developing Yakthung books and other teaching materials, Jagira got Radha Krishna Kaphle to help Muringla from the mid-1970s. After Muringla got a professional training from Kaphle, he and his colleagues, such as P. S. Muringla and Chandra Mangyung got engaged in writing Yakthung textbooks; they used to write books by hand then (see the handwritten books in figure 31). Immediately after they completed a textbook for grade one, Mangyung went back to village to teach (once his vacation was over) and P. S. Muringla got transferred to a different place in the government service. B. B. Muringla, not yet appointed by the government, stayed at a hotel to write other Limboo books, mainly supported by his father, Lal Man Nugo. Although Jagira invited B. B. Muringla to write Limboo textbooks in 1975, the Sikkimi Government officially appointed Muringla as a textbook writer only in April 1976, and his handwritten textbooks (see figure 31) were published in early 1976 (Limbu, 2017).

B. B. Muringla stated that he, in the process of printing Limboo textbooks and reference books, visited different presses in India, including Nepal. The more Muringla visited the printing presses, the more he learned about composing, arranging, designing, editing, formatting, and publishing processes. According to Muringla, a publisher named Frank Brothers (New Delhi) wanted to publish Limboo books though it was not lucrative for the publisher (from business point of view). In terms of the Yakthung language teaching, Yakthung scholars, researchers, and activists (both from Nepal and India) have been undertaking research on *Yakthung pa:n*, writing, script, literature, and Mundhum rhetorics. They have been conducting research and writing books in multiple areas to meet the needs and expectations of Yakthungs and Yakthung communities. Similarly, Yakthungs have been documenting their oral-performance-based rhetorics, oral-performative texts, and Mundhum rhetorics to mention a few. Although printing had been already popular across the world, Yakthungs did not yet have any press (printing machine) to print Yakthung textbooks, reference books, and teaching materials in the Sirijanga script. Thus, B. B. Muringla wrote Yakthung textbooks and teaching materials in the Sirijanga script by hand. According to Muringla, he wrote textbooks from Kindergarten to higher secondary level by his own hand and the print medium was still chirographic/lithographic (see figure 31).

According to Muringla, by studying the interests of students, he wrote comic books in Yakthung language in Sirijanga script as reference books. He translated Hindi and English comics into *Yakthung pa:n*. In terms of the development of Yakthung language and literacy, there is an immense contribution of the Government of Sikkim and Kendriya Sikchha Parisad, New Delhi (India). The Sikkimi Chief Minister Nara Bahadur Bhandari approved the teaching of *Yakthung pa:n* up to higher secondary level in the early 1980s. As I mentioned earlier, when B. B. Muringla's handwritten texts were taught at schools in the 70s and 80s in Sikkim, Yakthungs still did not have any press both in India and Nepal. Finally, under the supervision of Sanchaman Limbu, the first Sirijanga script printing press was established in Gangtok, Sikkim in 1982, and Yakthungs started printing textbooks, teaching materials, and other Yakthung books in a three-faced type (Kandangwa, 1999, p. 50–51). However, as the three-faced type was not scientific and did not embody the Sirijanga script and Yakthung phonology, it did not become as popular as Yakthungs expected (see also Laoti, 2005, pp. 146–47).

In relation to Yakthung studies, both Indian and Nepali Yakthungs have been extremely dependent to each other in a cross-national context; they have been collaborating and struggling to create outstanding Yakthung cultural and academic spaces. In reality, they have been working together as a nation (spiritual nation)—Yakthung laje though the colonizers divided them in the early 18th century. Meaning, the Khas Aryans, Indians, and Europeans divided Yakthungs into three countries in the Treaty of Sugauli in 1816; however, they still collaborate, create, and succeed as *phu-ne-nusa* forever. The Yakthung *phu-ne-nusa* collectively struggled to establish Shree Yakthung Hang Chumlung; they collectively struggled to network via the Patra-mitrata campaign; they collectively collaborated and succeeded in their journal and pamphlet publish campaign. They have been organizing International Yakthung conferences. These settings were/are some significant signs of delinking Khas Aryan, Indian, and Western colonization, relinking Sawa Yet Hang, Yet Hang, and Thibong Yakthung cultural traditions, and liking the historical cultural traditions and updating them to local, regional, and global spaces from the 21st century perspectives.

Yakthung *phu-ne-nusa* collaborated to document their history, story, and Mundhum rhetorics; they collectively campaigned to institutionalize their language, literature, and writing. These all campaigns accelerated the teaching of Yakthung language, literature, and writing in Sikkim. Currently, as I stated earlier, Yakthung language is taught up to MA level in the Department of Limboo at Sikkim University. Yakthung Suhangs of Sukkim (Sikkim) have been formally engaging in the construction, dissemination, and shaping of Yakthung social and academic institutions. They have been one of the successful Indigenous peoples in the world who became able to institutionally delink Indian, Khas Aryan, and Western cultural and linguistic colonization in a short span of time. Due to the collective Yakthung endeavor, they became able to denaturalize Western and Indian colonial construction of knowledge that Yakthung language, literacy, Mundhum, and Yakthung rhetorical traditions are inferior. Based on my consistent interactions with Sikkimi Yakthung language instructors, including graduate students, Sikkimi Yakthungs, have been critically engaging now our students, and future colleagues to enrich their understanding of Yakthung Suhang, Yet Hang, Thibong Yakthung Suhang, and Sawa Yet Hang histories, narratives, cultural traditions, and contemporary leading-edge local and global epistemic conventions. Hence, Yakthungs have been struggling to relink their ancestral Yakthung Suhang voices, Susuwa Lilim Yakthung cultural experiences and have been exploring them in the academic and social institutions. As Yakthungs, one of our core accountabilities is to link our Yakthung studies to local, regional, and global academic spaces and make Yakthung studies cross-culturally and transnationally visible. By mentoring our Yakthung students in academic spaces like Sikkim (in academic context), we have to prepare them as engaged local and global researchers, writers, and communicators who can accomplish the needs, demands, and expectations of the global communities. We, Yakthungs, should never forget that we have always been accountable to the re/shaping of the global communities. Historically, we have never been compartmentalized only within Yakthung laje, we always fought together and bled together with other global brothers and sisters (as global allies) for the glocal peace, progress, and prosperity.

Yakthung social institutions and their roles in Sikkim

Similarly, in relation to communal Yakthung social institutions and their space/s in Sikkim, Yakthungs have been advocating for their political identity, cultural spaces, Yakthung voice, and Mundhum rhetorics. Despite the fact that Yakthungs from Sikkim also did not have the favorable cultural and political situation after the execution of Tye Angsi Singthebe (including the suppression of Sikkimi Bhutia government), they implicitly or explicitly have been researching for their cultural, linguistic, and political identities. The Yakthungs of Sikkim have/had six different registered non-governmental social institutions, such as:

1   Sukhim Yakthung Sapsok Songjumbho (SYSS),
2   Sirijanga Yakthung Sakthim Phujumbho (SYSP),
3   Sukhim Yakthung Nichhamsa Sapsok Chumbho (SYNSC),
4   Yakthung Sapsok Saplon Chumbho,
5   Temen Yakthung Ma-Chumbho, and
6   Akhil Sikkim Kirat Limbu Chumlung.

Sukhim Yakthung Sapsok Songjumbho (SYSS) is a major organization of all Yakthungs or Yakthung social institutions in India. Sirijanga Yakthung Phujumbho (SYSP) deals with development and the preservation of Yakthung culture, to impart trainings to Yakthung youths and to research on various related objectives and areas of the Yakthung society. Sukhim Yakthung Nichhamsa Chumbho (SYNSC) is run by Limboo students from various colleges and schools in Sikkim. It publishes Yakthung magazine, such as *aani? Lakkhum* and newsletter *aani? Lakkhum ing*. Namdha Sukhim Yakthung Saplon Chumbho deals with publishing Limboo literary books, magazines with its main objectives being to work for Limboo communities to raise the voice on different issues. Temen Yakthung Ma-Chumbho is a national level agency, which works for the interest of Limboo community of an entire nation (India). Its main purpose is to unite Limboos of India in order to maintain strong and healthy relationship among Limboos. Moreover, it also networks, collaborates, and shares philosophical and theoretical ideas and practices on Mundhum rhetorics, culture, history, and so on with other Yakthung communities from Nepal, Bhutan, Burma, Thailand, and beyond. In terms of Akhil Sikkim Kirat Limbu Chumlung, Khamdak states:

> ... on May, 23rd 1973, the Akhil Sikkim Kirat Limbu Chumlung (ASKLC) was established in Tharpu, West Sikkim by Ashok Kumar Tsong. In its first meeting held on July, 19th 1973 at Soreng Bazar, West Sikkim, under the Chairmanship of Harka Dhoj Tsong, the Chumlung passed a resolution declaring that the "Tsongs (Limbus) were not Nepalis but one of the indigenous tribes of Sikkim" (Gurung, 2011, p. 129; Chaudhury, 2006, p. 25). Since then, the Akhil Sikkim Kirat Limbu Chumlung time and again kept on highlighting the concept of the historical testimony, "Lho-Men-Tsong-Sum," and expressing their aspirations and demands. (p. 902)

Currently, Akhil Sikkim Kirat Limbu Chumlung (Limboo social institution) does not exist anymore though it was the institution that led Yakthungs to quest their cultural, linguistic, and political identities in Sikkim.

Development of Yakthung language and literacies in other states of India

Currently, innumerous Yakthung scholars, historians, Yakthung progressive intellectuals, and activists collectively started delinking Khas Aryan, Indian, and Western cultural and linguistic colonization, and they started relinking Yet Hang, Thibong Yakthung Suhang and Sawa Yet Hang cultural traditions not only in Nepal, but across the world (India, Bhutan, Burma, Thailand, Hong Kong, USA, UK, Singapore, Canada, Portugal, and Israel, etc.). Yakthungs globally network with other Yakthungs from around the world to inquire, discover, and/or construct Yakthung cultural, linguistic, and political identities. Yakthungs, living in different parts of the world, also network with other local and global Indigenous peoples from around the world. By visiting several Indigenous museums, cultural programs, interviewing Mundhumists, sharing thoughts and ideas and exchanging documents, Yakthungs have been exploring who they had been, how their ancestors had struggled, how they are struggling now, what differences and commonalities they share with other Indigenous communities, and how they need to link their identities with other global (Indigenous) communities so that Yakthung (Indigenous) identities, voices, and knowledges become globally visible. In relinking or linking processes, Yakthungs are not only inquiring, communicating, exploring, constructing, and sharing Susuwa Lilim, Sawa Yet Hang, Yet Hang, and/or

Thibong Yakthung identities as compartmentalized Yakthungs, but also as constructively, creatively contributing global citizens in the context of the 21st century networked world.

When Khas Aryan banished Yakthungs after the Nun-Paani Sandhi in 1774, they (Yakthungs) immigrated as far as Assam (West Assam or border of Jalpaiguri) Nagaland, Manipur, Bangladesh, Burma, and Thailand. However, Assam, Jalpaiguri, and Dooars had (always have) been original Yakthung ancestral lands before other Yakthungs arrived there. The new Yakthung immigrants had to struggle for their survival in new places wherever they immigrated; they also had to struggle to adapt in new places. Due to the struggles in the new places, they were not able to preserve, disseminate, and institutionalize their writing system. However, they could preserve Yakthung Suhang cultural practices as much as possible; they preserved Mundhums in oral forms; they retransmitted their histories, stories, and narratives orally from one generation to the next. Similarly, the Yakthungs who migrated up to Assam, Arunachal Pradesh, Manipur, Nagaland, and Meghalaya, etc. were constantly networking with other Yakthung *phu-ne-nusa* from Yakthung laje, such as Limbuwan, Sikkim, Kalimpong, Darjeeling, Siliguri, and Jalpaiguri, etc. They could, to some extent, learn Yakthung traditional cultural practices, language, writing, and Mundhum rhetorics from the networks; some of their *phu-ne-nusa* (brothers and sisters) also joined them wherever they settled, for many Yakthungs, Yakthung laje was not a favorable place to live in (due to Khas Aryan's atrocities over them). Even though Yakthungs had learned about Yakthung traditional cultural practices from new Yakthung immigrants, they gradually started losing their writing, script, language, and Mundhum literacy.

When they were about to lose their language, script, writing, and literacy, Yakthungs started a new campaign to preserve their language, writing, and culture in Assam, Manipur, and Nagaland, etc. When I went to Assam in 2018 to study Yakthung culture, language, and literacy, Assame Yakthungs demonstrated their cultural practices in five different districts, such as Guwahati, Sonitpur, Biswanath, Golaghat, and Tinsukia. Many Yakthungs from different districts also participated in these programs. During my research in Assam, I got the opportunity not only to meet with historians, writers, leaders, and Yakthung activists, but also to observe the Assame Yakthung cultural traditions and practices. For instance, Yakthungs of Assam performed Yakthung cultural practices, such as *ke-lang, yeba/ma lang*, Yakthung cultural performances, *ya:lang* (traditional Yakthung dance), *Yakthung samlo*, Mundhums, and cultural dances. Through these different Yakthung cultural performances and activities, I could vividly capture how Yakthung cultural practices have been shifting over the time due to the geo-political locations and other cultural influences. I also observed that old Yakthung generations (age 50 and above) could speak *Yakthung pa:n*, middle age Yakthungs (age 30 to late 40s) could understand and barely communicate, and young generation Yakthungs did not speak at all.

In Assam, some Yakthung activists, such as Man Bahadur Thalang and Pratap Sing Pomo started advocating for the teaching of *Yakthung pa:n*; they used to go to Shree Yakthung Hang Chumlung to meet with Yakthungs from Nepal, Kalimpong, Sikkim, Darjeeling, Siliguri, and Jalpaiguri. According to Pratap Sing Pomo (2018) Yakthungs of Assam established some informal social institutions where Yakthung language was taught in informal setting in the 60s and 70s. Thereafter, Yakthung activists started advocating for their cultural and linguistic identities. Pratap Sing Pomo (2018) stated that many Yakthungs in the 60s, 70s, and even in the 80s, did not want to learn Yakthung language; they did not encourage other Yakthungs to learn the Sirijanga script and writing system, for they (Yakthungs) thought that only Satya Hangma followers would learn the Sirijanga script and writing system. As I stated elsewhere, Satya Hangma Panthi started the teaching and learning of *Yakthung pa:n* in informal setting since 1988 BS (1931) in Nepal and beyond; they (Satya Hangma followers) wanted to reform Yakthung cultural practices (see Satya Dharma Muchulka 1988 BS). They reformed some Yakthung cultural practices in such a way that they (Yakthung cultural practices) look/ed like Hindu cultural practices. According to Pomo, this was one of the reasons why Yakthungs did not encourage their children to read and writing in the Sirijanga script because many Yakthungs abhorred the Satya Hangma cultural practices (also see Chapter 7).

Pratap Sing Pomo and his colleagues founded a Yakthung social institution in Golaghat, Assam, India and taught Sirijanga writing system, Yakthung Mundhum rhetorics, and culture. Among many other members, Lal Bahadur Pomo (President), Hangpal Sing Libang (Vice President), Prithvi Bahadur Meyang (Treasurer), and Padam Bahadur Samba, etc. were some notable Yakthung community leaders and activists. They appointed Khadka Bahadur Mabo to teach Yakthung language and writing system. Similarly, they persuaded Yakthungs from other districts in Assam to teach and learn *Yakthung pa:n* and writing system (P. Pomo, personal communication, May 21, 2018). Due to the lack of proper orientation and communication on religions, such as Yuma Samyo, Satya Hangma (now, Kirat), and Christianity in Yakthung communities, Yakthungs have not been collaborating to the re/shaping of Yakthung language, culture, and writing system in Assam. As a result, as Pomo stated that Yakthungs could do as much as they wanted in relation to the development Yakthung language, literacy, and Mundhum rhetorics in Assam. Later, Yakthungs of Assam have learned from their Bodo and Assame neighbors about the importance of mother-tongue education, language, and culture. Assame Yakthung activists of the 21st century have seen how the Bodos and Assames have been progressing in relation to political, cultural, and academic spaces. Due to the influence of other ethnic or tribal communities, Assame Yakthungs have been advocating for their cultural, linguistic, and religious identities. Though they did not continue to speak Yakthung language, they currently understand the importance of their language, writing system, culture, and Mundhum rhetorics.

While I went to Assam, Lakhi Khapung, Chandra Khapung, Riwaz Ninglekhu, and Uman Khapung accompanied me during my research travel for more than a week. During my visit to Assam in 2018, Chandra Khapung was the General Secretary of Limboo Mahasabha Assam, Lakhi Khapung was the President of Limboo Mahasabha Sonitpur (now, he is the President of Limboo Mahasabha Asam, central committee), and Riwaz Ninglekhu was the Vice President of Limboo Mahasabha Sonitpur (now Vice President of Limboo Mahasabha, central committee). As the representatives of the Yakthung social institutions and Young activists of Assame Yakthung communities, they shared the current condition of Assame Yakthung Suhang narratives, stories, and histories. For instance, what Limbu (Yakthung) meant to them, how they lost their language, *Yakthung pa:n*, how they have been collectively collaborating to relink their language, writing system, and Mundhum epistemologies, and how they have been communally struggling to institutionalize Yakthung language, writing system, and Mundhum literacies in Assam, India. For your information, Limboo Mahasabha Assam is a Yakthung social organization like Kirat Yakthung Chumlung in Nepal. Having been influenced by the Bodos and Assame language and literacy, Assame Yakthungs or Limboo Mahasabha of Assam also realized that they ought to restore their language and literacy. Currently, they have been networking with Yakthungs and Yakthung social institutions from Nepal, Sikkim, Kalimpong, and beyond. Limboo Mahasabha Assam (central committee) and the district committees of Limboo Mahasabha Assam (there are 17 district committees) have founded many informal Yakthung schools in order to educate young Yakthungs, including non-Yakthungs. Some of the informal Yakthung schools in Assam are:

1   Borjan, Tinsukia, Assam
2   Monahari, Biswanath, Assam
3   Jaipur, Biswanath, Assam
4   Maitalu, Biswanath, Assam
5   Chunpura, Sodiya, Assam
6   Hatidubi, Golaghat, Assam
7   Podum Pathar, Golaghat, Assam
8   Borijan, Golaghat, Assam
9   Mathikhola, Golaghat, Assam
10 Pinakol, Sonitpur, Assam
11 Gangapur, Sonitpur, Assam
12 Medhipam Pathar, Sonitpur, Assam
13 Kalipur Devkota Sangha, Assam
14 Nikashi Baganpur Kirat Mang-him, Baksa, Assam

(Source: Lakhi Khapung, Birkha Yonghang, &
Man Bahadur Limboo, 2018)

Assame Yakthungs founded Borjan Limbu Language Learning Center in Tinsukia Borjan, Assam in 2014; Silonijan Limbu Language and Culture

Learning Center in Golaghat in 2017; Limboo Language Learning Center in Gangapur, Sonitpur in 2018; Limboo Language Learning Center in Medhipam, Garjuli, Sonitpur in 2018, and Limboo Language Learning Center in Bishwanath, Assam (2016). While I was in Assam for research purpose in 2018 (May), I got the opportunity to inaugurate two Yakthung Language Learning Centers in Gangapur and Medhipam, Assam.

During my research visit, I met Yakthungs and communicated in *Yakthung pa:n* (Limbu language) in order to explore the present site of Yakthung language speakers in Assam. What I found during my visit in relation to Yakthung language and literacy was that majority of elderly Yakthungs could speak *Yakthung pa:n* and were very fluent. On the other hand, middle age Yakthungs could barely communicate, but were great advocates of Yakthung language and literacy. For instance, among many other Yakthungs, I spoke with Riwaz Ninglekhu, Lakhi Khapung, Uman Khapung, and Ganesh Kumar Limbu; they could understand Yakthung language, but they were not fluent *Yakthung pa:n* speakers. Whereas, the young Yakthungs did not speak Yakthung language at all (meaning, young generations stopped speaking *Yakthung pa:n*). Having known the desperate situation of Yakthung language, culture, and Mundhum rhetorics, Limboo Mahasabha Assam, including Yakthung progressive intellectuals of Assam, founded the informal Yakthung schools and started teaching *Yakthung pa:n* in different districts of Assam. Finally, they collectively started the campaign to relink Yakthung Suhang culture, Mundhums, Oral Yakthung narratives, and writing and rhetorics. According to Chandra Khapung, Lakhi Khapung, and Riwaz Ninglekhu, Assame Yakthungs have been appealing the Indian Central Government and Assame Government to recognize the Assame Yakthungs as "STs" (scheduled tribes) to formally institutionalize Yakthung studies (in *Yakthung pa:n*) at Assame government schools and colleges just like Yakthungs have been doing in Sikkim.

At present, the main purpose of the informal education in Assam is to delink the local and global cultural and linguistic colonization and to relink Yet Hang and Thibong Yakthung culture, language, and literacy. With the purpose of delinking cultural and linguistic colonization, Assame Yakthungs mutually beguiled the campaign to reintroduce Yakthung language and literacy. For example, they began teaching Yakthung children, including non-Yakthung children (whoever are interested), to speak, read, and write in *Yakthung pa:n* (as a campaign). According to Man Bahadur Limboo (2018), Yakthungs have been teaching the Sirijanga script, writing system, and *Yakthung pa:n* on Sundays for an hour since 2014 in Tinsukia, Assam. In Tinsukia, I met with Yakthung children language learners (both Yakthungs and non-Yakthungs) who have been learning Yakthung language in the Limboo Language Learning Center, Tinsukia. According to Limboo, in the past, Yakthungs had similar type of social institutions (i.e. informal Yakthung school/s) in Assam, India, but teachers and/or volunteers were not well trained. As a result, either Yakthungs, including teachers and Yakthung language activists, were not able to persuade the community members (parents and children) the importance of Yakthung language and literacy.

According to Lakhi Khapung, Chandra Khapung, and Riwaz Ninglekhu, Limboo Mahasabha Assam (central committee) and Limboo Mahasabha Assam (district committees) train *Yakthung pa:n* teachers and volunteers. Currently, they (Limboo Mahasabha Assam) know the demands and expectations of learners as well as parents. Lakhi Khapung and Riwaz Ninglekhu mentioned that young children are showing great interests to learn and practice Yakthung language, writing, and culture and are also performing well. While I went to Tinsukia, Assam, I got the opportunity to interact with Yakthung students (there were a few non-Yakthung children, too), Yakthung language teachers, and parents, including community leaders. Currently, Yakthung children are learning to speak Yakthung language and are learning to write in the Sirijanga script; I made several documentary videos of my Assam visit and shared them on our (Ganga and Marohang Limbu's) GLOBAL NETWORK (a YouTube Channel) with the purpose to introduce Assame Yakthung cultural traditions and practices. These social institutions, such as Borjan Limbu Language Learning Center and Silonijan Limbu Language and Culture Learning Center occasionally invite Yakthung historians, writers, and scholars online and get their students to interact with them in *Yakthung pa:n*. Based on the above mentioned Limboo Mahasabha Assam activities, Assame Yakthungs (including non-Yakthungs) are in the process of delinking local para-colonization and global cultural and linguistic colonization; they are relinking traditional Yet Hang and Thibong Yakthung customary epistemologies in relation to language, writing system, culture, and Mundhum rhetorics. Although Yakthungs live in different corners of the world, they have evidently demonstrated that the physical and political borders do not interrupt their communication with other Yakthungs and Indigenous communities to relink their traditional Yet Hang, Thibong Yakthung, and Yakthung Suhang rhetorical traditions and link their local Yakthung epistemologies with other global audiences.

The Yakthungs from Assam, India are in the process of delinking, relinking, and linking Yakthung culture, language, and Mundhum rhetorics; they are in the process of recovering the Sawa Yet Hang epistemologies; they through various social institutions are in the process of rearticulating Thibong Yakthung epistemologies. Assame Yakthung Suhangs informally are orienting their Yakthung children and Yakthungs to relink their history, culture, language, literacy, and Mundhum rhetorics. They celebrate Yakthung feasts and festivals, such as *Yakwa Tangnam, Chasok Tangnam, Sisekpa Tangnam, Kakphekwa Tangnam,* and *Chasok Tangnam,* etc. They frequently perform Yakthung Mundhum activities and Yakthung cultural activities to preserve and introduce them to their children. In so doing, they have been delinking the para-colonial way of creating hierarchical spaces based on body, gender, language, and geo-political locations in India. They are challenging Khas Aryan, Indian, and Western body-based, caste-based, and race-based hegemony and politics. The Assame progressive Yakthung intellectuals know that the delinking, relinking, and linking approach is a process of repairing Khas Aryan, Indian, and Western colonial wounds; it is a process of healing Yakthungs and Yakthung culture from para-colonial traumas, and it is also a process of re/discovering Sawa Yet Hang, Yet Hang, and Thibong Yakthung Suhang rhetorical traditions. Their delinking, relinking, and linking approaches establish scholarly *Yakthung Chumlungdens* (Yakthung contact zones) for Yakthungs to collaborate, succeed, and disseminate Yakthung epistemologies to make their identities, subjectivities, and agencies visible in the local and global contexts.

Similarly, in 2018, I went to Dungrabasti, Kalimpong, India to meet and interact with Kalimponge Yakthung historians, scholars, teachers, and activists. Among many others, I got the opportunity to interview K. B. Sambahamphe (age 92 then, a WWII veteran) who worked all his life researching, documenting, and preserving Yakthung history, language, and literacies. Sambahamphe read his old Yakthung historical notes without using reading glasses, and his notes included many important Yakthung histories, such as the foundation of Shree Yakthung Hang Chumlung, Lalshor Sendang's teaching or preaching at Shree Yakthung Hang Chumlung, establishment of Zambuk Junior Basic School (the first school where Yakthung language and writing system was taught), King Sirijanga, and Tye Angsi Singthebe. According to Sambahamphe, although foundation of Yakthung language and literacy started through Shree Yakthung Hang Chumlung and Zambuk Junior Basic School in Kalimpong, the local government (West Bengal) and Indian Government did not recognize the formal institutionalization of Yakthung language and literacy in Kalimpong (West Bengal). Currently, according to Suraj Lungduyo (2018) who is also from Kalimpong, Kalimponge and Darjeelinge Yakthungs have been teaching *Yakthung pa:n* in the Sirijanga script only in informal setting (personal communication).

Present site of Yakthung language and literacy in Bhutan, Burma, Thailand, and beyond

According to Ranadhoj Subba (2019) and Krishna Bahadur Subba (2019), Bhutani government has not yet approved the teaching of Yakthung language in Bhutan. The Bhutani government still practices the Dzhongkha and English-only language policy. Despite the fact the Bhutani government has not approved the teaching of Yakthung language, Bhutani Yakthungs have been teaching the *Yakthung pa:n* and Sirijanga writing system in informal settings. Ranadhoj Subba mentioned that after the Bhutani government officially recognized the Druk Kirat Chhoetshog (Kirat religion) in May 24, 2018, they got the opportunity to learn and teach the Sirijanga script, writing system, and Samjik Mundhum. In the Kirat religion, the Kirat religion followers are required to read Samjik Mundhum, which is written in the Sirijanga script in *Yakthung pa:n*. In the interview, Ranadhoj Subba (2019) mentioned that *yo dharmale tadhako najik lyayo ra najikko tadha banayo;* meaning, the introduction of the Kirat religion both brought unity and disunity among Yakthungs in Bhutan. Subba mentioned that Yakthungs have a harsh debate and discussion on Yakthungs' religious identities, such as Yuma Samyo and/or Kirat Samyo in Bhutan (like other Yakthung communities across the world). The religious debates and discussions engaged Yakthungs in hatred and disunion in Yakthung communities ever since the foundation of Satya Hangma Panth (1988 BS) in Nepal and beyond, and Bhutani Yakthungs could not remain as an exception.

The Bhutani Yakthungs have a plan to build Yakthung *Mang-hims* (Kirati temples) in Bhutan not only to promote Kirat religion, but also to promote the teaching and learning of the *Yakthung pa:n,* writing, and Mundhum rhetorics (K. B. Subba, personal communication, March 20, 2019; R. Subba, personal communication, December 10, 2019). This setting, to some extent, is delinking the Bhutani Dzongkha and English-only language policy in Bhutan. Bhutanese Yakthungs' collective endeavors facilitate to relink Yet Hang and Thibong Yakthung Suhang epistemologies and Kirat wisdom in informal settings in Bhutan. Additionally, the growing network via social media has shaped the Bhutani Yakthung community like any other Yakthung communities or Kirat communities in the world. For instance, Bhutani Yakthungs communicate with *Yakthung phu-ne-nusa* from across the world to share Yakthung culture, histories, narratives, and Mundhum rhetorics. In doing so, they can imagine how they can shape the Bhutani Yakthung community. Currently, according to Ranadhoj Subba (2019) Druk Kirat Chhoetshog has 18 *samdangen warumsaba/ma,* 35 *mang sewasama,* and 55 *mang sewasaba.* As Subba mentioned the *samdangen warumsaba* have an advanced reading and writing skills in the Sirijanga script; the *Mang sewasaba/mas* are like *phedangmas* (Yakthung ritual performers); they also read Samjik Mundhum to perform Kirat religious rituals. According to Subba (2019), there are 75,000 Kirat religion followers in Bhutan that include Yakthungs, Rais, Magars, Gurungs, Lepchas, Tamangs, Sherpas, and Chhetris (spouses only). Whereas, there are also many Yakthungs who follow Yuma Samyo in Bhutan who are equally contributing to teach Yakthung language and writing system. In short, Bhutani Yakthungs are delinking local linguistic and cultural colonization and are relinking Yet Hang and Thibong Yakthung cultural traditions; they are documenting and disseminating Yakthung language, cultural literacy, and Mundhum rhetorics.

Similarly, Yakthungs, from Burma and Thailand, have been networking with Yakthungs from across the world. By sending their representatives to Nepal, they have been sharing their cultural, linguistic, and Mundhum practices. By representing Thai and Barmeli (Burmese) Yakthungs and their social institutions, Dr. Bharati Subba attended the International Limbu Conference in Dharan, Nepal in 2014 where she shared Thai and Barmeli Yakthung cultural traditions and current Yakthung cultural conditions. Dr. Subba, with the very purpose, went to Nepal to meet Yakthung scholars, writers, historians, Mundhumists, and activists in 2017 again. The Thai and Barmeli Yakthungs also organize Kirat Yayokha programs annually to introduce their children to Yakthung cultural traditions, language, and Mundhum literacies. They not only regularly network and collaborate with Yakthungs from across the world, but they also share their Thai and Burmeli Yakthung cultural traditions with other Yakthungs, via social media, such as Facebook, YouTube, SoundCloud, and Podcast, etc.

Overall, Yakthung academic institutions, social institutions, and Yakthungs collective network, from across the world, have been advocating for creating safer Yakthung global contact zones from where we (Yakthungs) intellectually and diplomatically expose who we had been, who we are, and who we should be in local, regional, and global contexts. Our social institutions and academic institutions consistently have been delinking the local, regional, and global colonial ideologies; they have been combating against the structural inequalities and systemic binaries of colonial knowledge construction. Yakthungs from other countries are fighting for their rights to self-determination so that their children can freely determine or pursue their social, linguistic, and cultural choices. In a nutshell, Yakthungs collectively are addressing both individual and collective rights, cultural rights, and identity. Yakthungs, from across the world, are seeking to create democratic, inclusive, and representational Yakthung Suhang Mundhum-based cultural, linguistic, academic, economic, and political spaces in the context of the 21st century world.

13 Shifting from chirography to digitocracy

Delinking, relinking, and linking Yakthung language and literacies

The Sirijanga script has a long history of development since its inception; later, King Maarang and King Sirijanga redesigned the script in the 6th and 9th centuries respectively (Subba, 1928). Similarly, Tye Angsi Singthebe (1704–1741) redesigned and popularized it in Yakthung laje in the mid-18th century. While Jobhansing Limbu, Chyangresing Phedangba, Ranadhoj Limbu, and Jit Mohan (1845–1857) documented Yakthung culture, literature, history, narratives, and Mundhum rhetorics in the 19th century, they also used the Old Sirijanga script (Old Sirijanga writing system shifted to the New Sirijanga script in the 20th century). The books and manuscripts documented by Jobhansing Limbu, Chyangresing Phedangba, Ranadhoj Limbu, and Jit Mohan were transported to the British Library, including other European libraries (Sprigg, 1959 implied). Since the teaching and learning of Yakthung language, writing, and Mundhum rhetorics were banned in Nepal from 1774–1990, Yakthungs, including other Kirat communities, almost forgot about their script and writing system.

Yakthungs, after World War I (WWI), founded a Yakthung social institution, Shree Yakthung Hang Chumlung in Dungrabasti, Kalimpong in 1925. The Yakthungs of Shree Yakthung Hang Chumlung for the first time named the script, "Sirijanga script." Though after the invention of the Sirijanga script, Yakthungs had documented books, grammar books (*Barnamala*), genealogy books, and Mundhum books in the Sirijanga script, the local colonizers destroyed all of them starting from 1774 until 1990 in Nepal; whereas, due to the execution of Singthebe in 1741, Yakthungs were reluctant to read and write in their language in Sikkim as well. After the Bhutia King approved the teaching of Yakthung pa:n in Sikkim in the late 1960s, Yakthungs got opportunity to formally teach and learn it, and now Yakthung studies is taught up to MA level in Sikkim; whereas, Yakthungs are teaching Yakthung pa:n as an optional subject up to elementary level in Nepal. Similarly, according to Kalpana Limbu (2020) Yakthungs have been teaching various subjects, such as science, math, moral science, Mundhum, etc. in Yakthung pa:n up to elementary level, and Yakthung pa:n is also taught at higher secondary school (10+2 levels) in Mangsebung, Ilam. Based on this background information, this chapter discusses the development of Yakthung language and literacy, such as how the Sirijanga writing system shifted from chirography to digitocracy in three decades (from 70s to 90s), and Yakthungs are delinking, relinking, and linking their language and literacies, and how Yakthungs revisited their literacy histories and are in the process of institutionalizing them in the context of the 21st century.

Limbu et al. (1845–1857) mentioned that Yakthungs found old damaged Yakthung book/s in Sikkim. They studied the book/s; they redocumented them; they wrote other Yakthung histories, narratives, and Mundhum rhetorics. Though Yakthungs found the old Yakthung book/s in Sikkim, the study and redocumentation of the books took place in Darjeeling from 1845 to 1857 (when I went to the British Library in London, I also found a book written in 1967, and it was a part of Hodgson collection). Even though Brian Hodgson lived in Nepal for decades, after his retirement, he requested Yakthungs and non-Yakthungs, to document Yakthungs histories, Mundhum rhetorics, and other important accounts in Darjeeling from 1845–1857. Limbu et al. (1845) state that they documented Yakthung histories, narratives, stories, Yakthung grammar books, and Mundhum rhetorics based on the damaged book/s Yakthungs found in Sukhim (Sikkim). In relation to Yakthung books, Ilamsing Limbu (a Sikkimi minister) had many old Yakthung books and materials written in the Old Sirijanga script, but Yakthungs could not use them for academic purposes. Meaning, they were not able to formally establish schools and teach Yakthung language under the Bhutia reign in Sukhim until late 1960s. According to Campbell when he requested for Yakthung (Limbu) books, Ilamsing Limbu gave some of the books to him. Based on Campbell's narrative, he wrote some articles on Yakthung syllabary. In his article, Campbell stated that Yakthung syllabary had 19 consonants and one vowel (Sprigg, 1959; see also figure 5). Though Campbell was not quite accurate in his discussion of the Yakthung syllabary, his article suggests that the books, that Campbell got from Ilamsing Limbu, were written in the Old Sirijanga script (see figure 5). Sadly, European colonizers, such as Campbell and Hodgson, transported Yakthung books to Europe for colonial purposes. That was one of the reasons why Yakthungs, including Khambus, Yakkhas, and Kõiches (Kõits), did not have any books. Second, the Khas Aryan-centric Nepali government continuously destroyed almost all Yakthung (including Indigenous) books in Nepal from 1774–1990.

After the Nun-Paani Sandhi, Khas Aryans banned the teaching of Yakthung language in Yakthung laje; they persistently had been destroying books and other Yakthung, other Indigenous cultural artifacts in Nepal for more than two centuries. As the Khas Aryan-centric-Nepali government captured, tortured, banished, or executed Yakthungs by accusing them of teaching their language, Yakthungs forgot their writing system in two centuries (see Limbu, et al. from 1845–1857; Satya Dharma Muchulka 1988 BS). Yakthungs, who were banished from Nepal, took books with them, but the colonial agents like A. Campbell and Brian Hodgson collected them for colonial purposes and transported them to Europe for colonial purposes. During my five-year long research, though I found the books that Hodgson transported to the UK in the British Library in London, I failed to find the books that Campbell collected from Ilamsing Limbu (Sikkim) in the early 1840s. Even though Yakthung books were preserved in the British Library for colonial purpose (now public can visit the library and read the materials), Yakthungs were not able to visit the library to study about their script, culture, language, and literacy for centuries (in the past).

During my research, I did not meet any scholars, historians, or Mundhumists who could claim that they had books written in the Old Sirijanga script. Many scholars showed me old books, but they were written in the New Sirijanga script (only after the foundation of Shree Yakthung Hang Chumlung in 1925). What I am stating here is that although Tye Angsi Singthebe (1704–1741) wrote books and Limbu et al. wrote books from 1845–1857, we neither had in Nepal nor in Sikkim. The first Yakthung book that we could find was *Tum Yakthung Ningwaphu Sapla* (1928) written by Bajbir Subba after the foundation of Shree Yakthung Hang Chumlung in Kalimpong. Thereafter, Yakthungs wrote dozens of books by hand, and they were all chirographic (see Chapter 7); meaning, the method of printing/publishing then was either lithography (process of printing) or carbon-copy (carbonated printing). The printing processes, such as chirographic texts, lithography, or carbon-copy, existed until the 1970s. By then (1970s), the mainstream communities, such as Nepali, Hindi, and so on, had modern printing presses. Some Yakthungs, such as Randhoj Nembang tried to design wooden blocks to print (see figure 23); however, it was neither scientific nor effective. Gradually, after the teaching of Limboo (Yakthung) language was approved in Sikkim, B. B. Muringla also wrote textbooks by hand in the 70s and 80s, he used to take the handwritten manuscripts to printing presses in Delhi. Muringla was one of the Yakthungs who enthusiastically worked all his life to redesign and/or shape the Sirijanga script. Before Muringla redesigned the modern Sirijanga script in the late 20th century, Yakthungs were encountering inconsistencies in the Sirijanga writing system. Sadly, Muringla also did not follow the Old Sirijanga script that Singthebe had redesigned in the 18th century, and Limbu et al. used in the 19th century. I met Muringla in 2017 and 2018, I asked him (Muringla) the reason why he did not use the Old Sirijanga script and writing system, and in the response Muringla mentioned that Imansing Chemjong did not tell him anything about the Old Sirijanga script, and he was not well informed of the Old Sirijanga script (Imansing Chemjong knew about the Old Sirijanga script in 1955 through R. K, Sprigg).

As I stated earlier, the teaching of *Yakthung pa:n* was approved in 1968 and teaching commenced from 1969 in Sikkim. Although the teaching of *Yakthung pa:n* was upgraded to an undergraduate degree in the early 1980s, Yakthungs still did not have their own modern printing press. As Yakthungs were in a desperate need of a press to publish textbooks, reference books, and other magazines, etc., Yakthung Saapsak Sangchumbho (a Yakthung organization) summoned a meeting on December 10, 1981, to discuss the issues of publishing Yakthung books; the meeting unanimously decided to establish a Yakthung printing press in Sikkim, India. The meeting also chose Sanchaman Limboo to undertake the responsibility. Yakthungs prepared all necessary materials for the print designs, and Sanchaman Limboo, in co-ordination with other Yakthung scholars, started the campaign at his own expense (Kandangwa, 1999, p. 51). Finally, Yakthungs had their own press in Gangtok (India) and in Damak (Nepal), and the Indian President, Gyani Zail Singh, awarded Sanchaman Limbu for introducing the first Sirijanga script printing press.

Even though Sanchaman Limboo received the award for introducing the Sirijanga script printing press, it was B. B. Muringla, including other Yakthungs, who spent most of his life redesigning and reshaping the modern Sirijanga script and writing system. Without his life-long contribution to the development of Yakthung language and literacy, the writing system of Yakthungs would remain incomplete for a long time. For instance, after the foundation of Shree Yakthung Hang Chumlung in 1925, Bajbir Subba published *Tum Yakthung Ningwaphu Sapla* in 1928. Other Yakthungs also wrote several Yakthung booklets in the Sirijanga script; however, most of them, from the late 1920s to mid-1970s, mimicked the Devanagari script. In this regard, B. B. Muringla played a vital role to shape the Sirijanga script and writing

Consonants ꗤꗥ ꗩꗦ, /kudhəksak-ha?/ व्यञ्जनवर्णहरू

Sirijanga	IPA	Sirijanga	IPA
ꗤ	/kə/	ꗤ	/nə/
ꗦ	/khə/	ꗦ	/pə/
ꗖ	/gə/	ꗖ	/phə/
ꗧ	/ghə/	ꗩ	/bə/
ꗨ	/ŋə/	ꗦ	/və/
ꗩ	/ʧə/	ꗩ	/mə/
ꗦ	/chə/	ꗩ	/jə/
ꗩ	/zə/	ꗦ	/rə/
ꗩ	/tə/	ꗩ	/lə/
ꗩ	/θə/	ꗩ	/wə/
ꗩ	/ðə/	ꗩ	/sə/
ꗩ	/dhə/	ꗦ	/hə/
			/?/

Vowel ꗤꗥ ꗩꗦ, /kubuŋsək-ha?/ स्वरवर्णहरू

Sirijanga	IPA	Sirijanga	IPA
ꗩ	/ə/	ꗩ	/uː/
ꗩ	/əː/	ꗩ	/e/
ꗩ	/a/	ꗩ	/eː/
ꗩ	/aː/	ꗩ	/ɔ/
ꗩ	/i/	ꗩ	/oː/
ꗩ	/iː/	ꗩ	/ɛ/
ꗩ	/u/	ꗩ	/ɛː/

Figure 32 The digitized new Sirijanga Script (Credit: Harkajang Kurumbang Limbu).

system. Although Muringla was not a linguist by training (academic degree implied), he gradually learned how to apply the spoken language into writing practice. During the interviews, Muringla (2017, 2018) told me that he knew how the Sirijanga script's shape and size should look like in writing in order to produce distinctive Yakthung sounds and to produce different meanings in *Yakthung pa:n*. Muringla further told me that he knew the weaknesses and strengths of the Sirijanga writing system that existed before he started writing textbooks. Later, as I mentioned above, Muringla, along with other Yakthungs, was able to revise, devise, and shape the Sirijanga syllabary in the late 20th century. Because of Muringla's contribution to the development of Sirijanga syllabary and writing system, Yakthungs (specially, Sikkimi Yakthungs implied) of the 21st century regard him the "Sirijanga III."

Gradually, in 2050 BS (1993), in the process of digitizing the Sirijanga script, Kirat Yakthung Chumlung (KYC), Nepal and Yakthung scholars like Arjun Limbu, Bikram Subba, and Suman Subba also played a significant role to the design of the Sirijanga script; they requested Karan Thapa to design the digital Sirijanga script (A. Limbu, personal communication, June 10, 2018; Kandangwa, 1999, p. 52). Arjun Limbu coordinated to design the digital Sirijanga script, for Arjun Limbu had a familiarity of the Sirijanga script and writing system. Finally, KYC, Nepal, with the help of Karan Thapa, became successful to design the first digital Sirijanga script in 2052 BS (see figure 32). Arjun Limbu (2015, 2017) mentioned that since it was the first Sirijanga script in a digital form, it was difficult to arrange the characters from both aesthetic, pragmatic, and spacing point of view.

After the Sirijanga digital font was developed, among many others, Yakthungs and non-Yakthungs started writing and publishing Mundhum books, Yakthung monographs, biographies, magazines, popular journals, and

Figure 33 The Sirijanga script (Source: *Tanchhokpa*).

articles, including textbooks, in this script (see figure 33, for an example). The digital Sirijanga script is used in academic institutions, social institutions, and social media across the world. Currently, students, educators, writers, and general Yakthungs and non-Yakthungs extensively use it to document texts as well as communicate with Yakthungs and non-Yakthungs in written form or in multimodal contexts. As societies change, technologies change, and our demands also exponentially change; henceforth, Yakthungs have also created the Sirijanga script (app) for the handheld devices, such as cell phones and tablets (see figure 34). As we have the Sirijanga fonts in our digital devices, communication in Yakthung has become easier than ever, and such network practices have shifted the traditional colonial ideology of superior and inferior languages and writing systems.

In the past, we (Yakthungs) believed that we were inferior, our language was inferior, and our culture was inferior. As a result, we did not want to talk about our Yakthung culture, food culture, language, and Mundhums, and we were not also allowed to read and write in our language. We (Yakthungs) were oriented to disregard our own language and culture; we were politically and ideologically oriented to ignore our own cultural, linguistic, and *khambong-lungbong* identities. The Khas Aryan-centric government, by force or coercion, caged our knowledge in the Khas Aryan social and academic institutions for centuries. Our Yet Hang and Thibong Yakthung wisdom was caged; our Yakthung Suhang intellect was imprisoned in the Khas Aryan, Indian, and Western social institutions. These ideological settings made us discount ourselves, culture, Mundhums, and writing system for centuries.

Currently, we attempt to research, write, and share in our language, but our practices still inform us of the Khas Aryan, Indian, and Western cultural practices as we inherited them for centuries (see also Anzaldua, 1987; Bizzell, 2003 in terms of Western academic and social epistemic practices). However, with the use of digital technologies and social media, Yakthungs are in the process of delinking, relinking, and linking processes; they are networking, collaborating, and creating newer Yakthung routes through which our Yakthung culture will relink Sawa Yet Hang epistemology, Susuwa Lilim Yakthung rhetorical wisdom, and Yakthung Suhang sagacity from the 21st century Yakthung perspective. In terms of chirographic and digital Sirijanga writing system, as digital publishing in *Yakthung pa:n* just started in the mid-1990s, there are also technical difficulties and debate over the digital Sirijanga digital fonts and writing system. Before Sirijanga font was designed in the digital Sirijanga font, Yakthung writing used to be chirographic (handwritten) until recently (1990s). Due to its newness (in relation to digitized font), there are still variations between the Nepali and Sikkimi Sirijanga writing systems. The variations, however, are largely with the conjoint characters that we have not been able to design as we write (by hand), such as *kemphreng*. The issue does not exist from the writing and reading perspective, for readers can read and understand, but the issue exists from the aesthetic point of view.

Figure 34 Smart Phone Keyboard in the Sirijanga Script.

Although Khas Aryan-centric government does not support Yakthungs to establish Yakthung colleges or universities in Nepal, we already have Yakthung studies up to graduate level in Sikkim, India. The Khas Aryan-centric Nepali government must wisely consider that the Khas Aryan-Only tradition is not something that can be preserved in a pristine, original form; it must come to life through interventions that better interprets the relationship between the past and present in Nepal. More importantly, when traditions change, our needs and expectations also change, and our Yakthung, including Indigenous, culture is changing, Yakthung tradition is changing, and our needs and expectations are shifting. We are now in the Yakthung epistemological playing field; we have our own Yakthung epistemic game, and the game should serve our purpose/s. In this game, we (Yakthungs) have to create our own Yakthung Suhang rules and regulations that will lead us to our *cho:tlung* (destination).

We (Yakthungs) have already begun to practice how we have been shifting from orality to chirography to digitocracy. We have begun to digitally maintain, preserve, and institutionalize our culture, Mundhum, and *khambong-lungbong* identities. Now is the time for us to elucidate a broader concept of Yakthung Mundhum-based epistemologies and *khambong-lungbong*-based identities. Gradually, we (Yakthungs) have to collectively demonstrate how Mundhum and *khambong-lungbong*-based Yakthung epistemologies facilitate the construction of Yakthung Suhang cultural, spatial, and linguistic knowledge. Similarly, we have to demonstrate what our Yakthung histories were/are, how they have changed over time, and how we must relink, revisit and reconstruct our Yet Hang, Thibong Yakthung, and *khambong-lungbong* identities. In the process of the relinking our identities, Sawa Yet hang narratives, Yet Hang, and Thibong Yakthung customary institutional epistemologies, Yakthung Mundhum rhetorics become regulatory factors to delink, relink, and link our multiple Yakthung Suhang identities in multiple fields. In conclusion, we, Yakthung scholars and *tutu-tumyahangs*, have to share our conceptual, theoretical, and empirical Yakthung Suhang Mundhumic insights with our younger generations; we have to share them with our local and global Indigenous *phu-ne-nusa* (brothers and sisters). In doing so, we mutually can address cultural, linguistic, and political inequalities. We have to look at Yakthung Mundhums, Yakthung Suhang narratives, Thibong Yakthung cultural assets, and performative Mundhum rhetorics as critical cases to reform our *khambong-lungbong*-based epistemologies so that our future generation can delink colonization, relink their Yakthung *khambong-lungbong* identities, and link their epistemologies from local to global contexts.

Part VII

Delinking, relinking, linking Yakthung writing and rhetorics and future directions

14 Conclusion

Yakthungs, from across the world, are relinking their Yet Hang and Thibong Yakthung epistemologies and are linking their Yakthung Suhang cultural identities, Mundhum rhetorics, and oral literacies to local and global contexts. While linking cultural, linguistic, and socio-political identities, Yakthungs not only link as Yakthung Suhangs, but they also link as contributing global Indigenous *phu-ne-nusa* (brothers and sisters). In the delinking, relinking, and linking processes, Yakthungs perform both as consumers of (Khas Aryan and Western) knowledge and producers of knowledge. Yakthungs are delinking the Khas Aryan, Indian, and Western politics of knowledge construction, they are in the process of relinking their traditional Yet Hang and Thibong Yakthung customary institutional epistemologies, and they are relinking their disconnected Yakthung Suhang indigeneity. This conclusion chapter offers how delinking, relinking, and linking methodology assists Yakthungs, including other Indigenous peoples, to strive and thrive for their collective upward movement and/or for the inclusion and equity in local and global communities in the context of the 21st century networked village.

The delinking, relinking, and linking methodology facilitates Yakthungs to network, collaborate, and contribute to the 21st century global village as local and global citizens. In delinking, relinking, and linking methodology, there is a possibility of bonding every contradiction and ambivalence as it rejuvenates a newer Indigenous epistemology and consciousness. The process of delinking, relinking, and linking approach opens up Yakthung Suhang insights to delink para-colonization and relink Yakthung traditional customary institutions (to a larger community) not as compartmentalized Yakthungs, but as contributing global citizens. It not only assists Yakthungs, Indigenous peoples, and minorities to see from their own customary cultural lenses, but also unchains them from the colonial hegemonies. Therefore, delinking, relinking, and linking approach is a source of relief from pain; pain caused by colonial oppression both in academic and popular institutions. In other words, delinking, relinking, and linking approach provides Yakthungs a relief from colonial pain. The relief starts in the form of inquiry—the inquiry of lost Yakthung histories and *khambong-lungbongsa* identities. The process of inquiry develops through the layers of inquiries, such as who we were, what we were, what vulnerabilities displaced our *khambong-lungbongsa* identity, and why/how we were divided as *niti* (traditional Yakthung customary institutional law and practice supporters) and *samariti* (Gorkha/Khas Aryan statutory law supporters). The delinking, relinking, and linking methodology engages us in heuristic and hermeneutic processes, such as why we (Yakthung) continue to remain fragmented in the name of politics and religion, and why we (Yakthungs) do not congregate to critically discuss, debate, and collectively challenge the para-colonial ideology. As I mention in this book, Khas Aryans, Indian, and Europeans created a disunity in Yakthung communities for centuries as our disunity was the proliferation of our adversaries.

Current Yakthung age is age of critical thinking and inquiries, and Yakthung critical thinking and inquiries will lead us to our communal *cho:tlung* (destination). Hence, the lines of critical thinking and inquiries are the process of seeking our *khambong-lungbong*, Sawa Yet Hang, Yet Hang, and Thibong Yakthung identities. In this process, the descendants of *niti* and *samariti* of yesterday and/or Kirat and Yuma (religions), including diverse Khas Aryan-centric political parties (so called Yakthung leaders) of today have to convene at *chumlungdens* where we must tell the stories of divide and rule, such as *niti* and *samariti*, politics, and religion, in our own Yakthung homeland. We must tell our hostile stories of why, how, and for whose purpose the Khas Aryans, Indians, and Westerners divided us, displaced us, and destroyed us, for stories convey information and have the power to change, and they also have relational knowledge from storyteller to story listeners (Cook-Lynn, 2007; Morris & Eldridge, 2020; Wilson, 2008). For Yakthungs, now is the time, we must critically imagine and answer these questions the way that our *niti* and *samariti phu-ne-nusa* never thought of, and we must bond with one another so that nothing can divide us again.

The Yakthungs have to ingeniously imagine the dreams of our Yet Hang and Thibong Yakthung ancestors, for the critical imagination is a process of reaching our *cho:tlung* (an ultimate destination); we (Yakthungs) must critically question, imagine, and reimagine to get to our *cho:tlung*. To get to the *cho:tlung*, we must embrace the collective cloud network, for digital cloud network is immune to political and physical border (global *Yakthung phu-ne-nusa* network implied). So, Yakthungs collectively must advocate for and fight for equal access to all kind of opportunities that mainstream cultures entertain (in our homelands). Though the Khas Aryan and Western colonial and political veils shrouded our identities, we are in the process of being and becoming Yakthung Suhang once again in the context of the 21st century globally networked village. We, together, must reclaim our Yakthung laje, restore our Yakthung customary institutional theories and practices, and relink our Yet Hang and Thibong Yakthung customary institutions from the 21st century perspective. For us, the Khas Aryan-centric politics is not only the issue; the issue for us is the stolen land (our ancestral land, Yakthung laje). Our issue is our being homelessness in our own ancestral home.

Basically, anyone who wants to belong in Yakthung laje have to follow the Sawa Yet Hang, Susuwa Lilim, and Yakthung Suhang customary norms and values in the context of the 21st century. Yakthung laje is not the land of exclusion, it is the land of inclusion, equity, and representation (Yakthung Mundhum implied). We (Yakthungs and non-Yakthungs) must value and validate Yakthung Suhang Mundhum rhetorics. We collectively must reconstruct a robust Yakthung Mundhum-based inclusion and equity, for it is our physical and spiritual home. In this home, Limbuwani peoples (all races who live in Limbuwan) must collectively engage in debates and discussions to address our homelessness, including other cultural, political, and religious problems. So, when Yakthung Suhangs, including other Indigenous peoples, engage in political, cultural, and religious contradictions, their continual communication, contradictions, and recursive inquiries will lead them to the footpath of their self-discovery or *cho:tlung*.

Delinking, relinking, and linking methodology leads Indigenous and minority audiences to a world, full of images and histories often depicting images of para-colonial violence, and finally self-discoveries. In my own case, I thought that I and other Yakthungs were literate in terms of the Yakthung cultures, histories, and Mundhums. I even thought that my research concentration would be too dry, and I also did not consider researching and writing in Yakthung writing, rhetoric, and literacies. In my five-year-long research journey, my research inquiries, interactions, debates, discussions, communications, and discoveries proved that my initial thoughts were wrong. Now, I realize how I was paralyzed by the Khas Aryan and Western ideologies; how the Khas Aryan, Indian, and Western ideologies impaired my Yakthung Suhang learning abilities. Furthermore, in relation to my academic journey, I have two bachelor's degrees, two master's degrees, and a PhD degree; I co-edited several books, published books, and published journal articles. I reviewed and edited journal articles as an editor in different venues. However, Khas Aryan, Indian, and Western ideologies still stun my consciousness. The colonial norms and values constantly appear in me; they make me unconsciously observe my own culture via the para-colonial lenses. They make me distrust my own Yakthung Suhang trusts (Yakthung cultural traditions and Mundhum rhetorics, etc.). Due to the Western and para-colonial orientations, I could not see my own Yakthung body, *khambong-lungbong* spaces, and Thibong Yakthung identities. Therefore, I theorized delinking, relinking, and linking methodology to inquire, explore and construct Yakthung historical and current cultural traditions. Via delinking, relinking, and linking methodology, I could see what I was not able to see in my life; I could feel what I and other *Yakthung phu-ne-nusa* have never felt; and I could discover what I thought was not discoverable. This delinking, relinking, and linking research approach gave me what the colonial culture could not provide me.

Currently, Yakthung laje cultural epistemic activities are quite uncomfortable not only as Yakthungs sink into contradictions and anger, but they also uncritically engage in hatred and exploitation (politics and religion implied). As a result, it is hard for Yakthungs to pave the communal way to get to their *cho:tlung*. The main problem Yakthungs are encountering with contradiction and exploitation is that Khas Aryan fear Yakthungs' unity in Yakthung laje. So, Khas Aryan-centric Nepali government creates situations in which Yakthungs get smeared in contradiction, hatred, and exploitation among themselves. More importantly, the Khas Aryans do not honor the Yakthung and Indigenous people's inclusion in the mainstream government, for they do not want to jeopardize their Khas Aryan hegemony in Nepal. Hence, the Khas Aryan-centric government creates murky situation in Indigenous and minority communities, and they divert Indigenous peoples and minorities from the major Indigenous peoples' cultural and political agenda. As a result, Yakthungs in the last a couple of centuries engaged in disunion and could not collectively fight against the Khas Aryan hegemony. Henceforth, they lived (still live) the lives of the second-class citizens or even worse than that in their own homeland, Yakthung laje. In the context of Yakthung discourse, Bhabha's concept of "unhome" rightly resonates that Yakthungs are unhomed in their own home. The Yakthung Suhangs' unhomed situation in Yakthung laje is not only to be homeless or poor, but it is also a psychological feeling of not feeling at home though they are in their own home.

Our struggle of Yakthung laje, Limbuwan must undergo a struggle of *mingso ingso* (name and identity) and Yakthung Suhang customary institutional identity and space. Yakthung laje, Limbuwan has always been the space of struggle; our Yet Hang and Thibong Yakthung ancestors had struggled here; they struggled for the existence of Yakthung laje; they bled for Yakthung laje and died for Yakthung laje. So, this is our spiritual home and physical home. Our current struggle must be the struggle of Yakthung Suhang *mingso ingso*. The Arun River, Tamor River, and Tista River constantly whisper to us to protect and prevail our *mingso ingso*; the Mt. Phaktanglung unshakably stands as an eyewitness of Sawa Yet Hang, Susuwa Lilim Yakthung, Yet Hang, and Thibong Yakthung Suhang civilizations. The rivers, mountain/s, and Mundhumic spaces have been awaiting us to relink our ancestors' visions, faiths, and aspirations. We must learn to spiritually communicate with Yakthung laje to restore our ancestors' visions and dreams and relink Susuwa Lilim Yakthung Mundhum rhetorics, Yakthung Suhang epistemic activities. The Yakthungs of the 21st century have an absolute crossroad of choice whether they want to be free through unity or remain to be victims through their disunity. The choice is not only their own inner struggle to acknowledge their own Yakthungness, but also re/shape their physical, intellectual, and spiritual spaces in mainstream spaces. Furthermore, Yakthungs ought to understand that there will never be a Yakthung space if Yakthungs are not united, or to achieve their space, Yakthungs must collectively and consistently advocate and fight for their language, literacy, and *khambong-lungbong* rights until the eventual restoration of their ancestral land (that was illegally and unconstitutionally stolen from them).

Currently, Yakthungs reside across the world, and their digital engagement practices or digital visibility is shaping their culture, language, and literacies, for in the digitally networked knowledge society, anyone in principle can produce content, share it with the rest of the world. By engaging in digital crowd and cloud spaces, they are shaping and reshaping their communities the way they want it to be. Via the digital engagement, they are re/creating knowledge, content, manage them, disseminating them, and institutionalizing them for their own benefits. Yakthungs' digital literacy facilitates Yakthungs to create their personal, professional, and collective identities, and they gradually will create their own network paths in order to meet their cultural, economic, and political expectations. In other words, Yakthungs, including other Indigenous peoples and minorities, must consistently advocate and continue to fight against the para-colonial hegemony until they obtain equal opportunities, such as cultural, linguistic, economic, bureaucratic, and political opportunities. In relation to Yakthung laje, we must advocate and combat against castic discrimination until we can become able to establish inclusion, equity, and representation in Nepal. In so doing, Yakthungs, including other Indigenous peoples and minorities will make their voices, identities, and agencies visible both in academic and social institutions. In this process, Yakthungs' delinking para-colonial politics enables to unlearn the Khas Aryan, Indian, and Western colonial politics of knowledge construction. Via digital engagement, Yakthung Suhangs learn that delinking, relinking, and linking approach will help them explore what Khas Aryan, Indian, and Western body-graphic, caste-graphic, and geo-graphic politics of knowledge construction are, and how to deprivilege and delink them. In this setting, they will further relink Yet Hang and Thibong Yakthung Suhang epistemologies and link their subjectivities from local to global levels in the context of the 21st century digital global village.

Despite the adverse political situations in Nepal, including in India, Bhutan, and Burma, Yakthungs have been researching and documenting Yakthung histories, narratives, and Mundhum rhetorics. They are in the process of paving Yakthung Indigenous relational pedagogy and Mundhum pedagogy (Mundhum-based learning). Our relational Yakthung Mundhum pedagogy focuses on learning in relationships with humans and non-humans (Yakthung Mundhum implied). This Mundhumic pedagogy liberates us from the well-structured Khas Aryan castic cage and Western racial cage. Yakthungs' network with other local and global Indigenous *phu-ne-nusa* not only de-privileges the Khas Aryan castic epistemologies, but it also delinks the Western systemic privileges based on race, gender, sexuality, and geo-political locations. Our customary institutional practices and Mundhum pedagogy introduce us to Yet Hang rhetorical traditions, and Mundhum discourse facilitates to relink Sawa Yet Hang Mundhum traditions, traditional Yet Hang, and Thibong Yakthung customary rhetorical traditions. Yakthung language, literacy, and Mundhum pedagogy heal us from the century-long physical and psychological scars inflicted by Khas Aryans, Indians, and

European colonizers (Limbu, 2017, pp. 587, 589). Mundhum rhetorics seeks the process of liberating suppressed Yakthung Suhang customary rhetorical epistemologies. It seeks the process of releasing the caged Yakthung Indigenous souls and minds from the para-colonial cages. As global Indigenous *phu-ne-nusa* (brothers and sisters), we need to mentor our younger *phu-ne-nusa* so that they can navigate the meaning of Yet Hang, Thibong Yakthung, and *khambong-lungbongsa* customary institutional identities. The *khambong-lungbong*-based mentorship will lead Yakthung *phu-ne-nusa* to acknowledge Mundhum-based inclusion, equity, and representation.

In relation to language and literacy, our Yakthungs' future belong to the delinking, relinking, and linking approach as Indigenous future depends on the newer delinking, relinking, and linking pedagogy. In other words, delinking, relinking, and linking methodology ethical guidance that directs us to the journey of being Yakthung, becoming Yakthung, and belonging to Yakthung laje, such as discovering who we were, who we are, and who we can be. Tyson (1999) rightly argues that double consciousness persists in de-colonized nations today in terms of Anglo-American para-colonial context. So, among many tasks that formerly colonized people ought to address is the rejection of colonial ideology, which defined them as inferior, and the reclamation of their pre-colonial past. Both tasks involve many complex problems of interest to postcolonial critics. Hence, in order to reject para-colonial ideology and to embrace their pre-colonial cultures, such as Yet Hang and Thibong Yakthung cultures, some Yakthungs write in their own language, but such writings may face the difficulty of surviving in a publishing industry and publicizing their theories and practices both in local and global contexts. Therefore, my delinking, relinking, and linking methodology embraces local and global cultures, but it advocates for minority peoples' inclusion and representation in the center of mainstream spaces. Furthermore, our local and regional Indigenous literacy visibility requires the use of a common writing system in Indigenous communities in the South Asian Himalayan region (since Yakthung studies taught up to M. A. or soon to be PhD, the Sirijanga script could be a probable common writing system). Unfortunately, uncritical Yakthungs claim the Sirijanga script as their own writing system, and they force other Indigenous communities to create their own scripts. For example, in Sikkim (India), including in Nepal, Yakthungs, Rai, Tamang, and Lepcha are creating their own scripts because their government/s (Indian government) is obligating them to have their own scripts and religion to re/claim their schedule tribe (ST) status or Indigenous status (clearly, this is one of the strategies how local para-colonizers divide and rule Indigenous peoples). However, to address this issue, we, Himalayan Indigenous peoples, ought to create a common script to have an alternative writing system so that we can read texts written in other ethnic languages.

Finally, Yakthung Suhangs have to constantly question, contest, and mutually negotiate on pedagogy that value, validate, and respect all cultures, languages, religions, genders, and sexualities. I hope that delinking, relinking, and linking methodology leads colonizers and Indigenous peoples towards the collective, ethno-relative (not ethno-centric), relational, ecological, and representational global pedagogy in which both Indigenous and mainstream communities have horizontal spaces. Therefore, there is an urgency of embracing delinking, relinking, and linking pedagogy that creates safer contact zones from where we, in para-colonial context, will flourish by helping, not hurting each other. This space will allow us to mutually negotiate our dissimilar spaces, identities, faiths, castes, creeds, colors, and sexual orientations; it will allow us to mutually re/construct our cultural, academic, and political subjectivities. As delinking, relinking, and linking methodology does not impair our subjectivities both in (customary institutional) theory and practice, it is time for us to embrace it as an alternative pedagogy to seek inclusion and equity. One day, this pedagogy, I hope, will compel oppressive cultures to embrace (Yakthung) Indigenous pedagogy to create more democratic, inclusive, and representational glocal cultures.

References

Angbuhang, A. A. (2069 BS). Phalgunanda, Satyadharma Muchulka and Women's Right. *Chumlunghim Abhilekh* (pp. 183–188). Lalitpur, Nepal: Kirat-Yakthung Chumlung.

Anzaldua, G. (1987). *Borderlands/La Frontera: New Mestiza.* San Francisco, USA: Aunt Lute Books.

Arora, B. (2008). Routing the commodities of the empire through Sikkim. *Indian Institute of Technology* (pp. 1–21).

Axtell, J. (1979). Ethnohistory: An Historian's Viewpoint. *Ethnohistory, 26*(1), 3–4.

Banepaali, A. (2075 BS). Newarko Parichaya ra Itihas. *Khopring.* Kathmandu, Nepal: Bhaktapur Bikas Sahayog Sangh.

Baral, B. & Tigela, K. (2008). *Limbuwanko Rajniti: Itihas, Bartaman, ra Dastabej.* Dharan, Nepal: Gorkha Book Dipo.

Bessarab, D. & Ng'andu, B. (2010). Yarning about Yarning as a Legitimate Method in Indigenous Research. *International Journal of Critical Indigenous Studies, 3*(1), 37–50.

Bhabha, H. K. (2004). *The location of culture.* London: Routledge.

Binkley, R. (2004). The Rhetoric of Origins and the Other: Reading the Ancient Figure of Anheduanna. In Lipson, C. S. & Binkley, R. (Eds), *Rhetoric before and beyond the Greeks.* New York: SUNY.

Bista, D. B. (1991). *Fatalism and Development: Nepal's Struggle for Modernization.* London: Sangam Books.

Bizzell, P. (2003). Editing the Rhetorical Tradition. *Philosophy and Rhetoric, 36*(2), 109–18.

Brown, G. & Yule, G. (1983). *Teaching the Spoken Language: An Approach Based on the Analysis of Conversation English.* New York, NY: Cambridge University Press.

Bruffee, K. A. (1986). Social Construction, Language, and the Authority of Knowledge: A Biographical Essay. *College English, 48*(8).773–790.

Brummett, B. (1979). Three Meanings of Epistemic Rhetoric. *SCA Convention.* 1–9.

Budhathoki, H. (2020). Who Are Khas and Aryan. Online. Personal Communication.

Campbell, A. (1842). On the Literature and Origin of Certain Hill Tribes in Sikkim. *Journal of the Asiatic Society of Bengal,* XI, 4–5.

Campbell, A. (1855). Notes on the Limboo Alphabet of the Sikkim Himalaya. *Journal of the Asiatic Society of Bengal,* XXIV, 202–203.

Caplan, L. (1970). *Land and Social Change in Eastern Nepal: A Study of Hindu-tribal Relations.* London, UK: Routledge.

Census of India. (1981). Series 19, Part XIII, A & B.

Chakrabarti, A. (2012). Migration and Marginalization in the 'Himalayan King-dom' of Sikkim. *Journal of Exclusion Studies, 2*(1),1–6.

Chattopadhyaya, B. (2015). Interrogating 'Unity in Diversity': Voices from India's Ancient Texts. *Social Scientists, 43*(9), 3–28.

Chemjong, I. S. (2003). *History and Culture of Kirat People (4th ed.)*. Kathmandu, Ne-pal: Kirat-Yakthung Chumlung.

Chemjong, I. S. (2003). *Kirat Mundhum Khahun: Sikchha (3rd ed.)*. Kathmandu, Ne-pal: Kirat-Yakthung Chumlung.

Chemjong, I. S. (2003). *Yakthung Chukmuk Samjik Mundhum: Kirat Darsanko Saramsa (Summary of Kirat Philosophy) (2nd ed.)*. Kathmandu, Nepal: Kirat-Yakthung Chumlung.

Chemjong, I. (2013, 2059 BS). *Kirat Sahityako Itihas*. Lalitpur: Kirat Yakthung Chumlung.

Chemjong, I. & Tholong, B. (1931). *Nisigek Yakthung Sapla*. Darjeeling: Buddhiraj Tembe.

Clandinin, D. J. (2006). Narrative Inquiry: A Methodology for Studying Lived Experience. *Research Studies in Music Education, 27*(1), 44–54.

Coombes, J. & Ryder, C. (2020). Walking Together to Create Harmony in Re-search: A Murri Woman's Approach to Indigenous Research Methodology. *QROM, 15*(1), 58–67.

Cook-Lynn, E. (2007). *New Indians, Old Wars*. Champaign: University of Illinois Press.

Cushman, E. (2012). *The Cherokee Syllabary: Writing the People's Perseverance*. Okla-homa: University of Oklahoma Press.

Cushman, E. (2013). Wampum, Sequoyan, and Story: Decolonizing the Digital Archive. *College English, 76*(2), 115–135.

Daniels, P. T., & Bright, L. (Eds.). (1996). *The world's writing systems*. Oxford Uni-versity Press.

Fisher, J. (1996). An Interview with Dor Bahadur Bista. *Current Anthropology, 37*(2), 349–356. Retrieved from *http://www.jstor.org.proxy2.cl.msu.edu/stable/2744356*

Gaur, A. (1984, 1987). *A History of Writing*. London, UK: The British Library.

Geia, L. K., Hayes, B., & Usher, K. (2013). Yarning/Aboriginal Storytelling: To-wards and Understanding of an Indigenous Perspective and Its Implications for Research Practice. *Contemporary Nurse, 46*(1), 13–17.

Giuseppe, F. (1790). Account of the Kingdom of Nepal. In *An Account of Kingdom of Nepaul* (pp. 307–322).

Gurung, B. & Dahal, K. (2064 BS). B. S. 1988 ko Satya Dharma Muchulka. In *Tapaswi Phalgunandako Jibanee* (pp. 64–68). Damak, Nepal: Jagat Bahadur Rai & Srimati Mahendra Rai.

Harkin, M. (2010). Ethnohistory's Ethnohistory: Creating a Discipline from the Ground Up. *Social Science History, 34*(2), 113–128.

Hoffmann, L. & Hahlweg, K. (1957). Sprigg, R. K. (London): Limbu Books in the Kiranti Script. *Akten Des Vierundzwanzigsten Internationalen Orientalisten-Kongresses Munchen*. Herbert Franke (Ed.). Deutsche Morgenlandische Gesellschaft E.V.: Wiesbaden, Germany.

Houston, S. (2004). Overture to the First Writing. In *The First Writing: Script In-vention as History and Process* (pp. 3–15). Cambridge, UK: Cambridge University Press.

Hukpa Chongbang, H. (2071 BS). *Tye Angsi Sirijangako Jibani Abam Itihasko Kehi Jhalak*. Damak, Nepal: Ot Printing Press.

Hufford, M. (1991). *American Folklife: A Commonwealth of Cultures*. Washington: American Folklife Center, Library of Congress.

Ingnam, B. & Ingnam, S. (2070 BS). *Tehrathum Jillama Subbangi Pratha*. Kathmandu, Nepal: Nepal Rajkiya Pragya Pratisthan.

Kainla, B. [GLOBAL NETWORK]. (2019, May 28). *Historical Development of Limbu Language and Writing*. [Video file]. Retrieved from *https://www.youtube.com/watch?v=Bx69Rgcx33g&t=1239s*.

Kainla, B. (2069 BS). Mundhum: Charcha-Paricharcha. *Chumlung Abhilekh* (pp. 200–207). Lalitpur, Nepal: Kirat-Yakthung Chumlung.

Kainla, B. (2070). Adim Limbu Pariwar, Kul, Bangsa ra Samaj Niyamanko Bidhibyabastha. *Lahadangna-Suhangpheba Mundhum*. Kathmandu, Nepal: Limbu Bhasha Tatha Sahitya Prakashan.

Kainla, B. (2015). Kathmandu. Nepal. History of Sirijanga Script. Personal Communication.

Kainla, B. [GLOBAL NETWORK]. (2015, January 04). *History of Limbu Language and Literacy*. [Video file]. Retrieved from https://www.youtube.com/watch?v=PF2RZlMpcqM&t=109s.

Kainla, B. (2049 BS). *Limbu Bhasa Ra Sahityako Samchhipta Parichaya*. Kathmandu, Nepal: Nepal Rajkiya Pragya Pratisthan.

Kainla, B. (2071 BS). Chhoto Mantabya. *Tye Angsi Sirijangako Jibani Abam Itihasko Kehi Jhalak*. Damak, Nepal: Ot Printing Press.

Kainla, B. (2049 BS). *Mahaguru Phalgunandaka Upadesharu Tatha Satyahangma Panthaka Bhajanmala*. Dharan, Nepal: Tanghang Limbu & Indra Hang Limbu.

Kandangwa, K. (1999). Limbu Bhasa Tatha Sahityako Samchhipta Parichaya: Pustak Samikchha. *Journal of Limbu Literature and Culture, 6*(6), 44–55.

Kelly, J. (2012). In memoriam: Richard Keith Sprigg (1922–2011). International Phonetic Association. *Journal of the International Phonetic Association, 42*(1), 119–120.

Khajum-Limbu, P. (2069 BS). Kipat: Utpani, Unmulan ra Prabhabh. *Chumlunghim Abhilekh* (pp. 313–316). Lalitpur, Nepal: Kirat-Yakthung Chumlung.

Khajum-Limbu, P. (2017). Limbuwanma Kipat Pratha: Unmulanpachhi Yasko Prabhab.*Yuma Manghim Udghatan Samaroh: Smarika 2017*. Darjeeling, India: Limbu/Subba Tribal Society.

Kimdang Limbu, G. (2018). Lansing, USA. Personal Communication.

Kimdang Limbu, G. [GLOBAL NETWORK]. (2018, March 2*). Kirat-Athpahariya Culture*. [Video file]. Retrieved from https://laje.youtube.com/watch?v=bz4 YpkmR3vk.

Kirat League ko Bibaran Patra (2008 BS). In Baral, B. & Tigela, K. (2008). *Limbuwanko Rajniti: Itihas, Bartaman, ra Dastabej*. Dharan, Nepal: Gorkha Book Dipo.

Kirati, B. (2018). Yakthung laje. Nepal. Personal communication.

Kirkpatrick, W. (1996/1811). *Account of The Kingdom of Nepaul*. New Delhi, India: Asian Educational Services.

Kovach, M. (2009). *Indigenous Methodologies: Characteristics, Conversations, and Contexts*. Toronto, ON: University of Toronto Press.

Laksamba, C. (2016). Limbus in the UK. *Nepali Sajha*. Retrieved from http://nepalisajha.com/limbus-in-the-uk-by-dr-chandra-laksamba/.

Lambert, L. (2014). *Research for Indigenous Survival: Indigenous Research Methodologies in the Behavioral Sciences.* Pablo, Montana: Salish Kootenai College Press.

Laoti, Y. (2005). *Adibashi Limbu Jaatiko Samchhipta Parichaya.* Kathmandu: Kanchan Printing Press.

Laoti, Y. [GLOBAL NETWORK]. (2016, December 28). *Imansing Chemjong.* [Video file]. Retrieved from https://laje.youtube.com/watch?v=0yy4DZ1Tuuw.

Laoti, Y. [GLOBAL NETWORK] (2016, December 28). *Limbu Language and Literacy.* [Video file]. Retrieved from https://laje.youtube.com/watch?v=tgIsCpOR73E&t=231s.

Laoti, Y. (2069 BS). Limbu Bhasha ra Sahityaka Lagi Patramitra Abhiyan. *Chumlunghim Abhilekh* (pp. 313–316). Lalitpur, Nepal: Kirat-Yakthung Chumlung.

Lavallee, L. (2009). Practical Application of an Indigenous Research Framework and Two Qualitative Indigenous Research Methods: Sharing Circles and Anishinaabe Symbol-based Reflections. *International Journal of Qualitative Methods, 8*(1), 21–40.

Lawoti, M. (2013). Challenging Dominant Scholarship. In Rajendra Subba's *Debates on Federal System: Based on Ethnicity and Viability: A Case of Limbuwan.* Kathmandu, Nepal: Kitabghar Prakashan.

Lawoti, M. (2017, 2018). Michigan. USA. The Khas Aryan Political Theories and Practices in Nepal. Personal Communication.

Limbu, A. (2019). Limbus' Traditional Headmanship *Subhangi*: An Overview of Its Emergence and Disappearance (1774–1964). *Journal of Global Literacies, Technologies, and Emerging Technologies, 5*(2), pp. 857–873.

Limbu, A. [GLOBAL NETWORK]. (2017, January 29). *Limbuwan Studies Center.* [Video file]. Retrieved from https://www.youtube.com/watch?v=XZCNqFTeaSY.

Limbu, A. (2017, 2018). Kathmandu. Nepal. Personal communication.

Limbu, A. (2020). Yakthung laje. Nepal. Updating Limbuwan Study Center. Personal Communication.

Limbu, A. J. (2017). Kathmandu. Nepal. History of Sirijanga Script. Personal Communication.

Limbu, A. J. [GLOBAL NETWORK]. (2016, January 150). *Historical Development of Limbu Language, Script, and Literacy.* [Video file]. Retrieved from https://laje. youtube.com/watch?v=jqzVlxXPjFE&t=1122s.

Limbu, J., Phedangba, C., Limbu, R., & Mohan. J. Collection of Brian Hodgson, (1845–1857). The British Library, London.

Limbu, M. (2000). *A Contrastive Analysis Between Pedape and Chhathare Limbu Verb Morphology.* Unpublished MA Thesis. Nepal: Tribhuvan University.

Limbu, M. (2013). Emerging Pedagogies in the Networked knowledge Communities: Interweaving and Intersecting Global Communities in the 21st Century Global Village. In Limbu, M. & Gurung, B. (Eds.), *Emerging Pedagogies in the Networked Knowledge Society: Practices Integrating Social Media and Globalization* (pp. 61–86). Hershey, PA: IGI Global.

Limbu, M. (2016). Politics of Rhetoric and Writing in the Non-Western World: Delinking, Relinking, and Linking Yakthung Epistemologies. *Mikphulla laje Inghang, 10*(10) 36–41.

Limbu, M. (2017). Delinking, Relinking, and Linking Methodologies: A Glimpse of Kirat-Yakthung (Limbu) Language, Writing, and Literacy. *Journal of Global Literacies, Technologies, and Emerging Pedagogies, 4(1)*, 560–593.

Limbu, M. & Jennings, C. (2017). Khaasaam: Delinking, Relinking, and Linking Yakthung Indigenous Mundhum (Music) Theories, Philosophies, and Practices. *Journal of Global Literacies, Technologies, and Emerging Pedagogies, 4(2)*, 637–642.

Limbu Limphungwa, N. P. (2019). Kirat Yakthung Chumlungko Sthapana: Yakthung Jagaranko Euta Ghumti. *Chumlunghim Smarika.* Dharan, Nepal: Chumlung Him Nirman Samiti.

Limbu Lumphungwa, N. P. (2017). Yakthung Laje. Nepal. Personal Communication.

Lipson, C. S. (2004). Ancient Egyptian Rhetoric: It All Comes Down to Maat. Lipson, C. & Binkley, R. (Eds.). *Rhetoric Before and Beyond the Greeks.* New York: SUNY.

Louis, R. P. (2007). Can You Hear Us Now? Voices from the Margin: Using Indigenous Methodologies in Geographic Research. *Geographic Research, 45(2),* 130–139.

Lumphungwa Limbu, B. (2075 BS). *Limbuwan Andolan: Bikas Kram-Bigat ra Bartaman.* Kathmandu, Nepal: Limbuwan Adhyayan Kendra Bijaypur.

Lungduyo, S. (2018). Yakthung Laje. Kalebung Thum. India. Personal Communication.

Lunminthang, M. (2016). Rethinking the Political History of Northeast India: Historical Review on Kuki Country. *Indian Historical Review, 43*(I), 63–82.

Lyon, A. (2004). Confucian Silence and Remonstration: A Basis for Deliberation? Lipson, C. & Binkley, R. (Eds.). *Rhetoric Before and Beyond the Greeks.* New York: SUNY.

Mabohang, P. & Sharma-Dhungel, B. (2047). *Samchhipta Nepal Itihas,* Lalitpur, Nepal: Kirat Prakashan tatha Abhilekh Kendra.

Mabuhang, A. (2063 BS). *Limbuwan.* Dharan, Nepal: Lal Bahadur Lumphungwa.

Mabuhang, A. (2069 BS). Itihasma Bijayapur ra Buddhikarna Raya. *Chumlunghim Abhilekh* (pp. 180–182). Lalitpur, Nepal: Kirat-Yakthung Chumlung.

Mabuhang, A., & Tunghang, B. (2070 BS). *Hodgson Pandulipima Gorkha-Khambuwan-Limbuwan Yuddha.* Dharan, Nepal: Bishwa Yakthung Mundhum Samaj.

Mabuhang, B. (2014). Demographic Rhetorics (Ethnic and Religious Diversity) in Nepal: Ninety Percent Hindus' or Eighty Percent Indigenous Peoples' Population! *Journal of Global Literacies Emerging Pedagogies and Technologies, 2*(4), 170–188.

Mabuhang, B. (2017). Indigenous People's Space and Identity in Nepal. Online Video Clip. *YouTube.* 5 January 2017. Web. 25 January 2017. Retrieved from https://laje.youtube.com/watch?v=kHQrc1lzc6g&t=297s.

May, S. (2008). *Language and Minority Rights: Ethnicity, Nationality, and the Politics of Language.* New York: Routledge.

McGuire-Adams, T. D. (2020). Paradigm Shifting: Centering Indigenous Research Methodologies, and Anishinaabe Perspective. *Qualitative Research in Sport, Exercise, and Health, 12*(1), 34–47.

Meroitic Writing System. Library.cornell.edu. 2004-04-04. Retrieved 2010–01–31.

Mignolo, W. (2007): Delinking, *Cultural Studies, 21*:2–3, 449–514.

Mignolo, W. (2007). Delinking: The Rhetoric of Modernity, the Logic of Coloniality and the Grammar of De-Coloniality. *Cultural Studies, 21*(2–3), 449–514.

Mignolo, W. (2009). Epistemic Disobedience, Independent Though and De-Colonial Freedom. *Theory, Culture, & Society, 27*(7–8),1–23.

Mishra, N. & Singh, S. K. (2002). Right of Indigenous People in the Contemporary World. *Status of Minorities in South Asia.* Delhi, India: Authorspress.

Morris, C. B. & Eldridge, L. A. (2020). The Heart of Indigenous Research Methodologies. *Studies in Art Education:* A Journal of Issues and Research, *61*(3), 282–285.

Muringla, B. B. (2017). Sikkim. History of Writing in the Sirijanga Script. Personal Communication.

Muringla, B. B. (2018). Sikkim. Updating History of Writing in the Sirijanga Script. Personal Communication.

Nagarajan, M. (1993). Kirata in the Later Medieval Art of Tamilnadu. *East and West, 43*(1–4), 295–299.

National Population and Housing Census 2011 (National Report). Central Bureau of Statistics. November 2012. Kathmandu.

Nembang, B. (1987). *Limbuwanko Ramkahani*. Siliguri, India: Chhitij Prakashan.

Noyes, D. (2004). Folklore. In Kuper, A. & Kuper, J. (Eds.). *The Social Science Encyclopedia* (pp. 375–378). New York: Routledge.

Pallo Kirat Limbuwan Rastriya Manchako Rajnaitik Abadharana (2066 BS).

Pallo Kirat Limbuwanka Magharu (2002 BS?).

Parker, J. (2005). The Gurkhas: The Inside Story of the World's Most Feared Soldiers. Headline Book Publishing. ISBN 978-0-7553-1415-7.

Pomo, P. S. (2018). Golaghat. Assam. India. Personal Communication.

Powell, M. (2002). Rhetorics of Survivance: How American Indians Use Writing. *College Composition and Communication, 53*(3), 396–434.

Powell, M. (2012). Stories Take Place: A Performance in One Act (2012 CCC Chair's Address). *CCC, 64*(2), 383–406.

Rai, S., Ghale, D. K., Limbu, S. Rai, B., & Thami, T. (2016). *Cases of Indigenous Peoples Rights Violation*. Kathmandu, Nepal: LAHURNIP.

Rai, V. S. (2018). Nepal. Khambu-Limbu History. Personal Communication.

Rai, V. S. [GLOBAL NETWORK]. (2019, November 15). *Khambu (Rai) History, Language, and Literacy*. [Video file]. Retrieved from https://www.youtube.com/watch?v=s813lUkS6Us&t=397s.

Regmi, R. C. (1965). *Land Tenure and Taxation in Nepal*. California: University of California, Berkeley.

Rigney, L. I. (1999). Internationalization of an Indigenous Anticolonial Cultural Critique of Research Methodologies: A Guide to Indigenous Research Methodology and Its Principles. *Wicazo sa Review, 14*(2), 109–121.

Risley, H. H. (1928). *Gazetteer of Sikkim*. New Delhi, India: D. K. Publishers Distributions Pvt. Ltd.

Rosati, P. E. (2017). The Cross-Cultural Kingship in Early Medieval Kamarupa: Blood, Desire and Magic. *Religions, 8*(10), 1–18.

Roy, K. (2015). The Wilderness in Kalidasa's Poetry: A Classical Ancient Formation. *Studies in People's History, 2*(2), 145–154.

Said, E. (1987) *Orientalism*. New York: Pantheon Books.

Sambahamphe, K. B. (2018). Yakthung laje. Kalebung Thum. India. Personal Communication.

Sambahamphe, K. B. [GLOBAL NETWORK]. (2018, May 23). *Lalshor Sendang*. [Video file]. Retrieved from https://www.youtube.com/watch?v=pGahDDccufY&t=445s.

Satya Dharma Muchulka. (1988 BS).

Schlemmer, G. (2003/04). New Post for the Sake of a Better Future: Re-inventing the history of the Kirat in East Nepal. *European Bulletin of Himalayan Research, 25/26*, 199-144.

Scharfe, H. (2002). Kharosti and Brahmi. *Journal of the American Oriental Society*, *122*(2), 391–393.

Schlemmer, G. (2003/2004). Inventing a Past for Inheriting a Future: New visions of history among the Kirant intellectuals of Nepal. *European Bulletin of Himalayan Research*, *25/26*, 119–144.

Schlemmer, G. (2010). Rai, Khambu, Subba, Kirant, etc.: Ethnic Labels or Political and Land Tenure Categories? Logic of Identification of an Ensemble of Populations in Nepal. In Culas, C. & Robinne, F. (Eds.). *Inter-Ethnic Dynamics in Asia: Considering the Other Through Ethnonyms, Territories and Rituals (*pp. 42–56). London, UK: Routledge.

Scott, R. L. (1867). On Viewing Rhetoric as Epistemic. *Central States Speech Journal. 18*. 9–17.

Singak Limbu, L. [GLOBAL NETWORK]. (2018, February 28). *A Short History of Kirat Yakthung Chumlung*. [Video file]. Retrieved from https://youtu.be/2yIBMo7D8nY.

Singak Limbu, L. (2069 BS). Kirat-Yakthung Chumlung: Bigat, Bartaman, ra Bhabishya. *Chumlunghim Abhilekh* (pp. 285–288). Lalitpur, Nepal: Kirat-Yakthung Chumlung.

Singak, B. (2069 BS). Sambhawana ra Chunouti Bich Ani?pan. *Chumlunghim Abhilekh* (pp. 313–316). Lalitpur, Nepal: Kirat-Yakthung Chumlung.

Smith, L. T. (1999, 2012). *Decolonizing Methodologies: Research and Indigenous Peoples*. New York, NY: Zed Books.

Sprigg, R. K. (1959). Limbu Books in the Kiranti Script. In Deutsche, F. H. (Ed.). *Akten Des Vierundzwanzigsten Internationalen Orientatalisten-Kongresses Munchen* (pp. 590–592). Wiesbaden, Germany. Deutsche Morgenlandische Gesellschaft.

Sprigg, R. K. (1989) Review of George van Driem "A grammar of Limbu" Bulletin of the School of Oriental and African Studies. 52, pp. 163–165.

Sprigg, R. K. (1989). GEORGE VAN DRIEM: A Grammar of Limbu. (Mouton Grammar Library, 4.) xxiii, 561pp., 2 maps. Berlin, New York and Amsterdam: Mounton de Gruyter, 1987. DM 148.

Sprigg, R. K. (1998) Original and Sophisticated Features of the Lepcha and Limbu Scripts. *Nepalese Linguistics, 15*(1–18), Kathmandu, Nepal: Tribhuvan University.

Subba, A. B. (2016). *History, Growth and Development of Limboo Language: A Present Context in Sikkim*. Darjeeling, India: Gamma Publication.

Subba, B. (1928). *Tum Yakthung Ningwaphu Sapla*. Darjeeling: Darjeeling Chumloong.

Subba, C. (1995). *The Culture and Religion of Limbus*. Kathmandu: KB Subba.

Subba, J. R. (2004). *Mahatma Sirijunga Singthebe the Great Social Awakener*. Sikkim: Sukhim Yakthung Mundhum Saplopa.

Subba, J. R. (2011). *History, Culture, and Customs of Limboo*. Bombay, India: Gyan Publishing House.

Subba, J. R. (2015). *History of the Kirata Empire: The Third Most Empire of the World Recovery and Reconstruction* (Vol. I). Gangtok, Sikkim: Sukhim Yakthung Sapsok Songjumbho.

Subba, K. (2019). Bhutan. Limbus of Bhutan. Personal Communication.

Subba, R. (2019). Bhutan. Present Scenario of Yakthung Language and Literacy in Bhutan. Personal Communication.

Subba, P. (2005). *Sikkimka Limboo ani Limboo Bhasha*. Gangtok, Sikkim: Capt. Bhupendrahang Limboo.

Subba, T. B. (1989). *Dynamics of Hill Society: The Nepalis in Darjeeling and Sikkim Himalayas*. New Delhi: Mittal Publications.

Subba, T. B. (1989, July 9–11). Limbu Ethnicity at Crossroads. *Society and Religion of the Ethnic Communities of North-Eastern India*. International Center for Buddhist Studies & Research, Siliguri.

Subba-Lawati, A. (2017). "Limbuwan"ko Samchhipta Itihaas ani Darjeelingka Yakthungbaharu. *Yuma Manghim Udghatan Samaroh: Smarika 2017* (pp. 58–66). Darjeeling, India: Limbu/Subba Tribal Society.

Thebe, A. (2069 BS). *Limbu Jatiko Tumyahang Nyaya Pranali (Prathajanit Kanun)*. Dharan, Nepal: Bishwa Yakthung Mundhum Samaaj.

Tibetan Alphabet. (2016, December 31). *Wikipedia*. Web. 25 Feb. 2017. Retrieved from https://en.wikipedia.org/wiki/Tibetan_alphabet.

Tuck, E. & Guishard, M. (2013). Uncollapsing Ethics: Racialized Scenism, Settler Coloniality, and an Ethical Framework of Decolonial Participatory Action Research. In T. M. Kress, C. S. Malott, & B. J. Portfilio (Eds.), *Challenging Status Quo Retrenchment: New Directions in Critical Qualitative Research* (pp. 3–27). Charlotte, Information Age Publishing.

Tuck, E. & Yang, K. Y. (2018). Series Editors' Introduction. In L. T, Smith, E. Tuck, & W. Yang (Eds.), *Indigenous and Decolonizing Studies in Education: Mapping the Long View* (pp. x-xxi). Routledge: Taylor & Francis Group, New York.

Tumbahang, G. B. (2007). *A Descriptive Grammar of Chhatthare Limbu*. Unpublished PhD Thesis. Tribhuvan University, Kirtipur, Nepal.

Tumbahang, M. K. (2013). *A Linguistic Study of Limbu Mundhum*. (Unpublished PhD Dissertation). Tribhuvan University, Kirtipur, Nepal.

Tumbahang, M. K. (2068 BS). *Limbu Jatiko Chinari*. Kirat Yakthung Chumlung, Lalitpur, Nepal.

Tyson, L. (1999). *A Critical Theory Today: A User-Friendly Guide*. New York, USA: Garland Publishing Inc.

Vansitart, E. (1890/1980). The *Goorkhas*. New Delhi: Arina Publishing House.

Van Driem, G. (1987). *A Grammar of Limbu*. Berlin: Mouton de Gruyter.

Villanueva, V. (1993). *Bootstraps: From an American Academics of Color*. Illinois: NCTE.

Vizenor, G. (1990). *Crossbloods: Bone Courts, Bingo, and Other Reports*. Minneapolis: U. of Minnesota Press.

Webster, J. D. (2001). A Sociolinguistic Study of Limbu. *Journal of Nepalese Literature, Art and Culture, 51*(82), Kathmandu: Royal Nepal Academy.

Wilson, S. (2008). *Research is ceremony: Indigenous research methods*. Black Point, N.S: Fernwood Publication.

Xu, G. Q. (2004). The Use of Eloquence: The Confucian Perspective. In Lipson, C. & Binkley, R. (Eds.). *Rhetoric Before and Beyond the Greeks*. New York: SUNY.

Yakthungba, S. (2060 BS). *Muhigum Angsimang Phalgunanda: Jiban Prasanga, Satyadharma Muchulka ra Dharmopadesh*. Kathmandu, Nepal: Nonim Publication.

Yakthumba, M. (2062 BS). *Maulik Kirat Dharma Sanskar: Lekh Tatha Antarbarta Sangraha*. Lalitpur, Nepal: Dhanjit Yebheng Limbu & Rajkumar Phompho Limbu.

Yakthumba, M. (2013). *Mundhum ra Mithakharu*. Kathmandu, Nepal: Manjul Phombo Yakthumba.

Yakthumba, M. [GLOBAL NETWORK]. (2017, October 15). *Kirat Yakthung History, Mundhum, and Culture*. [Video file]. Retrieved from https://www.youtube.com/watch?v=-TIXjL0ZQn4.

Index

OJED

OPEN JOURNALS IN EDUCATION

Stony Brook University OLD DOMINION UNIVERSITY MICHIGAN STATE UNIVERSITY MORGAN Emerson COLLEGE

California State University Northridge ARKANSAS STATE UNIVERSITY AIRC CIES Appalachian

Open Journals in Education (OJED) publishes high quality peer reviewed, open access journals based at research universities. OJED uses the Open Journal System platform, where readers can browse by subject, drill down to journal level to find the aims, scope, and editorial board for each individual title, as well as search back issues. None of the OJED journals charge fees to individual authors thanks to the generous support of our institutional sponsors. OJED journals benefit from the editorial, production, and marketing expertise of our team of volunteers.

Explore our journals at www.ojed.org

Higher Education Politics & Economics
Journal of Comparative and International Higher Education
Journal of Underrepresented & Minority Progress
Journal of Human Services
Journal of Interdisciplinary Studies in Education
Journal of Development Education
Journal of Trauma Studies in Education
Journal of School Administration Research and Development
Journal of Global Literacies, Technologies & Emerging Pedagogies
International Journal of Multidisciplinary Perspectives in Higher Education

OJED JOURNAL OF INTERNATIONAL STUDENTS STAR SCHOLARS NETWORK

.